1996
THE COMPLETE HANDBOOK OF
PRO BASKETBALL

① SIGNET SPORTS (0451)

FOR THE SPORTS FAN . . .

☐ **THE COMPLETE HANDBOOK OF PRO FOOTBALL: 1995 EDITION, edited by Zander Hollander.** The total TV guide, with 350 profiles, 28 scouting reports, schedules, rosters, all-time records. Plus features on Frank Gifford, Steve Young, the Super Bowl, Jacksonville and Carolina. (185048—$6.99)

☐ **THE COMPLETE HANDBOOK OF BASEBALL: 25th Anniversary Edition, 1995, edited by Zander Hollander.** Features 10 great moments of the past quarter-century, Bob Costas, David Cone, Reggie Jackson on the Maris chase. Plus 28 yearbooks in one, including more than 300 player profiles. (183894—$5.99)

☐ **THE ILLUSTRATED SPORTS RECORD BOOK: Third Edition, by Zander Hollander and David Schulz.** 400 historic records recreated in stories with rare photos. Included are Joe Montana's Super Bowl marks, Michael Jordan's NBA playoff feats, Jack Nicklaus' Masters triumphs, Wayne Gretzky's scoring standards, Nolan Ryan's strikeout and no-hit plateaus, Martina Navratilova's Wimbledon crowns, Mark Spitz's Olympic gold medals, Joe DiMaggio's hitting streak, Bill Hartack's Kentucky Derby winners, and much more! (171179—$5.99)

☐ **THE COMPLETE HANDBOOK OF PRO BASKETBALL: 1996 EDITION, edited by Zander Hollander.** Michael Jordan heads a lineup of features that include The Schoolboy Who Jumped to the Pros, Clyde Drexler, Penny Hardaway and 50 years of NBA highlights. Plus player profiles, scouting reports and tons of records.
(188446—$6.99)

Prices slightly higher in Canada

Buy them at your local bookstore or use this convenient coupon for ordering.

PENGUIN USA
P.O. Box 999 — Dept. #17109
Bergenfield, New Jersey 07621

Please send me the books I have checked above.
I am enclosing $_____ (please add $2.00 to cover postage and handling). Send check or money order (no cash or C.O.D.'s) or charge by Mastercard or VISA (with a $15.00 minimum). Prices and numbers are subject to change without notice.

Card #_____ Exp. Date _____
Signature_____
Name_____
Address_____
City _____ State _____ Zip Code _____

For faster service when ordering by credit card call **1-800-253-6476**

Allow a minimum of 4-6 weeks for delivery. This offer is subject to change without notice.

1996
THE COMPLETE HANDBOOK OF PRO BASKETBALL

EDITED BY
ZANDER HOLLANDER

AN ASSOCIATED FEATURES BOOK

A SIGNET BOOK

ACKNOWLEDGMENTS

By the time you read this, we trust there will be peace on the court and a season will begin.

For this 22nd edition of *The Complete Handbook of Pro Basketball*, we especially acknowledge the contributions of managing editor Eric Compton and art director Dot Cordineer. As ever, they met impossible deadlines. We also thank the writers on the facing page and Lee Stowbridge, Nat Andriani, Phyllis Hollander, Linda Spain, Deb Brody, Sandra Mapp, Carl Galian, the NBA's Alex Sachare, Brian McIntyre, Jan Hubbard, Matt Winick, Marty Blake and the team publicity directors, the CBA's Brent Meister, Elias Sports Bureau and Bill Foley, Laura Courtney and the rest of the crew at Westchester Book Composition.

Zander Hollander

PHOTO CREDITS: Cover—Wide World. Inside Photos: Michael Hirsch, Vic Milton, Wide World, UPI and the NBA club and college photographers, including Dave Cross, George Kalinsky, Steve Lipofsky, Mike Maicher, Tom Maguire, Gary Morrison, Dick Raphael, Mike Shields, Mark Simmons.

SIGNET
Published by the Penguin Group
Penguin Books USA Inc., 375 Hudson Street,
New York, New York 10014, U.S.A.
Penguin Books Ltd, 27 Wrights Lane,
London W8 5TZ, England
Penguin Books Australia Ltd, Ringwood,
Victoria, Australia
Penguin Books Canada Ltd, 10 Alcorn Ave.,
Toronto, Ontario, Canada M4V 3B2
Penguin Books (N.Z.) Ltd, 182-190 Wairau Road,
Auckland 10, New Zealand

Penguin Books Ltd, Registered Offices:
Harmondsworth, Middlesex, England

First Signet Printing, November 1995
10 9 8 7 6 5 4 3 2

Copyright © 1995 Associated Features Inc.
All rights reserved.

 REGISTERED TRADEMARK—MARCA REGISTRADA

Printed in the United States of America

Without limiting the rights under copyright reserved above, no part of this publication may be reproduced, stored in or introduced into a retrieval system, or transmitted, in any form, or by any means (electronic, mechanical, photocopying, recording, or otherwise) without the prior written permission of both the copyright owner and the above publisher of this book.

BOOKS ARE AVAILABLE AT QUANTITY DISCOUNTS WHEN USED TO PROMOTE PRODUCTS OR SERVICES. FOR INFORMATION PLEASE WRITE TO PREMIUM MARKETING DIVISION, PENGUIN BOOKS USA INC., 375 HUDSON STREET, NEW YORK, NEW YORK 10014.

CONTENTS

MICHAEL JORDAN & BUGS BUNNY RIDE AGAIN ▪ By Melissa Isaacson 6

CLYDE THE GLIDE'S ROCKET RIDE TO THE SUMMIT ▪ By Fran Blinebury 14

CELEBRATING 50 YEARS OF THE NBA ▪ By Joe Gergen 24

KEVIN GARNETT: THE SCHOOLBOY WHO JUMPED TO THE PROS 34

GOOD LUCK! TORONTO, VANCOUVER 38

THE MAKING OF THE MAGIC PENNY ▪ By Bill Fay 40

INSIDE THE NBA ▪ By Fred Kerber, Corky Meinecke & Scott Howard-Cooper 48

Boston Celtics	54	Dallas Mavericks	238
Miami Heat	67	Denver Nuggets	250
New Jersey Nets	80	Houston Rockets	263
New York Knicks	93	Minnesota Timberwolves	275
Orlando Magic	107	San Antonio Spurs	288
Philadelphia 76ers	120	Utah Jazz	301
Washington Bullets	132	Vancouver Grizzlies	313
Atlanta Hawks	143	Golden State Warriors	325
Charlotte Hornets	156	Los Angeles Clippers	339
Chicago Bulls	168	Los Angeles Lakers	352
Cleveland Cavaliers	180	Phoenix Suns	364
Detroit Pistons	194	Portland Trail Blazers	377
Indiana Pacers	204	Sacramento Kings	390
Milwaukee Bucks	216	Seattle SuperSonics	402
Toronto Raptors	227		

NBA College Draft 416
NBA Statistics 426
NBA Schedule 448
NBC TV Games 460
TNT/TBS Games 462
CTV Games 463

Editor's Note: The material herein includes trades and rosters up to the final printing deadline.

MICHAEL JORDAN and BUGS BUNNY RIDE AGAIN

By MELISSA ISAACSON

Michael Jordan will concede certain things. His timing isn't quite back. His jump shot may never be the same in the cursed new United Center. And his hairline, shaven or not, has been a memory for some time now.

Of course, none of that matters much, for if his comeback proved one thing, it's that he is still just as elusive and perhaps even more compelling than ever.

Game on the decline? Not while he's still capable of pulling in a 55-point game in Madison Square Garden out of the blue and seemingly on command.

Low profile? Not as long as the players' union can use him as a catalyst.

Taking it easy during the offseason? Keeping up with Bugs Bunny, he isn't loafing.

Jordan had a pretty good idea of what to expect when he announced to the world, via fax, last March: "I'm back." At the same time, he said he was embarrassed by the extent of the attention paid to the two-week waiting period which proceded it, a span that saw the Las Vegas odds on the Bulls winning another NBA title dip dramatically, the New York stock exchange fluctuate and the City of Chicago come virtually to a screeching halt.

"I hoped for him to return," said Bulls coach Phil Jackson. "I just never allowed myself to think it would actually become a reality."

Melissa Isaacson covered the Bulls as beat writer for the Chicago Tribune *for four years, including two of their championship seasons. She is also a columnist for the* Tribune *and author of* Transition Game: An Inside Look at Life with the Chicago Bulls.

Comeback: Michael Jordan had 35-point first half vs. Knicks.

Muggsy Bogues' Hornets: No match for Michael in playoffs.

A Bulls team wading in mediocrity and standing just three games above .500, suddenly became a contender again. And still, fans and non-fans alike demanded to know why. Sure, his 18-month baseball career was far from legendary and the sport was burdened by a seemingly endless strike. But even Jordan's detractors agreed that he was showing marked improvement as a hitter and outfielder and his intent was no longer questioned.

"I love basketball," he said solemnly of the sport in which he is acknowledged as one of the best ever. "I had a good opportunity to come back. I tried to stay away as much as I could. The more active I was in other sports, it kept my mind away from the game. When I was in baseball, I was a distance away. But when you love something for so long..."

When it came right down to it, Jordan said, he couldn't find an adequate substitute for basketball. "I think at the time I walked away from it, I probably needed it—mentally more so than anything," he said. "But I really truly missed the game. I missed my friends. I missed my teammates. I missed the atmosphere."

It would take him time, he warned, to get back to his "usual self," and indeed after that first game in Indianapolis, it was clear he knew from whereof he spoke. He shot 7-for-28 that afternoon for 19 points, and committed five turnovers. Two games later against Orlando, he was 7-for-23 for 21 points. And the next week, against a Philadelphia team 30 games below .500, he was 5-for-19 for 12 points.

Sandwiched in between, however, there was magic. In Boston, in just his second game back, he was 9-for-17 for 27 points. Two games later, Jordan scored 32 at Atlanta, including the game-winner, and the very next game, in New York, he was merely 21-for-37 for 55 points, including 35 at the half, and dished off the perfect game-winning assist at the buzzer.

"There are some players who are simply unique and transcend every aspect of the game and he's the only one in the history of the game who has had the impact he has had all the way around," said then-Knicks coach Pat Riley.

Could he possibly keep it up, a reporter asked Jordan almost fearfully. "I don't know," he shrugged. "That's the fun thing about it. Tomorrow, you don't know what I will do."

The rest of the league shuddered. "M.J. is M.J.," said Boston forward Xavier McDaniel. "Even if he says, 'I'm coming back at 38.' You're talking about one of the top three, four, five players who has ever played basketball."

At 32, there were those who wondered if Jordan wouldn't be quite as sharp, quite as quick upon his return. "Actually," said

McDaniel, "he may have gained a step. His legs are fresh."

Of course, it wouldn't be quite so easy, though Jordan was eager. "I think I have renewed appreciation for this," he said early in his comeback. "I've been there and what I'm trying to do is work myself back to that point. I know what's on the other side of the door and I'm trying to get there as soon as possible."

The United Center would prove to be a major stumbling block. His beloved Chicago Stadium reduced to a mere pile of rubble across Madison St., Jordan made no secret of the fact that he was not happy in the new arena. And his shooting, hovering around the 30 percent mark at home in eight regular-season games, reflected it. "I'd like to blow that place up," he cracked on more than one occasion, still certain that somehow, come playoff time, the old sparkle would return.

In practice, Jordan was relentless. "It was war," said Ron Harper. "The first few days M.J. was back, I went home dehydrated."

Jordan was tough on his new and old teammates physically, and he was just as hard on them mentally. "I told Luc [Longley] if he drops one more pass, I'm going to take his head off with the next one," he vowed unabashedly.

Despite the growing pains, however, the Bulls and Jordan entered the playoffs with high hopes and even higher expectations than others. But after dispatching Charlotte in four games, they would both meet their match against Orlando.

Jordan's surprisingly dismal performance in Game 1—in which he shot 8-of-22 and committed eight turnovers, including two in the final 10 seconds—precipitated his well-documented number change from 45 to 23 (as well as a $125,000 fine later levied on the Bulls) and only enhanced the perpetual hype surrounding him. But it proved to be only a temporary and superficial remedy as the Bulls were eliminated in the second round of the playoffs for the second consecutive year.

"I'm very disappointed I wasn't able to contribute like I have in the past to this city," Jordan said after his much-heralded but somewhat uneven 27-game return to basketball. "I think everyone is going to basically say Michael Jordan needs to go through a regular season just to maintain his consistency and get his skills back to where he needs to be. And my answer to that is, we'll never know. Maybe I do."

Scottie Pippen defended Jordan, saying that expectations were too high. "Michael is not surrounded with the players that he once had," he said. "Give him credit. He's probably the greatest player to ever play the game. He wasn't his old self but the people around him weren't the same. And when you're in that position, it's really not a good situation for him because people are asking him to do what he did before and it's just not happening."

Looking toward the 1995-96 season, Jordan expressed concern over the futures of Pippen and Jackson. And he made it clear that rebuilding wasn't on his agenda.

"It would be a challenge [to rebuild] but it depends on how low you have to go," he said. "You start rebuilding from ground-zero and you have to go through a lot of disappointments. We're not that far away. We haven't gone from the top to not making the playoffs. That's rebuilding to me, when you don't win 50 percent of your games."

So eager was Jordan for the controversial Pippen to stay that he said it would not bother him if he was not the highest-paid player on the team. "If money is an issue, he can make more than me. I don't care," Jordan said. "Winning is all that matters to me. Money comes and goes but history books you don't forget. If I was worried about money, I wouldn't be back. I'm not making any extra money by coming back."

As for his own deal, which will pay him approximately $3.9 million this coming season, Jordan said he will not necessarily seek a new contract. "I have one year left on my deal and usually that's the time for renegotiation," he said. "If [Bulls owner] Jerry [Reinsdorf] comes to me and wants to renegotiate, great. Would I go to him to renegotiate? Probably not. We've always had our understanding in that situation. I'd rather see him take care of Pippen and Phil and whoever else needs to be taken care of . . . and he can deal with me later. I'm not starving."

Indeed, Jordan, who made approximately $30 million from endorsements last year, will never go hungry. And his return to the NBA set off an even more enthusiastic marketing frenzy with his sponsors, prompting the president of Chicago Chevrolet Dealer Advertising Association to remark, "This is like Christmas in March."

Burt Manning, chairman and CEO of J. Walter Thompson Co. in New York, tried to put it in perspective but was also reduced to cliche. "If there weren't a Magic Johnson, I'd say he's magic," he said of Jordan. "Even with the little shots he took on gambling, it seems to just be the buzzing of a fly that went away."

Jordan's involvement in the upcoming animated feature film *Space Jam*, co-starring his colleague in Nike ads, Bugs Bunny, should only further enhance his appeal and exposure. His role is to help Bugs stop aliens from kidnapping earthlings.

But Jordan indicates all of that is secondary. Of foremost im-

The baseball fantasy was never fulfilled.

portance, as it always has been, is the game. And it is clear that his pride demands that the next time he retires, he wants no questions to accompany him.

"I'm looking forward to starting over and getting to know everybody in a season," he said before a typical offseason dominated by golf and interrupted only slightly by NBA labor negotiations. "What I did was try to get to know this team in 17 games and maybe that was part of the team's downfall, just trying to rush getting to know each other and understand each other, and we had a lot of different problems down the stretch between the two entities.

"But I'm looking forward to going through an 82-game season and seeing if we can correct what was a problem in the playoffs. I'm not afraid to go back and go through the basics to see where it leads me down the stretch . . . I need training camp."

Will Jordan ever again be the same? Even he is not sure. But he also is unafraid of taking the risk of trying.

"I'm very glad I came back," he said. "I'm disappointed because I felt we had a good opportunity to steal a championship, if you want to call it that. But I'm happy to be back to the game of basketball. I still love the game. I still have challenges to play the game.

"Last season was fun. It's been an eye-opening experience of revisiting some of those things that have been fun for me for years. In certain situations, I've been able to be my old self. And I've been able to learn from other situations. And that's part of the game and that's part of me. I will never feel I've conquered the game to the point where I don't make mistakes. If that is ever the case, that would be boring for me. I can learn from this like anyone else."

CLYDE THE GLIDE: A ROCKET RIDE TO THE SUMMIT

By FRAN BLINEBURY

Clyde the Glide.

It rolls off the tongue. It's smoother than butter. It's slicker than a scoop of ice cream sliding down the back of your throat.

It doesn't only describe the way Clyde Drexler plays basketball, but the way he goes through life. It's not only the perfect image of him cruising to the hoop for another slam dunk that barely rattles the backboard, but it's the picture of a man who has always been unflappable in the pursuit of his goals.

Clyde the Glide.

It was a nickname bestowed by a former classmate at the University of Houston—Jim Nantz, now an announcer with CBS Sports—because it rhymed and because it fit his style of play like a custom-tailored suit. But the more you saw of him down through the years, it occurred that it was a name he could wear more like a tattoo. It was actually part of him.

Michael Jordan always seems to explode to the hoop. Drexler simply gets there with all of the noise and bombast of a baby's whisper. Michael has always been about the show, while Clyde was always about only the result.

There was Drexler in the aftermath of the Houston Rockets' second straight NBA championship—and the first of his career—and he wasn't jumping up and down or doing a little victory dance in the middle of the court. He wasn't puffing on a long celebration cigar and he wasn't spilling bubbly all over himself and his team-

---

As a columnist for the Houston Chronicle, *Fran Blinebury has followed the glare of the Rockets as they soared to back-to-back championships.*

High-five says it for Clyde Drexler (r.) and Hakeem Olajuwon.

mates to mark the end of his 12-year professional quest for the title.

A hug. That was Drexler's emotional outlet. A warm embrace with teammate Hakeem Olajuwon that celebrated their long-time friendship as much as it did finishing off the Orlando Magic in a four-game sweep.

In fact, nearly an hour had gone by since the game had ended and the Rockets had wrapped up their back-to-back trick when another teammate, Kenny Smith, entered the interview room where Drexler was addressing the media, pulled a full bottle of champagne from behind his back and finally doused Clyde from head to toe, making him fall off a folding chair.

"Clyde wasn't into the party," Smith explained. "We're all in the locker room celebrating and spraying this stuff all over each other and he's out here taking care of business, just doing his job. But that's Clyde. That's what he's always all about."

When Drexler and Olajuwon finally hugged in the middle of the Rockets' victory celebration, it was the official closure on some unfinished business that had followed the pair of them around for a dozen years.

On a long-ago night in a hot gym known as "The Pit" in a place called Albuquerque, N.M., Drexler and Olajuwon had stood there helplessly and stunned as Dereck Whittenburg launched his airball and Lorenzo Charles' prayerful hands gathered it in and converted the dunk that gave North Carolina State the 1983 NCAA championship over the Phi Slama Jama fraternity of Houston in one of the greatest upsets of all time.

"Down through the years, Dream and I have talked about that North Carolina State game a lot," Drexler said. "We've been over it this way and that way. I think we've talked about it inside and out.

"We'd always talk about the things that happened. Certain plays that we both could have made. Little things that either one of us could have done. We talked about missed opportunities, about the fact that anything can happen and you shouldn't take anything for granted.

"We talked about how we wanted to win it all for [coach] Guy Lewis. All these years we've talked about how we wanted to make things right and win a championship together."

But outside of the annual NBA All-Star Game and in summer pick-up games, they never got a chance to play together for all those years. Drexler left school right after the N.C. State loss, was taken by the Portland Trail Blazers in the first round of the NBA draft and spent the next 11½ years carving out a reputation as the best basketball player the Pacific Northwest had ever seen.

Meanwhile, Olajuwon remained at the University of Houston one more year and then was selected No. 1 in the draft by the Rockets and never had to leave his adopted home to become one of the finest players in the NBA.

They would always get together when their teams would play during the regular season or they would schedule a dinner during the all-star break and talk wistfully about what it would be like to be reunited. But as the years slipped by, both Drexler and Olajuwon thought the possibility of a trade to bring them together was getting dimmer and dimmer.

That is, until Feb. 14, 1995, when the Rockets made the biggest trade in franchise history, sending Otis Thorpe to Portland and bringing Drexler, the prodigal son, back home to Houston.

How fitting. It was Valentine's Day and the Rockets were giving themselves and their fans a gift that was sweeter than a box of chocolates, more treasured than a bouquet of roses and, in the end, the heart that would help make them champions again.

There were so many reasons for outsiders to criticize the trade, which also brought Tracy Murray to Houston. The Rockets had given up their second-best rebounder and that department was already a glaring weakness. Thorpe was the only Rocket who could successfully set the pick on the pick-and-roll play that had become such an integral part of their offense. His large body was bothersome defensively to some of the league's top power forwards. His strong hands made him one of the league's best finishing men on the fastbreak. There were people throughout the NBA who believed the Rockets had sabotaged their own chances of repeating with the trade.

No less an authority than Charles Barkley said: "They're done. When Houston traded Otis Thorpe, it killed them."

And yet the trade was never ripped in Houston, where everybody knew and respected Clyde and understood that he would bring to the Rockets the thing that can't be measured in terms of statistics. He would give them heart and the hunger of an annual all-star and a 1992 Dream Team member who had not yet won a title.

So many years ago, on the asphalt playground at Houston's Sterling High School, Drexler had honed the skills that would take him to the University of Houston, to multi-millionaire status in the NBA and, eventually, to the Hall of Fame.

It was the late '70s and Drexler's hair was a lot bigger than his game. He had the flamboyant Afro. But he was then only learning to glide. On all sides of that playground, there were basketball goals. Drexler would race from goal to goal. He threaded his way past imaginary defenders. He would rise above the hot pavement to jam the ball through one of the bent rims. And then he would adjust his flight to avoid the goal standard that was waiting to flatten him if his aerial maneuver was just the slightest bit too casual.

It was fitting that, after all those years in exile, Clyde was returning to the place where he learned how to glide.

Houstonians had never forgotten the 6-7 guard whose only rivals for flying with such ease were Air Jordan and the rockets that were navigated by the NASA engineers just down the road.

The acquisition of Drexler was something that the Rockets had been considering since Rockets vice president of basketball operations Bob Weinhauer had met with Blazers president Bob Whitsitt during a college Christmas tournament in Hawaii. Drexler had made it known that he wanted out of Portland after having

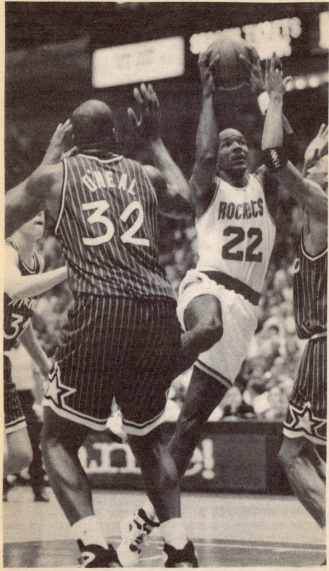
Shaq O'Neal's Magic couldn't stop Drexler and his Rockets.

heard his name come up in an offseason trade proposal that would have sent him to Miami.

But the prospects of Drexler coming home did not become real until the night of Feb. 6 when—coincidentally during a Rockets game at Portland—Houston's troubled guard Vernon Maxwell charged 11 rows up into the stands and slugged a fan. That was the culmination of a frustrating first half of the season for the defending champs and, a few days later, after an embarrassing loss to the Clippers, the deal was sealed.

It was a situation that was both exciting and uncomfortable for the Rockets. On one hand, you had Olajuwon delighted at being reunited with Drexler, and the fans of Houston were also thrilled. But you also had the other members of the team wondering how Drexler was going to be able to fit in smoothly in the middle of the season. Individuals wondered about how their playing time would be affected. They wondered who would have to adjust the most.

There was a period of adjustment. After Drexler joined the Rockets, the team went 17-18 to close out the regular season and the critics rose up again to say the Rockets had damaged their team chemistry. But again the critics were not watching closely. They did not see how Drexler stepped forward and carried the Rockets on his back during one stretch in March when Olajuwon was sidelined with anemia. During that span, Drexler averaged 30 points and 9.3 rebounds as the team's only go-to player, and it was that time that sold the rest of the Rockets on Clyde the Glide.

"You could see the possibilities," Olajuwon said. "I was watching from the sidelines and you could see all of the things that Clyde could bring to the team and the places he could take us."

What you could also see from inside the locker room was that Drexler never stepped forward until he was needed. He never tried to force his talents onto the team. He never wanted to step on toes and he succeeded.

"It's class," said Mario Elie, who also played with Drexler for a season in Portland and admitted to having initial reservations about the trade. "Clyde is a great person, a winner. He came in here and told me, 'Mario, I just want to fit in.' And that's what he did. By the way he does things, he's the leader out there. Always positive, never negative."

When the Rockets were on the ropes in the first round of the playoffs, down by seven points with 10 minutes to play in the deciding fifth game at Utah, it was Drexler who pulled them together and showed them how to win.

Clyde was finally feeling more at ease one week after Maxwell had faked a hamstring injury in a pout over playing time and asked for a leave of absence right in the middle of the playoffs. At last not having to worry about treading on Maxwell's feelings, Drexler had begun to step forward more boldly on the floor, and when the season was on the brink there in Salt Lake City, he pulled it back.

Drexler suddenly was everywhere, making steals by jumping into the passing lanes, getting every big rebound and leading the charge on the fastbreak as the Rockets came back to win.

"This is why we made the trade," said coach Rudy Tomjanovich. "You saw a superstar player rise to the occasion and take us to the next round."

But Drexler, as is his custom, refused to accept the individual accolades. Just doing his job, was all he'd say.

"Clyde has never been a showoff," said Eunice Scott, Drexler's mother. "That's just the way I taught him."

Indeed, he is one of the least colorful players in the NBA when it comes to being quoted. But that is not because he is incapable.

"I've worked hard all through my career at being boring," Drexler said with a smile. "I've worked very hard my whole career at saying nothing."

However, his game has always spoken volumes. Drexler was an eight-time all-star during his tenure with the Blazers and he led Portland to the Finals twice, against Detroit in 1990 and Chicago in 1992. But both times the Blazers lost and somehow the losing seemed to tarnish Drexler's image. That especially happened in 1992 when the series was billed as Jordan vs. Drexler, the battle to determine the best player in the league. Drexler tried too hard. He pressed at times and lost the one-on-one matchup.

But what is the disgrace in being the second-best player in the league behind Jordan?

"In his time, Clyde Drexler has been the most athletic player in the game with the exception of Michael Jordan," said no less an authority than Julius (Dr. J) Erving. "In an era without Jordan, everyone would be talking about Drexler."

Last June, the Rockets could never stop talking about Drexler for reasons that went way beyond his averages of 21 points, 6.5 rebounds and 4.6 assists in the playoffs.

"Clyde's influence on this team has been big, very big," Tomjanovich said. "Among the players, he is one of the most respected players in the league because his behavior is always top-notch, always classy. It's a big plus, but think about it the

Drexler drives past Magic's Nick Anderson in Game 4.

other way. If we got a guy who was a great player, but the personality isn't like that, think about what it does. Both things had to be in place for us to make that deal.

"We didn't make the trade knowing what was going to happen during the season. But if we didn't make it, I don't know if we would have even made the playoffs."

The Rockets not only made the playoffs, but they got by a 60-win team in Utah in the first round and their confidence surged.

Houston moved on to play Phoenix and Drexler was ejected early in the first game in a controversial run-in with veteran official Jake O'Donnell. It says much about Drexler's reputation and integrity throughout the league that after reviewing game films and conducting an investigation, the NBA office rescinded the automatic fine for an ejection against Drexler and instead suspended O'Donnell for the remainder of the playoffs.

The Rockets fell behind the Suns, 3-1, in the series for the second straight year and returned to Phoenix for another game on the brink. This time, Drexler came down with a severe case of the flu and never left his bed on game day. He was fed intravenously. The other Rockets left for the arena that evening believing that Drexler could not and would not play. They were desperate.

But less than an hour before the opening tip, the locker room door swung open and Clyde walked in, looking pale and weak.

"He walked up to me and said, 'Mario [Elie], I'm going to try, but I don't know how long I'll be able to last. I'm going to need you to carry me tonight.' I'll tell you, it was an inspiration to just see the man in the room. He lifted us all up."

Drexler took six shots in the game and missed them all. His four points came on free throws, but two of those were very big ones coming down the stretch and the Rockets escaped with an overtime win and went on to win the series.

While Olajuwon was dominating David Robinson in a battle of MVP centers in the Western Conference finals with San Antonio, Drexler was having his way with Vinny Del Negro and assorted other would-be Spurs defenders.

"It makes me laugh when they do so many things to try to stop you," Drexler said. "During the games, I try not to even think about it."

But the Spurs spent all last summer thinking about their frustration in trying to guard Drexler, and so did Orlando after he shined again in the Finals.

As the playoffs continued, national media members descended upon Houston and, looking for a new twist to the story, began visiting "Drexler's Barbecue" in the shadows of downtown. Asked what hand he had in the business, Clyde said, "I'm a customer. That's my mom and brother's business."

Drexler wasn't about to take any credit away from the rest of his family for the jobs they have done, even if the national media wanted to turn this into his joint. As far as they were concerned, Drexler prepared the meat, set the tables and dished out the spicy barbecue sauce. But he set the record straight.

Indeed, Drexler really is that quiet and unassuming. He loves to relax by playing golf or tennis, two more sports at which he excels, and merely by spending time with wife Gaynell and their three children, Austin, Adam and Elise. If you see him away from the court and not making another spectacular move to the hoop, you almost wouldn't believe he's an incredibly wealthy athlete, who is scheduled to make $9.75 million in salary this season alone.

He did everything but win title in 11 years at Portland.

But put a ball in his hand, turn on the lights and watch the show.

"The biggest thrill about winning this second championship for me," said Olajuwon, "was being able to win it with my good friend and he is a very big reason we did win it."

A class act had been added to the roster; the prodigal son had come home to his roots and performed like a hero, and when it was all over, he simply stood there in front of the cameras and smiled.

Clyde the Glide. So smooth.

CELEBRATING 50 YEARS OF THE NBA

By JOE GERGEN

With a nod to the future and a knack for turning former ruins into showplaces, pro basketball revisits Toronto this season. An original member of the alliance that formed the foundation of the National Basketball Association and the site for the inaugural game, Canada's largest city returns for the 50th season. Although many obstacles and a few detours were encountered on the journey from Huskies to Raptors, the final stage of the road has been paved with gold.

Of the four franchises that folded following the first season of the Basketball Association of America, Toronto is the third locale to undergo a basketball renaissance. Both Detroit and Cleveland have enjoyed aesthetic and financial success and the Pistons and Cavaliers, successors to the Falcons and Rebels, are housed in state-of-the-art arenas. While it may be the next century before the Raptors qualify for the playoffs, let alone contend for a championship, they will move into a plush basketball palace in time for the 1997-98 season.

The difference between then and now can be measured in the psychic distance from Maple Leaf Gardens, where the Huskies entertained the New York Knickerbockers on Nov. 1, 1946, to the SkyDome. The futuristic baseball facility, presumably with its retractable roof in the closed position, will serve as the Raptors' home court for the next two seasons. Now that the parquet floor

---

As a sportswriter and columnist for Newsday, *Joe Gergen has followed the NBA for more than a quarter of a century.*

CELEBRATING 50 YEARS • 25

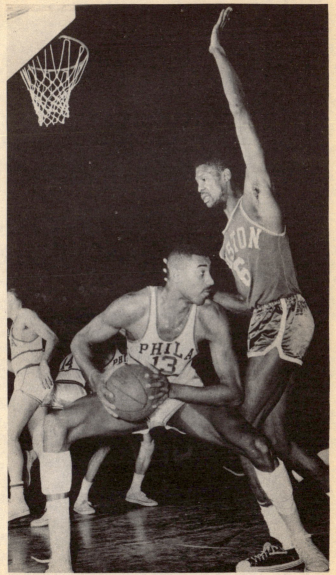

Wilt Chamberlain vs. Bill Russell: A classic rivalry.

has been passed from Boston Garden to the Fleet Center, Maple Leaf Gardens is the last of the league's initial edifices still hosting major sports events.

By spreading its wingspan from Miami in the Southeast to Vancouver—the other half of a two-pronged Canadian front—in the Northwest, the NBA is bigger than ever. Additionally, the exposure in the land of the sport's inventor sets the stage for international expansion. There's no better evidence of the game's growing popularity worldwide than the rise of Hakeem Olajuwon, the Nigerian native who has led the Houston Rockets to consecutive championships. He is among the swelling ranks of foreign-born stars enrolled in the league.

In its advance from zero to 50, the NBA has introduced lakes to Los Angeles, jazz to Utah and royalty to Sacramento. It has demonstrated keen foursight in the form of George Mikan's spectacles and Kareem Abdul-Jabbar's goggles. Its colorful history encompasses the Red period of Arnold Auerbach and William Holzman and the multihued impressionism of Dennis Rodman.

Faithful to that spirit, The Complete Handbook of Pro Basketball *hereby offers a compendium of matters large and small that have provided the NBA with its distinctive character through five decades.*

MOST CELEBRATED NUMBERS

100—Points scored by Wilt Chamberlain, Philadelphia Warriors, against the Knicks at Hershey, Pa., on March 2, 1962.

99—Uniform worn by George Mikan, Minneapolis Lakers, voted greatest player of the first half-century.

23—Jersey modeled by Michael Jordan during his three championship seasons with the Chicago Bulls, briefly changed to 45 late last season in the course of the 1995 playoffs and later resurrected, to the relief of thousands Jordan wannabes who had purchased his apparel.

16—Titles earned by the Boston Celtics, including an unprecedented eight in succession from 1959 through 1966.

MOST SIGNIFICANT HABERDASHERY

1) Hat worn by Eddie Gottlieb, founder, owner and first coach of the Philadelphia Warriors, under which he was said to keep his office and, in a later incarnation as consultant to the NBA, the entire league schedule, which he dutifully composed on scraps of paper.

George Mikan (99) was good cause for Laker celebration.

2) Hat owned by Maurice Podoloff, in which were slipped the names of three players left unemployed by the sudden expiration of the Chicago Stags three weeks before the start of the 1950-51 season. Picking first from the commissioner's fedora, the Knicks extracted the high-scoring Max Zaslofsky. The Warriors, next in line, drew forth experienced playmaker Andy Phillip. That meant the Celtics were stuck with a rookie guard from Holy Cross whom first-year coach Red Auerbach had spurned as a possible territorial draft choice. Thus, for the sum of $8,500, did Boston acquire the rights to Bob Cousy, destined to be the most flamboyant star in the league for the next decade.

LONGEST WINNING STREAK

33—Compiled by the Los Angeles Lakers from Nov. 5, 1971, through Jan. 7, 1972.

Lenny Wilkens smoked out Red Auerbach's cigar in 1995.

MOST COACHING VICTORIES

968—Len Wilkens, Seattle SuperSonics, Portland Trail Blazers, Seattle SuperSonics, Cleveland Cavaliers, Atlanta Hawks, 1969-present.

938—Arnold (Red) Auerbach, Washington Capitols, Tri-Cities Blackhawks, Boston Celtics, 1946-1966.

MOST HUMANITARIAN GESTURE

By Jack Twyman, Cincinnati Royals, who became the legal guardian for Maurice Stokes, a onetime Rookie of the Year, after the broad-shouldered forward became paralyzed in 1958. Confined to a wheelchair, Stokes lived until 1970, supported in part by an annual summer benefit game played by NBA stars at Kutsher's Country Club in New York's Catskill Mountains.

MOST FAMOUS RADIO CALL

"Havlicek Stole the Ball," by Johnny Most, Boston Garden, April 15, 1965, reacting to John Havlicek's interception of Hal Greer's inbounds pass with five seconds left in the seventh game of the Eastern Division finals, preserving a 110-109 victory and Boston's dynasty.

MOST FAMOUS PUBLIC-ADDRESS CALL

Tie between "Gola goal" and "Dipper Dunk!," both by Dave Zinkoff, PA announcer for the Philadelphia Warriors and Philadelphia 76ers.

MOST IMPORTANT SUGGESTION

A 24-second clock, by Dan Biasone, bowling alley proprietor and owner of the Syracuse Nationals. Adopted by the Board of Governors in 1954, it revolutionized the sport, eliminating the stalling tactics that had produced the sham of a 19-18 game between the Minneapolis Lakers and the Fort Wayne Pistons during the 1950-51 season. Before the decade was over, the same Lakers were victimized by the Celtics in Boston by the score of 173-139.

LOWEST WINNING PERCENTAGE

.110—Charged to Philadelphia 76ers, who won only nine of 82 games during the 1972-73 season.

MOST IRRITATING SIGHTS

1) Coach Red Auerbach lighting up a cigar in anticipation of an important victory for the Celtics. He performed the ceremony with exaggerated motions and inordinate care so that all the fans in Boston Garden would note the signal to start celebrating. It was, according to one of his stars, Bob Cousy, "the single most arrogant act in sports."

2) Movie stars gathered in the front row at The Forum during the Showtime era of the Los Angeles Lakers. The most notable of the celebrity fans, Jack Nicholson, occasionally followed the team on the road and, on the occasion of the team's first championship triumph at the expense of the Celtics in 1985, he mooned the patrons at Boston Garden from an upper-level box.

Magic Johnson and Larry Bird: Duels and derring-do.

MOST FRUSTRATED FRANCHISES

Tie among New Jersey Nets, Denver Nuggets, Indiana Pacers and San Antonio Spurs, the four surviving members of the American Basketball Association absorbed into the NBA in 1976. They have spent a combined 80 seasons in the league without any of the teams qualifying for the championship series. There is hope, however. Both the Pacers and Spurs advanced to the conference finals for the first time in 1995.

MOST COMPELLING RIVALRIES

1) Bill Russell, Boston Celtics, vs. Wilt Chamberlain, Philadelphia Warriors, San Francisco Warriors, Philadelphia 76ers, Los Angeles Lakers, 1959-69.

2) Magic Johnson, Los Angeles Lakers, vs. Larry Bird, Boston Celtics, 1979-1991.

CELEBRATING 50 YEARS • 31

MOST SUCCINCT COACHING PHILOSOPHY

Attributed to Charley Eckman, who began his career as a referee and became an announcer after guiding the Detroit Pistons for three seasons plus: "There are only two great plays—South Pacific and put the ball in the basket."

MOST CAREER POINTS

38,387—Kareem Abdul-Jabbar, Milwaukee Bucks, Los Angeles Lakers, 1969-89.

31,419—Wilt Chamberlain, Philadelphia Warriors, San Francisco Warriors, Philadelphia 76ers, Los Angeles Lakers, 1959-73.

MOST SHATTERING MOMENTS

1) Boston, Nov. 5, 1946—Shortly before a game between the Celtics and the Chicago Stags at Boston Arena, one of the glass backboards was broken by a shot credited to Chuck Connors, a 6-7 forward who later played first base for two major-league baseball teams but who would earn his greatest fame as an actor in the television series, "The Rifleman."

"The game would have been at the Boston Garden," he recalled years later, "but there was a rodeo there. We were taking our warm-up shots and I threw one up—maybe I was 30 feet out—and the next thing I knew the backboard was shattered. I didn't think I threw it that hard."

Talk about a brick! The start of the game was delayed for a half hour while workers rushed to the Garden and returned with another basket and backboard. The Stags went on to beat the Celtics, 57-55, and disgruntled Boston coach Honey Russell said, "They should give Chuck a bill for the backboard."

2) Kansas City, Nov. 13, 1979—Darryl Dawkins of the Philadelphia 76ers contributed to the legend in his own mind—that of rim-rocking Chocolate Thunder—when he threw down a dunk against the Kings at Kemper Arena and brought down the backboard. The 6-11, 258-pound center also bent the support pole for good measure. The undaunted Kings defeated the Sixers, 110-103, partially mollifying Kansas City general manager John Begzos, who threatened to send a bill for damages to the opponent.

3) Television commercials filmed by Shaquille O'Neal, the massive center of the Orlando Magic.

MOST ANXIOUS LANDING

By the Minneapolis Lakers, whose chartered flight from St. Louis to Minnesota on the night of Jan. 17, 1960 set down in a snow-covered Iowa cornfield. The electrical system in the DC-3 purchased by club owner Bob Short failed shortly after takeoff and the pilot, flying without lights or a radio, was guided by magnetic compass. But the plane drifted off course and the craft, low on fuel, had to be set down by the lights of a small town in western Iowa.

When the missing flight was reported on the radio back in Minneapolis, injured forward Steve Hamilton, the future major-league pitcher, cried in the belief he was the only surviving Laker. Despite five hours in the air without heat or lights, however, the occupants of the plane—including star forward Elgin Baylor, rookie power forward Rudy LaRusso and brash backcourt man Hot Rod Hundley—all returned safely. The DC-3 had slid about 100 yards in the smooth field and suffered no major damage.

Meanwhile, members of the party were picked up by residents of nearby Carroll, Iowa, and driven into town. "I had not been scared in the least when we were in the air or when we were landing," recalled coach Jim Pollard, whose mode of transportation turned out to be a hearse driven by the local mortician. "But when I saw that stretcher in the back of the car, I realized how close we had come, and I got the shakes for a few minutes."

A few months later, Short announced the Lakers were moving to Los Angeles, opening the NBA to the jet age.

GREATEST STEAL

By Arnold (Red) Auerbach, coach and GM of the Boston Celtics, in 1956 when he secured the rights to Bill Russell, center for the two-time NCAA champion San Francisco Dons, in a trade with the Hawks. He sent hometown favorite Easy Ed Macauley and Cliff Hagan to St. Louis for the Hawks' first-round pick (No. 2 overall) in the college draft and smiled when the Rochester Royals, as anticipated, opted for guard Sihugo Green of Duquesne. With his great shot-blocking ability and defensive presence, Russell changed the way the game was played and led the Celtics to 11 championships in the 13 years he played. He was selected Most Valuable Player five times.

SECOND GREATEST STEAL

Three years after the demise of the ABA, the NBA adopted one of the ridiculed league's "gimmicks," crediting three points for shots taken behind an arc drawn on the court. It drew the line at the funny red, white and blue basketball.

MOST ENDURING LEGACIES

1) Jim Paxson, Minneapolis Lakers, Cincinnati Royals, 1956-58; sons Jim Paxson, Portland Trail Blazers, Boston Celtics, 1979-89, and John Paxson, San Antonio Spurs, Chicago Bulls, 1983-1994.

2) Ernie Vandeweghe, New York Knicks, 1949-56; son Kiki Vandeweghe, Denver Nuggets, Portland Trail Blazers, New York Knicks, Los Angeles Clippers, 1980-1993.

3) Jimmy Walker, Detroit Pistons, Houston Rockets, Kansas City Kings, 1967-1976; son Jalen Rose, Denver Nuggets, 1994-present.

MOST DOMINATING PLAYOFF PERFORMANCE

By the Philadelphia 76ers, who won 12 of 13 games over three series en route to the 1983 championship. They narrowly missed fulfilling the prediction of center Moses Malone, who vowed the team would perform a clean sweep or, as he phrased it, win the title in "fo', fo' and fo'." The Sixers required only four games to defeat the Knicks in the first round and four games to overpower the Lakers in the NBA Finals but were pushed to five games by the Milwaukee Bucks in the Eastern Conference finals. The lone blemish was a 100-94 loss in Game 4 of the best-of-seven affair in Milwaukee.

MOST INSPIRATIONAL PLAYOFF PERFORMANCE

By the Houston Rockets, who overcame four teams that finished with better records during the regular season, four opponents that held a home-court advantage, en route to capturing their second consecutive title in 1995. Additionally, the Rockets were one loss from elimination against both Utah and Phoenix before advancing to meet and beat San Antonio in the Western Conference finals and then sweeping the Orlando Magic. They also set a playoff record by winning nine games on the road.

Meet Kevin Garnett: The Schoolboy Who Jumped to the NBA

He comes to the NBA with a size-52 suit and accolades galore.

He's 6-10, 220, and he can shoot 20-foot jumpers, is a tremendous leaper, slick ball-handler and passer, and runs with the speed of a 100-meter sprinter.

He attended his high-school prom last spring. He's 19 years old and will be a multi-millionaire on signing his contract with the Minnesota Timberwolves, who made him the fifth selection in the draft.

He is Kevin Garnett, the fifth player to enter the NBA without having played college basketball. The others: Moses Malone, Darryl Dawkins, Bill Willoughby and Shawn Kemp.

Is Garnett ready for the big jump? "I am prepared for this endeavor," he wrote in a letter to David Stern, NBA commissioner. "I know I will be among the finest players in the world."

The Wolves and the world can't expect him to be an overnight sensation. "He's talented enough to succeed in the NBA if mentally he's tough enough," says Dave Wohl, Miami Executive VP.

"He may not be ready physically, intellectually or emotionally," said Lee Rose, Milwaukee VP of player personnel. "But I only had to see him once."

"Everyone has to realize this is a 24-hour-day process," said Bob Whitsitt, the Portland GM who drafted Kemp for the Seattle SuperSonics in 1989. "You have to be willing to spend the years, not the days, to make it work."

No question that Garnett has to develop physically, especially his thin arms. "Unless you're built like Kemp, Dawkins and Malone, you've got one strike against you coming out of high school," said Cotton Fitzsimmons, now a Suns VP, who was Willoughby's first-year coach with the Atlanta Hawks. "They're in there with the men. For the first time in their lives, shots are being knocked back into their faces and they're being sent to the floor."

Kevin Garnett prepped at Chicago's Farragut Academy.

No. 5 in draft, Garnett talks to press in Minneapolis.

Garnett grew up in Mauldin, S.C., where he was Mr. Basketball through his junior year. His move, with his mother Shirley, to Chicago was triggered in part by an incident in which he and several friends were charged with assaulting a white student. As a first-time offender, he took part in a pretrial program and his record was cleared.

In the summer of 1994, he met William Nelson, the coach of Chicago's Farragut Academy, at a basketball camp and decided on the switch to Farragut for his senior year. There he moved into the national spotlight as he averaged 26 points, 18 rebounds, seven assists and six blocked shots.

Sought by many colleges, he narrowed his choices to North Carolina, Michigan and South Carolina. But he didn't achieve the qualifying score in the SAT or ACT that would have enabled him to receive a Division I scholarship.

He opted for the NBA draft and made a marked impression on NBA scouts at the predraft tryout camp. He'd been scouted previously at his high-school games. Whatever doubts there were about his youth, there was little question that he'd be an early first-round pick.

And now he enters the real world.

Moses Malone went from Petersburg (Va.) High to the pros.

GOOD LUCK! Toronto Raptors, Vancouver Grizzlies

Damn the puck, full speed ahead for roundball!

Although basketball will never replace hockey as the national sport of Canada, the Toronto Raptors and Vancouver Grizzlies launch a new era north of the border this season.

As the expansion entries in a 29-team NBA, the Raptors and Grizzlies begin with high hopes for hoops and with nicknames that befit them as the "hungriest teams in the NBA."

Raptors are predatory birds that prey on other animals; grizzlies, as Western Indian mythology notes, are bears that inspire awe and respect and are powerful, aggressive and fearless in battle.

Preparing for the challenge is a Toronto team that wishes it could revive the playing talent of ex-Detroit Piston superstar Isiah Thomas but will settle for him as VP of Basketball Operations. And the Raptors boast a highly regarded coach in Brendan Malone, formerly a leading assistant coach with the Pistons and New York Knicks.

Vancouver, representing the heritage of Western Canada's

Ex-Knick Greg Anthony: Grizzlies' No. 1 expansion pick.

British Columbia, comes armed for the fray with a front office guided by former college and pro coach Stu Jackson, who will be GM and VP of Basketball Operations. The Grizzlies will be coached by Brian Winters, a veteran of nine seasons in the NBA as a player for the Los Angeles Lakers and Milwaukee Bucks and nine years as an assistant under Lenny Wilkens.

The players? Stocked by expansion and college drafts, Toronto will feature ex-Bull B.J. Armstrong, its No. 1 expansion pick, and Arizona's Damon Stoudamire, No. 7 overall in the college draft. Vancouver leads with ex-Knick Greg Anthony, its first expansion pick, and Oklahoma State's Bryant (Big Country) Reeves, No. 5 overall in the college draft. (For scouting reports, player profiles and rosters, see page 227 for Toronto and 313 for Vancouver.)

Toronto's home court for the next two seasons will be the SkyDome; then the team will move into a renovated postal station near the waterfront that will be known as Air Canada Centre and will seat 22,500.

Vancouver will play downtown at General Motors Place, a new multi-purpose arena with 20,000-seat capacity.

Toronto's colors are red, purple, black and Naismith silver (Naismith for Dr. James Naismith, the Canadian who invented basketball in 1891). Vancouver's colors are red, brown and black.

Of course the color they'll be seeking—the most elusive of all—is NBA gold.

THE MAKING OF THE MAGIC PENNY

By BILL FAY

It's an odd twist that Penny Hardaway owes his fame to offense when, in fact, much of his life has been devoted to being defensive.

Hardaway was a *Parade* Magazine All-American his senior year at Treadwell High School in Memphis, Tenn. He was a first-team All-American at Memphis State. He was runnerup for Rookie of the Year his first season with the Orlando Magic and All-NBA first team in just his second year as a professional when he helped take the Magic to the NBA Finals.

All of those awards and the rewards that accompany them—a seven-year, $50-million contract from the Magic after his rookie year—are based on a sensational gift for getting the ball into the basket.

Hardaway has been compared to Magic Johnson since he first scored in the sports pages as a junior high-school star in Memphis. It's an apt comparison. He has the height, the court sense, the unique passing touch and the ability to score inside or outside that made Johnson a Laker superstar.

Consider, too, that Hardaway is teamed with mighty Shaq O'Neal. Together, they form the most respected inside-outside game in the NBA since... well, since Johnson fed Kareem Abdul-Jabbar's appetite for sky hooks in the 1980s. Johnson-Jabbar were NBA champions five times between 1980 and 1987.

"It's really nice to hear when people compare me with Magic,

A sportswriter for the Tampa Tribune *since 1977, Bill Fay has been the Magic beat man from the beginning in 1989.*

Penny Hardaway displays his Magic to Michael Jordan.

but it's because of my height and the fact we both play point guard,'' the 6-7 Hardaway said. ''You can't really put me in the same class with Magic until I've won the number of championships he's won. I'm not even close to that yet.''

He's getting closer, as Orlando's appearance in last year's NBA Finals indicates, but even when the Magic win a championship, Hardaway will be thinking defense—off-the-court defense.

It all goes back to a Sunday night in April 1991, his freshman year at Memphis State, when he was returning a wallet to his cousin, LaMarcus Golden. Hardaway and a friend, Terry Starks, were parked outside of Golden's house about to go in when a car pulled up and a man stepped out to ask directions. Suddenly, he

Penny made All-NBA first team in only second season.

pulled a gun and within seconds Hardaway was face down on a cold, wet driveway with a gun jammed against the back of his head.

"You do a lot of thinking in that kind of situation," he said.

As Hardaway lay there shivering from fright and the cold pavement, he thought about what got him into the situation. He had grown up in this neighborhood. It was inner-city Memphis. The homes there were called "shotgun houses" because you could see from the front door right through to the back door of the 20-by-50 foot structures. Crime was part of the daily scene, but he'd steered clear of any involvement, thanks largely to the woman who raised him, his grandmother, Louise Hardaway. She had nicknamed him "Pretty" as a baby but it sounded like "Penny" and that is what everybody came to call him.

"My grandmother was very strict about where I was and when I had to be home," Hardaway said. "I had to be in before dark every night. I'd see guys out walking and hanging out all hours of the night and I'd be thinking, 'Man, I wish I could be out there', but my grandmother never let me. She was real strict about that and I'm glad about it now.''

Everybody knew Hardaway in his neighborhood, including the bad guys, and they left him alone. They knew he had a future, a way out. But the gunman on that night in '91 may have been from a different turf. He took their wallets, a gold chain, a ring and their tennis shoes. He got back into his car, but when Hardaway and his friend stood up too quickly, he leaned out the window and fired several shots. The last one ricocheted off the pavement and lodged itself in Hardaway's right foot.

Hardaway has been on the defensive ever since.

"That night had an impact on me that will last the rest of my life," he said. "I notice everyone and everything now. I don't take anything for granted. You come from where I come from and you learn to be defensive, real defensive."

So that's how Hardaway is. He never lets his guard down. Not on the basketball court, in the locker room or just walking to his car. Everywhere he goes, he's watching, listening, waiting for someone to say something or do something to him.

"I see a lot of myself in Penny," said teammate Nick Anderson, who grew up in a hostile inner-city environment in Chicago. "I see a guy who's sensitive about a lot of things, especially criticism. He keeps his guard up so he's ready to come back fighting if somebody gets on him."

He was tall for his age, 6-4 as a 12-year-old, so basketball was a natural sport to pursue. It became obvious very quickly that height wasn't the only gift he had when playing with his peers.

"The game was so easy for him," said Jim Kern, who recruited Hardaway as a 12-year-old to play for the YMCA-sponsored AAU team in town. "He wasn't like most kids tall for their age. He was coordinated, could run, handle the ball, score, rebound, do anything. We didn't call him a guard, forward or center, we just put him out there and said, 'Go.' He made things happen."

Hardaway was fortunate to be part of a golden era for basketball in Memphis. Future NBA players Elliott Perry, Vincent Askew, Todd Day and Tony Dumas were part of the AAU program at that time. The team traveled to tournaments at Virginia Beach, Jacksonville, Indianapolis and Seattle. They won the AAU National tournament when Hardaway was 16.

"We would go just about anywhere that would have us," Kern

said. "And Penny was the man. I didn't do a whole lot of coaching with him. I think the only thing I ever said to him was 'You've got to shoot more,' but he wouldn't. He wanted everybody on the team to score. He always got a bigger thrill out of setting somebody else up than he did scoring himself."

His star was shining just as bright at Treadwell High School, so long as he was on the basketball court. In the classroom, he literally fell asleep. Teachers, coaches, friends and especially his grandmother warned him that the lack of effort academically could cost him a career in basketball, but he ignored them. He had to sit out the middle half of his senior year at Treadwell because of academic failures. He returned just before the playoffs, but his skills were rusty. Though his team reached the state tournament, they didn't win a championship.

"I wouldn't listen to anybody," Hardaway admitted. "I don't know what was going on in my head. I guess I thought I was so good at basketball, the teachers would just let me skate in the classroom. Even when I had to sit out, I didn't realize the grades would be a big deal until they told me I couldn't play my first year in college."

Hardaway signed to play at Memphis State, but was among the first casualties of the infamous Prop 48 amendment, which set stricter academic guidelines for athletes to qualify for a scholarship at a Division I school. As a result, he was grounded for a full season at Memphis State.

"It was tough, but it was a blessing," Memphis State coach Larry Finch said. "Penny finally realized the price he had to pay to be involved in something he loved. He really made up his mind that nothing was going to keep him from basketball again, and you know what? He made the dean's list his first semester here!"

The flip side of the defensive Hardaway is that he craves acceptance. He wants to be liked, respected and admired. It took awhile for that to happen in Orlando with the Magic and their fans. When Orlando was interviewing prospects for the 1993 NBA draft, the people's choice was Chris Webber. The team sent representatives and a limousine to meet Webber at the airport and alerted media from all over Central Florida for the occasion. When Hardaway came to town, the only people there to greet him were a cameraman and reporter from a local TV station. He had to bum a ride into town with them. They even stopped at Burger King to buy him some breakfast before his workout.

That workout, coming two weeks before the draft, went well, but sentiment inside and outside the organization was still very strong for Webber. John Gabriel, then the team's player personnel director, sensed the appeal of a Hardaway-O'Neal duo and asked the rest of the management team to reconsider Hardaway. The club brought him back the night before the draft for a closed workout with five other Magic players.

"That workout sealed the deal," Gabriel said. "Penny was fantastic. He did a little bit of everything, rebound, pass, score, and we all saw the possibilities for something really special happening if we got him here and made him our point guard for the next 10 years."

On draft night, a huge crowd gathered at Orlando Arena and cheered wildly when Webber was announced as the Magic's first pick. Moments later, the team announced a trade and introduced Hardaway as their pick. The crowd responded with resounding boos. They did it again at the first exhibition game when Hardaway debuted off the bench and made six turnovers, yet was announced as Subway Sub of the Game. Hardaway went into his shell after that.

"You see and hear bad things all your life growing up; you don't want to hear no more when you go someplace new," Hardaway said that night. "I want the fans in Orlando behind me, but if I have to, I'll go through the season by myself."

"He wanted to be wanted so much that I think he was worrying about that the whole time instead of worrying about doing the things he can do," Magic coach Brian Hill said.

The turnaround came, ironically, in a home game against Golden State and Webber. Hardaway had 23 points, eight rebounds, five assists and two blocks. The fans gave him a couple of standing ovations. One group unfurled a banner that read: "We Picked The Right One Baby, Uh Huh!"

The rest of his rookie season unfolded just as the Magic had hoped. Hardaway started at shooting guard with veteran Scott Skiles as the point guard. As the season wore on, he gradually got more and more minutes at point guard as Hill eased him into the role. By the first week in February, the change was made and Hardaway has been the Magic's starting point guard ever since. He helped the team reach its goal of 50 victories and the first playoff berth in Magic history his rookie season. He finished the year averaging 16 points, 6.6 assists and 5.4 rebounds while shooting 47 percent from the field. The only sore point came in the playoffs when the Magic were eliminated, 3-0, in the first round by the Indiana Pacers.

"Penny did everything we asked of him, but you knew he was only scratching the surface that rookie year," Hill said. "He was

He came close to being Rookie of the Year in 1993-94.

getting to know his own strengths and weaknesses as well as those of his opponents. I had a feeling he was going to burst into the elite status of guards in the league his second year.''

And that's exactly what happened, though once again, not without some personal torment. Hardaway, on the advice of his agents, was a holdout when training camp opened. Media reports put his contract demands in the $100-million range, a territory uncharted by any athlete. Some fans lashed out again at him and even his newest teammate, Horace Grant, encouraged Hardaway to get the contract issue settled quickly. ''There's a time for business and a time to be with your teammates at work and now is the time for him to be at work," Grant said five days into the holdout.

The issue was settled two days later when Hardaway received a deal that made him the highest-paid point guard in the league. He came to camp intent on proving his worth and once again wiping any tarnish off his reputation. When the Magic rolled off a team-record 10 wins in November, the issue was long forgotten. When they set another club record for victories with 13 in December, he was being talked about as a starter on the All-Star team. When Orlando finished the month of January 12-2, he had his first starting spot in the All-Star Game sewn up and the Magic had the best overall record in the NBA at 35-8.

"He can definitely be another Magic," Seattle scout and longtime NBA assistant Bob Kloppenburg said after seeing Hardaway in late January. "I really believe that. I don't know him so I don't know if he has the heart, but he has the game. Some of the passes he throws, he makes them look so easy. He has the whole package."

As the season continued, Hardaway's confidence increased to the point where he was able to lead Orlando to victory in games where O'Neal and Grant didn't play. He had 39 points, six assists and five rebounds and scored the winning basket on a steal and breakaway dunk in a nationally-televised game against Chicago. A few days later, when O'Neal and Grant were back, he had 13 points, 12 assists and seven rebounds in a win over New York.

"The best players can adjust to whatever their team needs," Hardaway said. "Before every game, I look at the matchups and try and figure out what we need that night. If we need scoring, I'll score, but with Shaq and Nick [Anderson] and Dennis [Scott], I usually don't have to do that. I have to get everybody involved, keep everybody happy. That's really the way I like to play."

He kept the Magic and their fans happy right up to the NBA Finals when neither he nor his teammates could figure out how to beat Houston. The Magic were swept out of the playoffs for the second straight year, albeit three rounds later than in their first trip. Hardaway was as vexed as any of his teammates by the Rockets' ability to come up with the big plays at the end of every game. He sees that as the next logical step in his career.

"I'm going into this offseason the same way I did last year: remembering how we lost, more so than how good a season we had," Hardaway said. "I've been to the state finals in high school, the last eight in the NCAA tournament and the NBA Finals and never won. I don't know how many more chances I'm going to get, but I'm going to find a way to win one."

INSIDE THE NBA

By FRED KERBER, CORKY MEINECKE and SCOTT HOWARD-COOPER

PREDICTED ORDER OF FINISH

ATLANTIC	CENTRAL	MIDWEST	PACIFIC
Orlando	Chicago	Houston	Phoenix
New York	Indiana	Utah	Seattle
Philadelphia	Cleveland	San Antonio	L.A. Lakers
Boston	Charlotte	Denver	Golden State
New Jersey	Atlanta	Dallas	Sacramento
Miami	Milwaukee	Minnesota	Portland
Washington	Detroit	Vancouver	L.A. Clippers
	Toronto		

EASTERN CONFERENCE: Orlando
WESTERN CONFERENCE: Houston
CHAMPION: Orlando

"Never underestimate the heart of a champion."

Good advice. That was the advice Houston Rockets coach Rudy Tomjanovich presented to the world on the eve of his club's quest for repeat status as NBA champions. The Rockets faced an incredible path to return to Eden. For starters, they had won just

---

Off-the-boards Fred Kerber is the veteran NBA beat man for the New York Post, *Corky Meinecke follows the Pistons for the Detroit Free Press and Scott Howard-Cooper covers the Lakers for the* Los Angeles Times. *Meinecke wrote the Central Division, Cooper the Midwest and Pacific, and Kerber the Atlantic and introduction.*

Warriors made Maryland's Joe Smith No. 1 in draft.

47 games and were seeded sixth in the West. No team ever arose from that lowly status of No. 6. No team until the Rockets last year, of course.

So how can you underestimate Houston's chance for a three-peat, especially with Hakeem Olajuwon, who simply devoured everything and everyone in sight when it mattered? How can you pick against the Rockets?

Well, it isn't easy. But this year—an expansion year that includes the NBA's first steps in modern times on foreign soil with the addition of Vancouver and Toronto, a year that sees the league hoping to come back from a first-ever, serious labor dispute that resulted in a summer lockout—it seems prudent to believe in Magic. Orlando's Magic.

The senses-numbing run for the Magic, which included a sensational 39-2 home record and then playoff victories against Boston, Chicago and Michael Jordan, plus a seven-game gut check against Indiana, came to an ignominious end in a four-and-out sweep defeat against Houston in the Finals.

"But they are a team that will be back and winning championships for many years to come," Olajuwon cautioned.

And Year One, the Year of the Magic, should be 1995-96.

The Magic took home more than just pain and some embarrassment after the Houston lightning warfare assault. The Magic took home some invaluable experience.

They made the climb to the Finals and then proceeded to show their age in various ways. Blowing a 20-point Game 1 lead. Shooting close to death from the foul line. Failing to REALLY establish their own doomsday weapon, Shaquille O'Neal. And other things that are the trademarks of greenhorns.

So the Magic watched and learned. And they stood huddled around coach Brian Hill at the end of Game 4, watching the Rockets launch themselves into a dizzying celebration. "I wanted them to remember that moment. I wanted them to see it, to get an idea of how it could be for them," Hill said.

The Magic could be getting that feeling this June.

They have the core talent. They have Shaq, the defending scoring champ who had to learn something about humility from Hakeem. They have Anfernee (Penny) Hardaway, who in his second year showed many of the comparisons to another point guard of repute, Magic Johnson, are legitimate. They have a potentially awesome long-range attack with Dennis Scott and Nick Anderson (who must exorcise his playoff demons).

They have rebounder and defender deluxe Horace Grant at power forward. The bench is frighteningly thin, populated by the likes of former CBAers Anthony Bowie and Donald Royal, but first reserve guard Brian Shaw has quality, versatility and, when teamed with Hardaway, can help the Magic find nightmare mismatches for opponents.

Getting there for Orlando won't be easy. At least when the

playoffs start. They should sleepwalk through the weak Atlantic Division, where only the Knicks, under new coach Don Nelson, figure to give chase. But after the regular season, Jordan and the Bulls, Reggie Miller and the Pacers, plus the Hornets of Alonzo Mourning and Larry Johnson, will be among those lining up to halt the Magic ride.

To get back to the Finals, Houston must first endure what figures to be a blistering regular-season run through the Midwest minefield, populated by the NBA's only two 60-victory teams last season, San Antonio and Utah. And, of course, the playoffs will bring out the Pacific contenders from Pheonix and Seattle and Los Angeles.

So bank on the Magic to win it all, ousting Houston in a reversal of 1994-95 form. Look for both to win their respective divisions with Phoenix taking the Pacific Division and Chicago returning to Jordan-induced prominence in the Central.

So a quick scan, division by division, starts in the Atlantic, where three new coaches reside and improvement, not serious title thoughts, looms as the goal for the bulk of the teams.

The one Atlantic team beyond Orlando dreaming of title rings remains the Knicks. When Pat Riley walked out on his contract with one year remaining, the Knicks vaulted into a short-list candidate search and pick a plum in Nelson. The sixth-winningest coach in history, with 817 victories, Nelson resigned at Golden State last season amid the furor surrounding the aftermath of the Chris Webber fiasco. Most predicted a year off for the Hall of Fame-bound coach. "I said it would have to be the right job for me to come back and this was the right job," Nelson assessed.

Making it right is Patrick Ewing, who fits the description of the big man Nelson has so longed to coach. No more Alton Lister. No more Paul Mokeski. Ewing, coming off perhaps the finest all-around season of his career, should fit nicely into a faster-paced tempo envisioned by Nelson. But the Knicks are an aging team, seen by many as going in reverse. Nelson thinks not. The Knicks, though, never got ample playing time for their young players under Riley and have many questions, most notably backup point guard to 34-year-old Derek Harper. The Knicks lost Greg Anthony to expansion.

Elsewhere in the Atlantic, Philadelphia may show the biggest turnaround. That shouldn't be hard. The Sixers only won 24 last season. But Philly has shooter extraordinaire Dana Barros, the ever-improving 7-6 Shawn Bradley and undersized though effective forward Clarence Weatherspoon. And the Sixers grabbed Jerry Stackhouse, billed as the "Next Jordan" with the third pick in the draft.

In Boston, it will be intriguing to note how self-hired coach M.L. Carr remains optimistic when confronted with today's players. And without Greece-bound Dominique Wilkins. Carr, Boston's basketball player personnel chief, interviewed his list of candidates for the Celtics' job. And then hired himself.

At press time, Miami, with all sorts of needs, was still without a coach. Pat Riley was in the wings, awaiting a settlement of tampering charges that would enable him to be a hoped-for miracle worker for the Heat.

In Washington, the Bullets have assembled a terrific half-team. The Bullets are good up front with last season's rookie plum, Juwan Howard, Webber and 7-7 behemoth Gheorghe Muresan. But alas, there are no worthwhile guards. The Bullets should still make strides on last season's 21 victories, but not enough to play in the postseason.

New Jersey, fighting rumors of a summer sale and subsequent move, will continue trying to coax Derrick Coleman to play every night while hoping point guard Kenny Anderson doesn't fall under the Jersey jinx.

In the Central, Michael is back. From the start this time. After Jordan dropped baseball and re-upped with Scottie Pippen and coach Phil Jackson in Chicago, the Bulls surged to 12 games over .500 and scored a first-round playoff victory over the Hornets. They'll be better this season with Michael playing all the way. But not good enough to get another ring.

Defending Central champ Indiana will be tougher than ever. Reggie Miller hits from the outside, the vastly improved Rik Smits scores inside, Derrick McKey closes down opponent scorers and the Davis boys, Dale and Antonio, work the glass. The Pacers, though, need bench help.

Cleveland hopes to avoid the injury mess that demolished them last year. Charlotte, with Kendall Gill back home after a trade to Seattle, hopes this is FINALLY the year (it's not). Atlanta, which can't live solely on the defensive pressure of guards Mookie Blaylock and Stacey Augmon, is trying to rebuild and has two late first, two mid-second-rounders. Milwaukee went to the wire before losing its playoff bid, but that should change behind the young guns, Vin Baker and Glenn Robinson. Doug Collins, who took over as coach in Detroit, has last season's super rookie Grant Hill, a terrific shooter in Allan Houston, the always potent, ever-classy Joe Dumars and then not a heckuva lot else. Toronto? Hey, the Raptors are in the league and have fingers—or claws—crossed on undersized guard Damon Stoudamire, 5-10.

INSIDE THE NBA • 53

Out West, Charles Barkley tried to deflect attention from the Suns' blowing a 3-1 playoff lead to Houston by talking retirement. He's back. Wow, what a stunner. Seattle is on depression watch. After terrorizing the league, again, the Sonics went meekly in the first round. Again. The Lakers, with youth and quickness that includes guard Nick Van Exel and forward Eddie Jones, who's back for his second year, stunned the world and ran off 48 victories and a playoff upset of Seattle. They bear watching as the NBA's darkhorse candidate.

After the Lakers, the Blazers are trying to rebuild in their new arena; Sacramento hopes this is the year Mitch Richmond shoots them into the playoffs despite the never-ending search for a center continuing, while Golden State, with Rick Adelman, late of Portland, now in charge, needs to rejuvenate with all that offense. And rejuvenation could come in the form of the draft's No. 1 pick, 6-10 Joe Smith out of Maryland. The Clippers? Well, they're the Clippers. They drafted Antonio McDyess of Alabama, a move praised by NBA observers as insightful and astute. So the Clippers promptly traded McDyess to Denver.

The Midwest has Hakeem and Co. figuring to get it done even in the regular season this time. Utah, behind the talent of the marvels known as Karl Malone and John Stockton, could surprise if Felton Spencer can successfully return from a torn Achilles. San Antonio, on those days Dennis Rodman is on time and playing, can fight with anyone. Denver got the replacement for iffy LaPhonso Ellis in McDyess but still must find a point with a legit point-guard mentality. Dallas will also make noise behind guards Jim Jackson, whose exclusion from the All-Star Game was a joke, co-Rookie of the Year (with Hill) Jason Kidd and forward Jamal Mashburn. Minnesota, with 19-year-old schoolboy Kevin Garnett, is trying to right years of wrongs, and Vancouver, well, the Grizzlies are in the same Canadian boat as Toronto.

BOSTON CELTICS

TEAM DIRECTORY: Chairman: Paul Gaston; Vice-Chairmen: Paul Dupee, Stephen Schram; Pres.: Red Auerbach; Exec. VP/GM: Jan Volk; Exec. VP/Dir. Basketball Oper./Head Coach: M.L. Carr; VP-Marketing/Communications: Tod Rosensweig; Dir. Pub. Rel.: Jeff Twiss; Dir. Publications and Inf.: David Zuccaro; Asst. Coaches: Don Casey, John Kuester, Dennis Johnson. Arena: Fleet Center (18,600). Colors: Green and white.

SCOUTING REPORT

SHOOTING: It's fair, at best. And now Dominique Wilkins has left for Greece. Dino Radja will score inside. Ditto Eric Montross, who displayed quality skills around the basket as a rookie. But once you step outside, the scoring and the shooting drops dramatically.

The Celtics are devoid of perimeter consistency. Dee Brown and Sherman Douglas are most effective in an open-court style, a style that new coach M.L. Carr promises this season, but occasionally, it's nice to bang home some jumpers. The Celtics are simply saddled with too many question-mark shooters.

PLAYMAKING: This will be a wait-and-see situation. If the Celtics go from 45 RPM to 77 RPM, there could be more excitement. As well as more turnovers, an area where they ranked 10th from the bottom last year.

The problem was that the overall offense was much too stagnant, lacking creativity beyond Douglas, who was 16th in the league with 6.9 assists per game. But after him, it was mediocre to poor as the Celtics placed 20th in assists. And there's not much coming from forward draftees Eric Williams (a scorer) or Junior Burrough (a rebounder).

REBOUNDING: Again, there's nothing special here. Montross will get his and Radja can grab an offensive rebound for a quick score. But on the defensive glass, the Celtics look like a talent-challenged team. And forget anything coming from the backcourt here because the Celtics are overburdened by a decided lack of size at guard.

Derek Strong, a former CBA player and a cast-off by several NBA teams, supplied some muscle. But the best way to sum up Boston's rebounding woes came through a comment about Strong

Eric Montross was given high marks in his rookie season.

by then-coach Chris Ford early last season. After watching Strong dominate the glass in a practice, Ford enthused to reporters, "You should have seen Derek Strong. He was getting everything off the boards. But then he was doing it against us, so take it with a grain of salt."

DEFENSE: Awful. The Celtics surrendered too many points (104.7), too many good shots (.484 opponent shooting percent-

CELTIC ROSTER

No.	Veterans	Pos.	Ht.	Wt.	Age	Yrs. Pro	College
7	Dee Brown	G	6-1	175	26	5	Jacksonville
20	Sherman Douglas	G	6-1	198	29	6	Syracuse
29	Pervis Ellison	F-C	6-10	235	28	6	Louisviiille
44	Rick Fox	G-F	6-7	231	26	4	North Carolina
U-5	Jay Humphries	G	6-3	185	33	11	Colorado
U-34	Xavier McDaniel	F	6-7	232	32	10	Wichita State
9	Greg Minor	G-F	6-6	210	24	1	Louisville
0	Eric Montross	C	7-0	270	24	1	North Carolina
40	Dino Radja	F	6-11	263	28	2	Croatia
U-31	Derek Strong	F	6-8	250	27	4	Xavier
4	David Wesley	G	6-0	196	24	2	Baylor

U-unrestricted free agent

Rd.	Rookie	Sel.No.	Pos.	Ht.	Wt.	College
1	Eric Williams	14	F	6-8	220	Providence
2	Junior Burrough	33	F	6-8	242	Virginia

age). And they ranked just 23rd in steals, 21st in blocked shots. Yep, that qualifies as awful.

And nowhere are the Celtics worse than in the transition game. They simply don't—or can't—get back. Even where they do, their halfcourt defense is just a notch above miserable. They are plagued at the forward spot, where Radja has appeared too one-dimensional as an offensive threat. Wilkins long has been an underrated defender, but age (35) is overtaking him. Carr promises an exciting, aggressive defensive style. Too bad he doesn't have exciting, aggressive defensive players.

OUTLOOK: Well, they'll have a new arena. Other than that, most aspects around the Celtics figure to be as grim and dreary as the old Boston Garden they are leaving behind. The team, on paper, is simply too inconsistent, with too many questions. Where will the rebounding come from? Who can step up and consistently knock down shots? How long will Carr's ultra-positive approach last when the losses begin mounting?

Boston has its bright spots, such as Radja's scoring, Douglas' creativity, Brown's quickness. But the bright spots don't outshine the dark, and the Celtics are hurtling into mediocrity at an alarming pace.

Dino Radja is a multiple force under the boards.

CELTIC PROFILES

SHERMAN DOUGLAS 29 6-1 198 — Guard

Remember how back in Miami they rapped him for creating too much for himself? Well, it's a good thing he never stopped or the Celtics' offense last year might have averaged about 31 points a game... Ended the season as, arguably, the Celtics' most important player... Never has been a classic drive-and-dish point guard, but his dashes to the basket bailed the Celtics out numerous times... Offense broke down a lot and this Syracuse product had little choice... Brought an offensive toughness that the Celtics were lacking... Had big-time trouble in the playoffs, though: shot .353. But don't forget the opposing point guard was Anfernee Hardaway... Sprained knee knocked him out of action early in season... Terrific after the All-Star Game. Stats took a quantum leap in every category... Season-high 18 assists against Bullets March 1. It was only the 13th time a Celtic ever had 18 assists... Career-high 22 assists came as a Celtic, April 3, 1994, at Philly. That was the third-highest ever by a Celtic... Celtics got him on Jan. 10, 1992, in trade with Miami for Brian Shaw... Heat drafted him on second round in 1989 after his standout Big East career... Born Sept. 15, 1966, in Washington, D.C.... Made $2.731 million in 1994-95.

Year	Team	G	FG	FG Pct.	FT	FT Pct.	Reb.	Ast.	TP	Avg.
1989-90	Miami	81	463	.494	224	.687	206	619	1155	14.3
1990-91	Miami	73	532	.504	284	.686	209	624	1352	18.5
1991-92	Mia.-Bos.	42	117	.462	73	.682	63	172	308	7.3
1992-93	Boston	79	264	.498	84	.560	162	508	618	7.8
1993-94	Boston	78	425	.462	177	.641	193	683	1040	13.3
1994-95	Boston	65	365	.475	204	.689	170	446	954	14.7
	Totals	418	2166	.485	1046	.667	1003	3052	5427	13.0

DINO RADJA 28 6-11 263 — Forward

Okay, okay, he's named after Fred and Wilma's dinosaur pet... But there's nothing else ancient about his game, especially on offense... Cemented himself as a legit scoring power forward... Also rebounds... Terrific around the basket. Nice up-and-under move. And he has the bulk to withstand and give poundings... Missed 15 games with a fractured finger... A 49-percent shooter, he was Boston's best rebounder and shot-blocker... Of course, being Boston's best rebounder and shot-blocker last year was like being the best swimmer in Death Valley... Defensively, well, that part of the game is coming... Maybe... Member of the 1988 silver medalist Yugoslavian (now Croatian) Olympic team... Celtics picked him on the second round in 1989 with the No. 40 overall pick... All-Rookie second team in 1993-94... Born April 24, 1967, in Split, Croatia... No college, but attended the Technical School Center for high school. Earned $2.145 million last year. So much for going nowhere without a college degree.

Year	Team	G	FG	FG Pct.	FT	FT Pct.	Reb.	Ast.	TP	Avg.
1993-94	Boston	80	491	.521	226	.751	577	114	1208	15.1
1994-95	Boston	66	450	.490	233	.759	573	111	1133	17.2
	Totals	146	941	.506	459	.755	1150	225	2341	16.0

DEE BROWN 26 6-1 175   Guard

His 1994-95 season? Been there, done that... With the exception of his eager acceptance of the new three-point distance, he pretty much had the same season he's had each year... Hit 126 of his three-pointers. In four previous seasons, he had made just 68... So there was at least one new wrinkle. But many of the old patterns, too... Showed flashes of brilliance ... Also showed grating flashes of inconsistency... Upped his scoring, lowered his shooting in the playoffs... Needs to lose the nice-guy mentality on the court. Some say he lacks the arrogance needed to be a top-flight scorer... No denying the quickness factor... Was the No. 19 pick in 1991 out of Jacksonville... Made the All-Rookie team but then nearly saw career wiped out the following season via a devastating knee injury... But he returned, in season after the ACL injury in preseason, and scored 23 points in his first game back... Slam Dunk champ his rookie season... Real name: DeCovan... Born Nov. 29, 1968, in Jacksonville, Fla.... Pocketed $2.5 million in 1994-95.

Year	Team	G	FG	FG Pct.	FT	FT Pct.	Reb.	Ast.	TP	Avg.
1990-91	Boston	82	284	.464	137	.873	182	344	712	8.7
1991-92	Boston	31	149	.426	60	.769	79	164	363	11.7
1992-93	Boston	80	328	.468	192	.793	246	461	874	10.9
1993-94	Boston	77	490	.480	182	.831	300	347	1192	15.5
1994-95	Boston	79	437	.447	236	.852	249	301	1236	15.6
	Totals	349	1688	.461	807	.829	1056	1617	4377	12.5

ERIC MONTROSS 24 7-0 270 Center

They asked a lot. And they got a lot... With Pervis Ellison hurt, with Acie Earl a dud, a lot of responsibility fell to this rookie... And he responded with a game that placed him high among the league's second echelon of centers... Was a little meek at times. Forgivable in a rookie... Celtics would like him to be more instinctive offensively. After all, Dean Smith is no longer calling the shots... Second on the team in games, rebounding and blocks... Serious foul trouble against Shaquille O'Neal in the playoffs. Serious trouble, period, against Shaq... Fourth-best rookie rebounder... There's something for the future here... Born Sept. 23, 1971, in Indianapolis, Ind.... Grandfather, Johnny Townsend, was standout in the pros during the late '30s and '40s... Celtics grabbed him at No. 9 out of North Carolina... Two-time second team All-American... Member of Tar Heels' 1993 NCAA championship team... Earned $800,000 last season.

Year	Team	G	FG	FG Pct.	FT	FT Pct.	Reb.	Ast.	TP	Avg.
1994-95	Boston	78	307	.534	167	.635	566	36	781	10.0

PERVIS ELLISON 28 6-10 235 Center

Swears this year will be different... Another season beset with knee problems... Played 55 games, started 11... In six seasons since being the No. 1 pick out of Louisville, by Sacramento, he has never played a full 82 games. Played less than 60 four times, less than 50 three times... And he can play. But one big question: does he really want to after all the setbacks?... Showed all the skills—rebounds, shot-blocking, low-post offense—that makes teams want to keep trying to get him sound... Missed first 19 games of the season because of chronic bad knee, then stepped in against Denver on Dec. 12 and scored 19 points and grabbed 10 rebounds... That's why teams will always gamble on him... Born April 3, 1967, in the Bronx, N.Y.... High school in Savannah, Ga.... Surgery for bone spurs in right foot and ankle killed his rookie season... Then came tendinitis in his big toe... Went from Kings to Bullets in three-team trade with Utah that landed Jazz Jeff Malone on June 25, 1990... Strained knees led to surgery on both knees during days with Bullets... Signed as a free agent by Boston and made $1.1

million last season... As a freshman, he was the NCAA Tournament MVP in leading Louisville to 1987 national title.

Year	Team	G	FG	FG Pct.	FT	FT Pct.	Reb.	Ast.	TP	Avg.
1989-90	Sacramento	34	111	.442	49	.628	196	65	271	8.0
1990-91	Washington	76	326	.513	139	.650	585	102	791	10.4
1991-92	Washington	66	547	.539	227	.728	740	190	1322	20.0
1992-93	Washington	49	341	.521	170	.702	433	117	852	17.4
1993-94	Washington	47	137	.469	70	.722	242	70	344	7.3
1994-95	Boston	55	152	.507	71	.717	309	34	375	6.8
	Totals	327	1614	.513	726	.697	2505	578	3955	12.1

DEREK STRONG 27 6-8 250   Forward

Headed into unrestricted free agency... If only he were a little taller. That listed 6-8 is just a bit generous... He can rebound. And he can help when given a chance. Career-high 16 rebounds against the Bulls on March 22... Shoulder problems... Averaged 5.4 rebounds in just 19.2 minutes... Offense is limited to moves around basket... Was college teammate at Xavier of all-star forward Tyrone Hill... CBA's Most Valuable Player in 1992-93... Drafted by Sixers in second round in 1990. Did a year in Spain and the USBL... After tryouts and waiver moves by 76ers and Bullets, he hit the CBA... Finally landed in the NBA with Milwaukee via 10-day contract. Stuck with Bucks... Traded to Celtics with Blue Edwards for Ed Pinckney and draft rights to Andrei Fetisov June 29, 1994... Born Feb. 9, 1968, in Los Angeles... Made $600,000 last year.

Year	Team	G	FG	FG Pct.	FT	FT Pct.	Reb.	Ast.	TP	Avg.
1991-92	Washington	1	0	.000	3	.750	5	1	3	3.0
1992-93	Milwaukee	23	42	.457	68	.800	115	14	156	6.8
1993-94	Milwaukee	67	141	.413	159	.772	281	48	444	6.6
1994-95	Boston	70	149	.453	141	.820	375	44	441	6.3
	Totals	161	332	.433	371	.794	776	107	1044	6.5

RICK FOX 26 6-7 231   Forward-Guard

Could be a starter this year... Injured a lot last season. Surgery to remove bone spurs from both ankles wiped out the last month and the playoffs... Has never quite lived up to the promise of his rookie season... But he is a good, active one-on-one defender with solid quickness... His shot improved and he benefited from nearer three-point line. Still, he's not what you'd call a pure shooter. Not by a long shot. Or a midrange shot... Decent finisher but prone to some absolutely galling mistakes... Typical swingman problem: ball-handling a little suspect for the two, bulk isn't enough for the three... But he did have a 14-rebound game last season... Real name is Ulrich... Never missed a game in four years at North Carolina. Tied school mark by playing in 140 games... Also left Tar Heels as the all-time leader in steals... Boston drafted him at No. 24 in 1991... Born July 24, 1969, in Toronto... Made $1.75 million in 1994-95.

Year	Team	G	FG	FG Pct.	FT	FT Pct.	Reb.	Ast.	TP	Avg.
1991-92	Boston	81	241	.459	139	.755	220	126	644	8.0
1992-93	Boston	71	184	.484	81	.802	159	113	453	6.4
1993-94	Boston	82	340	.467	174	.757	355	217	887	10.8
1994-95	Boston	53	169	.481	95	.772	155	139	464	8.8
	Totals	287	934	.471	489	.766	889	595	2448	8.5

GREG MINOR 24 6-6 210   Guard-Forward

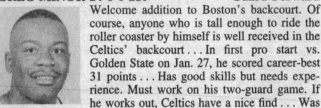

Welcome addition to Boston's backcourt. Of course, anyone who is tall enough to ride the roller coaster by himself is well received in the Celtics' backcourt... In first pro start vs. Golden State on Jan. 27, he scored career-best 31 points... Has good skills but needs experience. Must work on his two-guard game. If he works out, Celtics have a nice find... Was drafted by Clippers with 25th pick in 1994. Sent to Indiana as part of the Mark Jackson trade... Became free agent when he and Pacers couldn't work out a contract... Was the Metro Conference's Clutch Player of the Year as a senior at Louisville... Born Sept. 18, 1971, in Sandersville, Ga.... Celtics paid him $250,000 last year.

Year	Team	G	FG	FG Pct.	FT	FT Pct.	Reb.	Ast.	TP	Avg.
1994-95	Boston	63	155	.515	65	.833	137	66	377	6.0

DAVID WESLEY 24 6-0 196   Guard

Not bad as a backup point guard. But he certainly wasn't the answer to Boston's crying lack of height in the backcourt... Started 36 games... Season went down Feb. 27 when he was placed on the injured list because of swelling in his right knee. Underwent surgery and missed the final 31 games and the playoffs... Nice, steady player who needs to become more

instinctive running the offense. And he needs to develop a shot
... Moves the ball well and finds the open guy ... Undrafted out
of Baylor, Class of '92 ... Signed on as a free agent with the
Nets and spent a year as Kenny Anderson's backup after doing
the CBA in 1992-93 ... Latched on with Celtics, signing as a free
agent before the season and made $250,000 last year ... Born
Nov. 14, 1970, in Longview, Tex.

Year	Team	G	FG	FG Pct.	FT	FT Pct.	Reb.	Ast.	TP	Avg.
1993-94	New Jersey	60	64	.368	44	.830	44	123	183	3.1
1994-95	Boston	51	128	.409	71	.755	117	266	378	7.4
	Totals	111	192	.394	115	.782	161	389	561	5.1

JAY HUMPHRIES 33 6-3 185   Guard

Acquired in-season, Feb. 3, along with a second-round draft pick from Utah for Blue Edwards ... Rarely used with Celtics ... Rarely used with Utah for that matter ... Celtics took him more for his salary slot ... Had absolutely no chance to show Boston what he can—or can't—still do ... Offseason surgery wiped out his preseason and the first 15 games ...
Eleven-year veteran has played both guard spots ... Never a great
shooter, but always a sound, smart player ... No. 13 pick on first
round by Phoenix out of Colorado in 1984 ... Traded to Milwaukee for Craig Hodges and a second-round pick Feb. 25, 1988
... Went to Utah with Larry Krystkowiak for Edwards, Eric Murdock and a first-rounder June 24, 1992 ... Born Oct. 17, 1962,
in Los Angeles ... Made $1.9 million last year.

Year	Team	G	FG	FG Pct.	FT	FT Pct.	Reb.	Ast.	TP	Avg.
1984-85	Phoenix	80	279	.446	141	.829	164	350	703	8.8
1985-86	Phoenix	82	352	.479	197	.767	260	526	905	11.0
1986-87	Phoenix	82	359	.477	200	.769	260	632	923	11.3
1987-88	Phoe.-Mil	68	284	.528	112	.732	174	395	683	10.0
1988-89	Milwaukee	73	345	.483	129	.816	189	405	844	11.6
1989-90	Milwaukee	81	496	.494	224	.786	269	472	1237	15.3
1990-91	Milwaukee	80	482	.502	191	.799	220	538	1215	15.2
1991-92	Milwaukee	71	377	.469	195	.783	184	466	991	14.0
1992-93	Utah	78	287	.436	101	.777	143	317	690	8.8
1993-94	Utah	75	233	.436	57	.750	127	219	561	7.5
1994-95	Utah-Bos.	18	8	.235	2	.500	13	19	20	1.1
	Totals	788	3502	.476	1549	.782	2003	4339	8772	11.1

XAVIER McDANIEL 32 6-7 232 Forward

Maybe leaving the Knicks a couple of years ago wasn't such a hot idea... Never achieved the status the Celts hoped for when they signed him as a free agent away from the Knicks in 1992... Celtics, at end of season, bought out his contract, which paid him $2.64 million last year... Showed he can still score in the half-court and be effective down on the blocks... But he spent most of the season on the trading block... Was one of the few real leaders on the team... But suffered through career lows across the board... Great game face. Will take on anyone, any time, any place... One of only three men ever to lead the NCAA in scoring and rebounding the same season... Did that for Wichita State in 1985... Seattle made him the No. 4 pick in 1985. Immediate impact: All-Rookie team and sixth in the league in offensive rebounding... Was a devastating boarder with maniacal explosiveness and tenacity... Knee woes (surgery after 1987-88) took a fearsome toll... Traded by Sonics to Suns for Eddie Johnson and two first-round picks Dec. 7, 1990... Suns sent him to Knicks Oct. 1, 1991 for Trent Tucker, Jerrod Mustaf and draft picks... Played one year with Knicks... A super guy in the locker room... Born June 4, 1963, in Columbia, S.C.

Year	Team	G	FG	FG Pct.	FT	FT Pct.	Reb.	Ast.	TP	Avg.
1985-86	Seattle	82	576	.490	250	.687	655	193	1404	17.1
1986-87	Seattle	82	806	.509	275	.696	705	207	1890	23.0
1987-88	Seattle	78	687	.488	281	.715	518	263	1669	21.4
1988-89	Seattle	82	677	.489	312	.732	433	134	1677	20.5
1989-90	Seattle	69	611	.496	244	.733	447	171	1471	21.3
1990-91	Sea.-Phoe.	81	590	.497	193	.723	557	187	1373	17.0
1991-92	New York	82	488	.478	137	.714	460	149	1125	13.7
1992-93	Boston	82	457	.495	191	.793	489	163	1111	13.5
1993-94	Boston	82	387	.461	144	.676	400	126	928	11.3
1994-95	Boston	68	246	.451	89	.712	300	108	587	8.6
	Totals	788	5525	.489	2116	.718	4964	1701	13235	16.8

THE ROOKIES

ERIC WILLIAMS 23 6-8 220 Forward
Celtics hope he can follow in NBA footsteps of his Providence teammate, Michael Smith of Sacramento... Considered to have better offensive skills than Smith, who made impact with rebounding and defense... Scored over 1,000 points in his two

years with Friars... Did two years at Vincennes (Ind.) Junior College... Unanimous first-team Big East selection... Celtics made him No. 14 pick... Born July 17, 1972, in Newark, N.J.

JUNIOR BURROUGH 22 6-8 242 Forward
Second-round pick, No. 33, out of Virginia... Real name: Thomas... Fifth all-time scorer in Virginia history. Missed 2,000 points by 30... Honorable mention All-American as a senior... Good NBA size. Showed improvement each year... Cavs' leading rebounder (8.7 per) also considered strong defensively... Born Jan. 18, 1973, in Charlotte, N.C.

COACH M.L. CARR: Must have really bowled himself over in the interview... As Executive VP and Director of Basketball Operations, he conducted the search to find the replacement of Chris Ford. Wound up hiring himself... Has no coaching experience. But he is the eternal optimist... Played with the Celtics for six seasons as an enthusiastic, workhorse 6-6, 210-pound forward... Big on towel waving. Fired up the Boston Garden crowd with his white towel waving on the bench... With this team, he may be throwing in towels this season... Feuded with Ford over the style the team should be playing. Favors a decidedly up-tempo approach with lots of aggressive, attacking defense... Now all he needs are up-tempo players and aggressive, attacking defenders... In first year as VP of Basketball Operations, he brought in Dominique Wilkins, Pervis Ellison, David Wesley and Greg Minor... Member of Celtics' 1981 and '84 championship teams... Served the franchise as Director of Community Relations for three years. Was a member of the team's scouting department before that... Played with St. Louis of the ABA for one season out of Guilford College... Did three years with the Pistons before signing on with the Celtics as a free agent in 1979. Those were compensation days. So the Pistons were awarded Bob McAdoo while the Pistons sent two first-round picks to Boston. The Celtics later used those picks to make the staggering Robert Parish-Kevin McHale trade-draft... Initials stand for Michael Leon... Born Jan. 9, 1951, in Wallace, N.C.

GREATEST FIND

Celtic great Tom Heinsohn always had this problem with a Laker reserve forward. So when the forward was waived by the Lakers, Heinsohn ambled into the office of Celtic icon Red Auerbach and said it might not be a bad idea to put the guy in green.

Auerbach listened, and a $100 waiver fee later, Don Nelson was a Celtic.

Not a bad buy. Starting in 1965-66, Nelson played 11 years in Boston, scoring 9,968 points while missing only 21 games—he established a franchise-record streak by playing in 465 straight games from 1967-72. Nelson, who later also would earn a place among the greats in the coaching ranks, played for five Celtic championship teams and later saw his No. 19 jersey retired and hoisted among the rafters at fabled Boston Garden.

Nelson was a third-round pick by the Chicago Zephyrs out of Iowa in '63. After the Zephyrs moved to Baltimore, they sold Nelson to the Lakers. In two years as a reserve, he did enough to impress Heinsohn. And insure a storied future.

ALL-TIME CELTIC LEADERS

SEASON

Points: John Havlicek, 2,338, 1970–71
Assists: Bob Cousy, 715, 1959–60
Rebounds: Bill Russell, 1,930, 1963–64

GAME

Points: Larry Bird, 60 vs. Atlanta, 3/12/85
Assists: Bob Cousy, 28 vs. Minneapolis, 2/27/59
Rebounds: Bill Russell, 51 vs. Syracuse, 2/5/60

CAREER

Points: John Havlicek, 26,395, 1962–78
Assists: Bob Cousy, 6,945, 1950–63
Rebounds: Bill Russell, 21,620, 1956–69

MIAMI HEAT • 67

(Note: Miami was without a coach at press time.)

MIAMI HEAT

TEAM DIRECTORY: Managing Gen. Partner: Mickey Arison; VP-Player Personnel Dir.: Kevin Loughery; Dir. Pro Scouting: Chris Wallace; Dir. College and International Scouting: Tony Fiorentino; VP-Communications: Mark Pray; Coach: TBA; Arena: Miami Arena (15,200). Colors: Orange, red, yellow, black and white.

Glen Rice's shooting was highlighted by 56-point game.

SCOUTING REPORT

SHOOTING: They have Glen Rice. That makes them a better-than-average shooting team right there. And after Rice, Khalid Reeves showed in his first season that he's a legitimate perimeter threat. Billy Owens can be expected to produce a high percentage with his inside game and post-up ability against guards. But then there's a dropoff.

Kevin Willis is a 7-footer in love with the jump shot. Any jump shot. And of course, the Heat would prefer to see their 7-footer with his head in the general vicinity of the rim. The interior game, as it is on defense, is generally weak. If the Heat managed anything of significance inside, Rice might be able to produce awesome, instead of simply terrific, numbers. The Heat are expecting big things from European star Predrag Danilovic, whose slashing, driving game might be able to free up Rice some more.

PLAYMAKING: In an ideal world, Reeves would push the ball, Rice would shoot it in transition or, if the break opportunity isn't there, the Heat would work it inside for a Willis hook. That's in a perfect world. But Miami's world is far from perfect.

The Heat ranked sixth from the bottom in the league in assists. Reeves was, after all, a rookie and Bimbo Coles is far better known for his defense. With a shooter of Rice's ability, the Heat ideally would like to work inside-out. But too often the ball goes in and stays in. Only to go out. Of the basket.

REBOUNDING: The Heat placed right in the middle—13th—of the NBA in rebounding, despite the presence of Willis (10.9 per), who would have been the East's third-best rebounder had he played in enough games. Injuries kept him three games away. And in Owens (7.2 rpg), the Heat possessed the best rebounding guard in the NBA. So why so middle of the road?

Offensive rebounding, for starters. The Heat were highly susceptible to numerous-shot possessions by opponents. Willis just wasn't the ferocious boarder of past years and the departed-through-expansion John Salley was non-existent. Three times as a starter, Salley failed to get a rebound. The Heat have always lacked an inside horse. They're hoping their first-round pick, 6-9 Kurt Thomas of TCU, who led the nation in scoring and rebounding, can be that thoroughbred.

DEFENSE: Another middle-of-the-league area. And they played that way. The biggest problem for the Heat, as it has been for the

HEAT ROSTER

No.	Veterans	Pos.	Ht.	Wt.	Age	Yrs. Pro	College
U-2	Keith Askins	G-F	6-8	224	27	5	Alabama
7	Rex Chapman	G	6-4	195	28	7	Kentucky
12	Bimbo Coles	G	6-2	182	27	5	Virginia Tech
–	Predrag Danilovic	G	6-6	200	25	0	Serbia
U-21	Ledell Eackles	G	6-5	231	28	5	New Orleans
35	Kevin Gamble	G-F	6-6	225	29	8	Iowa
52	Matt Geiger	C	7-0	243	26	3	Georgia Tech
U-54	Brad Lohaus	F-C	6-11	235	31	8	Iowa
32	Billy Owens	G-F	6-9	225	26	4	Syracuse
3	Khalid Reeves	G	6-3	199	23	1	Arizona
41	Glen Rice	F-G	6-8	220	28	6	Michigan
42	Kevin Willis	F-C	7-0	240	33	11	Michigan State

U-unrestricted free agent

Rd.	Rookies	Sel.No.	Pos.	Ht.	Wt.	College
1	Kurt Thomas	10	F	6-9	230	Texas Christian
2	Terrence Rencher	32	G	6-3	185	Texas
2	George Banks	46	F	6-7	210	Texas-El Paso

franchise's history, is the decided lack of a shot-blocker. Want to drive the middle? Go ahead, there's no one to stop you if you can break down Rice and Owens and Reeves off the dribble. Wonder no more why the Heat were 17th in opposing shooting percentage, allowing .471. They were the only team in the league to have less than 300 rejects (298).

With Coles and Reeves, the Heat can apply some decent pressure with their first line of defense. But that always becomes a decidedly risky gamble. Just think of the awaiting nightmare if they get beaten.

OUTLOOK: The Heat are a team in transition. Again. They have a new coach—or should have one in Pat Riley once the tampering controversy is resolved. They have a new owner in shipping magnate Micky Arison, who bought out Billy Cunningham and Lewis Schaffel. They are a team without great hope for this year.

Oh, they'll have their moments. But those moments will be more losing than winning, despite the frequent torch jobs by Rice. They're trying to build a nucleus for upcoming years. They have some nice pieces in place, but too many of the same, tired problems remain. A team that came into the league with a five-year plan seems destined to turn it into a 10-year job. But they're counting on Riley to cut down on that hang time.

HEAT PROFILES

GLEN RICE 28 6-8 220   Guard-Forward

Caution: perennial all-star under construction. If not already complete... Yeah, he's a stud... Tied career high with 22.3 scoring average, ninth-best in NBA... Displayed why he's one of the game's best outside shooters on national TV when he nailed season league-high and franchise-record 56 points against Magic on Apr. 15... Still must improve putting ball on the floor but has quickest release east of Dodge... Showed he can nail the jumper in transition as well as coming off screens... Set franchise record for points in a season... Only Heat player to appear in all 82 games... Rebounding down to lowest total since his rookie season. But with that shot, who really cares? ... Member of Michigan's 1989 NCAA championship team... No. 4 pick by Heat in the '89 draft... Mr. Michigan in high school... Born May 28, 1967, in Flint, Mich.... 1994-95 salary: $2.6 million.

Year	Team	G	FG	FG Pct.	FT	FT Pct.	Reb.	Ast.	TP	Avg.
1989-90	Miami	77	470	.439	91	.734	352	138	1048	13.6
1990-91	Miami	77	550	.461	171	.818	381	189	1342	17.4
1991-92	Miami	79	672	.469	266	.836	394	184	1765	22.3
1992-93	Miami	82	582	.440	242	.820	424	180	1554	19.0
1993-94	Miami	81	663	.467	250	.880	378	184	1708	21.1
1994-95	Miami	82	667	.475	312	.855	378	192	1831	22.3
	Totals	478	3604	.459	1332	.835	2363	1067	9248	19.3

KEVIN WILLIS 33 7-0 240   Center-Forward

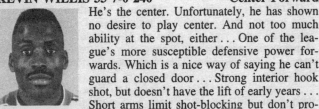

He's the center. Unfortunately, he has shown no desire to play center. And not too much ability at the spot, either... One of the league's more susceptible defensive power forwards. Which is a nice way of saying he can't guard a closed door... Strong interior hook shot, but doesn't have the lift of early years... Short arms limit shot-blocking but don't prohibit rebounds. Still averaged 10.9 boards, which would have been third-best in East had he played enough games... Suffered nagging back problem that kept him out of 14 games. Suspended for one other game for failing to comply with team rehab guidelines... Managed two 20-20 games... Runs court well. Occa-

MIAMI HEAT • 71

sionally will play a team game. Occasionally Halley's Comet stops by, too... Can hit jumper. But often falls in love with it, which is not good for a seven-footer, unless you're named Patrick Ewing... During 1991-92 season, he averaged 15.5 rebounds with two 30-board games... Acquired Nov. 6, 1994, after playing two games with Hawks, with a future first-rounder for Steve Smith and Grant Long... Earned $2.975 million last season... No. 11 pick on first round by Atlanta, out of Michigan State, in 1984... Born Sept. 6, 1962, in Los Angeles.

Year	Team	G	FG	FG Pct.	FT	FT Pct.	Reb.	Ast.	TP	Avg.
1984-85	Atlanta	82	322	.467	119	.657	522	36	765	9.3
1985-86	Atlanta	82	419	.517	172	.654	704	45	1010	12.3
1986-87	Atlanta	81	538	.536	227	.709	849	62	1304	16.1
1987-88	Atlanta	75	356	.518	159	.649	547	28	871	11.6
1988-89	Atlanta					Injured				
1989-90	Atlanta	81	418	.519	168	.683	645	57	1006	12.4
1990-91	Atlanta	80	444	.504	159	.668	704	99	1051	13.1
1991-92	Atlanta	81	591	.483	292	.804	1258	173	1480	18.3
1992-93	Atlanta	80	616	.506	196	.653	1028	165	1435	17.9
1993-94	Atlanta	80	627	.499	268	.713	963	150	1531	19.1
1994-95	Atl.-Mia.	67	473	.466	205	.690	732	86	1154	17.2
	Totals	789	4804	.501	1965	.695	7952	901	11607	14.7

VERNELL (BIMBO) COLES 27 6-2 182   Guard

If only he could shoot... Terrific defensive type who assumed starting point-guard mantle after trade of Steve Smith... Good ball distributor, he became Miami's all-time assist leader... Missed last 11 games with bad hamstring... Still the NBA's best player named Vernell... Had 2.67-to-1 assists-to-turnover ratio... Also had career best in steals... Good driver, good finisher... May one day create his own shot. Give him time. This was only his fifth season... A $902,000 bargain... Born Apr. 22, 1968, in Covington, Va.... Second-round pick by Kings in 1990, out of Virginia Tech... Heat made terrific pickup getting him for veteran (and long-since retired) Rory Sparrow June 27, 1990.

Year	Team	G	FG	FG Pct.	FT	FT Pct.	Reb.	Ast.	TP	Avg.
1990-91	Miami	82	162	.412	71	.747	153	232	401	4.9
1991-92	Miami	81	295	.455	216	.824	189	366	816	10.1
1992-93	Miami	81	318	.464	177	.805	166	373	855	10.6
1993-94	Miami	76	233	.449	102	.779	159	263	588	7.7
1994-95	Miami	68	261	.430	141	.810	191	416	679	10.0
	Totals	388	1269	.445	707	.802	858	1650	3339	8.6

BILLY OWENS 26 6-9 225   Guard-Forward

Has the skills. Needs the confidence... If he gets his head into game and displays the toughness needed, he could be a super stud... Recorded only the third triple-double in team history vs. T-Wolves on Jan. 5 (19 points, 10 rebounds, season-best 10 assists)... Has coast-to-coast ability, with rebounding and finishing skills. Could be a one-man break... Among league's best ball-handling forwards. Problem is, he plays guard... Lacks the outside touch of a legit shooting guard. And at the line? Hey, he's from Syracuse, okay? (.630 career)... Defensively, a question mark. But at 6-9, he doesn't get posted up much. Quick guards can give him fits, though... But he was the league's best rebounding guard... Assorted injuries knocked him out 12 games... Came to Heat from Warriors Nov. 2, 1994, along with rights to European star Predrag Danilovic for Rony Seikaly... Born May 1, 1969, in Carlisle, Pa.... Kings drafted him No. 3 in 1991... Traded to Warriors before '91 season for Mitch Richmond... $2.867-million wage earner in 1994-95.

Year	Team	G	FG	FG Pct.	FT	FT Pct.	Reb.	Ast.	TP	Avg.
1991-92	Golden State	80	468	.525	204	.654	639	188	1141	14.3
1992-93	Golden State	37	247	.501	117	.639	264	144	612	16.5
1993-94	Golden State	79	492	.507	199	.610	640	326	1180	15.0
1994-95	Miami	70	403	.491	194	.620	502	246	1002	14.3
	Totals	266	1610	.507	714	.630	2045	904	3941	14.8

REX CHAPMAN 28 6-4 195   Guard

Take his salary. Please... Which is what Miami did on draft night. Along with second-round draft pick Terrence Rencher in exchange for the draft rights to former second-round picks Jeff Webster and Ed Stokes... Made $2.004 million last year... In a career of dismal shooting, he shot a career low... And had more injuries, including a sore groin, fractured thumb, pulled abdominal muscle... Washington had been hoping for big things after a .498 injury-plagued 1993-94... Didn't happen... Tremendous athletic gifts. But rarely has he been able to put it together on the court... Made eight three-pointers in one game vs. Heat Nov. 12. That was a franchise record... Has played 70 games only once in last six seasons. Sixty games or less in four straight years... He's good when he's on. But then,

MIAMI HEAT • 73

who isn't?... Horrible defensively. And he's has never grasped the team game... First pick ever by Charlotte Hornets, No. 8 overall, after he left scandal-ridden Kentucky following his soph season in '88... Born Oct. 5, 1967, in Bowling Green, Ky.... Father Wayne played in ABA... Bullets got him Feb. 19, 1992 in trade for Tom Hammonds.

Year	Team	G	FG	FG Pct.	FT	FT Pct.	Reb.	Ast.	TP	Avg.
1988-89	Charlotte	75	526	.414	155	.795	187	176	1267	16.9
1989-90	Charlotte	54	377	.408	144	.750	179	132	945	17.5
1990-91	Charlotte	70	410	.445	234	.830	191	250	1102	15.7
1991-92	Char.-Wash.	22	113	.448	36	.679	58	89	270	12.3
1992-93	Washington	60	287	.477	132	.810	88	116	749	12.5
1993-94	Washington	60	431	.498	168	.816	146	185	1094	18.2
1994-95	Washington	45	254	.397	137	.862	113	128	731	16.2
	Totals	386	2398	.438	1006	.805	962	1076	6158	16.0

KHALID REEVES 23 6-3 199   Guard

Started slowly in rookie season under then-coach Kevin Loughery. Time picked up after then-coach became ex-coach... Terrific spot-up three-point shooter who spread defenses (67-of-171, 392). Showed much better range than expected after Heat made him the No. 12 pick out of Arizona... Good penetrate-and-dish guy. Already considered among better offensive-oriented point guards... Defense is questionable. What a surprise in a rookie... Needs to improve conditioning. By end of season, he ran through all the extra oxygen tanks... Knee tendinitis took him out of 14 games... Born July 15, 1972, in the Bronx, N.Y.... Parade All-American at Christ the King in Queens... Fell 75 points shy of 2,000 in college... Made $1.3 million in first season.

Year	Team	G	FG	FG Pct.	FT	FT Pct.	Reb.	Ast.	TP	Avg.
1994-95	Miami	67	206	.443	140	.714	186	288	619	9.2

MATT GEIGER 26 7-0 243   Center

Some guys just should go bald... Sort of looks like Charles Manson. If Squeaky Fromme becomes courtside regular, he's got to get a rug... Forced to play starting center for half the year due to team's lack of interior personnel... Runs floor well for a big man... Will never be mistaken for Hakeem Olajuwon defensively... Or Manson for that matter...

Did block 51 shots, though... But don't get excited. He is 7-feet, don't forget... Rebounding disappointment: 5.6 from a 7-foot starter? And that was his career best... Tends to drift mentally. When head's in game, he's nearly a competent NBA center. When not, he's closer to Henry Finkel... But overall not bad for a former second-round pick ('92 out of Georgia Tech) ... Made $1.402 million last season... Born Sept. 10, 1969, in Salem, Mass.

Year	Team	G	FG	FG Pct.	FT	FT Pct.	Reb.	Ast.	TP	Avg.
1992-93	Miami	48	76	.524	62	.674	120	14	214	4.5
1993-94	Miami	72	202	.574	116	.779	303	32	521	7.2
1994-95	Miami	74	260	.536	93	.650	413	55	617	8.3
	Totals	194	538	.548	271	.706	836	101	1352	7.0

KEVIN GAMBLE 29 6-6 225   Guard-Forward

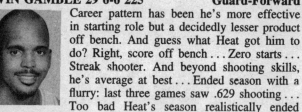

Career pattern has been he's more effective in starting role but a decidedly lesser product off bench. And guess what Heat got him to do? Right, score off bench... Zero starts... Streak shooter. And beyond shooting skills, he's average at best... Ended season with a flurry: last three games saw .629 shooting... Too bad Heat's season realistically ended about a month before... Decent ball-handler and passer, but gets in trouble off dribble. Gets in even more trouble against trapping defenses, especially when playing guard... If he improves his defense, he could rate as marginal... Good veteran for a young team... Born Nov. 13, 1965, in Springfield, Ill. ... Blazers took him on third round out of Iowa in '87. Didn't stick and became a CBA find by Celtics. Signed with Miami as a free agent for $650,000 Oct. 7, 1994... Wears No. 35 with Heat in honor of the late Reggie Lewis.

Year	Team	G	FG	FG Pct.	FT	FT Pct.	Reb.	Ast.	TP	Avg.
1987-88	Portland	9	0	.000	0	.000	3	1	0	0.0
1988-89	Boston	44	75	.551	35	.636	42	34	187	4.3
1989-90	Boston	71	137	.455	85	.794	112	119	362	5.1
1990-91	Boston	82	548	.587	185	.815	267	256	1281	15.6
1991-92	Boston	82	480	.529	139	.885	286	219	1108	13.5
1992-93	Boston	82	459	.507	123	.826	246	226	1093	13.3
1993-94	Boston	75	368	.458	103	.817	159	149	864	11.5
1994-95	Miami	77	220	.489	87	.784	122	119	566	7.4
	Totals	522	2287	.515	757	.812	1237	1123	5461	10.5

MIAMI HEAT • 75

BRAD LOHAUS 31 6-11 235 — Center-Forward

TCS: Tall Caucasian Syndrome... Prototypical three-point-shooting center... Once wandered into offensive paint and was asked for ID by teammates... Among lead leaders in treys (63-of-155) but didn't have enough conversions to qualify for league title... Can block a shot. Reportedly... And on Heat, if you block more than two, you're a defensive force... Low budget ($325,00) player whose pricetag, size and locker-room demeanor will keep him in the league... Miami is his fifth NBA stop in eight years, most spent in Milwaukee... Born Sept. 29, 1964, in New Ulm, Minn. (not to be confused with Old Ulm)... Heat signed him as free agent Oct. 7, 1994... Celtics originally brought him into NBA as a second-round pick out of Iowa in 1987.

Year	Team	G	FG	FG Pct.	FT	FT Pct.	Reb.	Ast.	TP	Avg.
1987-88	Boston	70	122	.496	50	.806	138	49	297	4.2
1988-89	Bos.-Sac.	77	210	.432	81	.786	256	66	502	6.5
1989-90	Minn.-Mil.	80	305	.460	75	.728	398	168	732	9.
1990-91	Milwaukee	81	179	.431	37	.685	217	75	428	5.3
1991-92	Milwaukee	70	162	.450	27	.659	249	74	408	5.8
1992-93	Milwaukee	80	283	.461	73	.723	276	127	724	9.1
1993-94	Milwaukee	67	102	.363	20	.690	150	62	270	4.0
1994-95	Miami	61	97	.420	10	.667	102	43	267	4.4
	Totals	586	1460	.443	373	.734	1786	664	3628	6.2

LEDELL EACKLES 28 6-5 231 — Guard

Fighting the Battle of the Bulge on the home front. And the waistline... Was in shape early and gave effective streak shooting and scoring off bench (scored 22 points vs. Bullets in late November)... As weight rose, minutes dropped. Or vice-versa... When in shape, he can score from anywhere on court. When not in shape, he can set off seismographs anywhere on court... His drives to basket often resemble bull charges... Became unrestricted free agent at season's end... Spent 1993-94 on suspended list with Indiana. If nothing else, he got his name back in people's minds... Born Nov. 24, 1966, in Baton Rouge, La.... Second-round pick of Bullets in '88 out of New Orleans, where he was American South Conference Player of the Year as a senior... Signed by Heat as a free agent Oct. 6, 1994... Made minimum $150,000 wage last season.

Year	Team	G	FG	FG Pct.	FT	FT Pct.	Reb.	Ast.	TP	Avg.
1988-89	Washington	80	318	.434	272	.786	180	123	917	11.5
1989-90	Washington	78	413	.439	210	.750	175	182	1055	13.5
1990-91	Washington	67	345	.453	164	.739	128	136	868	13.0
1991-92	Washington	65	355	.468	139	.743	178	125	856	13.2
1994-95	Miami	54	143	.439	91	.722	95	72	395	7.3
	Totals	344	1574	.447	876	.755	756	638	4091	11.9

KEITH ASKINS 27 6-8 224   Forward

MVPP—Most Valuable Practice Player... Valuable to Heat because of dedication, drive and locker-room influence... Another in a long string of Alabama (Class of '90) relative unknowns who have made a name in NBA... Good three-point shooter, especially from corners... Scrappy—some say dirty—on defense ... Because Heat team defense is so pitiful, he's considered a defensive stopper, more so than he would be anywhere else... Limited skills, but makes the most of them... Born Dec. 15, 1967, in Athens, Ala.... Undrafted, signed with Heat as a free agent Sept. 7, 1990... Tossed out of Game 2 of 1994 opening-round playoff series with Hawks and suspended for last three games in series for coming off bench in brawl... Made $406,000 last season.

Year	Team	G	FG	FG Pct.	FT	FT Pct.	Reb.	Ast.	TP	Avg.
1990-91	Miami	39	34	.420	12	.480	68	19	86	2.2
1991-92	Miami	59	84	.410	26	.703	142	38	219	3.7
1992-93	Miami	69	88	.413	29	.725	198	31	227	3.3
1993-94	Miami	37	36	.409	9	.900	82	13	85	2.3
1994-95	Miami	50	81	.391	46	.807	198	39	229	4.6
	Totals	254	323	.407	122	.722	688	140	846	3.3

PREDRAG DANILOVIC 24 6-6 200   Guard

European standout (you didn't really think he was from Brooklyn, did you?) whose rights were acquired by Heat in the Billy Owens-Rony Seikaly trade Nov. 2, 1994... Played in Italy for Buckler Beer/Knorr Bologna... Compared to Brian Winters, he can score off slashing dribble or hit medium-range outside shot... Serbian National Team member... Played in European championships with Laker Vlade Divac... Rare European player who actually plays defense... Was drafted on second round by Golden State in 1992... Grew up in Sarajevo.

THE ROOKIES

KURT THOMAS 23 6-9 230   **Forward**
Heat hope No. 10 pick can be the interior presence they've longed for... Led Division I in both scoring (28.9 points per) and rebounding (14.6) for Texas Christian as a senior. He became only the third player in NCAA history to accomplish that feat, joining the late Hank Gathers of Loyola Marymount and current NBAer Xavier McDaniel of Wichita State... Third team All-American ... Set TCU record with 12 blocked shots in one game... Born Oct. 4, 1972, in Dallas.

GEORGE BANKS 23 6-7 210   **Forward**
Second-rounder, No. 46 pick, raised his stock at the Portsmouth Invitational, where he was named to the All-Tourney team... Considered steady all-around type. Lots of points inside: two-year shooting at Texas-El Paso was .536... Needs some bulk but did average 8.4 rebounds... Led All-American Conference in rebounding his two years at UTEP... Born Oct. 9, 1972, in Rillito, Ariz.

TERRENCE RENCHER 22 6-3 185   **Guard**
All-time leading scorer in Southwest Conference history with 2,306 points, surpassing another U. of Texas product, Travis Mays... Fourth on Texas all-time assist list, too... Was selected by Washington at No. 32 on the second round and traded to Miami in draft-night deal for Rex Chapman... Born Feb. 19, 1973, in the Bronx, N.Y.

(Note: At press time, Pat Riley had not been signed as coach. Awaited was a settlement of the tampering charges made by the Knicks against the Heat. For reader interest, and in the likelihood that Riley will wind up with the Heat, his profile follows.)

COACH PAT RILEY: He walked away from the Knicks with one year remaining on his contract for a deal with Miami that would make him the highest-paid coach in NBA history... Failed to finish first last season for the only time in 13-year head-coaching career as Knicks placed second to Orlando in Atlantic Division... Did, however, notch his 13th 50-victory (55) season... Winningest coach in NBA playoff history with lifetime 137-77 mark... Lifetime record of 756-299 makes him ninth-winningest coach ever... After four seasons the time had come to leave New York. Players had grown more and more disenchanted with his heavy demands... Achieved four NBA championship rings and nine straight division titles with Lakers from 1981-90... Earned two other title rings: one as an assistant coach, one as a player with L.A.... Coach of the Year in 1990. Voted Coach of the Decade for the '80s... His father, Leon, was a pro baseball player. His brother, Lee, played in the NFL... Riley was a three-sport star—later drafted by the Dallas Cowboys—at Linton High in Schenectady, N.Y.... U. of Kentucky product was drafted at No. 7 by San Diego Rockets in 1967... Picked by Trail Blazers in 1970 expansion draft and sold to Lakers ... Ended playing career with Phoenix after nine seasons in NBA... Born March 20, 1946, in Rome, N.Y.

GREATEST FIND

In the Heat's short life span, there haven't been many flat-out steals. But the guy who comes closest to that description is power forward Grant Long.

Now in Atlanta following last year's early-season trade, Long served commendably for six seasons after being taken on the second round of the 1988 draft, the Heat's first venture into the selection process. By the time he left Miami, Long had placed himself atop the team's all-time steals list (666) and is still in the top four in games played and started, field goals, rebounds, assists, blocked shots and points.

OK, Bimbo Coles, no shooter, but everything else.

And he did all that while being undersized—he's listed at 6-9, 248 but don't believe it. All in all, not bad for a second-round pick.

ALL-TIME HEAT LEADERS

SEASON

Points: Glen Rice, 1,831, 1994–95
Assists: Sherman Douglas, 624, 1990–91
Rebounds: Rony Seikaly, 934, 1991–92

GAME

Points: Glen Rice, 56 vs. Orlando, 4/15/95
Assists: Sherman Douglas, 17 vs. Atlanta, 2/26/90
Rebounds: Rony Seikaly, 34 vs. Washington, 3/3/93

CAREER

Points: Glen Rice, 9,248, 1989–95
Assists: Sherman Douglas, 1,243, 1988–91
Rebounds: Rony Seikaly, 4,544, 1988–94

NEW JERSEY NETS

TEAM DIRECTORY: Chairman: Alan Aufzien; Vice Chairmen: David Gerstein, Jerry Cohen; Pres.-COO: Jon Spoelstra; Exec. VP/GM-Basketball Oper.: Willis Reed; Dir. Pub. Rel.: John Mertz; Coach: Butch Beard; Asst. Coach: Jerry Eaves. Arena: Brendan Byrne Meadowlands Arena (20,049). Colors: Red, white and blue.

SCOUTING REPORT

SHOOTING: You can make your own joke about the Nets' shooting being so bad that shooting the Nets is a good idea. It was the worst in the league last season. And it's not like they brought in Reggie Miller and Dell Curry during the offseason.

One of the biggest problems facing the Nets is the simple matter of shot selection. This team has a remarkable knack for launching some of the poorest conceived shots on the planet. Inside, they actually can score some, with Armon Gilliam showing common sense. But the perimeter? Forget it. Kenny Anderson loves to shoot. Too bad he can't connect. Derrick Coleman, when the spirit moves him, can be staggering inside or out. But the spirit moves him about once a month, if that often. The Nets pray Kevin Edwards can return to form after a season wiped out by an Achilles injury. He has a shot. More importantly, he has common sense.

PLAYMAKING: In Anderson, the Nets have one of the most remarkably creative guards on the planet. But that strength also displays one of the Nets' biggest weaknesses. Too often, all the Nets have is Anderson's creativity. Sets are not run properly and a typical scenario is watching Anderson forced into some sort of a mad dash as the shot clock runs down into single digits.

Too often, Anderson himself is to blame for the predicament as he simply holds on to the ball too long before making a set-saving play. But he's good enough to do it—he was second in the league in assists with 9.4 a game, bettered only by John Stockton. Chris Childs is more conventional and can get others involved as Anderson's backup. But with that conventional style comes one that's also too methodical and lacking creative instinct.

REBOUNDING: Say what you want about the Nets. And there's usually a lot to say, most of it bad. But they do rebound.

Only John Stockton topped Kenny Anderson in assists.

Always have, probably always will. Maybe it's the simple stockpile of big bodies. Maybe it's because they miss so many shots themselves. But last year was a typical season—they led the league most of the season until a late swoon dropped them to third.

They won't have Benoit Benjamin to ridicule in the Meadowlands anymore, so the Nets' first priority is finding a starting center to plug the gap. Jayson Williams remains undersized, last year's first-rounder Yinka Dare is a joke and Dwayne Schintzius hasn't done it yet, so there's no reason to expect he'll do it now.

NET ROSTER

No.	Veterans	Pos.	Ht.	Wt.	Age	Yrs. Pro	College
7	Kenny Anderson	G	6-1	168	25	4	Georgia Tech
42	P. J. Brown	C-F	6-11	240	26	2	Louisiana Tech
R-1	Chris Childs	G	6-3	195	27	1	Boise State
44	Derrick Coleman	F	6-10	258	28	5	Syracuse
11	Yinka Dare	C	7-0	265	23	1	George Washington
21	Kevin Edwards	G	6-3	210	30	7	DePaul
U-12	Eric Floyd	G	6-3	185	35	13	Georgetown
43	Armon Gilliam	F	6-9	245	31	8	UNLV
9	Sean Higgins	G-F	6-9	215	26	4	Michigan
U-4	Rick Mahorn	F	6-10	260	37	14	Hampton Institute
U-34	Chris Morris	F	6-8	220	29	7	Auburn
U-33	Dwayne Schintzius	C	7-2	285	27	5	Florida
2	Rex Walters	G	6-4	190	25	2	Kansas
U-55	Jayson Wiilliams	F	6-10	245	27	5	St. John's

R-restricted free agent
U-unrestricted free agent

Rd.	Rookie	Sel.No.	Pos.	Ht.	Wt.	College
1	Ed O'Bannon	9	F	6-8	217	UCLA

DEFENSE: They'll block shots. They'll hit the defensive boards. And they'll have the likes of P.J. Brown, one of the league's most underrated players, to throw against the hot guy. And maybe this year, rookie Ed O'Bannon's work ethic and good citizenship can help defensively. But after that, the Nets will do little.

They won't make too many steals; in fact, they were dead last by a mile in steals/turnover ratio last year. They won't get back in transition with any semblance of regularity. They certainly won't rotate or close out on the perimeter. The Nets' approach and execution on defense, overall, is remarkably mediocre. Sort of like the history of the team.

OUTLOOK: Incredibly, the outlook might be worse than last year. The team has utterly little direction. The star player is every coach's nightmare. Rumors of sales and coaching changes always abound. The shooting is so laughably bad, some fans are thinking of holding a telethon. Even in the woefully weak Atlantic Division, this team is in trouble. There simply is no way to dig out of the rubble caused by over a decade of poor decision-making and poorer planning. The outlook? Grim. On the good days.

NET PROFILES

DERRICK COLEMAN 28 6-10 258   Forward

Generation X poster child... Never was so much given to one, with so little in return... When he bounded onto the scene as the No. 1 pick in the 1990 draft out of Syracuse, he was projected as the next Karl Malone. Now the question is, will he be out of the league before Karl Malone?... Unquestioned ability. Can shoot with range, put the ball on the floor, rebound, block shots... Those are all things he can do. They are also things he doesn't do. Or does only when he feels like it... Was fat and out of shape most of the season, which contained his usual string of injuries. He missed 26 games... And despite all the nonsense, he averaged over 20 points and 10 rebounds for third straight year... Was on *Sports Illustrated* cover for story about spoiled athletes in NBA... Drives? Only at drive-through for Burger King last year... And classic response when it was noted that fellow co-captain Kenny Anderson should be more responsible: "Whoop de damn do."... Sickening part is, he made $4.212 million... Dream Team II member, a coach's nightmare... Born June 21, 1967, in Mobile, Ala. and raised in Detroit.

Year	Team	G	FG	FG Pct.	FT	FT Pct.	Reb.	Ast.	TP	Avg.
1990-91	New Jersey	74	514	.467	323	.731	759	163	1364	18.4
1991-92	New Jersey	65	483	.504	300	.763	618	205	1289	19.8
1992-93	New Jersey	76	564	.460	421	.808	852	276	1572	20.7
1993-94	New Jersey	77	541	.447	439	.774	870	262	1559	20.2
1994-95	New Jersey	56	371	.424	376	.767	591	187	1146	20.5
	Totals	348	2473	.461	1859	.770	3690	1093	6930	19.9

KENNY ANDERSON 25 6-1 168   Guard

The other half of the Nets' migraine... Was still depressed from broken wrist suffered in 1993. Wore cast throughout summer, so he didn't work out and reported out of shape. Legs and hamstrings were first to go... Took off a practice after getting in a snit with coach Butch Beard after he was yanked from game in which he stunk. On night of missed practice he was spotted at New York strip club... Blessed with ability far exceeding his heart and brains... Unquestionably one of the most exciting, gifted and creative penetrators and cutters in the league... But also unquestionably one of the worst defensive point guards on the planet... Maturity and commitment levels need an elevator... No serious shot to speak of. Shoots a lot. Misses a lot... Became Nets' all-time assists leader in fourth season... Had club season-high 40 points at Philadelphia Jan. 13 ... Still, Nets should have taken Dikembe Mutombo... No. 2 pick out of Georgia Tech in '91... Born Oct. 9, 1970, in Queens, N.Y.... NYC high-school legend made $3.463 million last season.

Year	Team	G	FG	FG Pct.	FT	FT Pct.	Reb.	Ast.	TP	Avg.
1991-92	New Jersey	64	187	.390	73	.745	127	203	450	7.0
1992-93	New Jersey	55	370	.435	180	.776	226	449	927	16.9
1993-94	New Jersey	82	576	.417	346	.818	322	784	1538	18.8
1994-95	New Jersey	72	411	.399	348	.841	250	680	1267	17.6
	Totals	273	1544	.413	947	.811	925	2116	4182	15.3

P.J. BROWN 26 6-11 240 Forward

Truly deserves a better fare... Has no right being a Net... Serious, dedicated athlete who maximizes skills and actually works hard... Shooting percentage improved from .415 to .446 but still needs to get better... Superior defensive talent. He'll take on the assignment that rightfully should belong to Derrick Coleman... Nets used him effectively on Joe Dumars one game... Rebounding could use a nudge upwards, but he is the small forward on a good rebounding team... Best competition comes at home against wife, Dee, in one-on-one games. She's former captain of Louisiana Tech women's team. He left there in '92 and was sleeper find at No. 29 on second round by Nets... Played a year in Greece after college to improve skills ... A great guy. Has one year left on his contract and they'll line up around the league to get him... Two years in league and he's one of the most professional guys on team, along with Armon Gilliam... Born Oct. 14, 1969, in Detroit... A $780,000 bargain ... Real name is Collier.

Year	Team	G	FG	FG Pct.	FT	FT Pct.	Reb.	Ast.	TP	Avg.
1993-94	New Jersey	79	167	.415	115	.757	493	93	450	5.7
1994-95	New Jersey	80	254	.446	139	.671	487	135	651	8.1
	Totals	159	421	.433	254	.708	980	228	1101	6.9

CHRIS MORRIS 29 6-8 220 — Forward

Knuckleheads Anonymous... Headed for unrestricted free agency and reminded team and anyone who cared with messages on his sneakers: "Trade me, please" or "I'm outta here." ... Another with a body by Fischer, ability by Zeus and brains by Tinkertoy... Incredibly bad shot selection... Absolutely no concept of defense... As consistent as March weather... Worst shooting season of career (.410)... Played shooting guard at times. Not well, but at times... Yes, he can do some things well: terrific offensive rebounder because of outstanding leaping ability. Unfortunately, though, that will put the ball in his hands ... Warms up with halfcourt shots... Longevity has placed him high on Nets' career offensive category lists... Thinks he deserves Scottie Pippen money... Born Jan. 20, 1966, in Atlanta ... No. 4 pick in '88 draft, out of Auburn... Made $2.06 million last season.

Year	Team	G	FG	FG Pct.	FT	FT Pct.	Reb.	Ast.	TP	Avg.
1988-89	New Jersey	76	414	.457	182	.717	397	119	1074	14.1
1989-90	New Jersey	80	449	.422	228	.722	422	143	1187	14.8
1990-91	New Jersey	79	409	.425	179	.734	521	220	1042	13.2
1991-92	New Jersey	77	346	.477	165	.714	494	197	879	11.4
1992-93	New Jersey	77	436	.481	197	.794	454	106	1086	14.1
1993-94	New Jersey	50	203	.447	85	.720	228	83	544	10.9
1994-95	New Jersey	71	351	.410	142	.728	402	147	950	13.4
	Totals	510	2608	.444	1178	.733	2918	1015	6762	13.3

REX WALTERS 25 6-4 190 — Guard

Biggest contribution may have been ripping Kenny Anderson for selfishness... Not that it made a difference, but it did make headlines ... Has a great career ahead as a coach. Unfortunately, not as a player... At 25, he admits his athleticism has declined. At least he's honest... A shooting guard who can't shoot... Short arms don't help... Good in open-floor game and can finish break. Problem is, when he's teamed with Anderson he doesn't get the ball to finish... Defensively challenged, okay?... But he did hold down Michael Jordan—for a half. M.J. had seven points by halftime. Then went off for 30 more... Halfcourt game is not exactly his strength... Turnover-prone, too... First-round pick, No. 16, in 1993, out of Kansas

... Born March 12, 1970, in Omaha, Neb. ... Made $845,000 last season.

Year	Team	G	FG	FG Pct.	FT	FT Pct.	Reb.	Ast.	TP	Avg.
1993-94	New Jersey	48	60	.522	28	.824	38	71	162	3.4
1994-95	New Jersey	80	206	.439	40	.769	93	121	523	6.5
	Totals	128	266	.455	68	.791	131	192	685	5.4

YINKA DARE 23 7-0 265   Center

Should have been Wesley Person ... Nets desperately needed perimeter shooter. But despite advice of Dare's college coach, their own scouts and coaches plus radio talk-show callers, they drafted this guy ... Played a valuable three minutes ... You can hold your breath longer ... And he has bad knees ... Nicknamed "Stinka" by teammates ... Five games into season, he went on injured list ... Most felt it was a scam. Until he required surgery on both knees ... Took one shot. In keeping with team policy, he missed ... Can allegedly block shots ... Left George Washington after two years. Really should have stayed ... Made $920,000, then was exposed in expansion draft ... Born Oct. 10, 1972, in Kano, Nigeria.

Year	Team	G	FG	FG Pct.	FT	FT Pct.	Reb.	Ast.	TP	Avg.
1994-95	New Jersey	1	0	.000	0	.000	1	0	0	0.0

ARMON GILLIAM 31 6-9 245   Forward

Doesn't belong on this team ... Voted Most Valuable Net by media ... Only Net to play in all 82 games ... Isn't their some kind of cruelty-pay clause somewhere? ... Religious type who tried to convert Jayson Williams. Gave him 12 bibles ... Most professional player on team, along with P.J. Brown ... Was very strong starting in Derrick Coleman's absence. Was third in scoring, second in rebounding on team ... Potent scorer with strong moves inside ... Can score with either hand and uses little jump hooks with effectiveness ... Learned to use both hands by tying the right behind his back and eating with his left ... Can hit up to 14 feet ... Good, strong positional rebounder ... Topped team in offensive boards ... What's the catch? Check out his defense. He has this problem rotating ... A 15.0 career scorer since leaving UNLV in 1987, when he was the No. 2 pick overall by Suns ... Traded to Charlotte with draft picks for Kurt Rambis Dec. 13, 1989... Went to Philly with Dave Hoppen for Mike Gminski Jan. 4, 1991. Sixers waived him and he signed as a free agent with Nets Aug. 11, 1993... Born May 28, 1964, in Pittsburgh... 1994-95 salary: $1.66 million.

Year	Team	G	FG	FG Pct.	FT	FT Pct.	Reb.	Ast.	TP	Avg.
1987-88	Phoenix	55	342	.475	131	.679	434	72	815	14.8
1988-89	Phoenix	74	468	.503	240	.743	541	52	1176	15.9
1989-90	Phoe.-Char.	76	484	.515	303	.723	599	99	1271	16.7
1990-91	Char.-Phil.	75	487	.487	268	.815	598	105	1242	16.6
1991-92	Philadelphia	81	512	.511	343	.807	660	118	1367	16.9
1992-93	Philadelphia	80	359	.464	274	.843	472	116	992	12.4
1993-94	New Jersey	82	348	.510	274	.759	500	69	970	11.8
1994-95	New Jersey	82	455	.503	302	.770	613	99	1212	14.8
	Totals	605	3455	.497	2135	.772	4417	730	9045	15.0

CHRIS CHILDS 27 6-3 195   Guard

Got a chance, made good... Recovering alcoholic by way of John Lucas' rehab. Also did the CBA route... One of the few bright spots for the Nets... Began season on injured list with foot injury... Twice recorded 14 assists in a game as backup point guard... Very good defensively... Ball moves better, more freely, when he's on court... Gets everyone involved ... But his shooting (.380) is erratic at best and he's very methodical. Fifth among rookies with 4.1 assists per... A $150,000 free-agent minimum-wage steal... Born Nov. 20, 1967, in Bakersfield, Cal.... CBA's Playoff MVP in 1994 for Quad City.

Year	Team	G	FG	FG Pct.	FT	FT Pct.	Reb.	Ast.	TP	Avg.
1994-95	New Jersey	53	106	.380	55	.753	69	219	308	5.8

KEVIN EDWARDS 30 6-3 210   Guard

Nets missed his scoring, shooting and professionalism... Played just 14 games before being cut down by Achilles tendon problems... Complained of soreness in preseason... Told to ice and stretch tendons. It didn't help. Knew it was serious in 14th game when he tried to block a shot, ironically, by Wesley Person (guy Nets should have drafted over Yinka Dare). Was told he'd be back by Christmas. Didn't return all season... And he was off to a great start... Shooting has made jump from low-to-mid 40s since he left DePaul in '88... College backcourt teammate of Rod Strickland... Born Oct. 30, 1965, in Cleveland

Heights, Ohio... No. 20 pick by Miami... Signed with Nets as a free agent July 8, 1993... Made $1.66 million last season.

Year	Team	G	FG	FG Pct.	FT	FT Pct.	Reb.	Ast.	TP	Avg.
1988-89	Miami	79	470	.425	144	.746	262	349	1094	13.8
1989-90	Miami	78	395	.412	139	.760	282	252	938	12.0
1990-91	Miami	79	380	.410	171	.803	205	240	955	12.1
1991-92	Miami	81	325	.454	162	.848	211	170	819	10.1
1992-93	Miami	40	216	.468	119	.844	121	120	556	13.9
1993-94	New Jersey	82	471	.458	167	.770	281	232	1144	14.0
1994-95	New Jersey	14	69	.448	40	.952	37	27	196	14.0
	Totals	453	2326	.435	942	.798	1399	1390	5702	12.6

DWAYNE SCHINTZIUS 27 7-2 285   Center

He's big. He's white. He's employed... Barely employed, though... Has never played more than 400 minutes in a season since leaving Florida as the No. 24 pick by Spurs in 1990... Too soft despite size... No toughness down low, as evidenced during streak of 11 starts in March... Decent hands for rebounds but not for shooting... Nice guy, quick wit, little game... Traded by Spurs to Kings with a second-rounder for Antoine Carr Sept. 23, 1991... Waived by Kings... Signed as a free agent with Nets Oct. 1, 1992. Nets matched '93 free-agent offer sheet from Milwaukee, inflating his salary... Born Oct. 14, 1968, in Brandon, Fla.... 1994-95 salary: $1.197 million.

Year	Team	G	FG	FG Pct.	FT	FT Pct.	Reb.	Ast.	TP	Avg.
1990-91	San Antonio	42	68	.439	22	.550	121	17	158	3.8
1991-92	Sacramento	33	50	.427	10	.833	118	20	110	3.3
1992-93	New Jersey	5	2	.286	3	1.000	8	2	7	1.4
1993-94	New Jersey	30	29	.345	10	.588	89	13	68	2.3
1994-95	New Jersey	43	41	.380	6	.545	81	15	88	2.0
	Totals	153	190	.403	51	.614	417	67	431	2.8

RICK MAHORN 37 6-10 260   Forward-Center

Never assume anything... He didn't play much early and everybody assumed he had nothing left... But when the Nets hit a center crisis late in the season, he actually showed effectiveness, enough to fuel speculation he'd be back... Clubhouse politician, absolutely wonderful team guy... Team's player rep... Had his best shooting year (.523) since before

Detroit's Bad Boy championship days... Game hasn't changed. Bangs, bumps, taunts. Got Patrick Ewing ejected... A coach in waiting for somebody... Last two games of season saw him get 13 rebounds, then 17 points, both season highs... Second-round pick, No. 35, by Washington in 1980 draft, out of Hampton Institute (Va.)... Traded to Detroit with Mike Gibson for Dan Roundfield, June 17, 1985... Picked by Minnesota in '89 expansion draft. Wouldn't report... Went on to Philly for draft package Oct. 27, 1989... Played a year in Italy before free-agent signing with Nets Nov. 9, 1992... Born Sept. 21, 1958, in Hartford, Conn.... Earned $800,000 in 1994-95.

Year	Team	G	FG	FG Pct.	FT	FT Pct.	Reb.	Ast.	TP	Avg.
1980-81	Washington	52	111	.507	27	.675	215	25	249	4.8
1981-82	Washington	80	414	.507	148	.632	704	150	976	12.2
1982-83	Washington	82	376	.490	146	.575	779	115	898	11.0
1983-84	Washington	82	307	.507	125	.651	738	131	739	9.0
1984-85	Washington	77	206	.499	71	.683	608	121	483	6.3
1985-86	Detroit	80	157	.455	81	.681	412	64	395	4.9
1986-87	Detroit	63	144	.447	96	.821	375	38	384	6.1
1987-88	Detroit	67	276	.574	164	.756	565	60	717	10.7
1988-89	Detroit	72	203	.517	116	.748	496	59	522	7.3
1989-90	Philadelphia	75	313	.497	183	.715	568	98	811	10.8
1990-91	Philadelphia	80	261	.467	189	.788	621	118	711	8.9
1992-93	New Jersey	74	101	.472	88	.800	279	33	291	3.9
1993-94	New Jersey	28	23	.489	13	.650	54	5	59	2.1
1994-95	New Jersey	58	79	.523	39	.796	162	26	198	3.4
	Totals	970	2971	.498	1486	.705	6576	1043	7433	7.7

JAYSON WILLIAMS 27 6-10 245   Forward

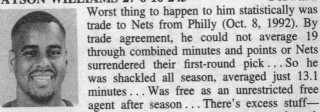

Worst thing to happen to him statistically was trade to Nets from Philly (Oct. 8, 1992). By trade agreement, he could not average 19 through combined minutes and points or Nets surrendered their first-round pick... So he was shackled all season, averaged just 13.1 minutes... Was free as an unrestricted free agent after season... There's excess stuff—clubhouse comedian, late hours, etc. But the guy can rebound. Averaged an offensive rebound every 5.49 minutes. That's terrific ... Ex-Net assistant Paul Silas convinced him he'd have long career if he just rebounded. So lots of teams were interested in him as free agent... No. 21 pick out of St. John's by Suns in 1991 ... Rights were sent to Philadelphia for future first-rounder Oct. 28, 1990... Born Feb. 22, 1968, in Ritter, S.C., but was schooled at Christ the King in Queens, N.Y. . . . Made $1.1 million last season.

Year	Team	G	FG	FG Pct.	FT	FT Pct.	Reb.	Ast.	TP	Avg.
1990-91	Philadelphia	52	72	.447	37	.661	111	16	182	3.5
1991-92	Philadelphia	50	75	.364	56	.636	145	12	206	4.1
1992-93	New Jersey	12	21	.457	7	.389	41	0	49	4.1
1993-94	New Jersey	70	125	.427	72	.605	263	26	322	4.6
1994-95	New Jersey	75	149	.461	65	.533	425	35	363	4.8
	Totals	259	442	.430	237	.588	985	89	1122	4.3

SEAN HIGGINS 26 6-9 215 — Guard

Seemed like a good idea at the time. So did the Edsel . . . Free-agent pickup out of Europe was supposed to be the find of the year. Was supposed to be able to shoot . . . Shot .385. He wasn't supposed to do that . . . GM Willis Reed talked him out of Greece. Any more decisions like that and Reed will talk himself out of a job . . . Really good shooter in practice, though . . . Was supposed to be a good defender, too . . . He's not, okay? . . . Too weak for small forward, too slow for off guard . . . A bust . . . Made $500,000 . . . Born Dec. 30, 1968, in Los Angeles . . . Father, Earle, played with Indiana in the ABA; Nets should have signed him instead . . . Spurs picked him on second round following his junior year at Michigan in 1990 . . . Had short stints in Orlando and Golden State before going to Europe . . . Member of Michigan's 1989 NCAA champs.

Year	Team	G	FG	FG Pct.	FT	FT Pct.	Reb.	Ast.	TP	Avg.
1990-91	San Antonio	50	97	.458	28	.848	63	35	225	4.5
1991-92	S.A.-Orl.	38	127	.458	31	.861	102	41	291	7.7
1992-93	Golden State	29	96	.447	35	.745	68	66	240	8.3
1994-95	New Jersey	57	105	.385	35	.875	77	29	268	4.7
	Totals	174	425	.435	129	.827	310	171	1024	5.9

THE ROOKIE

ED O'BANNON 23 6-8 217 — Forward

Super solid citizen. So what's he doing in New Jersey? . . . Only question about the MVP of UCLA's collegiate championship team is his surgically repaired left knee . . . On draft night, he said he wants to lead by example. This could be interesting in New Jersey, so long a home to NBA's prominent knuckleheads... First-team All-American was also collegiate Player of the Year ... Supremely gifted. Can shoot and run the lanes. Now, if the knee holds up... UCLA was 92-25 in the games he played... Born Aug. 14, 1972, in Los Angeles.

COACH BUTCH BEARD: Got the job through friendship with GM Willis Reed. Some friend... Succeeded Chuck Daly June 28, 1994, and finished first year with 30-52 record and lots of anxiety about job security... Hard worker who knows if this doesn't work out, another head job might be hard to find... Questionable late-game decisions, such as keeping small guards on court when size was needed. In his defense, though, some of his bigger guys shouldn't even be in league, let alone on court... Got little support from brass in confrontations with players. And that can cause a big decline in the respect department... He's a quick study. Was that way as a player with Hawks, Cavs, Sonics, Warriors and Knicks during nine-year career... Hawks picked him No. 10 out of Louisville in 1969... Spent six years as NBA assistant (four with Knicks, two with Nets) before head job at Howard University, where he was 45-69 in four years... Real first name is Alfred ... Born May 4, 1947, in Hardinburg, Ky.

GREATEST FIND

Coming up with a "find" or a "steal" in the Nets' NBA history is almost as difficult as uncovering great moments for the franchise in 1994-95. Guys who were supposed to be good, were good. Guys who were sleepers never woke up.

But the Nets did manage a steal in a trade—even though they eventually lost their booty, Chris Dudley, to free agency.

The man who made Shaquille O'Neal look deadly from the free-throw line, Dudley, after several so-what seasons in Cleveland, earned the label as the league's best backup center with the Nets. In his four years in New Jersey after being acquired from Cleveland for two second-round draft picks, Dudley established himself as a ferocious offensive rebounder and shot-blocker. His four-season rebound average with the Nets was 8.2 per.

Dudley, whose biggest claim to claim once was that he hailed from Yale, left the Nets after the 1992-93 season for the free-agent bucks of Portland.

ALL-TIME NET LEADERS

SEASON

Points: Rick Barry, 2,518, 1971–72 (ABA)
Bernard King, 1,909, 1977–78
Assists: Kevin Porter, 801, 1977–78
Rebounds: Billy Paultz, 1,035, 1971–72 (ABA)
Buck Williams, 1,027, 1982–83

GAME

Points: Julius Erving, 63 vs. San Diego (4 OT), 2/14/75 (ABA)
Mike Newlin, 52 vs. Boston, 12/16/79
Ray Williams, 52 vs. Detroit, 4/17/82
Assists: Kevin Porter, 29 vs. Houston, 2/24/78
Rebounds: Billy Paultz, 33 vs. Pittsburgh, 2/17/71 (ABA)
Buck Williams, 27 vs. Golden State, 2/1/87

CAREER

Points: Buck Williams, 10,440, 1981–89
Assists: Billy Melchionni, 2,251, 1969–75 (ABA)
Kenny Anderson, 2,116, 1991–95
Rebounds: Buck Williams, 7,576, 1981–89

NEW YORK KNICKS

TEAM DIRECTORY: Pres.: David Checketts; VP-GM: Ernie Grunfeld; Senior VP-Communications: John Cirillo; Dir. Pub. Rel.: Chris Brienza; Mgr. Publications and Inf.: Dennis D'Agostino; Dir. Scouting Services: Dick McGuire; Coach: Don Nelson. Asst. Coaches: Jeff Van Gundy, Bob Salmi, Jeff Nix, Don Chaney. Arena: Madison Square Garden (19,763). Colors: Orange, white and blue.

SCOUTING REPORT

SHOOTING: Wow, here's a stunner: The Knicks need a consistent perimeter game. They had John Starks leading the way with more made three-pointers (217) in one season last year than any man in history. Of course, Starks attempted more three-

At his peak, Patrick Ewing starts his 11th campaign.

pointers (611) in one season last year than any man in history. Like the saying goes, throw enough of it against the wall and some of it will stick.

Derek Harper is hardly a classic shooter, but he is astoundingly good in the clutch. In Patrick Ewing, the Knicks possess the best jump-shooting big man in history. He'll be back for more. Charles Oakley is accurate up to 15 feet. But after his return from toe surgery and especially in the playoffs, Oakley fell far too much in love with the outside. Hubert Davis is the team's best shot, but after two straight tentative efforts in the playoffs, the team must be concerned about his ability under pressure.

PLAYMAKING: When the Knicks pass and rotate and work for good shots, they can be overpowering. When they don't, when they hoist at will, they are so certifiably beatable as to be laughable.

In Harper, the Knicks have a smart, cool, veteran leader who knows where, when and how to deliver the ball. But Greg Anthony's departure through expansion leaves the team without a proven, capable backup. Charlie Ward? They hope he's the answer, but who knows? Those 44 minutes last year didn't quite impress too many folks. Ewing is adept at hitting cutters or spotting the double teams and passing to the perimeter.

When they play unselfish ball, the Knicks are dangerous. But when the ball stops moving, they're in trouble through the lack of creativity and consistency.

REBOUNDING: Always a Knick strength, always near the top of the league. So what happened last year, when they were the fifth-worst offensive rebounding team and only the 17th-best rebounding team overall? Plenty.

Start with Oakley's toe. That, in essence, killed him for the year. Then add in Ewing's achy knees, which affected his start and finish. Toss in a backcourt that didn't rebound. Add in 6-11 Smith, a small forward stationed on the perimeter and you begin to see how the Knicks slipped so badly.

Thank goodness ex-coach Pat Riley didn't suspend Anthony Mason (8.4 rpg) for more than five games. If the Knicks are to get back to being the Manhattan Maulers off the boards, it has to be like in previous years. Oakley must forsake the jump shot and there must be a rebound-by-committee approach.

DEFENSE: This should be intriguing. Over the past four years under Riley, when you thought of the Knicks, you thought of

KNICK ROSTER

No.	Veterans	Pos.	Ht.	Wt.	Age	Yrs. Pro	College
U-4	Anthony Bonner	F	6-8	225	27	5	St. Louis
7	Doug Christie	G-F	6-6	205	25	3	Pepperdine
44	Hubert Davis	G	6-5	183	25	3	North Carolina
33	Patrick Ewing	C	7-0	240	33	10	Georgetown
11	Derek Harper	G	6-4	206	34	12	Illinois
U-14	Anthony Mason	F	6-7	250	28	6	Tennessee State
34	Charles Oakley	F	6-9	245	31	10	Virginia Union
54	Charles Smith	F	6-10	244	30	7	Pittsburgh
3	John Starks	G	6-5	185	30	6	Oklahoma State
21	Charlie Ward	G	6-2	190	25	1	Florida State
32	Herb Williams	C-F	6-11	260	37	14	Ohio State
2	Monty Williams	F	6-8	225	24	1	Notre Dame

U-unrestricted free agent

defense. Plain, no-gimmicks, man-to-man, grunt-and-groan defense. But now with Don Nelson's promise of a more uptempo game, where will that leave the Knicks?

Probably with another set of defensive numbers that rank near the top of the league. Just like last year, when opponents shot a league-low .437 against New York and managed just 95.1 points, second-best behind slowdown Cleveland.

Those numbers figure to go up in a faster-paced game. But whether they're running or not, the Knicks will still be a formidable defensive unit because they know no other way. Harper will still hound. Smith will still be one of the toughest forwards to shoot over in the league. Ewing will be Ewing. The questions among the starters include whether or not Starks can get defense back in his mind and whether Oakley can come back from a lost season to play the macho game that made him an all-defensive selection two seasons ago.

OUTLOOK: If nothing else, the Knicks should be more exciting. They're probably not as close to championship timber as the brass would like the public to think. After a trip to the NBA Finals, they went out in the second round. But they are still a dangerous team and Nelson should come up with a wrinkle or two to keep them near the top.

They simply need consistency from the perimeter, and Nelson won't be the first coach to search for it in Madison Square Gar-

KNICK PROFILES

PATRICK EWING 33 7-0 240   Center

The Franchise will forever be reminded of The Layup... Made wonderfully strong move to hole and then blew buzzer layup in Game 7 of Eastern semis against Pacers, who won by two ... If there's one guy you didn't want to see that happen to on Knicks, it's him... Growling image is a facade. Super nice guy but his public image could use a lift... May have had his finest season in 10th NBA year... All-time Knick scoring leader became 50th player to crack 17,000 points. Also franchise king in blocks and steals and will become leader in games (needs one) and rebounds (needs 542) this season... Best jump-shooting big man ever... Has not been the ferocious defender he was earlier in career but still a force in middle... Underwent knee surgery in summer, causing slow start. Had another arthroscope this summer... Sore left calf held playoff scoring to just 19.0 ppg... Tied Bernard King's team record with five straight 30-point games in February... Born Aug. 5, 1962, in Kingston, Jamaica... Came to U.S. at age 12 and was Player of the Year at Rindge-Latin High in Cambridge, Mass.... Led Georgetown to NCAA title in '84 and two other championship-game appearances ... Was the first-ever lottery prize in '85... Made $4.486 million but is due for an $18-million balloon this season.

Year	Team	G	FG	FG Pct.	FT	FT Pct.	Reb.	Ast.	TP	Avg.
1985-86	New York	50	386	.474	226	.739	451	102	998	20.0
1986-87	New York	63	530	.503	296	.713	555	104	1356	21.5
1987-88	New York	82	656	.555	341	.716	676	125	1653	20.2
1988-89	New York	80	727	.567	361	.746	740	188	1815	22.7
1989-90	New York	82	922	.551	502	.775	893	182	2347	28.6
1990-91	New York	81	845	.514	464	.745	905	244	2154	26.6
1991-92	New York	82	796	.522	377	.738	921	156	1970	24.0
1992-93	New York	81	779	.503	400	.719	980	151	1959	24.2
1993-94	New York	79	745	.496	445	.765	885	179	1939	24.5
1994-95	New York	79	730	.503	420	.750	876	212	1886	23.9
	Totals	759	7116	.520	3832	.742	7873	1643	18077	23.8

DEREK HARPER 34 6-4 206   Guard

Every beat writer needs one. So does every team... Class act who'll answer every question politely, insightfully... Super devoted to his wife and three kids... Of course, it doesn't hurt that he can play... Back-to-back games became a problem with age and Pat Riley's penchant for death-march work... Great hands still make him a theft threat, but hand-check rules led to fewest steals (79) in career... Shot .574 on three-pointers in playoffs... Scored 30 points to seal Game 4 win over Cavs in first round... Knicks are concerned about minutes problem this year, though. Hence, they made offseason search for proven backup... Remains Mavs' all-time leader in assists and steals... Came to Knicks Jan. 6, 1994 in exchange for a first-rounder and Tony Campbell... Picked No. 11 after junior season at Illinois by Dallas in '83... Childhood idol was Walt Frazier, who now does Knick radio broadcasts... Born Oct. 13, 1961, in Elberton, Ga.... Made $2.382 million in 1994-95.

Year	Team	G	FG	FG Pct.	FT	FT Pct.	Reb.	Ast.	TP	Avg.
1983-84	Dallas	82	200	.443	66	.673	172	239	469	5.7
1984-85	Dallas	82	329	.520	111	.721	199	360	790	9.6
1985-86	Dallas	79	390	.534	171	.747	226	416	963	12.2
1986-87	Dallas	77	497	.501	160	.684	199	609	1230	16.0
1987-88	Dallas	82	536	.459	261	.759	246	634	1393	17.0
1988-89	Dallas	81	538	.477	229	.806	228	570	1404	17.3
1989-90	Dallas	82	567	.488	250	.794	244	609	1473	18.0
1990-91	Dallas	77	572	.467	286	.731	233	548	1519	19.7
1991-92	Dallas	65	448	.443	198	.759	170	373	1152	17.7
1992-93	Dallas	62	393	.419	239	.756	123	334	1126	18.2
1993-94	Dal.-N.Y.	82	303	.407	112	.687	141	334	791	9.6
1994-95	New York	80	337	.446	139	.724	194	458	919	11.5
	Totals	931	5110	.467	2222	.745	2375	5484	13229	14.2

ANTHONY MASON 28 6-7 250   Forward

Mase made his case... Took huge gamble and turned down Knicks' three-year, $9-million offer and played out final year of contract to become unrestricted free agent... Became not only the cream of the free-agent class but the NBA's runaway Sixth Man of the Year award winner... Spectacular ball-handling skills for a guy his size... Above-average defender and tireless rebounder... Wants the ball more. Maybe too much... Weak at foul line. Nothing beyond 15 feet... Exceptionally versatile. Plays either forward spot and in a pinch can play the stud centers because of his strength... Has razor-cut messages in hair ... But at least it's not dyed... Capable of a double-double any night... Suspended for second straight year by Pat Riley, this time for five games. Year before, it was three... NBA Cinderella story. Bounced around CBA, USBL and Turkey before sticking with Knicks. Had shots in Portland, New Jersey and Denver... Unheralded third-round pick by Blazers out of Tennessee State in 1988... Born Dec. 14, 1966, in Miami, but grew up in Queens, N.Y.... Made $1.2 million... Signed as a free agent by Knicks July 30, 1991.

Year	Team	G	FG	FG Pct.	FT	FT Pct.	Reb.	Ast.	TP	Avg.
1989-90	New Jersey	21	14	.350	9	.600	34	7	37	1.8
1990-91	Denver	3	2	.500	6	.750	5	0	10	3.3
1991-92	New York	82	203	.509	167	.642	573	106	573	7.0
1992-93	New York	81	316	.502	199	.682	640	170	831	10.3
1993-94	New York	73	206	.476	116	.720	427	151	528	7.2
1994-95	New York	77	287	.566	191	.641	650	240	765	9.9
	Totals	337	1028	.511	688	.665	2329	674	2744	8.1

CHARLES OAKLEY 31 6-9 245 Forward

Okay, Knicks got knocked out of the playoffs early. They have to trade. Guess who's name comes up?... For years, the prototype rebounding power forward... Toe surgery KO'd him for much of season, thus career lows across the board, including just 50 games... Saw streak of 268 straight games ended by pain in toe... Finally, an artificial insert was placed in joint... Never fully recovered although there were flashes here and there, such as season-high 17 rebounds vs. Denver Mar. 14... Disappointing playoffs. Became more a jump shooter and averaged below double-figure rebounds for only second time in 10 playoff appearances... Work ethic is legendary but may have dipped through unpublicized friction with Pat Riley ... Born Dec. 18, 1963, in Cleveland... Drafted by Cavs out of Virginia Union as No. 9 pick in '85 and was promptly traded to Bulls for Ennis Whatley and draft rights to Keith Lee... Became a Knick on June 27, 1988, in trade for Bill Cartwright... Made $2.2 million but signed extension for hefty down-the-line balloon.

Year	Team	G	FG	FG Pct.	FT	FT Pct.	Reb.	Ast.	TP	Avg.
1985-86	Chicago	77	281	.519	178	.662	664	133	740	9.6
1986-87	Chicago	82	468	.445	245	.686	1074	296	1192	14.5
1987-88	Chicago	82	375	.483	261	.727	1066	248	1014	12.4
1988-89	New York	82	426	.510	197	.773	861	187	1061	12.9
1989-90	New York	61	336	.524	217	.761	727	146	889	14.6
1990-91	New York	76	307	.516	239	.784	920	204	853	11.2
1991-92	New York	82	210	.522	86	.735	700	133	506	6.2
1992-93	New York	82	219	.508	127	.722	708	126	565	6.9
1993-94	New York	82	363	.478	243	.776	965	218	969	11.8
1994-95	New York	50	192	.489	119	.793	445	126	506	10.1
	Totals	756	3177	.494	1912	.739	8130	1817	8295	11.0

CHARLES SMITH 30 6-10 244   Forward

Knick fans' favorite whipping boy... Will never be forgiven for the memorable Chicago four-tap in Game 5 of '93 Eastern finals... Of course, it's rarely pointed out that no Knick was around to help him... Solid 12.7 scoring average, but a 6-10 guy should get more than 4.3 rebounds per... Good face-up jumper, solid low-post game... Always a power player, Knicks got him in mega three-team deal Sept. 22, 1992, and promptly placed him facing the basket... Averaged 16.1 points on .526 shooting the first two months of the season when Patrick Ewing was still recovering from knee surgery... Began making stronger moves late in year, something fans have cried for over three years... Very active in community. Started Charles Smith Foundation in hometown Bridgeport, Conn., to help needy kids in all areas... Players' union executive VP... Born July 16, 1965, in Bridgeport... Pitt, Class of '88... No. 3 pick by Sixers and wound up with Clippers via draft-night trade involving Hersey Hawkins... Made $2.857 million.

Year	Team	G	FG	FG Pct.	FT	FT Pct.	Reb.	Ast.	TP	Avg.
1988-89	L.A.Clippers	71	435	.495	285	.725	465	103	1155	16.3
1989-90	L.A.Clippers	78	595	.520	454	.794	524	114	1645	21.1
1990-91	L.A.Clippers	74	548	.469	384	.793	608	134	1480	20.0
1991-92	L.A.Clippers	49	251	.466	212	.785	301	56	714	14.6
1992-93	New York	81	358	.469	287	.782	432	142	1003	12.4
1993-94	New York	43	176	.443	87	.719	165	50	447	10.4
1994-95	New York	76	352	.471	255	.792	324	120	966	12.7
	Totals	472	2715	.482	1964	.777	2819	719	7410	15.7

JOHN STARKS 30 6-5 185 Guard

Was underpaid at $1.3 million, Knicks gave him a four-year $13-million-plus extension. Then he didn't earn it... Made more three-pointers in one season (217) than any man in history... Bad part is he took more three-pointers (611) than any man in history. And often they were simply awful shots... Fiery competitor who seemed to forget last season that it was defense that kept him in the league... Size was a real problem as bigger and stronger guards posted him on nightly basis, causing Knicks to alter whole defensive strategy and double-team more... Good ball-handler who can play point in a pinch ... Averaged 5.1 assists, so he doesn't always shoot... Will forever be associated with abysmal 2-of-18 Game 7 shooting in '94 Finals... Shot .450 in last year's playoffs—an improvement on .395 regular season... Four colleges. Last was Oklahoma State ... Not drafted in '88. Had free-agent spin with Warriors for a year, then knocked around CBA... Signed as free agent by Knicks, Oct. 1, 1990... Born Aug. 10, 1965, in Tulsa, Okla.

Year	Team	G	FG	FG Pct.	FT	FT Pct.	Reb.	Ast.	TP	Avg.
1988-89	Golden State	36	51	.408	34	.654	41	27	146	4.1
1990-91	New York	61	180	.439	79	.752	131	204	466	7.6
1991-92	New York	82	405	.449	235	.778	191	276	1139	13.9
1992-93	New York	80	513	.428	263	.795	204	404	1397	17.5
1993-94	New York	59	410	.420	187	.754	185	348	1120	19.0
1994-95	New York	80	419	.395	168	.737	219	411	1223	15.3
	Totals	398	1978	.423	966	.763	971	1670	5491	13.8

DOUG CHRISTIE 25 6-6 205 Guard-Forward

One question went through the minds of Knick observers regarding this swingman: What the heck did they get him for?... Reputation as a scorer was never on the line because he was never on the floor... Played 79 usually garbage-time minutes... Might have done handstands the day Pat Riley resigned... Displayed ball-handling skills, flashy moves and adept passing in L.A.... Lakers dealt him to Knicks in preseason for two second-round picks... Recovery from offseason ankle surgery kept him on injured list until Dec. 27... Teammates swore he excelled in practice... He swore to friends and relatives that he was on team... Fouled out in 11 minutes vs. Miami Feb. 17, fastest DQ in Knick history... No. 17 pick by Sonics, out of

Pepperdine, in 1992 ... Didn't sign and was traded to Lakers with Benoit Benjamin for Sam Perkins Feb. 22, 1993 ... Made $1.244 million last year ... Born May 9, 1970, in Seattle.

Year	Team	G	FG	FG Pct.	FT	FT Pct.	Reb.	Ast.	TP	Avg.
1992-93	L.A. Lakers	23	45	.425	50	.758	51	53	142	6.2
1993-94	L.A. Lakers	65	244	.434	145	.697	235	136	672	10.3
1994-95	New York	12	5	.227	4	.800	13	8	15	1.3
	Totals	100	294	.426	199	.713	299	197	829	8.3

HUBERT DAVIS 25 6-5 183   Guard

Wears a "Jesus" tattoo. So much for his hell-raising instincts ... Terrific shooter who will win you games in the regular season ... Playoffs are another matter ... Horribly tentative in postseason for second straight year. That's cause for concern ... But nicest guy you'll meet in league ... Just don't try to talk to him before a game. It's a Knick thing ... Only Knick in every 82 games ... Set career highs in virtually every offensive category ... Nephew of NBA great Walter Davis, but credits his dad with teaching him to shoot ... Fourth in NBA in three-point shooting (.455) ... Knicks took him out of North Carolina as the No. 20 pick in 1992 ... Born May 17, 1970, in Winston-Salem, N.C. ... Made $940,000 in 1994-95.

Year	Team	G	FG	FG Pct.	FT	FT Pct.	Reb.	Ast.	TP	Avg.
1992-93	New York	50	110	.438	43	.796	56	83	269	5.4
1993-94	New York	56	238	.471	85	.825	67	165	614	11.0
1994-95	New York	82	296	.480	97	.808	110	150	820	10.0
	Totals	188	644	.469	225	.812	233	398	1703	9.1

HERB WILLIAMS 37 6-11 260   Center

Perhaps the league's best backup center ... Knows role is limited, completely accepts it ... Classy veteran who is worth the $1-million pricetag for his locker-room demeanor alone ... Filled in admirably at outset of season when Patrick Ewing was recovering from knee surgery ... Then he fractured his hand and missed two months ... Still a tough rebounder and smart, positional defender ... Played in 1,000th career game Apr. 16 at Chicago ... First player in Ohio State history to score 2,000 points. Was 35th in NCAA history to get 2,000 points and

1,000 rebounds... No. 14 pick in 1981 draft by Pacers. Sent to Dallas for Detlef Schrempf Feb. 21, 1989... Signed by Knicks as a free agent Nov. 15, 1992... Born Feb. 16, 1958, in Columbus, Ohio... Still among Pacers' all-time point and rebound leaders.

Year	Team	G	FG	FG Pct.	FT	FT Pct.	Reb.	Ast.	TP	Avg.
1981-82	Indiana	82	407	.477	126	.670	605	139	942	11.5
1982-83	Indiana	78	580	.499	155	.705	583	262	1315	16.9
1983-84	Indiana	69	411	.478	207	.702	554	215	1029	14.9
1984-85	Indiana	75	575	.475	224	.657	634	252	1375	18.3
1985-86	Indiana	78	627	.492	294	.730	710	174	1549	19.9
1986-87	Indiana	74	451	.480	199	.740	543	174	1101	14.9
1987-88	Indiana	75	311	.425	126	.737	469	98	748	10.0
1988-89	Ind.-Dal.	76	322	.436	133	.686	593	124	777	10.2
1989-90	Dallas	81	295	.444	108	.679	391	119	700	8.6
1990-91	Dallas	60	332	.507	83	.638	357	95	747	12.5
1991-92	Dallas	75	367	.431	124	.725	454	94	859	11.5
1992-93	New York	55	72	.411	14	.667	146	19	158	2.9
1993-94	New York	70	103	.442	27	.643	182	28	233	3.3
1994-95	New York	56	82	.456	23	.622	132	27	187	3.3
	Totals	1004	4935	.469	1843	.698	6353	1820	11720	11.7

ANTHONY BONNER 27 6-8 225　　　　　　　　Forward

Sort of got the hint he wouldn't return with Knicks when they didn't even try to resign him entering his unrestricted free-agency year... Springs in his socks... Terrific athletic skills that don't always translate into statistics... Tough one-on-one defender, exceptionally strong offensive rebounder... A nightmare at the foul line, although his .657 was a career best... Hits an occasional jumper, but not enough to warrant steady placement in the rotation... But you could do a lot worse for a seventh man... Signed as a free agent by Knicks Oct. 5, 1993, after his rights were renounced by Kings, who picked him 23rd on first round in 1990 out of St. Louis... Born June 8, 1968, in St. Louis... Made $845,000 in 1994-95.

Year	Team	G	FG	FG Pct.	FT	FT Pct.	Reb.	Ast.	TP	Avg.
1990-91	Sacramento	34	103	.448	44	.579	161	49	250	7.4
1991-92	Sacramento	79	294	.447	151	.627	485	125	740	9.4
1992-93	Sacramento	70	229	.461	143	.593	455	96	601	8.6
1993-94	New York	73	162	.563	50	.476	344	88	374	5.1
1994-95	New York	58	88	.456	44	.657	262	80	221	3.8
	Totals	314	876	.469	432	.592	1707	438	2186	7.0

MONTY WILLIAMS 24 6-8 225　　　　　　　　　Forward

So you draft a scorer. And when you do play him, you tell him not to score. Makes sense, huh?... Now you know the frustration this guy felt as a rookie after Knicks selected him 24th out of Notre Dame... Slipped that low because many teams were frightened off by existing heart condition. But medical experts gave him the go-ahead and Knicks couldn't pass him up... Unfortunately, they also couldn't play him... He filled in as a starter when Charles Oakley went down with toe surgery and performed admirably and athletically... Started 23 games... Range must improve if he's to be a legit NBA star. Has all the necessary stuff around the basket and, unlike most of his teammates, can finish a break... Born Oct. 8, 1971, in Fredricksburg, Va.... Made $650,000 in first leg of five-year deal.

Year	Team	G	FG	FG Pct.	FT	FT Pct.	Reb.	Ast.	TP	Avg.
1994-95	New York	41	60	.451	17	.447	98	49	137	3.3

CHARLIE WARD 25 6-2 190　　　　　　　　　　Guard

Among regular courtside celebs at Knick games were Spike Lee, Woody Allen and this guy... How else to describe the 1994 Heisman Trophy winner who played all of 44 minutes as a rookie?... Knicks, though, are wild about his potential... Remember, at Florida State he only played half-seasons because of football... Showed ability in practice and preseason. But then only got to run around on court with guys more fit for Sweden than the NBA... Good decisions (when he can make them), good shot (when he can take them). You get the idea... Born Oct. 12, 1970, in Tallahassee, Fla.... No. 26 pick on first round in 1994... Made $550,000 last season.

Year	Team	G	FG	FG Pct.	FT	FT Pct.	Reb.	Ast.	TP	Avg.
1994-95	New York	10	4	.211	7	.700	6	4	16	1.6

COACH DON NELSON: Give the Knicks credit. They get names... Pat Riley resigned with one year left on his contract, so the Knicks went out and hired Nelson, the sixth-winningest coach in NBA history... But he has never won an NBA title... Led Dream Team II to the World Championships title and then saw everything come crashing down at Golden State... Admitted he mishandled the Chris Webber situation. Said he didn't communicate well enough. Webber demanded and received a trade and Warriors quit on the coach... He resigned with team struggling at 14-31... It's the only blot on a Hall of Fame career... Has 18-year record of 817-604 (.575)... After 14-year playing career that saw all but three seasons with Celtics, he was assistant coach for two months with Bucks... Ascended to head coaching job and held that 11 seasons, winning 540 games and seven divisional titles... Was GM most of that time, too... Took on two-headed job at Golden State (didn't coach the first year due to contractual clause). Left in his sixth season after 277 victories... As a coach and player, has been involved in more games, including playoffs, than any man in history (2,736)... All-American at Iowa, he was drafted on the third round (No. 19) by old Chicago Zephyrs, who moved to Baltimore but sold him to Lakers... After two years, he was waived by Lakers... Celtics got him for $100 waiver fee at recommendation of Tom Heinsohn... Played for five Celtic NBA title teams... His No. 19 was retired by Boston... Got a three-year deal with Knicks. With incentives, it's worth nearly $7 million... Born May 5, 1940, in Muskegon, Mich.

GREATEST FIND

The Knicks have had their share of luck throughout the years. How about getting Hall of Famer Willis Reed with their SECOND pick in a draft? But for a pure, straight-out find, the Knicks rarely struck gold the way they did with Anthony Mason, the reigning Sixth Man of the Year award winner.

Mason had a shot in Portland, where he went for a preseason fling as an undersized third-round selection, in New Jersey, where he barely left the bench, and in Denver, where a 10-day contract resulted in 21 minutes.

Mainly, Mason bounced around the CBA and the USBL. He even did a stint in Turkey. Finally, while playing on Long Island

Knicks know they can always count on Derek Harper.

in the USBL, he was spotted by Knick personnel who invited him for a summer-camp tryout.

By then, Mason was a physical specimen, a bulky 6-7, 250-pounder blessed with speed and ball-handling skills. Since signing on before 1991-92, Mason's improvement has been so steady that he became the cream of last summer's free-agent class.

ALL-TIME KNICK LEADERS

SEASON

Points: Patrick Ewing, 2,347, 1989–90
Assists: Mark Jackson, 868, 1987–88
Rebounds: Willis Reed, 1,191, 1968–69

GAME

Points: Bernard King, 60 vs. New Jersey, 12/25/85
Assists: Richie Guerin, 21 vs. St. Louis, 12/12/58
Rebounds: Harry Gallatin, 33 vs. Ft. Wayne, 3/15/53
Willis Reed, 33 vs. Cincinnati, 2/2/71

CAREER

Points: Patrick Ewing, 18,077, 1985–95
Assists: Walt Frazier, 4,791, 1967–77
Rebounds: Willis Reed, 8,414, 1964–74

ORLANDO MAGIC

TEAM DIRECTORY: Chairman: Rich DeVos; Exec. Vice Chairman: Cheri DeVos VanderWeide; Pres.: Bob VanderWeide; GM/COO: Pat Williams; Exec. VP: Jack Swope; VP-Basketball Oper.: John Gabriel; Dir. Publicity/Media Rel.: Alex Martins; Coach: Brian Hill; Asst. Coaches: Richie Adubato, Tree Rollins. Arena: Orlando Arena (15,151). Colors: Blue, silver, and black.

Shaq's goal: Extend that arm around the NBA trophy.

SCOUTING REPORT

SHOOTING: Inside is a near-unstoppable presence (at least for anybody not named Hakeem) in Shaquille O'Neal. Outside, there are three expert marksmen (at least when they're not in the Finals) in Nick Anderson, Dennis Scott and Anfernee (Penny) Hardaway. And in Hardaway, the Magic are blessed with an explosive first-step kind of guy who can and will dunk on anyone. So the Magic last year shot .502, the second-best mark in the league and tops in the East. No letup is in sight. Any wonder why opponents are nauseous thinking of the immediate future in the East?

Ah, but there is a blight. The foul line. Orlando shot a grade-school-like .669 at the line last season, making the league's finest offensive team the league's worst free-throw shooting team. And that has always been the Achilles heel opponents seek late in games. But the problem for opponents late in games is merely to still be in the game so that free throws matter.

PLAYMAKING: Exceptional. The Magic move the ball with precision. In his second year, Hardaway showed great improvement in simply recognizing the point-guard position. He was the assist king on a team where no fewer than eight players rang up at least 130 assists.

Inside, the veteran savvy and smarts of Horace Grant will keep the ball moving, back to the perimeter if needed. O'Neal is a capable and, usually, willing passer. And Orlando is blessed with 6-6 Brian Shaw off the bench. Forever, Shaw has battled the "Is he a one or two?" syndrome. When he's teamed with Hardaway, it really doesn't matter. What does matter then is Orlando has two steady, ball-handling guards who can score or get other guys involved. And as was the case with shooting, again, the Magic placed second only to Utah in this category league-wide.

REBOUNDING: They had Shaq, but they always needed a power forward. They tried Jeff Turner. They tried Anthony Avent. They still needed a power forward. Enter Grant, late of Chicago, wearer of three title rings. Enter an improvement on the glass that moved Orlando up to fifth in the league.

Grant's presence made Shaq that much more effective. And Shaq did for Grant in Orlando what Michael Jordan did for him in Chicago. Double teams often left Grant alone underneath, where he was the happy recipient of easy putbacks and follow-ups. Grant may even get some time to rest this season due to the addition of 6-10 rookie David Vaughn.

MAGIC ROSTER

No.	Veterans	Pos.	Ht.	Wt.	Age	Yrs. Pro	College
25	Nick Anderson	G-F	6-6	220	27	6	Illinois
R-10	Darrell Armstrong	G	6-1	180	27	1	Fayetteville
00	Anthony Avent	F	6-9	235	26	3	Seton Hall
U-14	Anthony Bowie	G	6-6	200	31	6	Oklahoma
54	Horace Grant	F	6-10	235	30	8	Clemson
R-43	Geert Hammink	F-C	7-0	262	26	2	Louisiana State
1	Anfernee Hardaway	G-F	6-7	200	24	2	Memphis State
32	Shaquille O'Neal	C	7-1	303	23	3	Louisiana State
U-30	Tree Rollins	C	7-1	255	40	18	Clemson
5	Donald Royal	F	6-8	210	29	5	Notre Dame
R-3	Dennis Scott	G-F	6-8	229	27	5	Georgia Tech
U-20	Brian Shaw	G	6-6	194	29	6	Cal-Santa Barbara
22	Brooks Thompson	G	6-4	193	25	1	Oklahoma State
31	Jeff Turner	F	6-9	244	33	9	Vanderbilt

R-restricted free agent
U-unrestricted free agent

Rd.	Rookie	Sel.No.	Pos.	Ht.	Wt.	College
1	David Vaughn	25	F	6-10	240	Memphis

DEFENSE: On the surface, the Magic's yield of 103.8 points a game was ghastly. But consider how many points they rang up, 110.9, a league-best. So when you consider the point differential margin, a plus 7.1, the Magic, like everywhere else, were solid on defense.

They have one of the best defensive forwards in the game in Grant. They have O'Neal in the middle ready to throw back shots. Hardaway and Shaw can apply good pressure and in Grant, the Magic possess the guy who always was the key to Chicago's vaunted pressure defense.

OUTLOOK: Hey, they've got Shaq and Penny, okay? That alone insures a successful season ahead. Throw in Grant, Anderson, Scott and Shaw and you have the nucleus of a team destined to dominate. Especially at home, where their 39-2 regular-season mark last year ranked as the second-best in history.

Yes, Orlando can be beaten (see: NBA Finals, 1995). But when they are passing the ball out of the double team, finding the open man on the perimeter and doing that while Shaq is establishing himself down low, they are darn near indefensible.

They have youth, they have speed, they have power, they have shooting, they have defense. They just don't have a championship. Yet. Give them time.

MAGIC PROFILES

SHAQUILLE O'NEAL 23 7-1 303   Center

Half man, half mountain, part grizzly bear... First in scoring, second in shooting, third in rebounds, sixth in blocks... And after Michael, first in endorsements... Salary ($4.8 million) plus endorsements brought him a mere $18.7 million pittance... Ruled the league until this guy named Hakeem showed up for the Finals... His 29.3 scoring title average marked the first time any Magic player led the league in any stat category... Game keeps improving as his offense becomes more varied. And he hits an occasional free throw... Rap singer too, to the delight of young fans, to the consternation of those without hearing problems... Size and strength simply frightening. Throw in quickness of a small forward and you've got an awesome package... Frustrated in Finals as Olajuwon and Rockets kept him farther out than he likes, then doubled and forced him to pass... Foul trouble diminished. Star status does that... Despite being outplayed by Olajuwon, he wasn't that far behind statistically in Finals: 28 points, 12.5 boards... Eastern All-Star starting center. Will hold that label for, oh, life... Scored 40 or more nine times last season... Born March 6, 1972, in Newark, N.J.... Left LSU after junior year and was No. 1 pick by Magic in 1992. Only possible person more popular than Mickey in Orlando... Was two-time first-team All-American and NCAA leader in rebounds as sophomore, blocks as junior.

Year	Team	G	FG	FG Pct.	FT	FT Pct.	Reb.	Ast.	TP	Avg.
1992-93	Orlando	81	733	.562	427	.592	1122	152	1893	23.4
1993-94	Orlando	81	953	.599	471	.554	1072	195	2377	29.3
1994-95	Orlando	79	930	.583	455	.533	901	214	2315	29.3
	Totals	241	2616	.583	1353	.558	3095	561	6585	27.3

ANFERNEE (PENNY) HARDAWAY 24 6-7 200   Guard

The smaller half of Orlando's dynamic duo... Yeah, real small: a 6-7 point guard... Pat Riley said the only other one like him has retired. He was referring to Magic Johnson... Astounding ball-handling, passing skills... A major problem with post-up ability against smaller points. And that means everybody else ... A mismatch a night... Top 20 in assists, scoring and steals. In his second year... With Shaq, people already talking dynasty... A real class-act guy, too, in addition to being so damn good it makes you sick... Second career triple-double Nov. 26 at Milwaukee (35 points, 12 assists, 10 rebounds). He's a triple-double waiting to happen... Shooting (.512) soaring over 50 percent... Great finisher on breaks... Terrific drive-and-dunk ability... Or drive and dish... A 35 percent threat from three-point range... Don't blame Finals sweep on him: averaged 25.5 points... Born July 18, 1971, in Memphis, Tenn.... Was picked No. 3 by Warriors, out of Memphis State, in 1993 and was sent to Magic with three first-rounders in mammoth draft-night trade for Chris Webber... Made $4.305 million in 1994-95.

Year	Team	G	FG	FG Pct.	FT	FT Pct.	Reb.	Ast.	TP	Avg.
1993-94	Orlando	82	509	.466	245	.742	439	544	1313	16.0
1994-95	Orlando	77	585	.512	356	.769	336	551	1613	20.9
	Totals	159	1094	.490	601	.758	775	1095	2926	18.4

NICK ANDERSON 27 6-6 220   Guard

Nick The Brick... May wear that label forever after blowing four (count 'em, four) free throws in the final :10.5 of regulation in Game 1 of NBA Finals... Magic lost that game in overtime. Lost series in a sweep. And no one felt worse than this guy, the first player ever drafted by Magic: No. 11 in 1989... Disappeared after that. Shot a Finals-awful .360, averaged 12.3 points... He'll be back... Solid regular season. Size and bulk can bully many two guards... And his touch can destroy from three-point range. Was 14th in NBA on treys... Had career high in assists... Team leader in career games played... Left Illinois after junior season... Wears No. 25 in honor of high-school pal Ben Wilson, who was shot to death... Says he'd be a cop if not playing ball... Born Jan. 20, 1968, in Chicago... Made $3.09 million in 1994-95.

Year	Team	G	FG	FG Pct.	FT	FT Pct.	Reb.	Ast.	TP	Avg.
1989-90	Orlando	81	372	.494	186	.705	316	124	931	11.5
1990-91	Orlando	70	400	.467	173	.668	386	106	990	14.1
1991-92	Orlando	60	482	.463	202	.667	384	163	1196	19.9
1992-93	Orlando	79	594	.449	298	.741	477	265	1574	19.9
1993-94	Orlando	81	504	.478	168	.672	476	294	1277	15.8
1994-95	Orlando	76	439	.476	143	.704	335	314	1200	15.8
	Totals	447	2791	.469	1170	.696	2374	1266	7168	16.0

HORACE GRANT 30 6-10 235   Forward

Somebody in Chicago should be fired. Or fired at... How in blazes could they just let him walk?... Signed with Magic as an unrestricted free agent in summer of '94. NBA challenged pact and then it was redone... Brought everything Orlando hoped for—except a title. But Magic got to the Finals... See? Somebody in Orlando other than Shaq does rebound... Shot .567 with his usual supply of dunks and putbacks plus a collection of mid-range jumpers... Third in the NBA in shooting, 14th in rebounding... Went over 5,000 rebounds for career during season-high 17-board game vs. Clippers Dec. 30... Had 13.7 points and 10.4 boards per in playoffs... And he was his usual defensive presence throughout. One of best help defenders in game... Bitter parting with Bulls. They actually held a press conference to trash him despite his contributions to three NBA titles... Born July 4, 1965, in Augusta, Ga., a few minutes before twin brother Harvey, a forward with Blazers... Bulls picked him No. 10 in '87 out of Clemson... Made $2.125 million in 1994-95.

Year	Team	G	FG	FG Pct.	FT	FT Pct.	Reb.	Ast.	TP	Avg.
1987-88	Chicago	81	254	.501	114	.626	447	89	622	7.7
1988-89	Chicago	79	405	.519	140	.704	681	168	950	12.0
1989-90	Chicago	80	446	.523	179	.699	629	227	1071	13.4
1990-91	Chicago	78	401	.547	197	.711	659	178	1000	12.8
1991-92	Chicago	81	457	.578	235	.741	807	217	1149	14.2
1992-93	Chicago	77	421	.508	174	.619	729	201	1017	13.2
1993-94	Chicago	70	460	.524	137	.596	769	236	1057	15.1
1994-95	Orlando	74	401	.567	146	.692	715	173	948	12.8
	Totals	620	3245	.534	1322	.677	5436	1489	7814	12.6

DENNIS SCOTT 27 6-8 229   Forward

He shoots, he scores. Not a whole heckuva lot else... And there wasn't much of that in the Finals. His shot might be showing up for the Finals any time now... Ended season with a 31-percent whimper against Houston in the championships... Took over the starting small forward spot in the second round of playoffs ... One of league's deadliest shooters. When he's on, of course... Eleventh in league in three-point accuracy during regular season... Blistered Knicks for 38 points off bench in just 31 minutes April 23 ... Began season on injured list with strained lower back ... Injuries kept him to just 72 combined games in his second and third seasons in the league ... Has fought weight problem since coming into league out of Georgia Tech after his junior year in 1990, when Magic made him No. 4 pick ... Earned $3.24 million in 1994-95 ... Born Sept. 5, 1968, in Hagerstown, Md.

Year	Team	G	FG	FG Pct.	FT	FT Pct.	Reb.	Ast.	TP	Avg.
1990-91	Orlando	82	503	.425	153	.750	235	134	1284	15.7
1991-92	Orlando	18	133	.402	64	.901	66	35	359	19.9
1992-93	Orlando	54	329	.431	92	.786	186	136	858	15.9
1993-94	Orlando	82	384	.405	123	.774	218	216	1046	12.8
1994-95	Orlando	62	283	.439	86	.754	146	131	802	12.9
	Totals	298	1632	.422	518	.779	851	652	4349	14.6

BRIAN SHAW 29 6-6 194   Guard

Magic's "other" free-agent windfall ... Brought reliable backup to Penny Hardaway and provided additional size and speed ... Plays both one and two, another luxury. And all he cost was $692,000 last year ... Overall shooting continued to be a bane, as it has for much of career ... But he makes up for it with smarts and very sound defense ... Was one of the real bright spots in Finals sweep. Averaged 12.5 points and hit 10-of-29 three-pointers ... When teamed with Hardaway, gives opponents super headaches because of size, speed and ball-handling backcourt combo ... Best assists average in four seasons ... Signed on Sept. 22 as Orlando scored coup over Florida rival Miami ... Drafted by Celtics on first round, No. 24, out of UC-Santa Barbara, in 1988 ... Played in Italy during contract snit in '89 ... Traded to Heat for Sherman Douglas Jan. 10, 1992 ... Born March 22, 1966, in Oakland.

Year	Team	G	FG	FG Pct.	FT	FT Pct.	Reb.	Ast.	TP	Avg.
1988-89	Boston	82	297	.433	109	.826	376	472	703	8.6
1990-91	Boston	79	442	.469	204	.819	370	602	1091	13.8
1991-92	Bos.-Mia.	63	209	.407	72	.791	204	250	495	7.9
1992-93	Miami	68	197	.393	61	.782	257	235	498	7.3
1993-94	Miami	77	278	.417	64	.719	350	385	693	9.0
1994-95	Orlando	78	192	.389	70	.737	241	406	502	6.4
	Totals	447	1615	.425	580	.790	1798	2350	3982	8.9

DONALD ROYAL 29 6-8 210 Forward

While Orlando was being humbled in the Finals, this guy started griping about his playing time... Yeah, like he was going to be the answer... Career highs in most major categories and scoring was only off a bit (9.1 compared to 9.2)... Decent defender, but his strength lies in his ability to get to the line... Good finisher, too. Has a knack for the ball... He's a complementary type who may have been spoiled by starting... He did begin the playoffs as the starting small forward. But usually, he just kept the position warm for Dennis Scott... After career-high minutes in regular season, he played one minute in Finals... Born May 22, 1966, in New Orleans... Cavs made him a third-round pick out of Notre Dame in 1987... After CBA stint, did a year with expansionist Timberwolves, played in Israel, was signed and released by Magic, played a year with Spurs. Returned to Orlando as a free agent Aug. 24, 1992... Made $1 million in 1994-95.

Year	Team	G	FG	FG Pct.	FT	FT Pct.	Reb.	Ast.	TP	Avg.
1989-90	Minnesota	66	117	.459	153	.777	137	43	387	5.9
1991-92	San Antonio	60	80	.449	92	.692	124	34	252	4.2
1992-93	Orlando	77	194	.496	318	.815	295	80	706	9.2
1993-94	Orlando	74	174	.501	199	.740	248	61	547	7.4
1994-95	Orlando	70	206	.475	223	.746	279	198	635	9.1
	Totals	347	771	.480	985	.765	1083	416	2527	7.3

ANTHONY AVENT 26 6-9 235 Forward

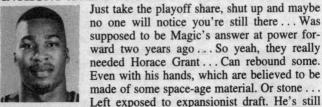

Just take the playoff share, shut up and maybe no one will notice you're still there... Was supposed to be Magic's answer at power forward two years ago... So yeah, they really needed Horace Grant... Can rebound some. Even with his hands, which are believed to be made of some space-age material. Or stone... Left exposed to expansionist draft. He's still with Magic... Never got off the bench in the Finals... First-round pick, No. 15, by Hawks out of Seton Hall in 1991. Rights traded to Bucks in three-way deal that involved Denver and sent Blair Rasmussen to Atlanta... Went to Italy for 1991-92... Magic gave up Anthony Cook and a conditional first-rounder for him Jan. 15, 1994 . . . Born Oct. 18, 1969, in Rocky Mount, N.C. . . . Made $800,000 in 1994-95.

Year	Team	G	FG	FG Pct.	FT	FT Pct.	Reb.	Ast.	TP	Avg.
1992-93	Milwaukee	82	347	.433	112	.651	512	91	806	9.8
1993-94	Mil.-Orl.	74	150	.377	89	.724	338	65	389	5.3
1994-95	Orlando	71	105	.430	48	.640	293	41	258	3.6
	Totals	227	602	.417	249	.673	1143	197	1453	6.4

ANTHONY BOWIE 31 6-6 200   Guard

Reliable but unspectacular . . . But Magic doesn't need spectacular with Shaq and Penny . . . At his best in the open court. Near invisible in halfcourt game . . . So yeah, he likes to try to get the tempo going . . . Strictly a role player, he seems to have learned it isn't mandatory to shoot every time you touch the ball . . . Good consistency the last two seasons with his shot: .481 and .480. And he has some range, although he's better going to the hole . . . Signed as a free agent Dec. 31, 1991 . . . Drafted on third round by Rockets in 1986, out of Oklahoma. Did time with Houston and San Antonio . . . Was CBA's MVP in 1988-89 . . . Born Nov. 9, 1963, in Tulsa, Okla. . . . Earned $900,000 last year.

Year	Team	G	FG	FG Pct.	FT	FT Pct.	Reb.	Ast.	TP	Avg.
1988-89	San Antonio	18	72	.500	10	.667	56	29	15	8.6
1989-90	Houston	66	119	.406	40	.741	118	96	284	4.3
1991-92	Orlando	52	312	.493	117	.860	245	163	758	14.6
1992-93	Orlando	77	268	.471	67	.798	194	175	618	8.0
1993-94	Orlando	70	139	.481	41	.837	120	102	320	4.6
1994-95	Orlando	77	177	.480	61	.836	139	159	427	5.5
	Totals	360	1087	.473	336	.818	872	724	2562	7.1

WAYNE (TREE) ROLLINS 40 7-1 255   Center

Began career in Bronze Age . . . Was the third-oldest player in the league last season, behind Moses Malone and Robert Parish . . . Retired and was minding own business as an assistant coach when injury struck Magic and he was forced to become player-coach in January 1994 . . . Magic liked him so much as Shaq's backup, they did an encore last year . . . One of the game's great defensive centers in his prime . . . His 2,542 career blocks place him fourth all-time in that category . . . Suffice to say he's no threat to John Stockton. His 660 career assists translate to one every 36.4 minutes... Was No. 14 pick by Hawks in 1977, out of Clemson... Played with Cavs, Pistons and Rockets at end of career before latching on as Orlando assistant in '93... Born June 16, 1955, in Winter Haven, Fla.... Was paid $735,000 in 1994-95.

Year	Team	G	FG	FG Pct.	FT	FT Pct.	Reb.	Ast.	TP	Avg.
1977-78	Atlanta	80	253	.487	104	.703	552	79	610	7.6
1978-79	Atlanta	81	297	.535	89	.631	588	49	683	8.4
1979-80	Atlanta	82	287	.558	157	.714	774	76	731	8.9
1980-81	Atlanta	40	116	.552	46	.807	286	35	278	7.0
1981-82	Atlanta	79	202	.584	79	.612	611	59	483	6.1
1982-83	Atlanta	80	261	.510	98	.726	743	75	620	7.8
1983-84	Atlanta	77	274	.518	118	.621	593	62	666	8.6
1984-85	Atlanta	70	186	.549	67	.720	442	52	439	6.3
1985-86	Atlanta	74	173	.499	69	.767	458	41	415	5.6
1986-87	Atlanta	75	171	.546	63	.724	488	22	405	5.4
1987-88	Atlanta	76	133	.512	70	.875	459	20	336	4.4
1988-89	Cleveland	60	62	.449	12	.632	139	19	136	2.3
1989-90	Cleveland	48	57	.456	11	.688	153	24	125	2.6
1990-91	Detroit	37	14	.424	8	.571	42	4	36	1.0
1991-92	Houston	59	46	.535	26	.867	171	15	118	2.0
1992-93	Houston	42	11	.268	9	.750	60	10	31	0.7
1993-94	Orlando	45	29	.547	18	.600	96	9	76	1.7
1994-95	Orlando	51	20	.476	21	.677	95	9	61	1.2
	Totals	1156	2592	.522	1065	.700	6750	660	6249	5.4

GEERT HAMMINK 26 7-0 262   Center

"Hammink": Dutch for "He who caddies for superstar rapper for life."... Backed up Shaq at LSU and is continuing that proud tradition in the pros... Played in one glorious regular-season game for seven minutes... He's big, okay?... Two years with Orlando have brought two appearances... Who the heck knows if he can play?... Injured list all last season... Made $260,000 ... Or $260,000 per made shot... Born July 12, 1969, in Arnhem, The Netherlands... Speaks Dutch, German and English fluently and speaks a little French and Italian... No. 26 pick by Magic in 1993.

Year	Team	G	FG	FG Pct.	FT	FT Pct.	Reb.	Ast.	TP	Avg.
1993-94	Orlando	1	1	.333	0	.000	1	1	2	2.0
1994-95	Orlando	1	1	.333	2	1.000	2	1	4	4.0
	Totals	2	2	.333	2	1.000	3	2	6	3.0

BROOKS THOMPSON 25 6-4 193   Guard

Gotta have garbage-time guys...Long-distance lefty shooter who was the 27th pick in the '94 draft...Not much time for guys behind Dennis Scott, Nick Anderson and even Jeff Turner on the depth chart...Started against Lakers April 2 and responded with 20 points...Supplies depth for Magic, frustration for himself because of limited opportunity situation...Set five school three-point records at Oklahoma State...Class of '94...Born July 19, 1970, in Dallas...Started college at Texas A&M....Made $650,000 in 1994-95.

Year	Team	G	FG	FG Pct.	FT	FT Pct.	Reb.	Ast.	TP	Avg.
1994-95	Orlando	38	45	.395	8	.667	23	43	116	3.1

JEFF TURNER 33 6-9 244   Forward

Yeah, yeah, he knows. He made the Olympic team over Charles Barkley in 1984...Steady role player. Nothing flashy; can hit a three-point shot and grab an occasional rebound...Defense has never been his strength...Nice guy who pointed out Magic players' unprofessionalism in late 1994. They laughed at him. They stopped laughing when they were swept in first round...Gets tossed in as a change of pace...Had career-low scoring. Magic simply loaded with better weapons...Was No. 17 pick by the Nets out of Vanderbilt in '84...Little used for three years. He went to Italy for two and then hooked up with Magic as a free agent July 11, 1989...Born April 9, 1962, in Bangor, Maine...Made $1.1 million last year.

Year	Team	G	FG	FG Pct.	FT	FT Pct.	Reb.	Ast.	TP	Avg.
1984-85	New Jersey	72	171	.454	79	.859	218	108	421	5.8
1985-86	New Jersey	53	84	.491	58	.744	137	14	226	4.3
1986-87	New Jersey	76	151	.465	76	.731	197	60	378	5.0
1989-90	Orlando	60	132	.429	42	.778	227	53	308	5.1
1990-91	Orlando	71	259	.487	85	.759	363	97	609	8.6
1991-92	Orlando	75	225	.451	79	.693	246	92	530	7.1
1992-93	Orlando	75	231	.529	56	.800	252	107	528	7.0
1993-94	Orlando	68	199	.467	35	.778	271	60	451	6.6
1994-95	Orlando	49	73	.410	26	.897	97	38	199	4.1
	Totals	599	1525	.469	536	.768	2008	629	3650	6.1

THE ROOKIE

DAVID VAUGHN 22 6-10 240 Forward
NBA body. NBA injuries in his past, though... Medically redshirted 1992-93 after partially torn ACL in his left knee... Still, Magic couldn't pass him up at No. 25 on the first round... Averaged 9.0 rebounds, 12.9 points as a senior when he missed five games with stress fracture in his left foot... Was nation's sixth-best rebounder as a senior... Twice led Memphis to Sweet 16 appearances... Born March 23, 1973, in Tulsa, Okla, but schooled in Nashville, Tenn.... Magic hope team's lone draft pick can be a quality backup to Horace Grant.

COACH BRIAN HILL: Forgive him if he gets a little paranoid. All he did was lead the Magic to the NBA Finals. And all he heard were whispers that Pat Riley or some other glamour type was going to take over... Guess he deserved it for being stand-up, decent guy... Despite rumors to contrary, he has a good relationship with Shaquille O'Neal. That's the biggest key to job security in Orlando... Kept it pretty simple and it paid off as Magic, until late-season injuries, terrorized the league... Believes in defense and intensity... Magic had NBA-best 39-2 record at home... Two-year record as head coach has produced a 107-57 record... Good communicator. Big on bulletin-board fodder. Always places Magic-related stories on board... Replaced Matt Guokas as head coach June 30, 1993... Two-sport standout (track, baseball) at Kennedy (Neb.) College... Assistant to Mike Fratello in Atlanta for four years. Three more years assisting Guokas in Orlando... Spent 14 years in the college ranks, eight as the head man at Lehigh... Brother, Fred, is Rutgers' baseball coach... Born Sept. 19, 1947, in East Orange, N.J.

GREATEST FIND

The CBA has been a proving/testing ground for many NBA players. Many are called, few are chosen to stay.

One such player is Donald Royal, who after his CBA stint did time with both Minnesota and San Antonio, with a short trip back to the lesser lights of lesser cities. Orlando even took a preseason look back in 1991.

After the Spurs waived him in the summer of '92, Orlando came calling for a second look. And the Magic is happy it did.

He surrendered his starting status in the playoffs, but for three seasons, Royal was a serviceable starting small forward. Last year, he started 68 games for the best team in the East, not too shabby an accomplishment for a guy whose resume includes Pensacola, Cedar Rapids, Tri-City and even Israel.

ALL-TIME MAGIC LEADERS

SEASON

Points: Shaquille O'Neal, 2,377, 1993–94
Assists: Scott Skiles, 735, 1992–93
Rebounds: Shaquille O'Neal, 1,122, 1992–93

GAME

Points: Shaquille O'Neal, 53 vs. Minnesota, 4/20/94
Assists: Scott Skiles, 30 vs. Denver, 12/30/90
Rebounds: Terry Catledge, 22 vs. Philadelphia, 11/13/91

CAREER

Points: Nick Anderson, 7,168, 1989–95
Assists: Scott Skiles, 3,176, 1989–94
Rebounds: Shaquille O'Neal, 3,095, 1992–95

PHILADELPHIA 76ERS

TEAM DIRECTORY: Owner: Harold Katz; GM/Coach: John Lucas; Dir. Player Personnel: Gene Shue; Dir. Scouting: Tony DiLeo; Dir. Pub. Rel.: Joe Favorito; Asst. Coaches: Ron Adams, Maurice Cheeks, Tom Thibodeau. Arena: The Spectrum (18,168). Colors: Red, white and blue.

SCOUTING REPORT

SHOOTING: Well, there's Dana Barros and Jeff Malone. And beyond that, there are a lot of wishes that there were somebody proven beyond Dana Barros and Jeff Malone. North Carolina's Jerry Stackhouse is being counted on to do a lot of wonderful things as a rookie. And he'll definitely get the chance to do it. Anybody who can hit the water from the shoreline will get the chance. Overall, Sixer shooting is simply poor. Clarence Weatherspoon is tough and effective down on the blocks. From the perimeter? Well, he's tough and effective down on the blocks. Willie Burton, a waiver steal last season, can light it up with anyone. But he is so naggingly inconsistent.

The Sixers are blessed with some quality people inside, but until they can come up with something from the perimeter—or get a healthy and rejuvenated Malone back from a lost season—it will be tough.

PLAYMAKING: A guard who can see the court, a guard who can see the court, John Lucas' kingdom for a guard who can see the court.

The Sixers had the fewest assists by far in the league last year and had a fewest number (3) of players with at least 100 assists. Barros proved his effectiveness from beyond the shortened three-point arc but left something to be desired as a set-up man, although he did average 7.5 assists per game. That wasn't nearly enough. The Sixers were dead last in the league in assists/turnover ratio. Stackhouse, the lone draft choice, will help keep the ball moving. But he won't be enough—unless, as billed, he truly is the next Air Jordan.

REBOUNDING: It got better because Shawn Bradley got better. And it will continue to get better as Bradley gets better.

There are some real workhouse studs, potentially, underneath for the Sixers. Last year's prized rookie, Sharone Wright, could

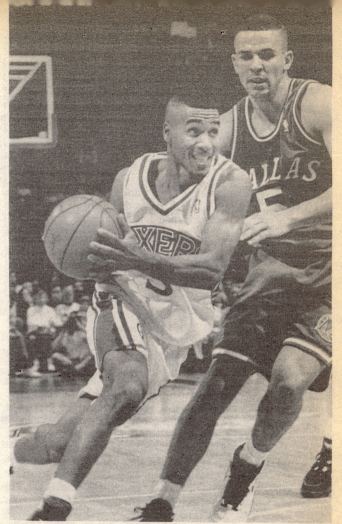

Dana Barros was chosen as NBA's Most Improved Player.

be a monster, but he needs to bulk up a bit and improve on his defensive approach, which in turn will get him better positioning underneath. And the Sixers are looking for help from anywhere. They were a wretched 19th in the league in rebounding last season.

76ER ROSTER

No.	Veterans	Pos.	Ht.	Wt.	Age	Yrs. Pro	College
R-21	Derrick Alston	F	6-11	225	23	1	Duquesne
U-3	Dana Barros	G	5-11	163	28	6	Boston College
76	Shawn Bradley	C	7-6	248	23	2	Brigham Young
U-9	Willie Burton	G-F	6-8	219	27	5	Minnesota
U-5	Corey Gaines	G	6-4	195	30	6	Loyola Marymount
20	Greg Graham	G	6-4	174	24	2	Indiana
U-14	Jeff Grayer	G	6-5	215	29	7	Iowa State
25	Jeff Malone	G	6-4	205	34	12	Mississippi State
23	Tim Perry	F	6-9	220	30	7	Temple
35	C. Weatherspoon	F	6-7	240	25	3	Southern Mississippi
–	Scott Williams	F	6-10	230	27	5	North Carolina
4	Sharone Wright	F	6-11	260	22	1	Clemson

R-restricted free agent
U-unrestricted free agent

Rd.	Rookie	Sel.No.	Pos.	Ht.	Wt.	College
1	Jerry Stackhouse	3	F-G	6-6	218	North Carolina

DEFENSE: The Sixers posted their finest points-per-game defensive yield (100.4) since the team was in Syracuse in 1955-56. Of course, the Sixers' lack of a quality offensive transition game helped that number, but a positive stat is a positive stat.

Bradley continued to emerge as a legitimate shot-blocker, a rear line of defense almost unto himself. But the young Sixers don't always seem to take advantage of his presence. They need to funnel more action into the middle, where Bradley can at least alter the situation or force the ball to be kicked outside.

OUTLOOK: Getting better all the time. And that is what they need: time. Bradley began to show that with experience there might be something there other than vertical size. Stackhouse will be tossed in and will undergo trial by fire, but from all accounts and advance notices, he'll be able to do it. But he suffers from one of the Sixers' most crippling ailments: inexperience. At the end of last season, the Sixers averaged a mere 2.7 years of league experience, which tied for the third-lowest mark in the league.

One factor that is decidedly in the Sixers' favor is divisional position. The Atlantic is the weakest division in the league. Playoffs this year? Maybe they can grab the eighth spot if somebody from the Central goes in the tank. And if they can find one more legitimate offensive weapon.

SIXER PROFILES

DANA BARROS 28 5-11 163 — Guard

Good things, small packages, etc. . . . The unrestricted free-agent all-star . . . Tremendous season as he proved to be Sixers' most effective weapon . . . Ended season with NBA-record 58 straight games with at least one three-point basket . . . Among top 20 in shooting, free-throw shooting, steals, assists and scoring . . . Team record .464 on three-pointers . . . His .899 from line was sixth-best mark in team history . . . Became just the third player under six feet to notch 50 points in one game when he torched Houston on March 14. Joined Michael Adams and Calvin Murphy . . . Great quickness. And durability. He didn't miss a game . . . Also had the highest percentage of total team assists ever by a Sixer (39.5) . . . His three-pointers usually come from original range, too . . . Still learning point-guard spot, though. Has natural two-guard mentality . . . Along with Willie Burton, he gave Sixers only seventh pair of teammates ever to have 50-point individual games in same season . . . Was No. 16 pick by Seattle out of Boston College in 1989 . . . Sonics traded him and Eddie Johnson to Charlotte for Kendall Gill Sept. 1, 1993 . . . Sixers got him, Sidney Green and draft rights to Greg Graham for Hersey Hawkins on Sept. 3, 1993 . . . Born April 13, 1967, in Boston . . . Made $937,500 in 1994-95.

Year	Team	G	FG	FG Pct.	FT	FT Pct.	Reb.	Ast.	TP	Avg.
1989-90	Seattle	81	299	.405	89	.809	132	205	782	9.7
1990-91	Seattle	66	154	.495	78	.918	71	111	418	6.3
1991-92	Seattle	75	238	.483	60	.759	81	125	619	8.3
1992-93	Seattle	69	214	.451	49	.831	107	151	541	7.8
1993-94	Philadelphia	81	412	.469	116	.800	196	424	1075	13.3
1994-95	Philadelphia	82	571	.490	347	.899	274	619	1686	20.6
	Totals	454	1888	.465	739	.855	861	1635	5121	11.3

SHAWN BRADLEY 23 7-6 248 — Center

He's getting there . . . Experience is bringing improvement. When he played 30 or more minutes, opponents shot 43 percent. When he didn't, opponents shot 51 percent . . . So there is hope for the future . . . Came on strong the last quarter of the season . . . Played in all 82 games . . . Far more active than first season. No longer just plops in middle and impersonates a lamp post... Had seven straight double-doubles from late March to early April, the most by a Sixer center in seven seasons... Fouled out just three times in last 44 games. Fouled out 15 times in first 38... Sixers still need to learn how to funnel opponents into him to best utilize his standout shot-blocking ability. Third in NBA in blocks average, second in overall total... Blocked 14 shots in one college game, tying NCAA record while at Brigham Young... Taken No. 2 in 1993, in between Chris Webber and Anfernee Hardaway... Played one year in college, spent two seasons on Mormon mission... Sixers were desperately trying to trade him. Then he picked up after deadline passed and those thoughts went south... Born March 22, 1972, in Landstuhl, West Germany... Made $3.51 million in 1994-95.

Year	Team	G	FG	FG Pct.	FT	FT Pct.	Reb.	Ast.	TP	Avg.
1993-94	Philadelphia	49	201	.409	102	.607	306	98	504	10.3
1994-95	Philadelphia	82	315	.455	148	.638	659	53	778	9.5
	Totals	131	516	.436	250	.625	965	151	1282	9.8

CLARENCE WEATHERSPOON 25 6-7 240   Forward

A four in a three's body... Toughness and work ethic are superior... For years, Sixers tried to win with an undersized power forward in Charles Barkley. Traded Sir Charles and immediately tried to win with this undersized power forward... His 4,159 three-season total points is second on Sixers' all-time list. Only Hersey Hawkins and Barkley had more after same time... A workhorse. Played 40 or more minutes 30 times in last 44 games... Passing skills continue to improve. Sixers were awful passing team but he was leader among non-point guards... Strength is on the low blocks. Perimeter game definitely needs improvement... Born Sept. 8, 1970, in Crawford, Miss.... No. 9 pick overall in the 1992 draft out of Southern Mississippi... Made team-high $4.0 million in 1994-95.

Year	Team	G	FG	FG Pct.	FT	FT Pct.	Reb.	Ast.	TP	Avg.
1992-93	Philadelphia	82	494	.469	291	.713	589	147	1280	15.6
1993-94	Philadelphia	82	602	.483	298	.693	832	192	1506	18.4
1994-95	Philadelphia	76	543	.439	283	.751	526	215	1373	18.1
	Totals	240	1639	.463	872	.718	1947	554	4159	17.3

JEFF MALONE 34 6-4 205 — Guard

Guard, did the Sixers need him... But season-long battle with heel problem limited him to a mere 19 games. Considering the Sixers only won 21, he was probably the luckiest guy on the team... Missed 41 straight games and then returned and scored 28 against Golden State on March 22... Then went out again... Missed more games last season than in his first 11 seasons combined (49)... Became the 48th player to crack the 17,000-point career barrier... Always a good, solid player. Known for his classic shot, but underrated defensively... Age and injury, however, have folks guessing about what he can bring this season... Was the No. 10 pick in the 1983 draft out of Mississippi State by the Bullets... After his glory years in Washington, he went to Utah in a three-way deal with Sacramento that involved Pervis Ellison and Jazz package of players and draft picks June 25, 1990... Came to Philly with a first-round pick for Jeff Hornacek and Sean Green Feb. 24, 1994... Born June 28, 1961, in Mobile, Ala.... Earned $1.93 million in 1994-95.

Year	Team	G	FG	FG Pct.	FT	FT Pct.	Reb.	Ast.	TP	Avg.
1983-84	Washington	81	408	.444	142	.826	155	151	982	12.1
1984-85	Washington	76	605	.499	211	.844	206	184	1436	18.9
1985-86	Washington	80	735	.483	322	.868	288	191	1795	22.4
1986-87	Washington	80	689	.457	376	.885	218	298	1758	22.0
1987-88	Washington	80	648	.476	335	.882	206	237	1641	20.5
1988-89	Washington	76	677	.480	296	.871	179	219	1651	21.7
1989-90	Washington	75	781	.491	257	.877	206	243	1820	24.3
1990-91	Utah	69	525	.508	231	.917	206	143	1282	18.6
1991-92	Utah	81	691	.511	256	.898	233	180	1639	20.2
1992-93	Utah	79	595	.494	236	.852	173	128	1429	18.1
1993-94	Utah-Phil.	77	525	.486	205	.830	199	125	1262	16.4
1994-95	Philadelphia	19	144	.507	51	.864	55	29	350	18.4
	Totals	873	7023	.485	2918	.871	2324	2128	17045	19.5

WILLIE BURTON 27 6-8 219 — Guard-Forward

Unceremoniously waived by Miami. Came back to haunt Heat with 53-point nuclear explosion on Dec. 13. That set a Spectrum record and were the most points by a Sixer since Wilt Chamberlain nailed 53 in 1967 against the Lakers... Never worked out in Miami, where he suffered recurring bouts of clinical depression. And where Heat continually drafted Big

Ten shooters, creating duplicity of talent... Arguably the most naturally talented player on the Sixers' roster... Never known for his defense. And never known for consistency, which has been the biggest rap... Went the month of February without a single 50-percent shooting game... Twice sprained right ankle, once in January, again in March, and that sliced his season apart... His .401 shooting was career low... Heat took him at No. 9 out of Minnesota in 1990 draft... Born May 26, 1968, in Detroit... Heat ate $1.052 million on his contract and Sixers paid him $146,190, pro-rated minimum wage.

Year	Team	G	FG FG	Pct.	FT	FT Pct.	Reb.	Ast.	TP	Avg.
1990-91	Miami	76	341	.441	229	.782	262	107	915	12.0
1991-92	Miami	68	280	.450	196	.800	244	123	762	11.2
1992-93	Miami	26	54	.383	91	.717	70	16	204	7.8
1993-94	Miami	53	124	.438	120	.759	136	39	371	7.0
1994-95	Philadelphia	53	243	.401	220	.824	164	96	812	15.3
	Totals	276	1042	.430	856	.785	876	381	3064	11.1

SCOTT WILLIAMS 27 6-10 230   Center-Forward

Can you say "backup"?... Wanted to prove to the league he was a starting player. Came to Philadelphia from Chicago as a free agent and promptly proved the world right. He's best suited an a reserve... Effectiveness drops after 18, 20 minutes... Still, he has his worth ... Good, sound and physical offensive rebounder... Underwent arthroscopic surgery on right knee at the end of the season... Plagued by all sorts by injuries: knee, finger, quad muscles... And still he had career highs in minutes, points, field goals, rebounds and steals... Best game came Feb. 20 against Golden State when he scored 17 points and grabbed career-high 20 rebounds... Born March 21, 1968, in Hacienda Heights, Cal.... Was one of the big finds of the '90s. Undrafted out of North Carolina in 1990, he was signed as a free agent by the Bulls. After three title rings, he came to Philly as a free agent July 28, 1994, for $1.5 million.

Year	Team	G	FG FG	Pct.	FT	FT Pct.	Reb.	Ast.	TP	Avg.
1990-91	Chicago	51	53	.510	20	.714	98	16	127	2.5
1991-92	Chicago	63	83	.483	48	.649	247	50	214	3.4
1992-93	Chicago	71	166	.466	90	.714	451	68	422	5.9
1993-94	Chicago	38	114	.483	60	.612	181	39	289	7.6
1994-95	Philadelphia	77	206	.475	79	.738	485	59	491	6.4
	Totals	300	622	.478	297	.686	1462	232	1543	5.1

SHARONE WRIGHT 22 6-11 260   Forward-Center

Looks like a mountain on bamboo stalks. Pro athlete's body, dancer's legs... Needed shoulder surgery at end of season... Seventh-best rebounder among all rookies. Which really wasn't all that hot because he was the No. 6 pick out of Clemson, where he left after junior year... One of only nine Sixer rookies ever to score 900 points... No range (What do you expect? He is 6-11). And may be a member of the United Federation of Foul-Line Brick Layers... But he displayed enough for Sixers to be optimistic... Excellent moves on the blocks, include a good turnaround jumper and an effective up-and-under spin move... Defensively? Hey, he was a rookie... Must improve conditioning. And put some meat on those calves while you're at it... Born Jan. 20, 1973, in Macon, Ga.... Made $2.02 million in 1994-95.

Year	Team	G	FG	FG Pct.	FT	FT Pct.	Reb.	Ast.	TP	Avg.
1994-95	Philadelphia	79	361	.465	182	.645	472	48	904	11.4

JEFF GRAYER 29 6-5 215   Guard-Forward

What might have been. Showed early promise in preseason and first month of 1988 as a Buck rookie, then tore up a knee... Was durable after that, but never quite the same player... A real good complementary player to have on a good team. Problem last year was that Sixers stunk... Can make shots, especially around the basket. But he never regained the explosiveness he once owned... Born Dec. 17, 1965, in Flint, Mich. ... Bucks took him on the first round, No. 13 overall, out of Iowa State in 1988... Played at Golden State for two seasons... Signed with Sixers as a free agent Jan. 5 for pro-rated minimum $150,000 after Warriors released him in offseason.

Year	Team	G	FG	FG Pct.	FT	FT Pct.	Reb.	Ast.	TP	Avg.
1988-89	Milwaukee	11	32	.438	17	.850	35	22	81	7.4
1989-90	Milwaukee	71	224	.460	99	.651	217	107	548	7.7
1990-91	Milwaukee	82	210	.433	101	.687	246	123	521	6.4
1991-92	Milwaukee	82	309	.448	102	.667	257	150	739	9.0
1992-93	Golden State	48	165	.467	91	.669	157	70	423	8.8
1993-94	Golden State	67	191	.526	71	.602	191	62	455	6.8
1994-95	Philadelphia	47	163	.428	58	.699	149	74	389	8.3
	Totals	408	1294	.457	539	.666	1252	608	3156	7.7

DERRICK ALSTON 23 6-11 225   Forward-Center

Not a bad second-round pick at all. After all, check out the size... Very athletic type. Can be used at any position in the frontcourt and his athleticism even allowed him to defend shooting guards at times... Made the most of his minutes and kept improving... First career start resulted in 22 points against Orlando. But don't get carried away. He'll probably never be a big scorer... Still, a nice solid second-round find... Born Aug. 20, 1972, in the Bronx, N.Y., but went to high school in Hoboken, N.J., across the river... Sixers took him No. 33 overall, out of Duquesne, and paid him minimum $150,000 for rookie season.

Year	Team	G	FG	FG Pct.	FT	FT Pct.	Reb.	Ast.	TP	Avg.
1994-95	Philadelphia	64	120	.465	59	.492	219	33	299	4.7

TIM PERRY 30 6-9 220   Forward

Wasted season. Career-low minutes, games. Didn't score double-figures in any of his 42 games... Has been a tribute to inconsistency offensively... The man who two years ago knocked down seven three-point shots in a row in the same game against Charlotte was 0-of-14 on trifectas last season... There is some ability here, but it's reserved almost exclusively to the defensive end. He can run and rebound and block some shots: he had 14 rebounds in his season-high 33-minute stint at Denver Feb. 23... Was the No. 7 pick out of Temple by Phoenix in 1988... Was part of the mega-deal involving Charles Barkley June 17, 1992. Came to Sixers with Andrew Lang and Jeff Hornacek for Sir Charles. He's all that's left in Philly from that trade... Born June 4, 1965, in Freehold, N.J. ... Made $1.75 million in 1994-95.

Year	Team	G	FG	FG Pct.	FT	FT Pct.	Reb.	Ast.	TP	Avg.
1988-89	Phoenix	62	108	.537	40	.615	132	18	257	4.1
1989-90	Phoenix	60	100	.513	53	.589	152	17	254	4.2
1990-91	Phoenix	46	75	.521	43	.614	126	27	193	4.2
1991-92	Phoenix	80	413	.523	153	.712	551	134	982	12.3
1992-93	Philadelphia	81	287	.468	147	.710	409	126	731	9.0
1993-94	Philadelphia	80	272	.435	102	.580	404	94	719	9.0
1994-95	Philadelphia	42	27	.346	22	.550	89	12	76	1.8
	Totals	451	1282	.485	560	.649	1863	428	3212	7.1

GREG GRAHAM 24 6-4 174   Guard

Another with "potential" ... Right, he hasn't done anything yet ... Eternal problem: Is he a one? Is he a two? Or is he really neither? ... Doesn't have the shot for the off-guard, doesn't have the ball-handling skills for the point ... Managed a career-high 20 points vs. Utah on Dec. 20 ... Shot 3-of-4 on three-pointers in that game, then went 2-of-3 vs. Phoenix on Jan 4. Rest of the year he was 1-of-21 ... Hornets took him No. 17 in 1993 but sent his draft rights to Philadelphia with Barros and Sidney Green for Hersey Hawkins, Sept. 3, 1993 ... Has never really lived up to rep that made him the Big Ten Defensive Player of the Year as a senior at Indiana or a mid-first-round draft choice ... Born Nov. 26, 1970, in Indianapolis ... Made $910,000 in 1994-95.

Year	Team	G	FG	FG Pct.	FT	FT Pct.	Reb.	Ast.	TP	Avg.
1993-94	Philadelphia	70	122	.400	92	.836	86	66	338	4.8
1994-95	Philadelphia	50	95	.426	55	.753	62	66	251	5.0
	Totals	120	217	.411	147	.803	148	132	589	4.9

COREY GAINES 30 6-4 195   Guard

Walking, talking tribute to luggage ... Six seasons in the CBA. Parts of five seasons in the NBA with the Nets, Sixers, Nuggets, Knicks and Sixers again ... Started college at UCLA, finished at Loyola Marymount ... No doubt had four different kindergartens ... Writer's cramp from all the free-agent contract signings ... Sixers signed him for minimum pro-rated wage on April 3 ... Solid, fundamental type. You could do a lot worse for a backup ... As always, showed he simply is not a shooter ... Decent defender. Was originally drafted by Sonics on the third round in 1988 ... Born June 1, 1965, in Los Angeles.

Year	Team	G	FG	FG Pct.	FT	FT Pct.	Reb.	Ast.	TP	Avg.
1988-89	New Jersey	32	27	.422	12	.750	19	67	67	2.1
1989-90	Philadelphia	9	4	.333	1	.250	5	26	10	1.1
1990-91	Denver	10	28	.400	22	.846	14	91	83	8.3
1993-94	New York	18	9	.450	13	.867	13	30	33	1.8
1994-95	Philadelphia	11	24	.471	5	.455	18	33	55	5.0
	Totals	80	92	.424	53	.736	69	247	248	3.1

THE ROOKIE

JERRY STACKHOUSE 20 6-6 218   Forward-Guard
The next Jordan? Some say so... Was the No. 3 pick in the draft, just like another famous North Carolina product who later chased minor-league fly balls... "An upper-echelon athlete," said Sacramento exec Geoff Petrie... Averaged 19.2 for Carolina. Under Dean Smith, that's like averaging 94 anywhere else... First team All-American... One of the draft's super sophs. Still has a lot of growth potential... Would bite the head off a rattlesnake to win ... Only third Carolina freshman ever to win MVP of ACC tourney, joining Phil Ford and Sam Perkins... Clippers wanted him at No. 2; he didn't want Clippers... Born Nov. 5, 1974, in Kinston, N.C.... *Sports Illustrated*'s College Player of the Year.

COACH JOHN LUCAS: Wasn't like this in San Antonio, huh? ... Two wonderfully winning seasons with the Spurs helped Lucas win the triple-threat job of head coach, general manager and VP of basketball operations... Didn't help him win more than 21 games in Philly, though... His life is a TV movie: drug addict who wastes No. 1 pick potential, recovers, sets up a rehab clinic in Houston and now helps others overcome the darkness and despair of substance abuse... After all that, basketball is just a game... Marvelously enthusiastic, motivational and a positive person... But please don't try to figure out his coaching. Utterly unorthodox. Rotations, substitutions, matchups? He sort of wings it at times... Players eventually catch his contagious spirit... Players' coach... Came out of Maryland as the No. 1 pick (Houston) in 1987. Career was twice suspended due to drug abuse... Also played with Warriors, Bullets, Bucks, Spurs and Sonics... Set NBA record with 14 assists in one quarter... Broke Pete Maravich's high-school scoring record... Was an All-American in tennis in college, winning three straight singles titles and playing on Junior Davis Cup team... Played World Team Tennis in the late '70s... Born Oct. 31, 1953, in Durham, N.C.

PHILADELPHIA 76ERS • 131
GREATEST FIND

They knew he could play coming out of West Texas State, so the 76ers figured he'd be worth a second-round pick. But no one ever envisioned just how well he could play. So, eventually, Maurice Cheeks became worth his weight in gold.

By the time the classy, low-key Chicago native called it a career after 1992-93, he had rewritten the defensive record books for point guards. A sure-bet future Hall of Famer, the 6-1 clutch player is the NBA's all-time steal leader with 2,310. During his prime, he was the league's prototypical point guard.

A four-time all-defensive first-team selection, Cheeks averaged 11.1 points and 6.7 assists in a 15-season career. He earned a championship ring with the '83 Sixers and holds the NBA record for most steals (8) in a playoff game.

ALL-TIME 76ER LEADERS

SEASON

Points: Wilt Chamberlain, 2,649, 1965–66
Assists: Maurice Cheeks, 753, 1985–86
Rebounds: Wilt Chamberlain, 1,957, 1966–67

GAME

Points: Wilt Chamberlain, 68 vs. Chicago, 12/16/67
Assists: Wilt Chamberlain, 21 vs. Detroit, 2/2/68
      Maurice Cheeks, 21 vs. New Jersey, 10/30/82
Rebounds: Wilt Chamberlain, 43 vs. Boston, 3/6/65

CAREER

Points: Hal Greer, 21,586, 1958–73
Assists: Maurice Cheeks, 6,212, 1978–89
Rebounds: Dolph Schayes, 11,256, 1948–64

WASHINGTON BULLETS

TEAM DIRECTORY: Chairman: Abe Pollin; Pres.: Susan O'Malley; Vice Chairman: Jerry Sachs; GM: John Nash; Dir. Communications: Matt Williams; Coach: Jim Lynam; Asst. Coaches: Bob Staak, Derek Smith. Arena: USAir Arena (18,756). Colors: Red, white and blue.

SCOUTING REPORT

SHOOTING: What's the word we're looking for? Wretched? Awful? Terrible? Lousy? Oh, well. Pick any one of those. They'll do.

The Bullets' perimeter game is a step away from invisible. In the other direction. The draft didn't help in that area, although the Bullets picked up another guy with inside force potential in North Carolina's Rasheed Wallace. And that's where the Bullets have concentrated their strength: inside. In Juwan Howard and Chris Webber, the Bullets have a certified, top-notch post-up attack. And Gheorghe Muresan, the 7-7 Romanian giant, can dunk and score on putbacks. But don't expect anything beyond six feet. Calbert Cheaney has been maddeningly inconsistent, an all-star-caliber shooter one night, a dead man the next. If the Bullets are serious about making some noise, they must find another shooter.

PLAYMAKING: Someone summed the Bullets up best when he said they are half a team. Up front, there's a nice, steady developing unit. In the backcourt, they are near chaos.

Doug Overton and Mitchell Butler were the best the Bullets had. And neither is a classic point guard, although each—more out of necessity than coaching desire—has played there. Scott Skiles, the incumbent point, was talking retirement. Around the draft, everybody was talking about a trade for Rod Strickland that would have solved the problem. But potential contractual snags killed that deal.

The Bullets' best playmaking, ironically, comes up front from two of Michigan's former Fab Five, Webber and Howard, who are skilled frontcourt passers. Now if they'll let the Bullets play three-on-three, it could be interesting.

REBOUNDING: The rebounding here is not as good as you'd think. It's not bad, but it's just not meeting the potential created by a 7-7, 6-8 and 6-10 frontline.

WASHINGTON BULLETS · 133

Controversial Chris Webber became a blistering Bullet.

The main problem exists on the offensive end, where the Bullets ranked 21st in efficiency last year. What the Bullets have on the starting line is quality, but once they hit the bench—especially if they're forced to go beyond Don MacLean—they're ragged at best. They need another big man to alleviate the do-it-all atmosphere around Webber and Howard.

BULLET ROSTER

No.	Veterans	Pos.	Ht.	Wt.	Age	Yrs. Pro	College
32	Mitchell Butler	G	6-5	210	24	2	UCLA
40	Calbert Cheaney	F-G	6-7	209	24	2	Indiana
00	Kevin Duckworth	C	7-0	285	31	9	Eastern Illinois
5	Juwan Howard	F-C	6-9	250	22	1	Michigan
34	Don MacLean	F	6-10	225	25	3	UCLA
22	Jim McIlvaine	C	7-1	240	23	1	Marquette
77	Gheorghe Muresan	C	7-7	303	24	2	Romania
14	Doug Overton	G	6-3	190	26	3	LaSalle
4	Scott Skiles	G	6-1	180	31	9	Michigan State
15	Kenny Walker	F	6-8	220	31	7	Kentucky
2	Chris Webber	F	6-10	250	22	2	Michigan

Rd.	Rookie	Sel.No.	Pos.	Ht.	Wt.	College
1	Rasheed Wallace	4	C	6-10	225	North Carolina

DEFENSE: Bad. But it has improved. It used to be pathetic.

On the perimeter, the Bullets are just bad defenders. Inside, they're tough. But let an opponent step out and the Bullets can be beaten easily. And in transition, the Bullets are markedly vulnerable.

Under coach Jimmy Lynam, the Bullets will trap and press but, as is the case in almost every category, they need help at the point there. Even last year with Skiles, who was the best the Bullets had, they simply didn't get enough pressure on the ball. Skiles' lack of speed forced him to play back, so opponents were able to get upcourt in a hurry and get into their sets far too easily.

OUTLOOK: If only they had another big man and a proven point guard. The Bullets could be dangerous with those two elements.

They went into the offseason with a point guard as their chief priority. So they drafted a center. They balked at the opportunity to land Strickland or even B.J. Armstrong, who went in the expansion draft. They'll keep looking. And until they find one, they'll keep looking for a way to sneak in the back door of the playoffs. There is enough talent for the Bullets to be fun to watch and to be competitive. But there isn't enough for them to be elite.

BULLET PROFILES

CHRIS WEBBER 22 6-10 250   Forward-Center

And just when it seemed he and Don Nelson were getting chummy... Forced Warriors into Nov. 17 trade for Tom Gugliotta and three first-rounders because of open feud with Nelson that led to downfall of legendary coach... Has all the physical gifts... Great passer— had three points, rebounds, assists triple-doubles... Led Bullets in scoring, rebounds, steals, minutes and was second in assists... Tremendous low-post game, no range to speak of... But the problem might not have all been Nelson's. There are concerns over his work ethic and commitment to learning... Bullets execs looked to slip out of town when he dislocated shoulder Dec. 22 at, of all places, Golden State. Missed 19 games with injury... One of the Michigan Fab Five. Called that real swell time-out against North Carolina in '93 NCAA Finals... Two NCAA finals, both losses... No. 1 pick in '93. Taken by Orlando, who turned around and traded him for Anfernee Hardaway, the No. 3 pick, and three first-rounders, June 30, 1993... Immediate impact. NBA's Rookie of the Year in 1993-94... Made $2.08 million in 1994-95... Born March 1, 1973, in Detroit... Real first name: Mayce.

Year	Team	G	FG	FG Pct.	FT	FT Pct.	Reb.	Ast.	TP	Avg.
1993-94	Golden State	76	572	.552	189	.532	694	272	1333	17.5
1994-95	Washington	54	464	.495	117	.502	518	256	1085	20.1
	Totals	130	1036	.525	306	.520	1212	528	2418	18.6

JUWAN HOWARD 22 6-9 250   Forward

They hoped he'd be good. Never even dreamed he'd be this good... Refined low-post game bringing comparisons to Maurice Lucas... Very tough, very smart player... He and Chris Webber are blocks for the future. Now if only the Bullets had some guards... Second on team in scoring and rebounding... Led all rookies in rebounds... Missed 10 games with ankle sprain late in season that knocked out any Rookie of the Year chance. Deserved consideration, though... Individual highs of 31 points, 15 rebounds... Missed first seven games in contract hassle. College teammate Webber was acquired and he quickly signed... Earned $1.309 million... Another Michigan Fab Five guy with two NCAA title-game appearances... Left school early, but went back and graduated with his class. First NBA player to do so... Was the No. 5 pick in the draft... Born Feb. 7, 1973, in Chicago... Person he'd most like to met: God. Bullets hoping that gathering doesn't come until after at least a 12-year career.

Year	Team	G	FG	FG Pct.	FT	FT Pct.	Reb.	Ast.	TP	Avg.
1994-95	Washington	65	455	.489	194	.664	545	165	1104	17.0

CALBERT CHEANEY 24 6-7 209 Guard-Forward

Nice guy. Too nice. And it affects his game... Can you say "softee?"... Flip a coin to see which guy shows up. The accurate, dangerous swingman who can work down low or the inconsistent lout who couldn't hit the water from a canoe... Greatly benefited from the three-point line moving in. Made one trifecta as a rookie. Made 96 last year... Played 50 minutes at Boston March 1... Some nights, he looks like an all-star... College Player of the Year as a senior at Indiana... Bullets made him the sixth pick in '93... Born July 17, 1971, in Evansville, Ind.... Made $2.4 million in 1994-95.

Year	Team	G	FG	FG Pct.	FT	FT Pct.	Reb.	Ast.	TP	Avg.
1993-94	Washington	65	327	.470	124	.770	190	126	779	12.0
1994-95	Washington	78	512	.453	173	.812	321	177	1293	16.6
	Totals	143	839	.460	297	.794	511	303	2072	14.5

KEVIN DUCKWORTH 31 7-0 285 Center

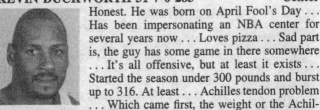

Honest. He was born on April Fool's Day... Has been impersonating an NBA center for several years now... Loves pizza... Sad part is, the guy has some game in there somewhere... It's all offensive, but at least it exists... Started the season under 300 pounds and burst up to 316. At least... Achilles tendon problem... Which came first, the weight or the Achilles? Who cares?... Suspended twice by team for failure to keep in shape... Also had surgery for calcium deposits in left ankle... Then got all screwed up with confidence and outlook and such. Tried to drown sorrows in pepperoni and anchovies... This

WASHINGTON BULLETS • 137

is his contract year coming up... Don't forget he helped Portland to two Finals appearances... Good low-post offense... Born April 1, 1964, in Harvey, Ill.... Second-round pick by San Antonio out of Eastern Illinois in 1986... Traded by Spurs to Portland for Walter Berry on Dec. 18, 1986... Bullets got him for Harvey Grant on June 24, 1993. Paid him $2.612 million last year... He trains dogs. Supply your own joke.

Year	Team	G	FG	FG Pct.	FT	FT Pct.	Reb.	Ast.	TP	Avg.
1986-87	S.A.-Port.	65	130	.476	92	.687	223	29	352	5.4
1987-88	Portland	78	450	.496	331	.770	576	66	1231	15.8
1988-89	Portland	79	554	.477	324	.757	635	60	1432	18.1
1989-90	Portland	82	548	.478	231	.740	509	91	1327	16.2
1990-91	Portland	81	521	.481	240	.772	531	89	1282	15.8
1991-92	Portland	82	362	.461	156	.690	497	99	880	10.7
1992-93	Portland	74	301	.438	127	.730	387	70	729	9.9
1993-94	Washington	69	184	.417	88	.667	325	56	456	6.6
1994-95	Washington	40	118	.442	45	.643	195	20	283	7.1
	Totals	650	3168	.469	1634	.737	3878	580	7972	12.3

DON MacLEAN 25 6-10 225   Forward

Somebody's minutes had to go down with Juwan Howard showing up... And then there was the injury... Sore knees and fractured right thumb knocked him out of 43 games... He's a scorer... He didn't score last year. That sort of complicated the problem even more. Defensively bankrupt... They said he had an ego problem at UCLA (Class of '92)... They're starting to say the same thing around the Bullets... Does have a good knack for three-point plays and just getting to the line... Not much range, though... Good offensive reserve type, but needs minutes to be effective... Was voted the Most Improved Player in his second year... Was the No. 19 pick by Pistons, who traded him to Clippers with William Bedford for Olden Polynice and draft picks on June 24, 1992... Clippers then sent him and Bedford to Bullets for John Williams on Oct. 8, 1992... Born Jan. 16, 1970, in Palo Alto, Cal.... Made $740,000 in 1994-95.

Year	Team	G	FG	FG Pct.	FT	FT Pct.	Reb.	Ast.	TP	Avg.
1992-93	Washington	62	157	.435	90	.811	122	39	407	6.6
1993-94	Washington	75	517	.502	328	.824	467	160	1365	18.2
1994-95	Washington	39	158	.438	104	.765	165	51	430	11.0
	Totals	176	832	.475	522	.809	754	250	2202	12.5

GHEORGHE MURESAN 24 7-7 303   Center

Of the Triteni, Romania Muresans, not the ones from Brooklyn... When he stretches his arms, he blocks out the sun... Wonderful find for Bullets on second round, No. 30 pick, of the 1993 draft... Marked improvement in second year. But he's never gonna win any sprint races. Unless opponents' shoelaces are tied together... Can't run floor. But, boy, can he clog up the middle... Plodding, clumsy and foul-prone. But he's working on it... Gives Bullets a real low-post presence at both ends... Alters tons of shots... Getting a little soft-touch shot down... Speaking less and less with an interpreter. Will probably order sweat socks for lunch, though... Made $1.15 million in 1994-95... Born Feb. 14, 1971, in Triteni, Romania... Attended Cluj University... Registered 30-point game against Celtics April 9.

Year	Team	G	FG	FG Pct.	FT	FT Pct.	Reb.	Ast.	TP	Avg.
1993-94	Washington	54	128	.545	48	.676	192	18	304	5.6
1994-95	Washington	73	303	.560	124	.709	488	38	730	10.0
	Totals	127	431	.555	172	.699	680	56	1034	8.1

DOUG OVERTON 26 6-3 190   Guard

Capable point-guard backup was forced into starter's role for last 20 games when Scott Skiles was injured... Lowered his turnovers as a starter... But he's just not a starting point guard if Bullets are to be serious about winning... Only Bullet in all 82 games... Decent all-around skills. Except for shooting, where he's simply too erratic... But he did lead the team in three-point shooting at .424. It's those pesky two-pointers that give him trouble... Scored in double figures in each of the last 10 games, including career-high 30 against Orlando on April 19... Posted 14.2 points and 6.2 assists as a starter... Second-round pick by Pistons, No. 40 overall, out of LaSalle in 1991... Did a year in the CBA before Bullets signed him as a free agent Oct. 19, 1992... A $550,000 wage earner last year... Born Aug. 3, 1969, in Philadelphia.

Year	Team	G	FG	FG Pct.	FT	FT Pct.	Reb.	Ast.	TP	Avg.
1992-93	Washington	45	152	.471	59	.728	106	157	366	8.1
1993-94	Washington	61	87	.403	43	.827	69	92	218	3.6
1994-95	Washington	82	207	.416	109	.872	143	246	576	7.0
	Totals	188	446	.430	211	.818	318	495	1160	6.2

MITCHELL BUTLER 24 6-5 210   Guard

If this Butler did it, you can bet it wasn't on offense... Shooting plunged to .421 after hopeful rookie season of .495... Bullets tried him at point. Wasn't horrible... It's defense, though, that will keep him employed for a while... Can handle the ball and is more suited for up-tempo game... Arthroscopic surgery on left knee at season's end... Undrafted out of UCLA in 1993... Signed as a free agent by Bullets, Oct. 5, 1993... Shot .665 from the line. And that was a BIG improvement over rookie year... Born Dec. 15, 1970, in Los Angeles... Made $400,000 in 1994-95.

Year	Team	G	FG	FG Pct.	FT	FT Pct.	Reb.	Ast.	TP	Avg.
1993-94	Washington	75	207	.495	104	.578	225	77	518	6.9
1994-95	Washington	76	214	.421	123	.665	170	91	597	7.9
	Totals	151	421	.455	227	.622	395	168	1115	7.4

JIM McILVAINE 23 7-1 240   Center

Can't teach height... Can't seem to teach him how to stay out of foul trouble, either... Shot-blocking defensive type. He recorded at least one block in all 24 games where he played over 10 minutes... Ankle sprains throughout season... Might have been better off in Europe for a year, playing and gaining experience... Was the Bullets' second-round pick in 1994, out of Marquette... Became a restricted free agent at end of season... Born July 30, 1972, in Racine, Wis.... Made $200,000 in 1994-95.

Year	Team	G	FG	FG Pct.	FT	FT Pct.	Reb.	Ast.	TP	Avg.
1994-95	Washington	55	34	.479	28	.683	105	10	96	1.7

SCOTT SKILES 31 6-1 180   Guard

End of the line?... Claimed 1994-95 would be his last year. But of course, he had not yet picked up a paycheck from the private sector... Missed last 20 games with surgery-requiring torn right wrist ligaments... Sixth in NBA in free-throw shooting... Fiery competitor. Sees the floor, makes good decisions... He's got to be a coach some day... Nice sta-

140 • THE COMPLETE HANDBOOK OF PRO BASKETBALL

tistical season. Was 13th in assists and 13th in three-point shooting. Was Bullets' only consistent long-range threat... Drawbacks? He's simply not quick enough for up-tempo game... Ranked fourth all-time in free-throw shooting at .890 for career... Had 15-assist game against Nets... Born March 5, 1964, in LaPorte, Ind.... Michigan State, '86... Drafted No. 22 on first round by Milwaukee. Traded June 22, 1987, from Bucks to Pacers for a second-round pick... Magic grabbed him in expansion draft of '89 and he helped hold team together for five seasons... Bullets gave up a first-rounder for him and a second on July 29, 1994... Made $2.125 million in 1994-95.

Year	Team	G	FG	FG Pct.	FT	FT Pct.	Reb.	Ast.	TP	Avg.
1986-87	Milwaukee	13	18	.290	10	.833	26	45	49	3.8
1987-88	Indiana	51	86	.411	45	.833	66	180	223	4.4
1988-89	Indiana	80	198	.448	130	.903	149	390	546	6.8
1989-90	Orlando	70	190	.409	104	.874	159	334	536	7.7
1990-91	Orlando	79	462	.445	340	.902	270	660	1357	17.2
1991-92	Orlando	75	359	.414	248	.895	202	544	1057	14.1
1992-93	Orlando	78	416	.467	289	.892	290	735	1201	15.4
1993-94	Orlando	82	276	.429	195	.878	189	503	815	9.9
1994-95	Washington	62	265	.455	179	.886	159	452	805	13.0
	Totals	590	2270	.436	1540	.890	1510	3843	6589	11.2

KENNY WALKER 31 6-8 220   Forward

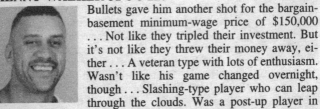

Bullets gave him another shot for the bargain-basement minimum-wage price of $150,000... Not like they tripled their investment. But it's not like they threw their money away, either... A veteran type with lots of enthusiasm. Wasn't like his game changed overnight, though... Slashing-type player who can leap through the clouds. Was a post-up player in college (Kentucky, '86) whom Knicks drafted No. 5 in 1986 and tried to make a small forward. Didn't work out... Played two years in Europe after Knicks released him in '91... Last two years with Bullets... Former Slam Dunk champ... Born Aug. 18, 1964, in Roberta, Ga.

Year	Team	G	FG	FG Pct.	FT	FT Pct.	Reb.	Ast.	TP	Avg.
1986-87	New York	68	285	.491	140	.757	338	75	710	10.4
1987-88	New York	82	344	.473	138	.775	389	86	826	10.1
1988-89	New York	79	174	.489	66	.776	230	36	419	5.3
1989-90	New York	68	204	.531	125	.723	343	49	535	7.9
1990-91	New York	54	83	.435	64	.780	157	13	230	4.3
1993-94	Washington	73	132	.482	87	.696	289	33	351	4.8
1994-95	Washington	24	18	.429	21	.750	47	7	57	2.4
	Totals	448	1240	.485	641	.749	1793	299	3128	7.0

THE ROOKIE

RASHEED WALLACE 21 6-10 225　　　　　　　　　Center
Another of the super sophs... Left North Carolina after his sophomore season and promptly was scooped up by Bullets at No. 4 ... According to Minnesota exec Kevin McHale, who knows a thing or two about NBA big men, "He's a big-time talent... needs to physically mature but he's got a great upside." ... That upside included a 16.6 scoring average that included 33 against No. 1 pick Joe Smith of Maryland in the ACC tourney... Gives Washington the athleticism it needs in the middle... Born Sept. 17, 1974, in Philadelphia.

COACH JIM LYNAM: Honest, he did good... Forget the 21-61 record that tied the franchise's worst mark for defeats. Remember that he had no guards to work with... Considered a motivator and a teacher, Lynam now has two young studs to motivate and teach in Chris Webber and Juwan Howard... Even Webber liked him... Big on preparation and communication... His friend, John Nash, Bullet GM, worked with him in Philly and brought him to Bullets... Career NBA head coaching mark of 267-325 with Clippers (which should never count against a guy's record), Sixers and Bullets... Led Sixers to 53-victory season in 1989-90... Assistant in Portland in 1981-82... Did 10 college years at Fairfield, American and St. Joseph's (Pa.), his alma mater and where he's a member of school Hall of Fame... Born Sept. 15, 1941, in Philadelphia.

GREATEST FIND

Rarely can the 11th pick in any draft be classified as a "find." But when that 11th pick landed in the second round, as it did back in 1963, and when that 11th pick follows the likes of Tom Hoover, Bill Green and Roger (The Rifle) Strickland, then, yeah, an 11th pick can be a find.

Especially when the 11th pick turns out to be Gus Johnson.

Immediately, Johnson made his impact felt as a member of the 1963-64 all-rookie team for Baltimore. But he didn't stop there. "Honeycomb," a standout defensive forward (he twice was all-defense first team), ranks as the fifth-greatest scorer in Bullets' history with 9,781 points. He also ranks among the franchise all-time leaders in games, field goals, rebounds and free throws.

Johnson, a 6-6 forward out of Idaho, passed away in April 1987.

ALL-TIME BULLET LEADERS

SEASON

Points: Walt Bellamy, 2,495, 1961–62
Assists: Kevin Porter, 734, 1980–81
Rebounds: Walt Bellamy, 1,500, 1961–62

GAME

Points: Earl Monroe, 56 vs. Los Angeles, 2/3/68
Assists: Kevin Porter, 24 vs. Detroit, 3/23/80
Rebounds: Walt Bellamy, 37 vs. St. Louis, 12/4/64

CAREER

Points: Elvin Hayes, 15,551, 1972–81
Assists: Wes Unseld, 3,822, 1968–81
Rebounds: Wes Unseld, 13,769, 1968–81

ATLANTA HAWKS

TEAM DIRECTORY: Pres.: Stan Kasten; GM: Pete Babcock; Dir. Pub. Rel.: Arthur Triche; Coach: Lenny Wilkens; Asst. Coaches: Dick Helm, Jerry Powell. Arena: The Omni (16,368). Colors: Red, white, gold, black and yellow.

Stealthy Mookie Blaylock had finest offensive season.

SCOUTING REPORT

SHOOTING: The Hawks are still suffering from Dominique Wilkins withdrawal. They have plenty of scoring options, but none they can count on all the time. The first option should be shooting guard Steve Smith, who has the perfect combination of size (6-8), range (the old three-point line) and imagination (he went to Michigan State, Magic Johnson's school). The trouble is, Smith sometimes nods off. The next best shooter on the team—mid-range, anyway—might be power forward Grand Long. But the Hawks prefer he stay close to the basket, the better to convert misses by Stacey Augmon, Mookie Blaylock and Ken Norman.

If rookie Alan Henderson is as good as advertised in the post—a 23-point average and 59-percent shooting in his senior year at Indiana—Long won't have to come inside. Henderson's techniques might also rub off on center Andrew Lang, whose post-up game still needs polishing.

Craig Ehlo remains responsible for off-the-bench scoring bursts, but he could be pushed by Donnie Boyce, a 6-5 rookie from Colorado.

PLAYMAKING: After Blaylock and Smith, there's not much creativity. Unselfishness, yes. Creativity, no. And while Blaylock and Smith sometimes concentrate too much on scoring, they're not nearly as bad as Norman, who will be the death of coach Lenny Wilkens if Hawks GM Pete Babcock can't trade him somewhere.

Augmon has enough problems without having to worry about becoming a better passer. He was shifted from shooting guard to small forward, and the adjustment wasn't a smooth one. But Wilkins still preferred him at small forward over Norman.

The best playmaker off the bench is Jim Les, which tells you how far the Hawks have to go.

REBOUNDING: There's no problem with Long, who isn't happy if he isn't bumping with somebody under the basket. He led the Hawks in all rebounding categories, which doesn't say much for centers Lang, who averaged just 5.6 rebounds, and Jon Koncak. But Lang did average 6.5 rebounds in the Hawks' last 12 games, and he seems poised for a run at double-figures.

Augmon sometimes gets overpowered by bigger small forwards, but he does much better than Norman. Smith towers over most shooting guards, but his rebounding numbers don't reflect the advantage. If only Smith had Ehlo's nose for the ball.

HAWK ROSTER

No.	Veterans	Pos.	Ht.	Wt.	Age	Yrs. Pro	College
U-22	Greg Anderson	F-C	6-10	230	31	7	Houston
R-2	Stacey Augmon	G-F	6-8	205	27	4	UNLV
10	Mookie Blaylock	G	6-1	185	28	7	Oklahoma
3	Craig Ehlo	G	6-7	206	34	12	Washington State
U-32	Jon Koncak	C	7-0	250	32	10	SMU
28	Andrew Lang	C	6-11	250	29	7	Arkansas
U-14	Jim Les	G	5-11	175	32	7	Bradley
43	Grant Long	F	6-9	248	29	7	Eastern Michigan
4	Ken Norman	F	6-8	223	31	8	Illinois
41	Blair Rasmussen	C	7-0	250	32	8	Oregon
8	Steve Smith	G	6-8	213	26	4	Michigan State
–	Anthony Webb	G	5-7	133	32	10	North Carolina State
U-1	Ennis Whatley	G	6-3	180	33	9	Alabama

R-restricted free agent
U-unrestricted free agent

Rd.	Rookies	Sel.No.	Pos.	Ht.	Wt.	College
1	Alan Henderson	16	F	6-9	225	Indiana
2	Donnie Boyce	42	G	6-5	195	Colorado
2	Troy Brown	45	F	6-8	238	Providence
2	Cuonzo Martin	57	G	6-6	215	Purdue

DEFENSE: When Blaylock and Augmon were the Hawks' starting backcourt, opponents found that getting over halfcourt was a challenge. It isn't the same with Smith, but Blaylock still topped the 200 mark in steals. Get sloppy around Mookie, and the ball goes the other way. Not so with Smith, who has neither the interest nor the ability to lock anybody up. Ehlo remains a solid defender, in spite of his age and several horrible experiences with Michael Jordan.

Long is a hard-nosed post defender, but a little short. Lang is big enough, but a little soft. He won't knock you down in the post, but he will swat layup attempts by driving guards into the third row. Henderson went to the Bobby Knight School of Defense, but he might be a little thin.

OUTLOOK: No surprises. That's what Wilkens and the Hawks are looking for after the mess of last season, which began with a blockbuster trade—Smith and Long from Miami for longtime Hawks' power forward Kevin Willis—and the shifting of Augmon. Factor in the loss of small forward Danny Manning to Phoenix, and you had the makings of a disaster.

Familiarity, if nothing else, should make the Hawks a much more competitive and dangerous team—maybe not a contender, but a team capable of beating any team in the league.

HAWK PROFILES

MOOKIE BLAYLOCK 28 6-1 185   Guard

The operative word here is *steal*... That describes his game, and the manner in which he was obtained from New Jersey on Nov. 3, 1992—the darkest day in the career of Nets GM Willis Reed, who sent the Mookster to Atlanta in exchange for Rumeal Robinson... Ouch... Registered his 1,000th career steal on March 22. Only three other players in league history got there faster... Over 200 thefts in each of last three seasons... When he got five or more last season, Hawks were 9-0... Also led Hawks in scoring team-high 29 times, which translated into career-best 17.2 scoring average... Assists dipped from 8.9 to 7.7, but much of that has to do with Kevin Willis going to Miami—and the closer three-point line, of course... Set Hawks record for most treys taken (555) and made (199)... Shot .425 overall, which must be improved if the Hawks are to contend... Drafted 12th, out of Oklahoma, in '89 by Nets... Born March 20, 1967, in Garland, Tex.... Made $2.1 million in 1994-95.

Year	Team	G	FG	FG Pct.	FT	FT Pct.	Reb.	Ast.	TP	Avg.
1989-90	New Jersey	50	212	.371	63	.778	140	210	505	10.1
1990-91	New Jersey	72	432	.416	139	.790	249	441	1017	14.1
1991-92	New Jersey	72	429	.432	126	.712	269	492	996	13.8
1992-93	Atlanta	80	414	.429	123	.728	280	671	1069	13.4
1993-94	Atlanta	81	444	.411	116	.730	424	789	1118	13.8
1994-95	Atlanta	80	509	.425	156	.729	393	616	1373	17.2
	Totals	435	2440	.418	723	.741	1755	3219	6078	14.0

STEVE SMITH 26 6-8 213   Guard

Ego took massive beating... Was basically ignored by Dream Team II coach Don Nelson, then was dealt with Grant Long to Miami for Kevin Willis... Played well enough to convince Lenny Wilkens to move Stacey Augmon to small forward, but Hawks have right to expect more... Still the biggest tease this side of Madonna... Did have first back-to-back 30-point nights, against New Jersey and Denver. Did have 20 games of 20 or more points, in which the Hawks were 16-4... No

ATLANTA HAWKS • 147

longer thought of as the next-best thing to Magic Johnson. Flopped as point in Miami, and won't get chance in Atlanta unless Mookie Blaylock changes address... Terrific three-point shooter, and equally devastating inside... Might be the worst defensive guard in the history of the world. Part of that has to do with wobbly knees... Drafted fifth, out of Michigan State, by Heat in '91... Born March 31, 1969, in Highland Park, Mich.... Made $1.93 million in 1994-95.

Year	Team	G	FG	FG Pct.	FT	FT Pct.	Reb.	Ast.	TP	Avg.
1991-92	Miami	61	297	.454	95	.748	188	278	729	12.0
1992-93	Miami	48	279	.451	155	.787	197	267	766	16.0
1993-94	Miami	78	491	.456	273	.835	352	394	1346	17.3
1994-95	Mia.-Atl.	80	428	.426	312	.841	276	274	1305	16.3
	Totals	267	1495	.446	835	.817	1013	1213	4146	15.5

GRANT LONG 29 6-9 248 Forward

Changed uniforms, but game remained the same... Loves to bang, loves to rebound. Every minute, every night... If a couple of inches taller, would be making trillions... Led Hawks in all rebounding categories—offensive (190), defensive (405), total (595) and average (7.5)... Had a nice mid-range jumper to go with decent post-up game... Got career-high 33 points against Sixers... Were Mookie Blaylock and Stacey Augmon elsewhere, would get credit for thefts—1.34, not bad for a power forward... Dealt with buddy Steve Smith to Hawks for Kevin Willis. He and center Rony Seikaly, who was dealt to Golden State, were the last original members of the Heat... Second-round pick, out of Eastern Michigan, in '88. Led upstart Hurons to Sweet 16 of NCAA tournament in '88... Nephew of former NBA guard John Long and cousin of Pistons' Terry Mills... Born March 12, 1966, in Wayne, Mich.... Made $1.48 million in 1994-95.

Year	Team	G	FG	FG Pct.	FT	FT Pct.	Reb.	Ast.	TP	Avg.
1988-89	Miami	82	336	.486	304	.749	546	149	976	11.9
1989-90	Miami	81	257	.483	172	.714	402	96	686	8.5
1990-91	Miami	80	276	.492	181	.787	568	176	734	9.2
1991-92	Miami	82	440	.494	326	.807	691	225	1212	14.8
1992-93	Miami	76	397	.469	261	.765	568	182	1061	14.0
1993-94	Miami	69	300	.446	187	.786	495	170	788	11.4
1994-95	Mia.-Atl.	81	342	.478	244	.751	606	131	939	11.6
	Totals	551	2348	.478	1675	.767	3876	1129	6396	11.6

KEN NORMAN 31 6-8 223   Forward

Quickly established himself as main target on Lenny Wilkens' dart board... Was so dismal and disruptive that Wilkens opted for guard Stacey Augmon at small forward... Hawks gambled that unhappy year in Milwaukee was just a bad mesh between Norman and Bucks boss Mike Dunleavy. Turns out that any authority figure is unacceptable to the Snake, which is what he prefers to be called... Fortunately for Hawks, all they gave up was Roy Hinson's salary slot... Unfortunately, four years remain on a six-year, $16-million pact signed with Bucks... Made $1.9 million last season... Drafted 19th, out of Illinois, by Clippers in '87. Did first year at Wabash Valley (Ill.) ... Left as Clips' all-time leading scorer. Not something you'd really brag about... Born Sept. 5, 1964, in Chicago.

Year	Team	G	FG	FG Pct.	FT	FT Pct.	Reb.	Ast.	TP	Avg.
1987-88	L.A. Clippers	66	241	.482	87	.512	263	78	569	8.6
1988-89	L.A. Clippers	80	638	.502	170	.630	667	277	1450	18.1
1989-90	L.A. Clippers	70	484	.510	153	.632	470	160	1128	16.1
1990-91	L.A. Clippers	70	520	.501	173	.629	497	159	1219	17.4
1991-92	L.A. Clippers	77	402	.490	121	.535	448	125	929	12.1
1992-93	L.A. Clippers	76	498	.511	131	.595	571	165	1137	15.0
1993-94	Milwaukee	82	412	.448	92	.503	500	222	979	11.9
1994-95	Atlanta	74	388	.453	64	.457	362	94	938	12.7
	Totals	595	3583	.489	991	.574	3778	1280	8349	14.0

STACEY AUGMON 27 6-8 205   Guard-Forward

Stock dropped dramatically... Shifted from starting shooting guard to starting small forward after Steve Smith got comfortable, and it wasn't a happy experience... Scoring dipped from 14.8 to 13.9, and shooting from a career-best .510 to .453... Spent less time in open court, which also cut mightily into his steals—100, 49 fewer than in 1993-94... Did score a career-high 36 points against the Blazers, but that was a blip on the screen... Also tied career best with 12 boards against Pistons, but everybody rebounds against Pistons... Any trade talks instigated by Hawks usually include his name... Drafted ninth, out of UNLV, by Hawks in '91... Born Aug. 1, 1968, in Pasadena,

ATLANTA HAWKS • 149

Cal. . . . Made $1.6 million in 1994-95.

Year	Team	G	FG	FG Pct.	FT	FT Pct.	Reb.	Ast.	TP	Avg.
1991-92	Atlanta	82	440	.489	213	.666	420	201	1094	13.3
1992-93	Atlanta	73	397	.501	227	.739	287	170	1021	14.0
1993-94	Atlanta	82	439	.510	333	.764	394	187	1212	14.8
1994-95	Atlanta	76	397	.453	252	.728	368	197	1053	13.9
	Totals	313	1673	.488	1025	.727	1469	755	4380	14.0

ANDREW LANG 29 6-11 250   Center

If he doesn't average in double figures this season, probably never will. But don't bet against him . . . Finally put Jon Koncak on the bench, starting the final 52 games. Hawks went 29-23. In last 12, he averaged 12.2 points, 6.5 rebounds and 1.9 blocks . . . Final numbers: 9.7 points, 5.6 rebounds . . . Will have to do much better than 5.6 rebounds, even if it means knocking teammate Grant Long out of the way . . . Must get back to 201 blocks, his total from final year with Suns. Had 136 last season . . . Suns dealt him, Jeff Hornacek and Tim Perry to Philly for Charles Barkley . . . Bolted after a season, signing free-agent deal with Hawks Sept. 7, 1993 . . . Was second-round pick, out of Arkansas, by Suns in '88 . . . Born June 28, 1966, in Pine Bluff, Ark. . . . Made $1.59 million in 1994-95.

Year	Team	G	FG	FG Pct.	FT	FT Pct.	Reb.	Ast.	TP	Avg.
1988-89	Phoenix	62	60	.513	39	.650	147	9	159	2.6
1989-90	Phoenix	74	97	.557	64	.653	271	21	258	3.5
1990-91	Phoenix	63	109	.577	93	.715	303	27	311	4.9
1991-92	Phoenix	81	248	.522	126	.768	546	43	622	7.7
1992-93	Philadelphia	73	149	.425	87	.763	436	79	386	5.3
1993-94	Atlanta	82	215	.469	73	.689	313	51	504	6.1
1994-95	Atlanta	82	320	.473	152	.809	456	72	794	9.7
	Totals	517	1198	.491	634	.737	2472	302	3034	5.9

ANTHONY (SPUD) WEBB 32 5-7 133   Guard

His contributions were undrerrated in Sacramento; maybe that'll change in Atlanta . . . Comes to Hawks in offseason deal for Tyrone Corbin . . . Set Kings' franchise record by shooting 93.4 percent from the line, which also led the league . . . Became the fourth King to finish No. 1 in the NBA in that category . . . Does a great job of using his quickness to compensate for size disadvantage... Blows past his man to get down the lane or relies on a pull-up jumper... But only recorded double-figure assists four times... The trade that brought him from Atlanta for Travis Mays in the summer of 1991 was a steal for Kings... Played with Nate McMillan and Vinny Del Negro at North Carolina State before Detroit took him in the fourth round in 1985... Born July 13, 1963, in Dallas... Made $2.071 million last season.

Year	Team	G	FG	FG Pct.	FT	FT Pct.	Reb.	Ast.	TP	Avg.
1985-86	Atlanta	79	199	.483	216	.785	123	337	616	7.8
1986-87	Atlanta	33	71	.438	80	.762	60	167	223	6.8
1987-88	Atlanta	82	191	.475	107	.817	146	337	490	6.0
1988-89	Atlanta	81	133	.459	52	.867	123	284	319	3.9
1989-90	Atlanta	82	294	.477	162	.871	201	477	751	9.2
1990-91	Atlanta	75	359	.447	231	.868	174	417	1003	13.4
1991-92	Sacramento	77	448	.445	262	.859	223	547	1231	16.0
1992-93	Sacramento	69	342	.433	279	.851	193	481	1000	14.5
1993-94	Sacramento	79	373	.460	204	.813	222	528	1005	12.7
1994-95	Sacramento	76	302	.438	226	.934	174	468	878	11.6
	Totals	733	2712	.454	1819	.846	1639	4043	7516	10.3

JON KONCAK 32 7-0 250   Center

Most famous contract in history of NBA—five years, $13.2-million—expired, as may his career... Lenny Wilkens turned him into a spectator, registering 19 DNP-CDs. Most came in second half, when Andrew Lang finally assumed control of center position... Started 17 straight, averaging 4.4 points and 4.8 rebounds ... But the rest of the time, zip. Registered career lows in points (2.9) and rebounds (184) total... Did expand game, adding medium-range jumper to sorry post-up skills... Maintained pleasant disposition in the face of constant ridicule about contract... Born May 17, 1963, in Cedar Rapids, Iowa... Drafted fifth, out of SMU, in '85 by Hawks... Has Olympic gold, from '84 Games... Made $2.6 million in 1994-95.

Year	Team	G	FG	FG Pct.	FT	FT Pct.	Reb.	Ast.	TP	Avg.
1985-86	Atlanta	82	263	.507	156	.607	467	55	682	8.3
1986-87	Atlanta	82	169	.480	125	.654	493	31	463	5.6
1987-88	Atlanta	49	98	.483	83	.610	333	19	279	5.7
1988-89	Atlanta	74	141	.524	63	.553	453	56	345	4.7
1989-90	Atlanta	54	78	.614	42	.532	226	23	198	3.7
1989-90	Atlanta	77	140	.436	32	.593	375	124	313	4.1
1991-92	Atlanta	77	111	.391	19	.655	261	132	241	3.1
1992-93	Atlanta	78	124	.464	24	.480	427	140	275	3.5
1993-94	Atlanta	82	159	.431	24	.667	365	102	342	4.2
1994-95	Atlanta	62	77	.412	13	.542	184	52	179	2.9
	Totals	717	1360	.469	581	.599	3584	734	3317	4.6

ATLANTA HAWKS • 151

CRAIG EHLO 34 6-7 206 — Guard-Forward

Might be closing in on the end of a nice career ... Both knees gave out last season, limiting him to 49 games—fewest since 1986-87, the year he joined Cavs ... Placed on injured list after having arthroscopic surgery on left knee. Activated Nov. 29 after missing 12 games ... Went through procedure again on Feb. 24, this time on right knee. Returned March 23, but wasn't 100 percent for playoffs ... Hawks were 26-23 when he played ... Followed Lenny Wilkens to Atlanta, even though Wilkens made him play Michael Jordan straight up in Cleveland ... Drafted in third round, out of Washington State, by Rockets in '83 ... Did time in CBA. Cavs signed him as free agent in '87 ... Born Aug. 11, 1961, in Lubbock, Tex. ... Made $2.65 million in 1994-95.

Year	Team	G	FG	FG Pct.	FT	FT Pct.	Reb.	Ast.	TP	Avg.
1983-84	Houston	7	11	.407	1	1.000	9	6	23	3.3
1984-85	Houston	45	34	.493	19	.633	25	26	87	1.9
1985-86	Houston	36	36	.429	23	.793	46	29	98	2.7
1986-87	Cleveland	44	99	.414	70	.707	161	92	273	6.2
1987-88	Cleveland	79	226	.466	89	.674	274	206	563	7.1
1988-89	Cleveland	82	249	.475	71	.607	295	266	608	7.4
1989-90	Cleveland	81	436	.464	126	.681	439	371	1102	13.6
1990-91	Cleveland	82	344	.445	95	.679	388	376	832	10.1
1991-92	Cleveland	63	310	.453	87	.707	307	238	776	12.3
1992-93	Cleveland	82	385	.490	86	.717	403	254	949	11.6
1993-94	Atlanta	82	316	.446	112	.727	279	273	821	10.0
1994-95	Atlanta	49	191	.453	44	.620	147	113	477	9.7
Totals		732	2637	.459	823	.685	2773	2250	6609	9.0

GREG (CADILLAC) ANDERSON 31 6-10 230 — C-F

Only NBA player to still dress like Huggy Bear ... Delightful personality, a perfect fit in any locker room ... If only he could catch the ball and remember all the plays ... Signed with Hawks Dec. 15 after Pistons declined to pick up option year. Got $450,000 from Pistons, another $110,000 from Hawks for 51 games ... Season highs: 17 points vs. Nets, 12 rebounds vs. Suns ... Came to Pistons from Italy. Also had stops in Denver, Milwaukee, New Jersey and San Antonio ... Drafted

23rd, out of Houston, by Spurs in '87. Career-best 13.7 points in 1988-89, the season before David Robinson arrived... Born June 22, 1964, in Houston... Brother, Mike, played QB at Grambling.

Year	Team	G	FG	FG Pct.	FT	FT Pct.	Reb.	Ast.	TP	Avg.
1987-88	San Antonio	82	379	.501	198	.604	513	79	957	11.7
1988-89	San Antonio	82	460	.503	207	.514	676	61	1127	13.7
1989-90	Milwaukee	60	219	.507	91	.535	373	24	529	8.8
1990-91	Mil.-N.J.-Den.	68	116	.430	60	.522	318	16	292	4.3
1991-92	Denver	82	389	.456	167	.623	941	78	945	11.5
1993-94	Detroit	77	201	.543	88	.571	571	51	491	6.4
1994-95	Atlanta	51	57	.548	34	.479	188	17	148	2.9
	Totals	502	1821	.492	845	.560	3580	326	4489	8.9

THE ROOKIES

ALAN HENDERSON 22 6-9 225   Forward
Left Indiana as all-time leader in blocks and rebounds... Averaged career-best 23 points as senior, also leading Hoosiers in four other categories... Shot 59 percent... Drafted 16th... Figures to be Grant Long's backup at power forward... Born Dec. 12, 1972, in Indianapolis... Father is cardiologist.

DONNIE BOYCE 22 6-5 195   Guard
Would probably have been first-rounder if hadn't suffered broken leg in Big Eight tournament... Went in second, at 42... Colorado's all-time leader in scoring (1,995) and starts (107)... Played at Proviso East in suburban Chicago with fellow first-rounders Michael Finley and Sherell Ford... Born Sept. 2, 1973, in Chicago.

TROY BROWN 24 6-8 238   Forward
Played way into draft at Portsmouth Invitational, averaging 20.3 points and 13.7 rebounds in three games... Drafted 45th... Spent five years at Providence. Redshirted fourth year because Friars had Michael Smith and Dickey Simpkins... Averaged 12 points... Born April 3, 1971, in Lynn, Mass.

CUONZO MARTIN 24 6-6 215 Guard

Was main reason Purdue returned to NCAA tourney despite losing Glenn Robinson... Averaged career-best 18.4 points, up from 5.8 as frosh... Led Big Ten in three-point shooting (47 percent)... Team captain since sophomore season... Second-to-last pick (57th)... Born Sept. 23, 1971, in St. Louis.

COACH LENNY WILKENS:  Had terrific season, despite winning 15 fewer games than in 1993-94, his first in Atlanta... Got rid of knucklehead Kevin Willis, passed Red Auerbach on all-time victory list and was named head coach of Dream Team III, which will compete next summer in Atlanta Olympics... Became all-time winningest coach on Jan. 6, when Hawks defeated Bullets at the Omni. Lit up cigar, a la Auerbach... Finished season at 968 wins. Auerbach quit at 938... Not known for bark, but evidence of big bite... Taught Hawks how to play defense. They gave up 96.2 in 1993-94, 95.3 last season. Before that, no Hawks team yielded an average of less than 100... Already in Hall of Fame, current president of NBA Coaches Association... Also a terrific player, among the all-time leaders in assists (3,285) in 15-year career. Starred at Providence College. Drafted in first round by Hawks in '60... Also coached Sonics, Blazers and Cavs. Guided Seattle to NBA title in '79... Winning percentage is .543... Dabbled in front office as VP, GM and Director of Player Personnel... Born Oct. 28, 1937, in Brooklyn, N.Y.

GREATEST FIND

This will be limited to the Hawks' tenure in Atlanta, which dates to 1968 and includes only a handful of players capable of getting fans from the street and into the Omni.

Dominique Wilkins was one of those players, but his success was hardly a surprise. Word of Wilkins' spectacular play didn't have to travel very far. He came to the Hawks from the University of Georgia, with a strong fan base already intact.

Spud Webb, on the other hand, wasn't expected to be around

Hawks responded to Indiana's Alan Henderson as No. 16.

long—not at 5-7, which was stretching things a bit. He came to the Hawks after failing to impress the Pistons in rookie camp in the summer of '85. They decided not to invite their fourth-round pick to training camp, figuring he'd only take time away from first-round pick Joe Dumars.

And a love affair with Omni fans ensued. Webb's arrival coincided with the first of four straight 50-win seasons. He became a national celebrity almost immediately, stealing the Slam Dunk crown from Wilkins in '86. And the fun continued until July 1, 1991, when Webb was traded to the Sacramento Kings—which Hawks boss Pete Babcock admits to being his biggest mistake.

That mistake has been corrected.

Spud is back.

ALL-TIME HAWK LEADERS

SEASON

Points: Bob Pettit, 2,429, 1961–62
Assists: Glenn Rivers, 823, 1986–87
Rebounds: Bob Pettit, 1,540, 1960–61

GAME

Points: Dominique Wilkins, 57 vs. Chicago, 11/10/86
Dominique Wilkins, 57 vs. New Jersey, 4/10/86
Lou Hudson, 57 vs. Chicago, 11/10/69
Bob Pettit, 57 vs. Detroit, 2/18/61
Assists: Mookie Blaylock, 23 vs. Utah, 3/6/93
Rebounds: Bob Pettit, 35 vs. Cincinnati, 3/2/58
Bob Pettit, 35 vs. New York, 1/6/56

CAREER

Points: Dominique Wilkins, 23,292, 1982–94
Assists: Glenn Rivers, 3,866, 1983–91
Rebounds: Bob Pettit, 12,851, 1954–65

CHARLOTTE HORNETS

TEAM DIRECTORY: Owner: George Shinn; Pres.: Spencer Stolpen; VP-Basketball Oper.: Bob Bass; Dir. Pub. Rel.: Harold Kaufman; Coach: Allan Bristow; Asst. Coaches: T.R. Dunn, Bill Hanzlik, John Bach. Arena: Charlotte Coliseum (23,698). Colors: Teal, purple and white.

SCOUTING REPORT

SHOOTING: This should be the least of the Hornets' problems, what with the post-up abilities of Alonzo Mourning and Larry Johnson and the long-range accuracy of Sixth Man candidate Dell Curry and small forward Scott Burrell.

But it became a problem in the playoffs, when Burrell wasn't available because of a Achilles tendon injury and Johnson began setting for mid-range jumpers. That turned Muggsy Bogues into a must-score point guard, and the pressure got to be too much. He either passed up jumpers or missed them, and the Hornets were eliminated by Chicago.

That led to the oddest of trades—Hersey Hawkins and David Wingate to Seattle for Kendall Gill, who complained his way out of Charlotte two years ago. There was talk of the Hornets sending Gill to Portland for Rod Strickland and Aaron McKie, but labor unrest stalled that report. If Gill stays, the Hornets again have a slasher.

PLAYMAKING: In this area, the Hornets couldn't be happier with Bogues. Few are better in transition, and he's developed into a competent halfcourt point guard. On the break or in pick-and-roll situations, he usually makes the right decisions.

The Hornets seem determined to turn Tony Bennett into a competent backup. He missed all but three games with a foot injury, which put the Hornets in a terrible fix when Michael Adams was shelved. And to think the Hornets gave up on Elliott Perry, just because Bennett's contract was guaranteed. Gill can create for others, but it doesn't always make him happy.

REBOUNDING: Shame on the Hornets. In their seven seasons in the NBA, they've never outrebounded their opponents. Last season, they were better only than the Pistons, Clippers and Timberwolves—none of whom had a center whose boarding skills

Another 20-plus ppg season for Alonzo Mourning.

were comparable to Mourning, 13th in the league with a 9.9 average.

Part of the problem was a spinal injury to bruiser Kenny Gattison, who missed 61 games. Johnson and Burrell never picked up the slack, and age finally caught up with veteran center Robert Parish. That's why the Hornets drafted UCLA center George Zidek, who ate up Arkansas' Corliss Williamson in the NCAA title game.

But the Hornets may not be able to do anything about L.J., who was too short to begin with. Now that his explosiveness comes and goes, he's a rebounding liability.

HORNET ROSTER

No.	Veterans	Pos.	Ht.	Wt.	Age	Yrs. Pro	College
23	Michael Adams	G	5-10	175	32	10	Boston College
R-25	Tony Bennett	G	6-0	175	26	3	Wisc.-Green Bay
1	Tyrone Bogues	G	5-3	144	30	8	Wake Forest
24	Scott Burrell	G-F	6-7	218	24	2	Connecticut
30	Dell Curry	G	6-5	208	31	9	Virginia Tech
13	Kendall Gill	G	6-5	200	27	5	Illinois
4	Darrin Hancock	G-F	6-5	205	23	1	Kansas
2	Larry Johnson	F	6-7	250	26	4	UNLV
33	Alonzo Mourning	C	6-10	240	25	3	Georgetown
00	Robert Parish	C	7-1	230	42	19	Centenary
U-12	Greg Sutton	G	6-2	170	27	2	Oral Roberts
U-43	Joe Wolf	F-C	6-11	230	30	7	North Carolina

R-restricted free agent
U-unrestricted free agent

Rd.	Rookie	Sel.No.	Pos.	Ht.	Wt.	College
1	George Zidek	22	C	7-0	250	UCLA

DEFENSE: Thanks to new assistant Johnny Bach, it got better. Slowing things down helped a great deal, too. With the Hornets relying on post-ups rather than the passing game, opponents' scoring dipped to a franchise-low 97.3.

Mourning should again be a pain in the paint, blocking or altering shots. He averaged 2.9 blocks last season, second to Philadelphia's Shawn Bradley in the Eastern Conference. Zidek is bigger (7-0) than Mourning, but he won't approach those figures.

Bogues can be a pest on the perimeter and Gill has the arms of an octopus, but the Hornets' guard play is so-so. Burrell and his backup, Darrin Hancock, bring toughness and tenacity to small forward. But with Gattison gone via expansion, the Hornets will continue to get beat up by power forwards.

OUTLOOK: Stable, the Hornets are not. They lost executive Dave Twardzik to the Warriors, and there was some question as to whether Allan Bristow would return to the bench. Bach wanted to join old friend Doug Collins in Detroit, but was prohibited from doing so by Hornets owner George Shinn and team president Spencer Stolpen.

The key is Johnson. If his explosiveness is a constant, the Hornets will be a contender. If not, they're staring at another first-round elimination.

CHARLOTTE HORNETS • 159
HORNET PROFILES

LARRY JOHNSON 26 6-7 250   Forward

Came back from back woes to play 81 games and 3,234 minutes, but explosiveness made only cameo appearances... Often settles for outside jumpers, which explains dip in shooting percentage—.480, lowest in four-year career... When healthy and frisky, is impossible to stop inside... Whispers about his new below-the-rim game surfaced during World Championships in Toronto... Averaged 18.8 points, 7.2 rebounds and 4.6 assists, but Hornets expect more from eight-year $69-million investment... Did have flashes of brilliance, getting a career-high 39 points against the Knicks and a triple-double (23 points, 10 rebounds and 10 assists) against the Wolves... Missed 31 games in 1993-94, during which Hornets were 9-22... Hopes to someday be as popular as "Grandmama"... Rookie of the Year in '92... Was No. 1 overall pick in '91 after being named College Player of the Year at UNLV... Born March 14, 1969, in Tyler, Tex.... Made $3.7 million in 1994-95.

Year	Team	G	FG	FG Pct.	FT	FT Pct.	Reb.	Ast.	TP	Avg.
1991-92	Charlotte	82	616	.490	339	.829	899	292	1576	19.2
1992-93	Charlotte	82	728	.526	336	.767	864	353	1810	22.1
1993-94	Charlotte	51	346	.515	137	.695	448	184	834	16.4
1994-95	Charlotte	81	585	.480	274	.774	585	369	1525	18.8
	Totals	296	2275	.502	1086	.777	2796	1198	5745	19.4

ALONZO MOURNING 25 6-10 240   Center

Tried to be more media friendly, but that's just not him... And by the looks of things, angry is very good... Only one of four players to lead team in four major categories—points (21.3), rebounds (9.9), blocks (2.92) and shooting percentage (.519)... Didn't make Hornets very happy by waiting until the start of training camp to acknowledge that big toe was aching. Missed first two games of season... Posted nine of the Hornets' 12 30-point games... Playoff highlight remains last-second jumper that eliminated Celtics in '93 first round... Post game is solid, and figures to get better. How can it not? Spends summers scrimmaging against fellow Georgetown alums Patrick Ewing and Dikembe Mutumbo... Drafted No. 2 overall in '92... Big East Player of the Year, Defensive Player of the Year and NCAA

160 • THE COMPLETE HANDBOOK OF PRO BASKETBALL

tournament MVP in '92... Born Feb. 8, 1970, in Chesapeake, Va.... Made $3.84 million in 1994-95.

Year	Team	G	FG	FG Pct.	FT	FT Pct.	Reb.	Ast.	TP	Avg.
1992-93	Charlotte	78	572	.511	495	.781	805	76	1639	21.0
1993-94	Charlotte	60	427	.505	433	.762	610	86	1287	21.5
1994-95	Charlotte	77	571	.519	490	.761	761	111	1643	21.3
	Totals	215	1570	.512	1418	.768	2176	273	4569	21.3

DELL CURRY 31 6-5 208　　　　　　　　　Guard

Repeated as top scorer among those players who never got a start, but fell short in bid for second straight Sixth Man award... Wasn't the same after missing 10 straight games late in the season with a sprained left ankle... Shooting percentage dipped to .441, lowest in seven seasons with the Hornets and worst since rookie year... Can catch and shoot with anyone... When he shot 50 percent from the field, Hornets were 22-6... Holds team record with 13 triple attempts and six makes... Was 15th pick, out of Virginia Tech, in '86 by Utah... Went to Cavs in three-way deal before 1987-88 season, then picked by Hornets in expansion draft... Born June 25, 1964, in Harrisonburg, Va.... Made $1.34 million in 1994-95.

Year	Team	G	FG	FG Pct.	FT	FT Pct.	Reb.	Ast.	TP	Avg.
1986-87	Utah	67	139	.426	30	.789	78	58	325	4.9
1987-88	Cleveland	79	340	.458	79	.782	166	149	787	10.0
1988-89	Charlotte	48	256	.491	40	.870	104	50	571	11.9
1989-90	Charlotte	67	461	.466	96	.923	168	159	1070	16.0
1990-91	Charlotte	76	337	.471	96	.842	199	166	802	10.6
1991-92	Charlotte	77	504	.486	127	.836	259	177	1209	15.7
1992-93	Charlotte	80	498	.452	136	.866	286	180	1227	15.3
1993-94	Charlotte	82	533	.455	117	.873	262	221	1335	16.3
1994-95	Charlotte	69	343	.441	95	.856	168	113	935	13.6
	Totals	645	3411	.462	816	.853	1690	1273	8261	12.8

TYRONE (MUGGSY) BOGUES 30 5-3 144　　　Guard

Nothing was more painful than watching him pass up, or miss, open jumpers in Hornets' first-round playoff loss to Bulls... That prompted Hornets to pursue B.J. Armstrong, among other point guards, before the draft... Search will continue, no doubt... Had another terrific regular season, posting a career-high scoring average of 11.1... But dip in assists

CHARLOTTE HORNETS • 161

(675, from 780) reflected change in rules and Hornets' committment to post-up plays for L. J. and 'Zo . . . Still fifth in NBA in assists, at 8.7 . . . One of two original Hornets . . . Drafted 12th, out of Wake Forest, by Bullets in '87 . . . Went to Hornets in expansion draft . . . Born Jan. 9, 1965, in Baltimore . . . Played at Dunbar High with the late Reggie Lewis, David Wingate and Reggie Williams . . . Made $1.12 million in 1994-95.

Year	Team	G	FG	FG Pct.	FT	FT Pct.	Reb.	Ast.	TP	Avg.
1987-88	Washington	79	166	.390	58	.784	136	404	393	5.0
1988-89	Charlotte	79	178	.426	66	.750	165	620	423	5.4
1989-90	Charlotte	81	326	.491	106	.791	207	867	763	9.4
1990-91	Charlotte	81	241	.460	86	.796	216	669	568	7.0
1991-92	Charlotte	82	317	.472	94	.783	235	743	730	8.9
1992-93	Charlotte	81	331	.453	140	.833	298	711	808	10.0
1993-94	Charlotte	77	354	.471	125	.806	313	780	835	10.8
1994-95	Charlotte	78	348	.477	160	.889	257	675	862	11.1
	Totals	638	2261	.460	835	.813	1827	5469	5382	8.4

MICHAEL ADAMS 32 5-10 175   Guard

A good idea gone bad, all because of injury . . . Second game of season, strained left hamstring. Missed 32 games . . . Played 21, then missed 20 of the final 27—14 with a torn muscle in left calf . . . Appeared in just 29 games, fewest since rookie season in 1985-86. String of seven straight seasons averaging in double figures ended at 6.5 . . . Got off just 81 triples, making 29. Still all-time leader in three-point attempts with 2,816. Has made a trey in last 79 games he has played . . . Drafted third, out of Boston College, by Kings in '85. Waived. Then signed and waived by Bullets. Signed again, traded to Denver with Jay Vincent for Darrell Walker and Mark Alarie in '87 . . . Back to Bullets in '91 in swap of first-rounders . . . Born Jan. 19, 1963, in Hartford . . . Made $1.24 million in 1994-95.

Year	Team	G	FG	FG Pct.	FT	FT Pct.	Reb.	Ast.	TP	Avg.
1985-86	Sacramento	18	16	.364	8	.667	6	22	40	2.2
1986-87	Washington	63	160	.407	105	.847	123	244	453	7.2
1987-88	Denver	82	416	.449	166	.834	223	503	1137	13.9
1988-89	Denver	77	468	.433	322	.819	283	490	1424	18.5
1989-90	Denver	79	398	.402	267	.850	225	495	1221	15.5
1990-91	Denver	66	560	.394	465	.879	256	693	1752	26.5
1991-92	Washington	78	485	.393	313	.869	310	594	1408	18.1
1992-93	Washington	70	365	.439	237	.856	240	526	1035	14.8
1993-94	Washington	70	285	.408	224	.830	183	480	849	12.1
1994-95	Charlotte	29	67	.453	25	.833	29	95	188	6.5
	Totals	632	3220	.415	2132	.850	1878	4142	9507	15.0

SCOTT BURRELL 24 6-7 218 Forward

Shed always-hurt label by averaging 11.5 points in first 65 games, then blew out Achilles tendon March 29 at Philadelphia... That took him out of running for Most Improved, but Hornet doctors indicated he would be ready for the start of training camp... Third on team in rebounding (5.7), second in blocks (40)... Developed into a three-point threat, making 98-241 (.409) and finishing third in All-Star Weekend's Long-Distance shootout... Best distance used to be 60 feet, six inches. Twice drafted by Mariners and Blue Jays, threw 90 mph in minors... Rugged defender, which drew attention to scouts attending U-Conn games... Drafted 20th in '93... Born Jan. 12, 1971, in Hamden, Conn.... Made $845,000 in 1994-95.

Year	Team	G	FG	FG Pct.	FT	FT Pct.	Reb.	Ast.	TP	Avg.
1993-94	Charlotte	51	98	.419	46	.657	132	62	244	4.8
1994-95	Charlotte	65	277	.467	100	.694	368	161	750	11.5
	Totals	116	375	.453	146	.682	500	223	994	8.6

JOE WOLF 30 6-11 230 Forward-Center

Came home after a season with Elmar Leon of the Spanish League... Appeared in 63 games, averaging 1.4 points and 2.0 rebounds in 9.3 minutes... Got six starts, in which Hornets were 4-2... Big body, decent touch. That's about it... Drafted 13th, out of North Carolina, by Clippers in '87... Averaged 5.8 points and 3.7 rebounds in three seasons with Clippers... Went to Denver as unrestricted free agent. Two years of about the same, but posted career-best numbers—7.3 points, 5.4 rebounds—in 1990-91... Two games with Boston in 1992-93, then 21 with Blazers. Then to Europe... Born Dec. 17, 1964, in Kohler, Wisc.... Brothers John and Jeff also played college hoops, Jeff at North Carolina... Made $150,000 in 1994-95.

Year	Team	G	FG	FG Pct.	FT	FT Pct.	Reb.	Ast.	TP	Avg.
1987-88	L.A. Clippers	42	136	.407	45	.833	187	98	320	7.6
1988-89	L.A. Clippers	66	170	.423	44	.688	271	113	386	5.8
1989-90	L.A. Clippers	77	155	.395	55	.775	232	62	370	4.8
1990-91	Denver	74	234	.451	69	.831	400	107	539	7.3
1991-92	Denver	67	100	.361	53	.803	240	61	254	3.8
1992-93	Bos.-Port.	23	20	.455	13	.813	48	5	53	2.3
1994-95	Charlotte	63	38	.469	12	.750	129	37	90	1.4
	Totals	412	853	.416	291	.786	1507	483	2012	4.9

KENDALL GILL 27 6-5 200   Guard

Returns to Charlotte after two seasons in Seattle... Acquired for Hersey Hawkins in June trade... Athletic, talented player always seems to get more attention for something other than his game... In first time around in Charlotte, it was speculation about his being unhappy that all the attention went to Alonzo Mourning and Larry Johnson. In Seattle, it was a desire to get away from coach George Karl... Culmination last season was his missing five games after being diagnosed with clinical depression... Sonics paid a heavy price to get him from Hornets: Dana Barros, Eddie Johnson and what became a 1994 lottery pick... Charlotte—the city and the team—wasn't exactly heartbroken to see him go, even though he was the No. 5 pick in 1990... Handles the ball well enough to be emergency point guard and plays defense... Born May 25, 1968, in Chicago and went down the state to attend Illinois... 1994-95 salary: $2.6 million.

Year	Team	G	FG	FG Pct.	FT	FT Pct.	Reb.	Ast.	TP	Avg.
1990-91	Charlotte	82	376	.450	152	.835	263	303	906	11.0
1991-92	Charlotte	79	666	.467	284	.745	402	329	1622	20.5
1992-93	Charlotte	69	463	.449	224	.772	340	268	1167	16.9
1993-94	Seattle	79	429	.443	215	.782	268	275	1111	14.1
1994-95	Seattle	73	392	.457	155	.742	290	192	1002	13.7
	Totals	382	2326	.454	1030	.770	1563	1367	5808	15.2

ROBERT PARISH 42 7-0 230   Center

Another good idea gone bad... Took it easy during the regular season, with the idea of turning it on in playoffs. One problem. Nothing left in tank... Made 81 appearances, but averaged just 4.8 points in 16.7 minutes. When he played 20 minutes, production jumped to 7.4... Did get up for old teammates, getting season-high 12 rebounds against Celts... Became eighth player to get 14,000 rebounds... Signed two-year deal with option, $5.5 million of which is guaranteed. Safe bet that Hornets won't pick up option... Second on all-time list of games played (1,494), behind Kareem Abdul-Jabbar's 1,560... In 19 seasons, he's averaged 15.3 points and 9.6 rebounds... Parish-Bird-McHale arguably best frontcourt ever... Born Aug. 30, 1953, in Shreveport, La.... Drafted eighth, out of Centenary, in

'76 by Warriors. Traded to Celts in '80 ... Made $1.925 million in 1994-95.

Year	Team	G	FG	FG Pct.	FT	FT Pct.	Reb.	Ast.	TP	Avg.
1976-77	Golden State	77	288	.503	121	.708	543	74	697	9.1
1977-78	Golden State	82	430	.472	165	.625	680	95	1025	12.5
1978-79	Golden State	76	554	.499	196	.698	916	115	1304	17.2
1979-80	Golden State	72	510	.507	203	.715	783	122	1223	17.0
1980-81	Boston	82	635	.545	282	.710	777	144	1552	18.9
1981-82	Boston	80	669	.542	252	.710	866	140	1590	19.9
1982-83	Boston	78	619	.550	271	.698	827	141	1509	19.3
1983-84	Boston	80	623	.546	274	.745	857	139	1520	19.0
1984-85	Boston	79	551	.542	292	.743	840	125	1394	17.6
1985-86	Boston	81	530	.549	245	.731	770	145	1305	16.1
1986-87	Boston	80	588	.566	227	.735	851	173	1403	17.5
1987-88	Boston	74	442	.589	177	.734	628	115	1061	14.3
1988-89	Boston	80	596	.570	294	.719	996	175	1486	18.6
1989-90	Boston	79	505	.580	233	.747	796	103	1243	15.7
1990-91	Boston	81	485	.598	237	.767	856	66	1207	14.9
1991-92	Boston	79	468	.535	179	.772	705	70	1115	14.1
1992-93	Boston	79	416	.535	162	.689	740	61	994	12.6
1993-94	Boston	74	356	.491	154	.740	542	82	866	11.7
1994-95	Charlotte	81	159	.427	71	.703	350	44	389	4.8
	Totals	1494	9424	.538	4035	.722	14323	2129	22883	15.3

TONY BENNETT 26 6-0 175   Guard

Hard to believe Hornets liked him better than Elliott Perry... Missed first 79 games after rupturing plantar fascia in pickup game over the summer... Tried rest, rehab. Didn't work ... Finally underwent surgery on Jan. 20 ... Came off the bench in final three games of season, averaging 4.7 points and 1.3 assists ... Didn't seem to lose any quickness. Of course, mighty slow to begin with... Was 35th pick, out of Wisconsin-Green Bay, in '92. Played for his dad... Born June 1, 1969, in Green Bay... Wisconsin's Mr. Basketball as high-school senior ... Made $224,000 in 1994-95.

Year	Team	G	FG	FG Pct.	FT	FT Pct.	Reb.	Ast.	TP	Avg.
1992-93	Charlotte	75	110	.423	30	.732	63	136	276	3.7
1993-94	Charlotte	74	105	.399	11	.733	90	163	248	3.4
1994-95	Charlotte	3	6	.462	0	.000	2	4	14	4.7
	Totals	152	221	.412	41	.732	155	303	538	3.5

GREG SUTTON 27 6-2 170 — Guard

Signed Nov. 16, after Hornets were convinced that Tony Bennett might miss the entire season ... Proved to be a competent backup for Muggsy Bogues, averaging 13 minutes and five points ... Makes sound decisions, but still can't shoot. And probably never will ... Averaged 8.8 points and 12.5 minutes in four preseason games in Dallas, but that wasn't good enough for Mavs ... Spent time in Greece and CBA after being waived by San Antonio in '92 ... Was 49th pick, out of Oral Roberts, in '91 draft. NAIA Player of the Year ... Born Dec. 3, 1967, in Douglass, Okla. ... Made $139,500 in 1994-95.

Year	Team	G	FG	FG Pct.	FT	FT Pct.	Reb.	Ast.	TP	Avg.
1991-92	San Antonio	67	93	.388	34	.756	47	91	246	3.7
1994-95	Charlotte	53	94	.409	32	.711	56	91	263	5.0
	Totals	120	187	.398	66	.733	103	182	509	4.2

DARRIN HANCOCK 23 6-5 205 — Guard-Forward

Was basically a spectator until Scott Burrell went down with season-ending Achilles tendon injury. Got seven starts, averaging 7.3 points and 17 minutes ... Very athletic, very active, very raw ... Turned pro after junior season at Kansas, spent 1993-94 season in France ... In one year with Jayhawks, he was named Big Eight All-Newcomer team and played in Final Four. Enrolled at Kansas after two years at Garden City (Kan.) Community College. Had committed to UNLV, didn't make grades ... Didn't play organized basketball until eighth grade ... Born Nov. 3, 1971, in Birmingham, Ala. ... Made $150,000 in 1994-95.

Year	Team	G	FG	FG Pct.	FT	FT Pct.	Reb.	Ast.	TP	Avg.
1994-95	Charlotte	46	68	.562	16	.410	53	30	153	3.3

THE ROOKIE

GEORGE ZIDEK 22 7-0 250 — Center

Opened eyes in NCAA title game by holding Arkansas' Corliss Williamson to 12 points and four rebounds, while getting 14 and six himself... Drafted No. 22... Prepared for UCLA with three years on Czech Junior National team... Father, Jiri, was coach ... Pac-10 All-Academic team, with 3.77 GPA... Born Aug. 2, 1973, in Zlin, Czechoslovakia.

COACH ALLAN BRISTOW:  Head was on the chopping block, but was saved by stars Larry Johnson and Alonzo Mourning. They told owner George Shinn that coaching wasn't the Hornets' problem... Now has foot back in the front office with departure of Dave Twardzik to Golden State. New personnel guy, Bob Bass, doesn't figure to have as much pull as Twardzik did with Shinn and team president Spencer Stolpen... Did the right thing the previous season by hiring defensive whiz Johnny Bach, formerly of the Bulls. Bach is back, but only because Shinn refused to let him out of the final year of pact to join old buddy Doug Collins in Detroit... That cost Bach some bucks... Is slowly abandoning beloved passing game for post-ups and pick-and-rolls for stars L. J. and 'Zo... Will get the credit he deserves when Hornets add a point guard who can consistently make open jumper... Mentor of Doug Moe, for whom he was an assistant for seven seasons... Played with four teams in 10-year NBA career. Averaged 7.8 points and 4.0 rebounds... Spent one season as Hornets' exec before assuming coaching duties in '92... Second-round pick, out of Virginia Tech, by Sixers in '73... Born Aug. 23, 1951, in Richmond, Va.

GREATEST FIND

Hornet fans probably can't decide between Muggsy Bogues and Dell Curry, the only remaining players from the 1988 expansion draft.

Both were longshots to succeed, even with a first-year team. Bogues was said to be way too short and Curry was considered a one-dimensional player whose dimension (outside shooting) couldn't make up for his many other shortcomings.

But Bogues developed into one of the league's most feared point guards, devastating in the open court and more than capable in a halfcourt set. Teams tried to post him up, but the presence of Alonzo Mourning kept that tack from being a game-to-game experience.

As for Curry, he lived up to his billing as a deadly outside shooter. He also proved to be more than adequate on defense, which convinced voters that he was a worthy Sixth Man award winner in 1993-94. And had he not missed 10 straight games late last season with a sprained left ankle, he may have repeated.

Because Bogues and Curry are consummate teammates, they probably won't mind sharing Greatest Find.

ALL-TIME HORNET LEADERS

SEASON

Points: Larry Johnson, 1,810, 1992–93
Assists: Tyrone Bogues, 867, 1989–90
Rebounds: Larry Johnson, 899, 1991–92

GAME

Points: Johnny Newman, 41 vs. Indiana, 1/25/92
       Hersey Hawkins, 41 vs. Golden State, 2/9/94
Assists: Tyrone Bogues, 19 vs. Boston, 4/23/89
Rebounds: Larry Johnson, 23 vs. Minnesota, 3/10/92

CAREER

Points: Dell Curry, 7,149, 1988–95
Assists: Tyrone Bogues, 5,065, 1988–95
Rebounds: Larry Johnson, 2,796, 1991–95

CHICAGO BULLS

TEAM DIRECTORY: Chairman: Jerry Reinsdorf; VP-Operations: Jerry Krause; Dir. Media Services: Tim Hallam; Coach: Phil Jackson; Asst. Coaches: Jim Rodgers, Tex Winter, Jim Cleamons. Arena: United Center (21,500). Colors: Red, white and black.

SCOUTING REPORT

SHOOTING: You know Michael Jordan's jump shot will return to normal, but he's already proven that he can't elevate as he did before putting away his sneakers and picking up a baseball glove. That means his days as a plus-.500 shooter are likely over. But he will do much better than .411, his percentage during the Bulls' last 17 regular-season games.

Jordan, Scottie Pippen and Steve Kerr are three-point threats, and there's no reason why Toni Kukoc shouldn't be. And you would think that shooting guard Ron Harper would find the range after his '94-95 Brickfest in which he shot .282 from outside the three-point arc. The Bulls also liked what they saw of Jud Buechler, a slasher who is also capable of hitting three-point shots.

Some things don't change. The Bulls will again operate without a post-up threat. And until they get one, their chances of moving past the Magic aren't good.

PLAYMAKING: This is what Jordan should turn to if he finds that getting off shots against double- and triple-teams is too exhausting. He has the skills and the savvy of a premier playmaker, but his pride often gets in the way of what's best for the team.

Kukoc and Pippen are also terrific passers, but Kukoc spends most of his time trying to figure out how to stay out of Jordan's way. Pippen's game also shrinks a bit when Jordan is on the court, but when that happens he makes up for it defensively.

Luc Longley could be one of the league's best passing centers, but Jordan doesn't really trust him—and if Jordan doesn't trust you, you rarely see the ball.

REBOUNDING: Big guys abound in the Bulls' locker room—Longley, Will Perdue, Bill Wennington and Dickey Simpkins—but no one comes close to stimulating the board skills of former Bull Horace Grant. Since Grant left for Orlando, every key rebound seems to go to the other team.

Pippen and Jordan are terrific rebounders for their positions,

Scottie Pippen soars . . . with or without Michael Jordan.

but if your team's best board men are a shooting guard and a small forward, trouble is just around the corner. That's probably why the Bulls took a chance in the first round on Alabama power forward Jason Caffey, whom most projected as a second-rounder.

DEFENSE: The Dobermans—Bulls assistant Tex Winter's nickname for Jordan and Pippen—will probably be turned loose again. And when they get tired, versatile Pete Myers can take

BULL ROSTER

No.	Veterans	Pos.	Ht.	Wt.	Age	Yrs. Pro	College
U-30	Jud Buechler	G-F	6-6	220	27	5	Arizona
9	Ron Harper	G	6-6	198	31	9	Miami (Ohio)
23	Michael Jordan	G	6-6	198	32	10	North Carolina
25	Steve Kerr	G	6-3	180	30	7	Arizona
U-42	Larry Krystkowiak	F	6-9	240	31	9	Montana
7	Toni Kukoc	F-G	6-10	230	27	2	Croatia
13	Luc Longley	C	7-2	265	26	4	New Mexico
U-20	Pete Myers	F-G	6-6	180	32	7	Ark.-Little Rock
32	Will Perdue	C	7-0	240	30	7	Vanderbilt
33	Scottie Pippen	G-F	6-7	210	30	8	Central Arkansas
8	Dickey Simpkins	F	6-9	248	23	1	Providence
34	Bill Wennington	C	7-0	260	32	8	St. John's

U-unrestricted free agent

Rd.	Rookie	Sel.No.	Pos.	Ht.	Wt.	College
1	Jason Caffey	20	F	6-8	225	Alabama
2	*Dragan Tarlac	31	F	6-10	260	Greece

*Will play in Greece this year

over. But extending a team's defense from baseline to baseline means you must have a stopper in the event nobody comes up with a steal or a deflection. The Bulls have no stopper. At least not one nearly as good as Grant, who must have the lead in every nightmare of Bulls GM Jerry Krause. Or even as good as former center Bill Cartwright, whose elbows discouraged many from taking the ball inside.

The Bulls may also have trouble defending point guards, what with the loss of B.J. Armstrong to expansion. In the glory years, Jordan could take most point guards out of the zone. That's not the case anymore.

OUTLOOK: Jordan may be older and slower and less likely to dunk over Knicks center Patrick Ewing, but he won't be rusty this time. This time, he'll have the entire summer and training camp to get ready for the regular season. And 82 games to get ready for the playoffs, not just 17.

With Jordan back, a Central Division title seems almost a lock, with the best record in the Eastern Conference a definite possibility, providing coach Phil Jackson can keep everybody from revolting against His Airness, who isn't always the most understanding and patient teammate.

BULL PROFILES

MICHAEL JORDAN 32 6-6 198   Guard

World became right again on March 18, 1995 ... Put down bat, put on sneakers and tried to drag the Bulls back into the Finals. Proved to be too big of a job, even for His Airness ... Highlight of 17-game regular season was 55-point strafing of John Starks and the Knicks at Madison Square Garden ... Lost a little off leap, which sometimes meant passing instead of finishing. In series against Magic, many of those passes wound up in the hands of the enemy ... Racked up the points (26.9), but was NBA's equivalent of a .200 hitter—.411 from the field, easily the lowest in a 10-year career ... Was also tough on teammates, center Luc Longley and forward Toni Kukoc in particular. He could make mistakes, they couldn't ... Left Bulls in a fix by retiring a few days before start of 1993-94 training camp. Took up baseball, bought a bus, joined the White Sox' A team, the Birmingham Barons ... You know the rest: Big wheel at North Carolina and in '84 Olympics. Bulls' third-round pick in '84. Reason Bulls won three straight titles ... Put Nike on map, sold millions of burgers for McDonald's ... Born Feb. 17, 1963, in Brooklyn, N.Y. ... Made $3.85 million in 1993-94.

Year	Team	G	FG	FG Pct.	FT	FT Pct.	Reb.	Ast.	TP	Avg.
1984-85	Chicago	82	837	.515	630	.845	534	481	2313	28.2
1985-86	Chicago	18	150	.457	105	.840	64	53	408	22.7
1986-87	Chicago	82	1098	.482	833	.857	430	377	3041	37.1
1987-88	Chicago	82	1069	.535	723	.841	449	485	2868	35.0
1988-89	Chicago	81	966	.538	674	.850	652	650	2633	32.5
1989-90	Chicago	82	1034	.526	593	.848	565	519	2753	33.6
1990-91	Chicago	82	990	.539	571	.851	492	453	2580	31.5
1991-92	Chicago	80	943	.519	491	.832	511	489	2404	30.1
1992-93	Chicago	78	992	.495	476	.837	522	428	2541	32.6
1994-95	Chicago	17	166	.411	109	.801	117	90	457	26.9
	Totals	684	8245	.514	5205	.845	4336	4025	21998	32.2

SCOTTIE PIPPEN 30 6-7 210   Forward-Guard

Gave farewell speech to teammates and media after Bulls were eliminated by the Magic. Figured he or Toni Kukoc were history and was positive that GM Jerry Krause wouldn't sent Croatian Sensation packing ... Remains one of the game's most elegant and versatile players, capable of something special every night. But with Michael back, has to pick and choose spots... Carries around two big pieces of baggage—migraine headache in Game 7 loss to Pistons in '90 conference finals, refusal to play closing seconds of Game 3 win over Knicks in '94 semis because play was called for Kukoc... Was everything to Bulls, leading in points (1,692), rebounding (8.1), assists (5.2), steals (2.94) and blocks (1.13)... Registered 14th career triple-double, made career-high six triples against Hornets... Was fifth pick, out of Central Arkansas, in '87. Went to Bulls in draft-day deal with Sonics (Olden Polynice and No. 1)... Born Sept. 25, 1965, in Hamburg, Ark.... Made $2.2 million in 1994-95.

Year	Team	G	FG	FG Pct.	FT	FT Pct.	Reb.	Ast.	TP	Avg.
1987-88	Chicago	79	261	.463	99	.576	298	169	625	7.9
1988-89	Chicago	73	413	.476	201	.668	445	256	1048	14.4
1989-90	Chicago	82	562	.489	199	.675	547	444	1351	16.5
1990-91	Chicago	82	600	.520	240	.706	595	511	1461	17.8
1991-92	Chicago	82	687	.506	330	.760	630	572	1720	21.0
1992-93	Chicago	81	628	.473	232	.663	621	507	1510	18.6
1993-94	Chicago	72	627	.491	270	.660	629	403	1587	22.0
1994-95	Chicago	79	634	.480	315	.716	639	409	1692	21.4
	Totals	630	4412	.489	1886	.688	4404	3271	10994	17.5

TONI KUKOC 27 6-10 230   Forward

Should be distrustful of Americans by now. Hailed as one of the best playmakers on the planet, and Bulls make him play power forward... That only made fans long for former Bull Horace Grant, the main reason Orlando was able to eliminate Chicago in six games... Just when he was getting used to playing with Scottie Pippen, Michael returned. At that point, couldn't get rid of ball quick enough... Did make strides from rookie season, improving from 10.9 points to 15.7, second to Pippen. Boosted shooting percentage from 43 to 50 percent, but closer three-point line didn't help much (62-198, .313)... Has knack for hitting big shots at the buzzer... Had two games of 30 or more points, and first career triple-double... Olympic silver medalist with '92 Croatians, '88 Yugoslavians... Born Sept. 18, 1968, in Split, Croatia... Made $3.26 million in 1994-95.

Year	Team	G	FG	FG Pct.	FT	FT Pct.	Reb.	Ast.	TP	Avg.
1993-94	Chicago	75	313	.431	156	.743	297	252	814	10.9
1994-95	Chicago	81	487	.504	235	.748	440	372	1271	15.7
	Totals	156	800	.473	391	.746	737	624	2085	13.4

STEVE KERR 30 6-3 180   Guard

Looks in the mirror and sees John Paxson... Played well enough to convince Bulls that B.J. Armstrong was expendable... Nobody took greater advantage of closer three-point line. Led league with .524 shooting percentage, but was eliminated in first round of All-Star Weekend three-point shootout... Should be even more dangerous after a cameo with Jordan, providing Michael is compelled to pass out of triple teams with more than three seconds left on the shot clock... OK ballhandler, defender... Bounced from Phoenix to Cleveland to Orlando before catching on with Bulls... Recovered from serious knee injury at Arizona, where he starred with Spurs forward Sean Elliott... Suns' second-round pick in '88... Born Sept. 27, 1965, in Beirut, Lebanon... Made $620,000 in 1994-95.

Year	Team	G	FG	FG Pct.	FT	FT Pct.	Reb.	Ast.	TP	Avg.
1988-89	Phoenix	26	20	.435	6	.667	17	24	54	2.1
1989-90	Cleveland	78	192	.444	63	.863	98	248	520	6.7
1990-91	Cleveland	57	99	.444	45	.849	37	131	271	4.8
1991-92	Cleveland	48	121	.511	45	.833	78	110	319	6.6
1992-93	Clev.-Orl.	52	53	.434	22	.917	45	70	134	2.6
1993-94	Chicago	82	287	.497	83	.856	131	210	709	8.6
1994-95	Chicago	82	261	.527	63	.778	119	151	674	8.2
	Totals	425	1033	.485	327	.836	525	944	2681	6.3

LUC LONGLEY 26 7-2 265   Center

Had all summer to think about the gimme he missed in closing moments of Bulls' season-ending loss to Orlando... Figured to distance himself from Will Perdue and Bill Wennington, but missed first 22 games with a stress fracture in left leg... Just another face in the crowd after that, but did have six games of 14 points. Only three double-figure rebound games, and that has to improve... As it is, famous only for being first Australian to play in the NBA... Acquired from Minnesota on Feb. 23, 1994, for Stacey King, who is no better on tundra than he was in Chicago... Was seventh pick, out of New Mexico, by Wolves in '91... Member of 1988 and '92 Aussie Olympic teams... Born Jan. 19, 1969, in Melbourne, Australia...

Made $1.59 million in 1994-95.

Year	Team	G	FG	FG Pct.	FT	FT Pct.	Reb.	Ast.	TP	Avg.
1991-92	Minnesota	66	114	.458	53	.663	257	53	281	4.3
1992-93	Minnesota	55	133	.455	53	.716	240	51	319	5.8
1993-94	Minn.-Chi.	76	219	.471	90	.720	433	109	528	6.9
1994-95	Chicago	55	135	.447	88	.822	263	73	358	6.5
	Totals	252	601	.459	284	.736	1193	286	1486	5.9

WILL PERDUE 30 7-0 240   Center

Was destined to follow in path of Greg Kite, bouncing from town to town in search of the 12th seat on the bench... Revived career instead, starting every game he played (78) and boosting averages from 2.7 and 2.9 in 1993-94 to 8.0 and 6.7. Did it while wearing Silence of the Lambs mask, protection from a broken nose... Wasn't on the playoff roster in '94. Was fifth on depth chart behind Bill Cartwright, Luc Longley, Bill Wennington and Scott Williams. And were those four not available, Phil Jackson would have gone with all-guard lineup... Still mechanical, still clumsy. But occasionally proficient... Was 11th pick, out of Vanderbilt, in '88... Born Aug. 29, 1965, in Melbourne, Fla.... Made $1.05 million in 1994-95.

Year	Team	G	FG	FG Pct.	FT	FT Pct.	Reb.	Ast.	TP	Avg.
1988-89	Chicago	30	29	.403	8	.571	45	11	66	2.2
1989-90	Chicago	77	111	.414	72	.692	214	46	294	3.8
1990-91	Chicago	74	116	.494	75	.670	336	47	307	4.1
1991-92	Chicago	77	152	.547	45	.495	312	80	350	4.5
1992-93	Chicago	72	137	.557	67	.604	287	74	341	4.7
1993-94	Chicago	43	47	.420	23	.719	126	34	117	2.7
1994-95	Chicago	78	254	.553	113	.582	522	90	621	8.0
	Totals	451	846	.507	403	.612	1842	382	2096	4.6

RON HARPER 31 6-6 198   Guard

Was traded for Danny Ferry, has become Danny Ferry... This is what the Bulls got for $2.4 million: 19.9 minutes, 6.9 points, .426 shooting... In last season with Clippers, he was 15th among scorers at 20.1... What happened? Maybe age, maybe jitters, probably no clue as to what he was supposed to do in that triangle offense... With Jordan back, numbers certain to drop lower than GM Jerry Krause's jowels. Four more years left on pact. What's that in dog years?... For Wayne Embry's benefit, here's a recap of that Ferry-Harper deal: Harper and first-round pick (Loy Vaught) for Ferry and Reggie Williams... Was eighth pick, out of Miami and Ohio, by Cavs in '86... Born Jan. 20, 1964, in Dayton.

Year	Team	G	FG	FG Pct.	FT	FT Pct.	Reb.	Ast.	TP	Avg.
1986-87	Cleveland	82	734	.455	386	.684	392	394	1874	22.9
1987-88	Cleveland	57	340	.464	196	.705	223	281	879	15.4
1988-89	Cleveland	82	587	.511	323	.751	409	434	1526	18.6
1989-90	Clev.-LAC	35	301	.473	182	.788	206	182	798	22.8
1990-91	L.A. Clippers	39	285	.391	145	.668	188	209	763	19.6
1991-92	L.A. Clippers	82	569	.440	293	.736	447	417	1495	18.2
1992-93	L.A. Clippers	80	542	.451	307	.769	425	360	1443	18.0
1993-94	L.A. Clippers	75	569	.426	299	.715	460	344	1508	20.1
1994-95	Chicago	77	209	.426	81	.618	180	157	530	6.9
	Totals	609	4136	.450	2212	.721	2930	2778	10816	17.8

BILL WENNINGTON 32 7-0 260   Center

Did Will Perdue a huge favor by suffering sprained left ankle during preseason, forcing him to miss first seven games of regular season... Didn't matter one way or the other to Wennington, who relished a backup role. Meant everything to Perdue, who got the starting job and kept it... What a team guy, eh?... Is a Piston killer. Got season-high 16 points at the Palace in December. Also got season-high nine rebounds, which he later matched against Pacers... Got a nice mid-range jumper, and is a better athlete than you think. Still gets pushed around, though... Did two years in Italy before signing free-agent pact with Bulls on Sept. 9, 1993... Came through with 7.1 points in '94, a career best. Slipped to 5.0, but that was Perdue's doing... Was 16th pick, out of St. John's, by Dallas in '85... Born April 26, 1963, in Montreal... Member of '84 Canadian Olympic team... Made $1 million in 1994-95.

Year	Team	G	FG	FG Pct.	FT	FT Pct.	Reb.	Ast.	TP	Avg.
1985-86	Dallas	56	72	.471	45	.726	132	21	189	3.4
1986-87	Dallas	58	56	.424	45	.750	129	24	157	2.7
1987-88	Dallas	30	25	.510	12	.632	39	4	63	2.1
1988-89	Dallas	65	119	.433	61	.744	286	46	300	4.6
1989-90	Dallas	60	105	.449	60	.800	198	41	270	4.5
1990-91	Sacramento	77	181	.436	74	.787	340	69	437	5.7
1993-94	Chicago	76	235	.488	72	.818	353	70	542	7.1
1994-95	Chicago	73	156	.492	51	.810	190	40	363	5.0
	Totals	495	949	.461	420	.773	1667	315	2321	4.7

PETE MYERS 32 6-6 180   Guard

Bulls didn't think they needed him until Ron Harper started playing like Valerie Harper... GM Jerry Krause hustled him back into town on Nov. 18, with Bulls at 4-4... Didn't duplicate first season with Bulls—7.9 points, 45 percent shooting—but minutes dropped from 24.8 to 17.9... Played 71, hustled 71... Still collected three DNP-CDs... Hasn't done much to improve as perimeter shooter, but has moments around the basket and is a pest on defense... Began career in Chicago in '86, then bounced from San Antonio to Philadelphia to New Jersey and San Antonio again before returning to Windy City... Sixth-round pick, out of Arkansas-Little Rock, in '86... Born Sept. 15, 1963, in Mobile, Ala.... Made $545,000 in 1994-95.

Year	Team	G	FG	FG Pct.	FT	FT Pct.	Reb.	Ast.	TP	Avg.
1986-87	Chicago	29	19	.365	28	.651	17	21	66	2.3
1987-88	San Antonio	22	43	.453	26	.667	37	48	112	5.1
1988-89	Phil.-N.Y.	33	31	.425	33	.688	33	48	95	2.9
1989-90	N.Y.-N.J.	52	89	.396	66	.660	96	135	244	4.7
1990-91	San Antonio	8	10	.435	9	.818	18	14	29	3.6
1993-94	Chicago	82	253	.455	136	.701	181	245	650	7.9
1994-95	Chicago	71	119	.415	70	.614	139	148	318	4.5
	Totals	297	564	.430	368	.670	521	659	1514	5.1

DICKEY SIMPKINS 23 6-9 248   Forward

Clone of former teammate Corie Blount... Biggest contribution was coming down with bogus injury when Michael decided to hang up spikes... Bulls GM Jerry Krause probably wishes he drafted Simpkins' teammate at Providence, Michael Smith... Made 59 appearance with five starts... Averaged 3.5 points and 2.6 rebounds, and shot just .424 from the field... Born April 6, 1972, in Washington, D.C.... Mom is Dr. Barbara Simpkins, administrative supervisor for D.C. public schools... Real name is LuBara Dixon. Older brother dubbed him Dickey, sparing him grade-school beatings... Was 21st pick in '94... Made $650,000 in 1994-95.

Year	Team	G	FG	FG Pct.	FT	FT Pct.	Reb.	Ast.	TP	Avg.
1994-95	Chicago	59	78	.424	50	.694	151	37	206	3.5

JUD BUECHLER 27 6-6 220   Guard-Forward

Wasn't supposed to do much beyond sit at the end of the bench and clap for Scottie and B.J. and even Luc . . . But proved to be a nice addition, at times a better option than Mr. Big Bucks, Ron Harper . . . One of those tweeners, though . . . Decent athlete, solid fundamentals . . . Double figures in five games, including season-high 17 against Dominique Wilkins and Celtics . . . Had trouble with right knee, missing first six games and 11 more near end of season . . . Was second-round pick by Seattle in '90, but never played for Sonics. Caught on with Nets, then went from there to San Antonio and Golden State . . . Spent parts of three seasons with Warriors, getting career-high 19 against Mavs in '93 . . . Played at Arizona . . . Born June 19, 1968, in San Diego . . . Made $150,000 in 1994-95.

Year	Team	G	FG	FG Pct.	FT	FT Pct.	Reb.	Ast.	TP	Avg.
1990-91	New Jersey	74	94	.416	43	.652	141	51	232	3.1
1991-92	N.J.-S.A.-G.S.	28	29	.408	12	.571	52	23	70	2.5
1992-93	Golden State	70	176	.437	65	.747	195	94	437	6.2
1993-94	Golden State	36	42	.500	10	.500	32	16	106	2.9
1994-95	Chicago	57	90	.492	22	.564	98	50	217	3.8
	Totals	265	431	.446	152	.652	518	234	1062	4.0

THE ROOKIES

JASON CAFFEY 22 6-5 255   Forward
Was destined for lottery, some think, until suffered broken foot in preseason . . . Still played 31 games for Alabama, averaging 12.1 points and eight rebounds . . . Second-team All-SEC . . . 20th pick . . . Will battle Dickey Simpkins for playing time . . . Born June 12, 1973, in Mobile, Ala.

DRAGAN TARLAC 22 6-10 260   Forward
Won't be available to the Bulls this season . . . Has another year remaining with Olympiakos in Greece. Plays with former NBA star Eddie Johnson and former Hawk Alexander Volkov . . . Has played in 17 European championship games, averaging 11.6 points and 6.7 rebounds . . . Born May 9, 1973, in Belgrade, Yugoslavia . . . Drafted 31st.

COACH PHIL JACKSON: Last year of contract, will make fortune—if Michael doesn't send him to the loony bin first... Bulls may have eliminated Magic if Jordan didn't press and ignore some teammates. If it happens again, Bulls are again pretenders... Nice resume. Won 200th game faster than any man in history. One of only 10 to win title as player and coach. First coach since Red Auerbach to win at least three straight... Kept Bulls above .500 without Jordan and Horace Grant... Six-year coaching record: 342-150, .695... Took over in '89, after Doug Collins' wacky ways got the best of the Jerrys—owner Reinsdorf and GM Krause... Before assisting Collins, coached Albany to CBA crown in '84... Big on mind games, on and off the court... Decided against becoming a minister and signed with Knicks after starring at North Dakota under Bill Fitch... Second-round pick in '67... Injured when Knicks won title in '70, but contributed to '73 championship... Played 13 seasons despite back problems, which today has him walking like Fred Sanford... Was also an assistant with Nets... Born Sept. 17, 1945, in Deer Lodge, Mont.

GREATEST FIND

The Bulls didn't find Michael Jordan. He fell in their laps, courtesy of the Portland Trail Blazers. Scottie Pippen took some work, but scouts expected him to be a bonafide first-rounder. Same with Horace Grant, chosen five spots behind Pippen at No. 10.

Jerry Sloan was another story.

He came to the Bulls in 1967, in the expansion draft—a second-year player out of Evansville who averaged 5.7 points for the Baltimore Bullets. He came with Johnny Kerr, who became the first Bulls coach. They won 33 games, made the playoffs. In 1970-71, they began a streak of four straight 50-plus win seasons.

The constant was Sloan, a two-time all-star and four-time member of the league's All-Defensive team. For 10 seasons, there was never any question as to who was the toughest Bull. He retired after 1975-76, then returned to coach Bulls for two-and-a-half seasons. Then he went to Utah, and turned the Jazz into contenders.

And his No. 4 jersey hangs in the United Center.

ALL-TIME BULL LEADERS

SEASON

Points: Michael Jordan, 3,041, 1986–87
Assists: Guy Rodgers, 908, 1966–67
Rebounds: Tom Boerwinkle, 1,133, 1970–71

GAME

Points: Michael Jordan, 69 vs. Cleveland, 3/28/90
Assists: Ennis Whatley, 22 vs. New York, 1/14/84
 Ennis Whatley, 22 vs. Atlanta, 3/3/84
Rebounds: Tom Boerwinkle, 37 vs. Phoenix, 1/8/70

CAREER

Points: Michael Jordan, 21,998, 1984–93, 1994–95
Assists: Michael Jordan, 4,025, 1984–93, 1994–95
Rebounds: Tom Boerwinkle, 5,745, 1968–78

CLEVELAND CAVALIERS

TEAM DIRECTORY: Chairman: Gordon Gund; Pres./Team Division: Wayne Embry; Dir. Player Personnel: Gary Fitzsimmons; Sr. Dir. Pub. Rel.: Bob Price; Dir. Media Rel.: Bob Zink Coach: Mike Fratello; Asst. Coaches: Ron Rothstein, Jim Boylan, Sidney Lowe. Arena: Gund Arena (20,562). Colors: Blue, black and orange.

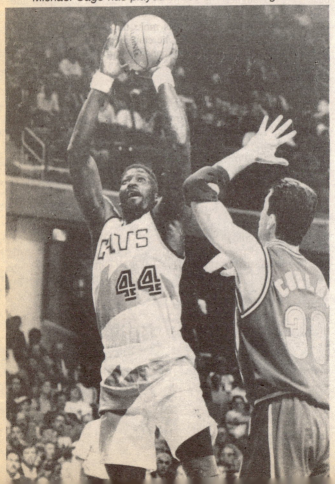

Michael Cage has played in 493 consecutive games.

SCOUTING REPORT

SHOOTING: Maybe this season, the Cavs' shots won't be preceeded by a lot of dribbling and waiting. Maybe this season, coach Mike Fratello will have enough healthy and able bodies to ditch his infamous milk-the-shot-clock offense.

For that to happen, for the Cavs to again be counted among the living, center Brad Daugherty must be healthy. He didn't play the last 30 games of 1993-94 or all of last season because of a back injury. Daugherty is a sure thing in the post or in pick-and-rolls with point guards Mark Price or Terrell Brandon. Having Daugherty down low also means more three-point opportunities for Danny Ferry, who needs all he can get.

Losing Gerald Wilkins to expansion will be a huge blow if Fratello can't resurrect the career of Harold Miner, who never lived up to expectations in Miami. If Miner remains a bust, Fratello's options at guard are incumbent Bobby Phills or Florida State rookie Bob Sura, who might be the second coming of Craig Ehlo.

PLAYMAKING: Price and Brandon are capable of much more than just setting up isolation plays for themselves or others. Fratello isn't likely to go to a run-and-gun offense, but he could. Price and Brandon would probably welcome a transition game—especially Price, a classic pull-up-and-shoot-it type.

Before Daugherty went down, he was considered among the game's best passing big men. That shouldn't change, as long as his back can handle the pounding in the post. After that, the pickings are slim. Ferry's passing skills are often overlooked, mostly because he's usually getting toasted at the other end by any number of people. Chris Mills and Hot Rod Williams would rather shoot than pass.

REBOUNDING: Only two teams were better on the boards than the Cavs, who outrebounded opponents by over two a game (40 to 37.8). Williams and Tyrone Hill were mainly responsible. Hill parlayed terrific rebounding and a much-improved offensive game into an All-Star Game berth. He was the toughest player on a team made up almost entirely of tough guys.

Things don't get any easier for opponents when Fratello goes to the bench. Veteran power forward Michael Cage averaged seven rebounds in 25 minutes, and figures to do the same this season. To their frontline the Cavs have added Donny Marshall, a 6-7 rookie from Connecticut who figures to be just as tough as starter Mills.

CAVALIER ROSTER

No.	Veterans	Pos.	Ht.	Wt.	Age	Yrs. Pro	College
10	John Battle	G	6-2	190	32	10	Rutgers
1	Terrell Brandon	G	5-11	180	25	4	Oregon
44	Michael Cage	F-C	6-9	240	33	11	San Diego State
U-9	Tony Campbell	F-G	6-7	215	33	11	Ohiio State
U-5	Steve Colter	G	6-3	175	33	8	New Mexico State
43	Brad Daugherty	C	7-0	263	30	9	North Carolina
U-30	Greg Dreiling	C	7-1	265	31	9	Kansas
35	Danny Ferry	F	6-10	236	29	5	Duke
32	Tyrone Hill	F	6-9	245	27	5	Xavier
24	Chris Mills	F	6-6	216	25	2	Arizona
—	Harold Miner	G	6-5	214	24	3	USC
14	Bobby Phills	G	6-5	217	25	4	Southern
25	Mark Price	G	6-0	178	31	9	Georgia Tech
U-31	Fred Roberts	F	6-10	218	35	11	Brigham Young
18	John Williams	F-C	6-11	245	33	9	Tulane

U-unrestricted free agent

Rd.	Rookies	Sel.No.	Pos.	Ht.	Wt.	College
1	Bob Sura	17	G	6-5	200	Florida State
2	Donny Marshall	39	F	6-7	230	Connecticut

DEFENSE: Nobody did it better last season. The Cavs held opponents under 100 points a franchise-best 62 times. In the 24-second era, only one other team in NBA history—Syracuse, in 1954-55—had a better defensive yield (89.68 to the Cavs' 89.83). In back-to-back games last season, the Cavs held Atlanta and the Clippers to 68 points.

The Cavs may not approach those numbers this season, especially if Daugherty returns and their shot attempts take a big jump. But they figure to be just as capable of limiting opponents to 46 percent shooting.

Hill, Williams and Phills are outstanding one-on-one defenders, but Fratello preaches team defense, with the emphasis on tenacity and togetherness. If Sura and Marshall buy into that, they'll play. If they don't, they won't.

OUTLOOK: Everything depends on Daugherty. If he can stay healthy and productive, the Cavs' margin of error should decrease greatly. Last season, they outscored their opponents 90.5-89.8, and that's no way for a team to live night after night.

With Daugherty, a contender. Without him, more woe.

CAVALIER PROFILES

MARK PRICE 31 6-0 178   Guard

On the verge of becoming a backup. Many think it should be in Atlanta, under old Cavs coach Lenny Wilkens... Injury bug again crawled into locker. Missed 27 games with broken right wrist, 34 overall... Led Cavs with 15.8 scoring average, but shot .413—lowest since rookie season (.408 in 1986-87)...
But with Brad Daugherty and Gerald Wilkins sidelined for season—and with Cavs playing crawl-it-up-the-floor offense—it was understandable... Required to take shots with four hands in face and shot clock about to expire... Nothing changed at free-throw stripe (148-162, .914). All-time leader at .906 (1883-2078). Had string of 34 from Dec. 13 to Jan. 14... Finished 19th in three-point shooting (103-253). Until suffering injury, he was favorite to three-peat in three-point contest at All-Star Weekend... Set Cavs' record with seven triples against Celts. In that game, he scored season-high 36 in just 27 minutes... Born Feb. 15, 1964, in Bartlesville, Okla.... Dad Denny coaches Phillips U. in Enid, Okla.... Brother Brent was a Bullet ... Second-round steal ('86 by Mavs)... Cavs then stole him from Mavs... Made $3.2 million in 1994-95.

Year	Team	G	FG	FG Pct.	FT	FT Pct.	Reb.	Ast.	TP	Avg.
1986-87	Cleveland	67	173	.408	95	.833	117	202	464	6.9
1987-88	Cleveland	80	493	.506	221	.877	180	480	1279	16.0
1988-89	Cleveland	75	529	.526	263	.901	226	631	1414	18.9
1989-90	Cleveland	73	489	.459	300	.888	251	666	1430	19.6
1990-91	Cleveland	16	97	.497	59	.952	45	166	271	16.9
1991-92	Cleveland	72	438	.488	270	.947	173	535	1247	17.3
1992-93	Cleveland	75	477	.484	289	.948	201	602	1365	18.2
1993-94	Cleveland	76	480	.478	238	.888	228	589	1316	17.3
1994-95	Cleveland	48	253	.413	148	.914	112	335	757	15.8
	Totals	582	3429	.479	1883	.906	1533	4206	9543	16.4

BRAD DAUGHERTY 30 7-0 263   Center

Only Clinton had tougher year... Spent entire season on injured list (back) after missing final 29 games in 1993-94... Tried rest, therapy. Finally had two herniated discs removed on Dec. 5. Keeping fingers crossed... When healthy, one of league's best passing centers. When healthy, pick-and-roll with Mark Price is unstoppable... Never healthy... Has played in 311 of Cavs' last 492 regular-season games. That's 63 percent. Not good... Would like to add to milestones. In 1993-94, went over 2,000 assists, 10,000 points and 5,000 rebounds... Never has been much of a shot-blocker, but never had to be with Larry Nance and Hod Rod Williams around... With Nance retired, will need to become more of a shot-blocking and defensive presence ... Born Oct. 19, 1965, in Black Mountain, N.C.... Didn't break a sweat, but last year made $3.8 million anyway... Is the reason why the Sixers don't trade top picks anymore. Philly thought power forward Roy Hinson was more of a sure thing in '86.

Year	Team	G	FG	FG Pct.	FT	FT Pct.	Reb.	Ast.	TP	Avg.
1986-87	Cleveland	80	487	.538	279	.696	647	304	1253	15.7
1987-88	Cleveland	79	551	.510	378	.716	665	333	1480	18.7
1988-89	Cleveland	78	544	.538	386	.737	718	285	1475	18.9
1989-90	Cleveland	41	244	.479	202	.704	373	130	690	16.8
1990-91	Cleveland	76	605	.524	435	.751	830	253	1645	21.6
1991-92	Cleveland	73	576	.570	414	.777	760	262	1566	21.5
1992-93	Cleveland	71	520	.571	391	.795	726	312	1432	20.2
1993-94	Cleveland	50	296	.488	256	.785	508	149	848	17.0
1994-95	Cleveland					Injured				
	Totals	548	3823	.532	2741	.747	5227	2028	10389	19.0

TERRELL BRANDON 25 5-11 180 Guard

Won't be kept down on the bench anymore, not after averaging a career-best 13.3 points and 5.4 assists in 67 games, 41 of which were starts... But appears to be as jinxed as anybody else in the locker room. Missed last 10 games with a stress fracture of right leg. Also missed four games with sprained wrist... And began 1993-94 by missing first nine games with mononucleosis... Tormented Penny Hardaway with career-high 31 points and 12-of-15 shooting on Feb. 15. Twelve days later, got 26 against Kenny Smith and Sam Cassell in Houston ... Also during that stretch, he had nine rebounds vs. Pistons... Shreds interior defenses with quickness and decisiveness... Improved shooting percentage from .420 to .448, but still needs work on jumper. Like Mark Price, often got stuck with low-percentage, shot-clock-beating shots... Eleventh pick in '92 draft, from

Oregon... Born May 20, 1970, in Portland, Ore.... Made $997,000 in 1994-95.

Year	Team	G	FG	FG Pct.	FT	FT Pct.	Reb.	Ast.	TP	Avg.
1991-92	Cleveland	82	252	.419	100	.806	162	316	605	7.4
1992-93	Cleveland	82	297	.478	118	.825	179	302	725	8.8
1993-94	Cleveland	73	230	.420	139	.858	159	277	606	8.3
1994-95	Cleveland	67	341	.448	159	.855	186	363	889	13.3
	Totals	304	1120	.442	516	.839	686	1258	2825	9.3

JOHN WILLIAMS 33 6-11 245 Forward-Center

Numbers indicate an off season. Dropped in scoring (12.6 from 13.7), rebounding (6.9 from 7.6) and shooting (.452 from .478). Numbers lie... Spent entire season out of position, due to Brad Daugherty's injury and everyone else's incompetence... Like most Cavs, couldn't play full season. Missed eight games (bronchial infection, hamstring, flu, ankle)... Missed '94 playoffs with broken right hand, which kept the Cavs from making things interesting against the Jordan-less Bulls... Cavs' all-time leader with 1,200 blocked shots, but dropped from 130 to 101 (1.36). Had career-high 182 blocks in 1991-92... Not known as a rebounder, but had 16 games of 10 or more. Twice grabbed 13... Point-shaving scandal at Tulane a distant memory, but explains why Cavs got him with 45th pick in '85... Made $3.8 million, part of the seven-year, $26.5-million offer sheet from the Heat that Cavs matched in 1986... Born Aug. 9, 1962, in Sorrento, La.

Year	Team	G	FG	FG Pct.	FT	FT Pct.	Reb.	Ast.	TP	Avg.
1986-87	Cleveland	80	435	.485	298	.745	629	154	1168	14.6
1987-88	Cleveland	77	316	.477	211	.756	506	103	843	10.9
1988-89	Cleveland	82	356	.509	235	.748	477	108	948	11.6
1989-90	Cleveland	82	528	.493	325	.739	663	168	1381	16.8
1990-91	Cleveland	43	199	.463	107	.652	290	100	505	11.7
1991-92	Cleveland	80	341	.503	270	.752	607	196	952	11.9
1992-93	Cleveland	67	263	.470	212	.716	415	152	738	11.0
1993-94	Cleveland	76	394	.478	252	.728	575	193	1040	13.7
1994-95	Cleveland	74	366	.452	196	.685	507	192	929	12.6
	Totals	661	3198	.482	2106	.730	4669	1366	8504	12.9

TYRONE HILL 27 6-9 245   Forward

Reason why the Cavs should buy a Concorde. Took a limo from Cleveland to New York after charter flight inexplicably fell thousands of feet. Got mad when Cavs wouldn't let him take limo back to Cleveland... That spat overshadowed terrific season: 13.8 points, 10.9 rebounds, and first All-Star appearance. Playing with sprained finger, got four rebounds and two points in six minutes... Wouldn't be a Cav if he wasn't injured. Missed 12 games (chip fracture, right hand)... Established career bests with 14 defensive rebounds (vs. Nets) and 10 offensive rebounds (vs. Sixers). Also scored career-high 29 points vs. Mavs... Always been nasty on the boards and defensively. Finesse in the offensive low post definitely something new... Traded from Golden State in 1993 because Warriors needed cap room for Chris Webber. Warriors got 16th pick in '94, which turned out to be Clifford Rozier. Not a good deal... Warriors picked him No. 11, out of Xavier, in '90... Made $2.8 million last year... Born March 17, 1968, in Cincinnati.

Year	Team	G	FG	FG Pct.	FT	FT Pct.	Reb.	Ast.	TP	Avg.
1990-91	Golden State	74	147	.492	96	.632	383	19	390	5.3
1991-92	Golden State	82	254	.522	163	.694	593	47	671	8.2
1992-93	Golden State	74	251	.508	138	.624	754	68	640	8.6
1993-94	Cleveland	57	216	.543	171	.668	499	46	603	10.6
1994-95	Cleveland	70	350	.504	263	.662	765	55	963	13.8
	Totals	357	1218	.513	831	.659	2994	235	3267	9.2

CHRIS MILLS 25 6-6 216   Forward

Continues to prove NBA experts wrong. Shouldn't have lasted until No. 22 in 1993 draft... Played 80 games, started 79... Scoring average jumped from 9.4 to 12.3. Also evolved as a three-point threat (94-240, .392), but needs a little more work on inside game and mid-range jumper... Overall low percentage (.420) can be attributed to size and inexperience... Rebounding average dropped from 5.1 to 4.6, but rebounding demon Tyrone Hill was the reason for that... Like most Cavs, solid on defense. And absolutely fearless, no matter the situation... Had career-high 26 points against Hornets that featured four triples. That was one of eight 20-point-plus performances... Cavs' minutes leader with 2,814... Made

CLEVELAND CAVALIERS • 187

$845,000 last year ... Pac-10 Player of the Year at Arizona, but began college career at Kentucky ... Born Jan. 25, 1970, in Los Angeles.

Year	Team	G	FG	FG Pct.	FT	FT Pct.	Reb.	Ast.	TP	Avg.
1993-94	Cleveland	79	284	.419	137	.778	401	128	743	9.4
1994-95	Cleveland	80	359	.420	174	.817	366	154	986	12.3
	Totals	159	643	.420	311	.799	767	282	1729	10.9

BOBBY PHILLS 25 6-5 217   Guard

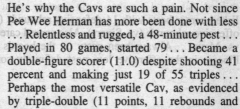

He's why the Cavs are such a pain. Not since Pee Wee Herman has more been done with less ... Relentless and rugged, a 48-minute pest ... Played in 80 games, started 79 ... Became a double-figure scorer (11.0) despite shooting 41 percent and making just 19 of 55 triples ... Perhaps the most versatile Cav, as evidenced by triple-double (11 points, 11 rebounds and 10 assists) against Miami. Also scored career-high 24 points at Madison Square Garden ... Patiently waited for opportunity since March 19, 1992, when he was signed to a 10-day contract out of the CBA ... Scored first basket at Gund Arena, the Cavs' new home ... Was second-round pick of the Bucks (45th overall, out of Southern), in '91 ... Father, Bobby II, is Dean of Agriculture and Home Economics at Southern in Baton Rouge, La. ... Born in Baton Rouge, Dec. 20, 1969 ... Jumped from $312,000 in 1993-94 to $1.5 million.

Year	Team	G	FG	FG Pct.	FT	FT Pct.	Reb.	Ast.	TP	Avg.
1991-92	Cleveland	10	12	.429	7	.636	8	4	31	3.1
1992-93	Cleveland	31	38	.463	15	.600	17	10	93	3.0
1993-94	Cleveland	72	242	.471	113	.720	212	133	598	8.3
1994-95	Cleveland	80	338	.414	183	.779	265	180	878	11.0
	Totals	193	630	.438	318	.743	502	327	1600	8.3

MICHAEL CAGE 33 6-9 240   Forward-Center

Could have signed with Pistons, but wanted to put consecutive-game streak to the real test: Cleveland, new home of the Ace bandage ... What jinx? Played in every game, extending streak to 493. That's second to Suns' A.C. Green's 731 ... In 21 starts, averaged 11.3 rebounds and 8.3 points ... Change of scenery also did wonders for his free-throw shooting.

After making less than 50 percent in final two seasons in Seattle, he hit 53-of-88 (.602)... Experienced a flashback against the Knicks, getting 20 rebounds against Charles Oakley and Anthony Mason. Stole 1987-88 rebounding crown from Oakley with 30 on the final night... Went from Clippers to Seattle in June 1988 in three-team, draft-day deal that included Hersey Hawkins and Charles Smith. Missed just two games with Sonics... Averaged career-best 15.7 points with Clippers in 1986-87. Never averaged double-figures with Sonics... The 14th pick (Clippers, out of San Diego State) in '84... Born Jan. 28, 1962, in West Memphis, Ark.... Made $1.6 million last year.

Year	Team	G	FG	FG Pct.	FT	FT Pct.	Reb.	Ast.	TP	Avg.
1984-85	L.A. Clippers	75	216	.543	101	.737	392	51	533	7.1
1985-86	L.A. Clippers	78	204	.479	113	.649	417	81	521	6.7
1986-87	L.A. Clippers	80	457	.521	341	.730	922	131	1255	15.7
1987-88	L.A. Clippers	72	360	.470	326	.688	938	110	1046	14.5
1988-89	Seattle	80	314	.498	197	.743	765	126	825	10.3
1989-90	Seattle	82	325	.504	148	.698	821	70	798	9.7
1990-91	Seattle	82	226	.508	70	.625	558	89	522	6.4
1991-92	Seattle	82	307	.566	106	.620	728	92	720	8.8
1992-93	Seattle	82	219	.526	61	.469	659	69	499	6.1
1993-94	Seattle	82	171	.545	36	.486	444	45	378	4.6
1994-95	Cleveland	82	177	.521	53	.602	564	56	407	5.0
	Totals	877	2976	.513	1552	.674	7208	920	7504	8.6

DANNY FERRY 29 6-10 236   Forward

Finally made contribution, thanks to rash of injuries and 22-foot three-point line... Still not much of a return on an investment that has five years and $29.2 million remaining... Still too weak to play power forward, too slow to play small forward. Would be more of a threat if somebody in the low post commanded a double team... Did have a better year than Ron Harper, whom the Cavs dealt with two first-round picks and a second-rounder for Ferry and Reggie Williams on Nov. 16, 1989... Played in every game, improving scoring average from 5.0 to 7.5. Was 21st in three-point percentage (94-223, .403)... In back-to-back games in February, scored 45 points—20 against the Knicks, a career-best 25 against the Nets. Before last season, career best was 17, against New York... Son of former Bullets GM Bob Ferry... Picked second overall, out of Duke, by Clips in '89, went to Italy instead... Born Oct. 17, 1966, in Hyattsville, Md.... Made $4.04 million last year.

Year	Team	G	FG	FG Pct.	FT	FT Pct.	Reb.	Ast.	TP	Avg.
1990-91	Cleveland	81	275	.428	124	.816	286	142	697	8.6
1991-92	Cleveland	68	134	.409	61	.836	213	75	346	5.1
1992-93	Cleveland	76	220	.479	99	.876	279	137	573	7.5
1993-94	Cleveland	70	149	.446	38	.884	141	74	350	5.0
1994-95	Cleveland	82	223	.446	74	.881	143	96	614	7.5
	Totals	377	1001	.442	396	.852	1062	524	2580	6.8

HAROLD MINER 24 6-5 214   Guard

"Baby Jordan" is hoping for a rebirth in Cleveland... One thing to remember, Harold. When you put your head down and plow into a stationary defender, there's a charge... Offensively gifted specimen who's still working on that defense thing three years after coming out of Southern Cal.... Individual moves to die for; team concept to gag for... Won the Slam Dunk championship at All-Star Weekend... One of only three players to capture that honor twice, joining Michael Jordan and Dominique Wilkins. Comparisons end right there... Fewest games of his career last season: 45. But he missed 25 games with assortment of ails... Cavs, desperately in need of offense, see a tremendous upside, the same kind of potential that made Miami select him at No.12 in 1992. Miami let him go for two second-round picks last June... Born May 5, 1971, in Inglewood, Cal. ... Made $1.459 million in 1994-95.

Year	Team	G	FG	FG Pct.	FT	FT Pct.	Reb.	Ast.	TP	Avg.
1992-93	Miami	73	292	.475	163	.762	147	73	750	10.3
1993-94	Miami	63	254	.477	149	.828	156	95	661	10.5
1994-95	Miami	45	123	.403	69	.726	117	69	329	7.3
	Totals	181	669	.461	381	.779	420	237	1740	9.6

JOHN BATTLE 32 6-2 190   Guard

Has all sorts of obstacles—size, age and a pair of bad knees... Made 28 appearances, and it was a struggle. Averaged 10 minutes, 4.1 points and shot 38 percent... Still has two years remaining on six-year pact signed in '91. Averaged 10.3 points in first season with Cavs, but hasn't approached that since... Came to Cleveland as an unrestricted free agent from

Atlanta. Best of six seasons was 1990-91 (13.6 points)... Biggest accomplishment in Cleveland: a career-high 14 assists against Utah in 1993-94... Terrific shooter, but doesn't handle ball well enough to play point... Was drafted in fourth round by Hawks in '85... A star at Rutgers... Born Nov. 9, 1962, in Washington, D.C.... Made $1.33 million last year.

Year	Team	G	FG	FG Pct.	FT	FT Pct.	Reb.	Ast.	TP	Avg.
1985-86	Atlanta	64	101	.455	75	.728	62	74	277	4.3
1986-87	Atlanta	64	144	.457	93	.738	60	124	381	6.0
1987-88	Atlanta	67	278	.454	141	.750	113	158	713	10.6
1988-89	Atlanta	82	287	.457	194	.815	140	197	779	9.5
1989-90	Atlanta	60	275	.506	102	.756	99	154	654	10.9
1990-91	Atlanta	79	397	.461	270	.854	159	217	1078	13.6
1991-92	Cleveland	76	316	.480	145	.848	112	159	779	10.3
1992-93	Cleveland	41	83	.415	56	.778	29	54	223	5.4
1993-94	Cleveland	51	130	.476	73	.753	39	83	338	6.6
1994-95	Cleveland	28	43	.377	19	.731	11	37	116	4.1
	Totals	612	2054	.464	1168	.793	824	1257	5338	8.7

GREG DREILING 31 7-1 265   Center

Have big body, will travel... Signed in 1994 as unrestricted free agent after one year with the Mavs. Previous seven seasons were with Indiana. Was the Pacers' second-round pick (26th overall) in '86... Takes up space, and that's about it... Played 58 games with Cavs, with three starts. Averaged 1.9 points and 2.2 rebounds, but did have career-high 12 rebounds against the Timberwolves... In first start with Cavs, tied career-best with three blocks. Yes, three... Played for Kansas team that went to the Final Four in '86. Began career at Wichita State... Born Nov. 7, 1963, in Wichita, Kan.... Made $150,000 in 1994-95.

Year	Team	G	FG	FG Pct.	FT	FT Pct.	Reb.	Ast.	TP	Avg.
1986-87	Indiana	24	16	.432	10	.833	43	7	42	1.8
1987-88	Indiana	20	8	.471	18	.692	17	5	34	1.7
1988-89	Indiana	53	43	.558	43	.672	92	18	129	2.4
1989-90	Indiana	49	20	.377	25	.735	87	8	65	1.3
1990-91	Indiana	73	98	.505	63	.600	255	51	259	3.5
1991-92	Indiana	60	43	.494	30	.750	96	25	117	2.0
1992-93	Indiana	43	19	.328	8	.533	66	8	46	1.1
1993-94	Dallas	54	52	.500	27	.711	170	31	132	2.4
1994-95	Cleveland	58	42	.412	26	.634	116	22	110	1.9
	Totals	434	341	.468	250	.667	942	175	934	2.2

TONY CAMPBELL 33 6-7 215   Guard-Forward

Keeps hanging around, and nobody knows how... Can score in bunches—9.7 points in just 20.4 minutes with the Mavs in 1993-94—but does little else well. And when not hitting, keeps shooting... Played 78 games with the Cavs, scoring 17 or more points in 10... Season-high 23 vs. the Nets... Averaged 6.0 points, lowest since third season with the Pistons... Averaged over 20 points in two of three seasons with the expansion Timberwolves... Former Ohio State star... Began career as No. 20 pick by Pistons in 1984... Has one championship ring (Lakers, 1988)... Born May 7, 1962, in Teaneck, N.J.... Got diploma from Teaneck High, which produced NBA commissioner David Stern... Made $650,000 in 1994-95.

Year	Team	G	FG	FG Pct.	FT	FT Pct.	Reb.	Ast.	TP	Avg.
1984-85	Detroit	56	130	.496	56	.800	89	24	316	5.6
1985-86	Detroit	82	294	.484	58	.795	236	45	648	7.9
1986-87	Detroit	40	57	.393	24	.615	58	19	138	3.5
1987-88	L.A.Lakers	13	57	.564	28	.718	27	15	143	11.0
1988-89	L.A.Lakers	63	158	.458	70	.843	130	47	388	6.2
1989-90	Minnesota	82	723	.457	448	.787	451	213	1903	23.2
1990-91	Minnesota	77	652	.434	358	.803	346	214	1678	21.8
1991-92	Minnesota	78	527	.464	240	.803	286	229	1307	16.8
1992-93	New York	58	194	.490	59	.678	155	62	449	7.7
1993-94	N.Y.-Dal.	63	227	.443	94	.783	186	82	555	8.8
1994-95	Cleveland	78	161	.411	132	.830	153	69	469	6.0
	Totals	690	3180	.456	1567	.790	2117	1019	7994	11.6

THE ROOKIES

BOB SURA 22 6-5 200   Guard

First ACC player to amass 2,000 points, 700 rebounds, 400 assists and 200 steals... Will battle Harold Miner and Bobby Phills for playing time at shooting guard... Needs to get game under control... Drafted 17th, out of Florida State... ACC Rookie of the Year... Born March 25, 1973, in Wilkes-Barre, Pa.

DONNY MARSHALL 23 6-7 230   Forward

Drafted 39th... Came up big in NCAAs, getting 25 against Cincinnati and season-high 27 in win over Maryland... Scoring average went from 1.9 to 7.8 to 12.4 to 15.8 in four seasons at Connecticut... May be the next Cavalier to take minutes from embattled Danny Ferry... Born July 17, 1972, in Detroit.

COACH MIKE FRATELLO: Should have been Coach of the

Year... Lost it to Bob Hill in the last two months of the season, after the Cavs dropped 14 of their last 15 road games—the result of adding point guard Terrell Brandon to an injured list that already included Brad Daugherty and Gerald Wilkins... And Brandon's exit coincided with the return of Mark Price, who missed 34 games with a broken wrist... Even without Daugherty and Wilkins, the Cavs built a 16-10 road record... In December, the Cavs won a team-record 11 straight games, third-longest last season behind San Antonio (15) and Utah (14)... Convinced players that walking it up and milking the clock were necessary, a plan everyone bought into. It resulted in a points-against average of 89.3, lowest in the league... In only 20 games were Cavs' opponents able to score 100 or more points... Two-year record: 90-74, .549... Seems to be less tightly wound, but injuries lowered expectations. Team played hard every second, regardless of the situation... Produced four 50-win seasons in seven years with Hawks... Coach of the Year in 1986-87... Worked under Hubie Brown and Kevin Loughery, with college stops at James Madison, Rhode Island and Villanova... Graduate of Montclair (N.J.) College... Born Feb. 24, 1947, in Hackensack, N.J.... Named Cavs' coach on June 17, 1993.

GREATEST FIND

Those who have followed the Cavs since they entered the league probably have a soft spot in their heart for Bobby (Bingo) Smith, an original Cav and key player on the only Cleveland team to play in the Eastern Conference finals—the 1975-76 Cavs, who lost in seven games to the eventual champion Boston Celtics.

But even though the Cavs got Smith from San Diego in the expansion draft, he was a first-round pick.

Not so with Mark Price, who was deemed to small to play in the NBA. He stayed on the board until the 25th pick in 1986, well into the second round. And not long after he was drafted by the Dallas Mavericks, they sent him to the Cavs for a second-round pick in '89 (Jeff Hodge) and other considerations.

And this is what Price has given to the Cavs: nine seasons, a 16.4 scoring average, four All-Star appearances and a role with Dream Team II.

ALL-TIME CAVALIER LEADERS

SEASON

Points: Mike Mitchell, 2,012, 1980–81
Assists: John Bagley, 735, 1985–86
Rebounds: Jim Brewer, 891, 1975–76

GAME

Points: Walt Wesley, 50 vs. Cincinnati, 2/19/71
Asissts: Geoff Huston, 27 vs. Golden State, 1/27/82
Rebounds: Rick Roberson, 25 vs. Houston, 3/4/72

CAREER

Points: Brad Daugherty, 10,389, 1986–95
Assists: Mark Price, 4,206, 1986–95
Rebounds: Brad Daugherty, 5,227, 1986–95

DETROIT PISTONS

TEAM DIRECTORY: Managing Partner: Bill Davidson; Pres.: Tom Wilson; VP-Player Personnel: Rick Sund; Dir. Scouting: John Hammord; Dir. Pub. Rel.: Matt Dobek; Coach: Doug Collins; Asst. Coaches: Alvin Gentry, Brian James. Arena: The Palace of Auburn Hills (21,454). Colors: Red, white and blue.

SCOUTING REPORT

SHOOTING: Put Hakeem Olajuwon in the middle and the Pistons would destroy everybody. Actually, all they need is somebody in the post that commands constant double-teams, leaving Joe Dumars, Allan Houston or Terry Mills open at the three-point arc.

If Otis Thorpe, presumed coming from Portland before the lockout, isn't that guy, nothing much will change. Only Grant Hill takes the ball to the hole, meaning the Pistons will again be at or near the bottom in free-throw attempts. And until Hill demonstrates that he can consistently hit mid-range shots, three or more players will be waiting for him at the basket.

Houston got most of the attention for improving his scoring average from 8.5 to 14.5, but Mills is probably the team's best pure shooter. New coach Doug Collins will let him fire away from the outside, but only if he mixes it up inside on defense.

PLAYMAKING: Creativity hasn't been a part of the Pistons' offense since Isiah Thomas left Motown to run the expansion Toronto Raptors. Lindsay Hunter was said to be the second coming of Isiah, but he creates only for himself. When Hunter suffered a broken foot last season, then-coach Don Chaney eventually turned to Dumars. He proved to be a calming influence and a guiding force, but in times of stress maintained his shooting-guard mentality. That was great for him, but not so great for Hill, who didn't see the ball enough.

Collins seems to be leaning toward an offense that features Hill at the point, something Collins often did with Scottie Pippen in Chicago. That will be a good idea only if Hill remembers to create for himself when the game's on the line.

REBOUNDING: The Pistons haven't done much of this since Dennis Rodman was traded to San Antonio and Bill Laimbeer

Grant Hill: Co-Rookie of Year with Jason Kidd.

retired. They've been pitiful at both ends for two seasons, during which time they've tried to make do with Mark West, Oliver Miller, Ivano Newbill, Eric Leckner, Olden Polynice and Cadillac Anderson.

West figures to open the season at center, but Collins could decide to shift Mills from power forward. Either way, the presence of Thorpe would be a key factor.

Hill did his share of rebounding (6.4) for a small forward, but Collins expects much more. Collins will also get after Houston, who at 6-6 should be one of the better rebounding shooting guards in the league.

PISTON ROSTER

No.	Veterans	Pos.	Ht.	Wt.	Age	Yrs. Pro	College
17	Bill Curley	F	6-9	245	23	1	Boston College
4	Joe Dumars	G	6-3	195	32	10	McNeese State
33	Grant Hill	F	6-8	225	23	1	Duke
20	Allan Houston	G	6-6	200	24	2	Tennessee
1	Lindsey Hunter	G	6-2	170	24	2	Jackson State
U-32	Negele Knight	G	6-1	182	28	5	Dayton
U-45	Eric Leckner	C	6-11	265	29	5	Wyoming
2	Mark Macon	G	6-5	185	26	4	Temple
6	Terry Mills	F	6-10	250	27	5	Michigan
41	Mark West	C	6-10	246	34	12	Old Dominion

U-unrestricted free agent

Rd.	Rookies	Sel.No.	Pos.	Ht.	Wt.	College
1	Theo Ratliff	18	F	6-10	215	Wyoming
1	Randolph Childress	19	G	6-1	188	Wake Forest
2	Lou Roe	30	F	6-7	220	Massachusetts
2	Don Reid	58	F	6-8	250	Georgetown

DEFENSE: Thorpe would upgrade the Pistons' interior defense from constantly porous to occasionally porous. They still don't have anybody capable of shutting down average centers, let alone great ones. But they did add a presence in the post—6-10 rookie Theo Ratliff, who left Wyoming with more career blocks (425) than anybody in NCAA history with the exception of Georgetown's Alonzo Mourning.

The main defensive burden again falls to Hill, who will be in the "Doug House" if he doesn't average over two steals and a block a game. Hill will also be responsible for stopping the opponents' hot scorer. That means covering everybody from point guard to power forward. He should get some help from rookie Lou Roe, who developed a tough-as-nails reputation at Massachusetts.

OUTLOOK: Much depends on the arrival of Thorpe. The Pistons should get his best, considering he's in the last year of a contract. Thorpe would solve two major problems—defense and rebounding—but he can't do anything about the team's lack of quality depth.

Collins insisted that Hill merely "scratched the surface" last season. If that's the case, the Pistons could make a run at a .500 record and the last spot in the playoffs. But a serious injury to Hill or Thorpe, and the Pistons are back on the lottery trail.

PISTON PROFILES

GRANT HILL 23 6-8 225 — Guard-Forward

Perfect in every way, which makes Pistons' 28-win season tough to understand... Spent most of the season deferring to captain Joe Dumars, who gladly took most of the important fourth-quarter shots. New coach Doug Collins vows that Hill "won't hide" anymore in crunch time... Must develop outside jumper, the only flaw in his game... Started in All-Star Game... Shared Rookie of the Year honors with Mavs' point guard Jason Kidd... Averaged 19.9 points, 6.4 rebounds and 5.0 assists... Registered Pistons' first triple-double since 1987 with 21 points, 11 rebounds and 10 assists against the Magic... Set unofficial record with two "Late Night With David Letterman" appearances. Also did Jay Leno, and posed for what seemed like several thousand magazine covers... Son of Calvin, former NFL star, and Janet, former college suitemate of First Lady Hillary Rodham Clinton... Played in three Final Fours at Duke and was ACC Player of the Year as a senior... Born Oct. 5, 1972, in Dallas... Made $2.75 million in 1994-95.

Year	Team	G	FG	FG Pct.	FT	FT Pct.	Reb.	Ast.	TP	Avg.
1994-95	Detroit	70	508	.477	374	.732	445	353	1394	19.9

ALLAN HOUSTON 24 6-6 200 — Guard

One of the reasons why Don Chaney no longer coaches the Pistons. Only after the Pistons were ravaged by injuries did Chaney turn to Houston, who scored just eight points and registered six DNP-CDs in November... After All-Star break, he had 15 games of 25 or more points... Set club record with 158 three-pointers... Improved scoring average from 8.5 to 14.5 and shooting percentage from 41 to 46 percent. Also among leaders in three-point percentage (42)... Nobody has a prettier jumper, and few are better finishers—a result of off-season sessions with strength coach Arnie Kander, who added eight inches of vertical leap... Still needs work defensively, but upgraded from lousy to adequate... Didn't complain about Chaney because of what father, Wade, went through at Tennessee... Born April 4, 1971, in Louisville, Ky.... Second only to Pete Maravich in SEC scoring... No. 11 pick in 1993... 1994-95 salary: $958,000.

Year	Team	G	FG	FG Pct.	FT	FT Pct.	Reb.	Ast.	TP	Avg.
1993-94	Detroit	79	272	.405	89	.824	120	100	668	8.5
1994-95	Detroit	76	398	.463	147	.860	167	164	1101	14.5
	Totals	155	670	.438	236	.846	287	264	1769	11.4

JOE DUMARS 32 6-3 195   Guard

Transition from shooting guard to point guard wasn't an easy one... For one thing, he was too heavy to keep up with the likes of Kenny Anderson and Mookie Blaylock. For another, his passing options were limited... Again struggled with injuries and apathy... Three games into last season, he tied an NBA record with 10 three-pointers against the woeful Wolves. Then completely lost long-range touch, shooting just 31 percent from outside the arc... Shot 43 percent overall, lowest mark in an otherwise stellar career... Another career-low: 67 games played... May have been worn down by commitment to Dream Team II... MVP of the 1989 Finals... Before the '85 draft, he was told by the Mavs that he and fellow Louisiana native Karl Malone would wind up in Dallas... Went instead at No. 18 to the Pistons, who were hoping centers Bill Wennington or Uwe Blab would still be on the board. Honest... Born May 5, 1963, in Natchitoches, La.... Made $1.1 million, but will get nearly $7 million this season and $4 million in '96-97.

Year	Team	G	FG	FG Pct.	FT	FT Pct.	Reb.	Ast.	TP	Avg.
1985-86	Detroit	82	287	.481	190	.798	119	390	769	9.4
1986-87	Detroit	79	369	.493	184	.748	167	352	931	11.8
1987-88	Detroit	82	453	.472	251	.815	200	387	1161	14.2
1988-89	Detroit	69	456	.505	260	.850	172	390	1186	17.2
1989-90	Detroit	75	508	.480	297	.900	212	368	1335	17.8
1990-91	Detroit	80	622	.481	371	.890	187	443	1629	20.4
1991-92	Detroit	82	587	.448	412	.867	188	375	1635	19.9
1992-93	Detroit	77	677	.466	343	.864	148	308	1809	23.5
1993-94	Detroit	69	505	.452	276	.836	151	261	1410	20.4
1994-95	Detroit	67	417	.430	277	.805	158	368	1214	18.1
	Totals	762	4881	.469	2861	.844	1702	3642	13079	17.2

LINDSEY HUNTER 24 6-2 170   Guard

Still clueless after two seasons... Master of the meaningless speed-dribble, often with the shot clock near zero... Is heading down the path of Rumeal Robinson, who never understood that a point guard is supposed to create for others, not just himself... We shouldn't be too critical, however. He didn't get point-guard tutoring at Jackson State, and was allowed to make the same mistakes over and over by Don Chaney's staff... Missed 41 games with a broken right foot. Played last two months of the season, but never got over the injury mentally... Scoring average dropped from 10.3 to 7.5, assist average from 4.8 to 3.8 ... Moving in the arc didn't help, either. Three-point percentage remained at an abysmal 33 percent... Takes it up strong, but seldom finishes... Lousy defender, too... Pistons' fans are wondering what possessed former VP Billy McKinney to take Hunter instead of Nick Van Exel or Sam Cassell... Born Dec. 3, 1970, in Utica, Miss.... Made $1.17 million last season.

Year	Team	G	FG	FG Pct.	FT	FT Pct.	Reb.	Ast.	TP	Avg.
1993-94	Detroit	82	335	.375	104	.732	189	390	843	10.3
1994-95	Detroit	42	119	.374	40	.727	75	159	314	7.5
	Totals	124	454	.375	144	.731	264	549	1157	9.3

TERRY MILLS 27 6-10 250   Forward

Looks an awful lot like boxer George Foreman, but doesn't care to mix it up inside... Defensively he's the NBA's equivalent of former punching bag Gerry Cooney... Might be only player with stretch marks, the result of dropping from 284 to 262 to 250 pounds. Is becoming more serious about offseason training, but still has a ways to go... Among Pistons, only Allan Houston has a sweeter outside shot, and nobody was better in November—20 or more points in 10 of 13 games, and eight double-doubles... But packed it in after the Pistons fell out of the playoff race, finishing up with 15.5 points and 7.8 rebounds, down from 17.3 and 8.4 in 1993-94... Missed seven games in March with foot problems; some in the front office didn't believe it to be that serious... Signed as restricted free agent when Nets decided against matching five-year, $9.5-million pact in 1992... Drafted by Bucks (16th in 1990, from Michigan), but held out. Played briefly in Greece, then dealt to Denver for Danny Schayes. Midway through rookie season, he was sent to New Jersey... Born Jan. 25, 1970, in Los Angeles... Made $1.9 million in 1994-95.

Year	Team	G	FG	FG Pct.	FT	FT Pct.	Reb.	Ast.	TP	Avg.
1990-91	Den.-N.J.	55	134	.465	47	.712	229	33	315	5.7
1991-92	New Jersey	82	310	.463	114	.750	453	84	742	9.0
1992-93	Detroit	81	494	.461	201	.791	472	111	1199	14.8
1993-94	Detroit	80	588	.511	181	.797	672	177	1381	17.3
1994-95	Detroit	72	417	.447	175	.799	558	160	1118	15.5
	Totals	370	1943	.472	718	.782	2384	565	4755	12.9

MARK WEST 34 6-10 246   Center

Didn't smile very much, and with good reason. Three reasons, actually... Traded from the Valley of the Sun to Mounds of Snow, suffered knee injury, which ended consecutive-game streak at 521, and went from title contender to lottery regular... Minutes went from 15 to 23, and that was asking way too much... Stopped believing in Don Chaney after Chaney played him 23 minutes in first game back from injury... Did beef up stats, averaging 7.5 points and 6.1 rebounds in 67 games. Final year in Phoenix: 4.7 points, 3.6 rebounds... Trails only Artis Gilmore (.599) in career shooting... Suns got him from Cleveland in the 1988 deal that also included best friend Kevin Johnson; Cavs got Larry Nance and Mike Sanders... Born Nov. 5, 1960, in Ft. Campbell, Ky.... Made $1.5 million; will jump to $2 million in final year of pact.

Year	Team	G	FG	FG Pct.	FT	FT Pct.	Reb.	Ast.	TP	Avg.
1983-84	Dallas	34	15	.357	7	.318	46	13	37	1.1
1984-85	Mil.-Clev.	66	106	.546	43	.494	251	15	255	3.9
1985-86	Cleveland	67	113	.541	54	.524	322	20	280	4.2
1986-87	Cleveland	78	209	.543	89	.514	339	41	507	6.5
1987-88	Clev.-Phoe.	83	316	.551	170	.596	523	74	802	9.7
1988-89	Phoenix	82	243	.653	108	.535	551	39	594	7.2
1989-90	Phoenix	82	331	.625	199	.691	728	45	861	10.5
1990-91	Phoenix	82	247	.647	135	.655	564	37	629	7.7
1991-92	Phoenix	82	196	.632	109	.637	372	22	501	6.1
1992-93	Phoenix	82	175	.614	86	.518	458	29	436	5.3
1993-94	Phoenix	82	162	.566	58	.500	295	33	382	4.7
1994-95	Detroit	67	217	.556	66	.478	408	18	500	7.5
	Totals	887	2330	.589	1124	.574	4857	386	5784	6.5

MARK MACON 26 6-5 185 — Guard

Has only two problems—can't make an open shot, and has no idea what is or isn't a good shot. Should enroll in the Nate McMillan School of Occasional Shooting... Began season as starter, ended it as benchwarmer. Got lapped by Allan Houston, whose jumper is pretty and accurate and everything Macon's is not... Lost some zest for the game, but remained the Pistons' most dogged defender. Even with new handchecking rules, he had no problems locking up most shooting guards... Problems can be traced to Temple, where John Chaney not only gave him the license to shoot, but the license to miss as well... Came to Detroit with Marcus Liberty (Nov. 19, 1993) only because that's the only way the Pistons could get rid of Alvin Robertson, who had attempted to strangle VP of basketball operations Billy McKinney... Born April 14, 1969, in Saginaw, Mich.... 1994-95 salary: $1.7 million.

Year	Team	G	FG	FG Pct.	FT	FT Pct.	Reb.	Ast.	TP	Avg.
1991-92	Denver	76	333	.375	135	.730	220	168	805	10.6
1992-93	Denver	48	158	.415	42	.700	103	126	358	7.5
1993-94	Den.-Det.	42	69	.375	23	.676	41	51	163	3.9
1994-95	Detroit	55	101	.381	54	.794	76	63	276	5.0
	Totals	221	661	.385	254	.732	440	408	1602	7.2

THE ROOKIES

THEO RATLIFF 22 6-10 215 — Forward
Will be backup at power forward... Entered Wyoming at 6-7, 170 pounds... Left with 425 blocked shots, second-best total in NCAA history behind former Georgetown star Alonzo Mourning... Needs another 30 pounds... Born April 17, 1973, in Demopolis, Ala.... Was 18th pick.

RANDOLPH CHILDRESS 23 6-1 188 — Guard
Second-team All-American as a senior at Wake Forest... Didn't have a great shooting percentage, going 41.5 and 43.8 his last two seasons. But nice range... No. 1 in school history in three-pointers and No. 2 in scoring... Pistons got him with 19th pick... Born Sept. 21, 1972, in Washington, D.C.

LOU ROE 23 6-7 220   Forward

Slid to 30th pick, which surprised many . . . Is expected to torment Grant Hill in practice . . . Three-year starter at U-Mass, Atlantic 10 tournament MVP his senior season . . . Actually had better junior year, scoring 28 each against Kentucky and North Carolina . . . Born July 14, 1972, in Atlantic City, N.J.

DON REID 22 6-8 250   Forward

Answer to two trivia questions . . . Who was 58th and last player selected in draft? Who converted Allan Iverson's miss at the buzzer to give Georgetown a 53-51 win over Weber State in NCAA tournament? . . . Typical Hoya. Tough, dedicated . . . Averaged 7.2 points, 5.7 rebounds . . . Born Dec. 30, 1973, in Largo, Md.

COACH DOUG COLLINS: Said he would leave TNT only  for the perfect job. This is it, and not just because of a five-year, $6.5-million contract . . . Will have the final say in all personnel matters, with president Tom Wilson and vice president of finance Ron Campbell handling contract talks . . . Staff includes former Celtic assistant Don Casey and Alvin Gentry, interim coach of the Heat for the final 34 games last season . . . Reunited with his college coach at Illinois State, longtime Piston executive Will Robinson . . . Was fired by Chicago in July 1989 after leading Bulls to Eastern Conference finals. Lost to the Pistons in six games after leading 2-1 . . . Downfall was said to be power struggle with Bulls GM Jerry Krause . . . Didn't jump back into coaching because of children . . . His son, Chris, plays at Duke, while daughter Kelly is a three-sport star in Northbrook, Ill. . . . Vows to turn Grant Hill into Scottie Pippen, a player capable of playing four positions . . . Will be Coach of the Year, former Pistons coach Chuck Daly predicts . . . Was 35 when got Bulls' job. Is 43 now, and professes to be much smarter and more mature. We'll see . . . Was an all-star in four of his eight seasons with Philadelphia. Averaged 17.9 points and shot 50 percent from the field in 415 games . . . Career was cut short because of several knee injuries . . . A key player for Sixers in loss to Portland in 1977 Finals, but is most remembered for making clutch free throws in the closing moments of 1972 Olympics title game against Soviet Union—which the USA lost in a controversial finish.

GREATEST FIND

They thought Dennis Rodman was overwhelmed by the competition. They thought he wasn't prepared to make the biggest step, from the NAIA (Southeastern Oklahoma State) to the NBA. They watched him struggle in the Chicago predraft camp, and projected him as a fringe player or worse, despite his 6-8, 210-pound frame.

What they didn't know is that asthma—not the competition—was getting the best of Rodman. Fortunately for the Pistons, Mike Abdenour was the camp's trainer. And when he told general manager Jack McCloskey how sick Rodman was, that gave the Pistons an edge over the field. They took advantage, selecting Rodman in the second round (27th overall) of the 1986 draft.

Stroke of luck, or genius?

The Pistons don't really care, not after Rodman helped them win two straight NBA titles. Along the way, he was a two-time Defensive Player of the Year. And before he could win the Sixth Man award, the Pistons moved him into the starting lineup.

ALL-TIME PISTON LEADERS

SEASON

Points: Dave Bing, 2,213, 1970–71
Assists: Isiah Thomas, 1,123, 1984–85
Rebounds: Bob Lanier, 1,205, 1972–73

GAME

Points: Kelly Tripucka, 56 vs. Chicago, 1/29/83
Assists: Kevin Porter, 25 vs. Phoenix, 4/1/79
 Kevin Porter, 25 vs. Boston, 3/9/79
 Isiah Thomas, 25 vs. Dallas, 2/13/85
Rebounds: Dennis Rodman, 34 vs. Indiana, 3/4/92

CAREER

Points: Isiah Thomas, 18,822, 1981–94
Assists: Isiah Thomas, 9,061, 1981–94
Rebounds: Bill Laimbeer, 9,330, 1982–94

INDIANA PACERS

TEAM DIRECTORY: Owners: Herb Simon, Melvin Simon; Pres.: Donnie Walsh; VP-Basketball: Billy Knight; Media Rel. Dir.: David Benner; Coach: Larry Brown; Asst. Coaches: Gar Heard, Billy King. Arena: Market Square Arena (16,530). Colors: Blue and yellow.

SCOUTING REPORT

SHOOTING: All-Star Reggie Miller and Rik Smits can score in bunches, but after that it's a guessing game for coach Larry

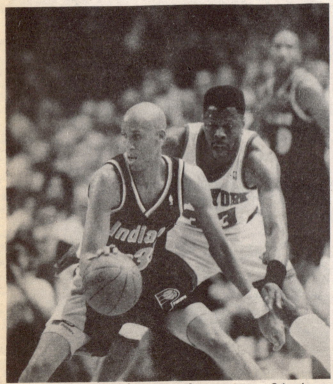

Reggie Miller got past Knicks, but then came Orlando.

Brown. He can't always count on small forward Derrick McKey, and the Davises—power forwards Dale and Antonio—are not much more than dunkers. Point guard Mark Jackson can score, but when he concentrates on shooting it takes away from his playmaking ability.

The X-Factor used to be veteran shooting guard Byron Scott, but even he fell off, which made the Pacers' decision to expose him to the expansion draft easier. Scott's departure opens the door for Indiana prep legend Damon Bailey, who missed all of last season with surgery on both knees, or second-round pick Fred Hoiberg of Iowa State. The Pacers' first-rounder, Georgia Tech point guard Travis Best, can also fill it up.

Brown may take a closer look at small forward Duane Ferrell, who was supposed to be the sleeper of the 1994 free-agent market. Ferrell's minutes were gobbled up by Sam Mitchell, the Pacers' most fearless shooter next to Miller.

PLAYMAKING: They don't come much better than Jackson, whose main emphasis is making everybody else play better. He usually gets the ball to the right man at the right time, whether in transition or the halfcourt game. Backup Haywoode Workman may get pushed by Best, who assumes the role of longtime Pacer favorite Vern Fleming.

That's about it for the Pacers' creativity. If Miller isn't catching and shooting, he isn't effective. The same goes for Smits. McKey is an above-average passer, but he tends to make mistakes at the most inopportune times.

The key is the coaching of Brown. His teams pass well because it is demanded of them.

REBOUNDING: Overshadowed in the Pacers' Game 7 defeat at Orlando in the Eastern Conference finals was the brilliance of Dale Davis, who took 15 rebounds from a team that featured Horace Grant and Shaquille O'Neal. And that was with a bad right shoulder, which required surgery after the season. Three times it popped out of place, the last time during the playoffs. He played anyway, with the benefit of a harness.

Nor was it smooth sailing for the Pacers' other Davis, Antonio. He missed 37 games with a bad back, forcing Smits to hit the boards harder—and he did, averaging a career-best 7.7 rebounds per game. What the Davises and Smits don't get often ends up in the hands of the 6-10 McKey. Miller and Jackson are solid rebounders for their positions, making the Pacers a tough team to deal with even when they're not shooting well.

PACER ROSTER

No.	Veterans	Pos.	Ht.	Wt.	Age	Yrs. Pro	College
R-22	Damon Bailey	G	6-3	201	24	1	Indiana
33	Antonio Davis	F-C	6-9	230	27	2	Texas-El Paso
32	Dale Davis	F	6-11	230	26	4	Clemson
27	Duane Ferrell	F	6-7	215	30	7	Georgia Tech
U-10	Vern Fleming	G	6-5	185	33	11	Georgia
44	Scott Haskin	F	6-11	250	25	1	Oregon State
13	Mark Jackson	G	6-1	180	30	8	St. John's
U-54	Greg Kite	C	6-11	263	34	12	Brigham Young
9	Derrick McKey	F	6-10	225	29	8	Alabama
31	Reggie Miller	G	6-7	185	30	8	UCLA
U-5	Sam Mitchell	F	6-7	210	32	6	Mercer
45	Rik Smits	C	7-4	265	29	7	Marist
U-41	LaSalle Thompson	F-C	6-10	260	34	13	Texas
U-3	Haywoode Workman	G	6-3	180	29	4	Oral Roberts

R-restricted free agent
U-unrestricted free agent

Rd.	Rookies	Sel.No.	Pos.	Ht.	Wt.	College
1	Travis Best	23	G	5-11	182	Georgia Tech
2	Fred Hoiberg	52	G	6-4	203	Iowa State

DEFENSE: The only wink link in the Pacers' defense is Jackson, who has trouble moving quickly in any direction, but especially laterally. When Jackson's shortcomings affect the Pacers' scheme, Brown simply turns to Workman.

Losing 25 pounds did wonders for Smits, but he remains foul-prone. Two quick ones and he's on the bench. Fortunately for the Pacers, both Davises play decent defense on centers—even the ones as big as O'Neal and as quick as Hakeem Olajuwon.

McKey is a small forward's worst nightmare—tall, rangy and persistent. He was especially bothersome to Pistons rookie Grant Hill, who was co-winner of Rookie of the Year. McKey is one of the main reasons why Hill spent most of the summer honing his jumper.

OUTLOOK: The Pacers are at the crossroads, which must be a frightening proposition for Brown and Miller—the two who have the most to lose if the Pacers are to the '90s what Mike Fratello's Hawks were to the '80s. The Hawks won 50 or more games for four straight seasons, and had nothing to show for it.

Taking the next step will require much more from Miller, who had a so-so regular season and then totally disappeared in Game 7 against the Magic. Miller must dominate from beginning to end, and the Davises must stay healthy. And it wouldn't be asking too much for Smits to pick it up another notch, either.

PACER PROFILES

REGGIE MILLER 30 6-7 185   Guard

Was where he wanted to be, back in Game 7 of Eastern Conference finals—a chance to atone for scoreless fourth quarter of Pacers' loss to Knicks in '94 conference final. Again goes scoreless in fourth, gets only 13 in 105-81 loss to Magic... Not good, especially after referring to Knicks as "choke artists" in previous series. Said that after scoring Pacers' last eight points in 18.9 seconds of Game 1... Has replaced Vinnie Johnson as game's best catch-it-and-shoot-it scorer. Also a terrific slasher, when motivated... Still had a tendency to stick foot in mouth, as evidenced by comment about Knicks... First player in NBA history to make 100 or more three-pointers in six straight seasons. Made 195 last season, a team record. Has 1,035 triples, second only to Dale Ellis' 1,119... Top five in free-throw shooting (.897), but failed to get 100 steals for first time in six years... Born Aug. 24, 1965, in Riverside, Cal.... Made $3.2 million in 1994-95... Was 11th pick, out of UCLA, in '87.

Year	Team	G	FG	FG Pct.	FT	FT Pct.	Reb.	Ast.	TP	Avg.
1987-88	Indiana	82	306	.488	149	.801	190	132	822	10.0
1988-89	Indiana	74	398	.479	287	.844	292	227	1181	16.0
1989-90	Indiana	82	661	.514	544	.868	295	311	2016	24.6
1990-91	Indiana	82	596	.512	551	.918	281	331	1855	22.6
1991-92	Indiana	82	562	.501	442	.858	318	314	1695	20.7
1992-93	Indiana	82	571	.479	427	.880	258	262	1736	21.2
1993-94	Indiana	79	524	.503	403	.908	212	248	1574	19.9
1994-95	Indiana	81	505	.462	383	.897	210	242	1588	19.6
	Totals	644	4123	.493	3186	.879	2056	2067	12467	19.4

RIK SMITS 29 7-4 265   Center

Opened eyes in seven-game duel with Knicks' Patrick Ewing, leading Pacers in scoring (22.6) and shooting (60 percent). Also fared well against Orlando Magic bully Shaquille O'Neal when zebras weren't blowing their whistles... Improvement traced to weight loss. Trimming down took pressure off knees, allowed more time in games and practices... If gets good

208 • **THE COMPLETE HANDBOOK OF PRO BASKETBALL**

low-post position, will score at will. If not, can hit mid-range jumper... More vocal about getting the ball, especially in clutch situations... Beat Magic with last-second shot in overtime of Game 4... Becoming a much better rebounder, but still prone to fouls... Career highs in scoring (17.9) and rebounding (7.7), second on the team in blocks (79) and shooting (.526)... Scored 30 or more points six times... Born Aug. 23, 1966, in Eindhoven, Holland. Hence nickname: "The Dunkin' Dutchman"... Was No. 2 pick, out of Marist, in 1988... Made $3.25 million in 1994-95.

Year	Team	G	FG	FG Pct.	FT	FT Pct.	Reb.	Ast.	TP	Avg.
1988-89	Indiana	82	386	.517	184	.722	500	70	956	11.7
1989-90	Indiana	82	515	.533	241	.811	512	142	1271	15.5
1990-91	Indiana	76	342	.485	144	.762	357	84	828	10.9
1991-92	Indiana	74	436	.510	152	.788	417	116	1024	13.8
1992-93	Indiana	81	494	.486	167	.732	432	121	1155	14.3
1993-94	Indiana	78	493	.534	238	.793	483	156	1224	15.7
1994-95	Indiana	78	558	.526	284	.753	601	111	1400	17.9
	Totals	551	3224	.514	1410	.767	3302	800	7858	14.3

DALE DAVIS 26 6-11 230   Forward

Only Pacer to rise to the occasion in Game 7 vs. Magic. Played possessed, getting 14 points and 15 rebounds... And that was with a bad right shoulder, upon which doctors operated after the season. Popped out of socket several times during the season, including playoffs... Was third in conference in shooting percentage (.563) behind Shaquille O'Neal and Horace Grant. True, many of his attempts were no-chance-of-missing dunks. But is improving around the basket... For third straight season, blocked over 100 shots... First Pacer to get 20 or more rebounds three times... Had 27 double-doubles, best on team... Was 13th pick, out of Clemson, in '91... ACC's leading rebounder for three straight seasons... Born March 25, 1969, in Toccoa, Ga.... Salary jumped from $688,000 in 1993-94 to $4.05 million last year.

Year	Team	G	FG	FG Pct.	FT	FT Pct.	Reb.	Ast.	TP	Avg.
1991-92	Indiana	64	154	.552	87	.572	410	30	395	6.2
1992-93	Indiana	82	304	.568	119	.529	723	69	727	8.9
1993-94	Indiana	66	308	.529	87	.529	718	100	771	11.7
1994-95	Indiana	74	324	.563	138	.533	696	58	786	10.6
	Totals	286	1090	.553	499	.537	2547	257	2679	9.4

MARK JACKSON 30 6-1 180   Guard

Went through some growing pains, which is mandatory with Larry Brown, but delivered in last month of season and in playoffs... Improved turnover ratio from 2.48-1 in the first 47 games to 3.75 to one. Twice had games of 17 assists... Remains a liability on defense, incapable of keeping up with the Kenny Andersons of the NBA... Rescued from the Clippers, escaping before the crash. Pacers sent Malik Sealy, Pooh Richardson and a No. 1 (Eric Piatkowski) to Clippers for Jackson and the rights to Greg Minor... Had been dispatched to the Clips after five-year stint in New York. That deal resulted in new homes for Stanley Roberts (Orlando to Clippers) and Charles Smith (Clippers to N.Y.)... Born April 1, 1965, in Brooklyn, N.Y.... Was 18th pick, out of St. John's, in '87... Made $2.3 million in 1994-95.

Year	Team	G	FG	FG Pct.	FT	FT Pct.	Reb.	Ast.	TP	Avg.
1987-88	New York	82	438	.432	206	.774	396	868	1114	13.6
1988-89	New York	72	479	.467	180	.698	341	619	1219	16.9
1989-90	New York	82	327	.437	120	.727	318	604	809	9.9
1990-91	New York	72	250	.492	117	.731	197	452	630	8.8
1991-92	New York	81	367	.491	171	.770	305	694	916	11.3
1992-93	L.A. Clippers	82	459	.486	241	.803	388	724	1181	14.4
1993-94	L.A. Clippers	79	331	.452	167	.791	348	678	865	10.9
1994-95	Indiana	82	239	.422	119	.778	306	616	624	7.6
	Totals	632	2890	.460	1321	.761	2599	5255	7358	11.6

ANTONIO DAVIS 27 6-9 230   Forward-Center

Sidelined from early December to mid-February with ruptured disc, forcing Pacers to hold their breath for 37 games. Before surgery, shot 39 percent in 13 games. After surgery, shot 46 percent and averaged 7.9 points and 6.2 rebounds... No relation to Dale, but the same type of player—tough, smart, relentless ... Drafted out of UTEP in second round of '90 draft, but opted for three years in Europe. No word on how many foreigners he demoralized... Came home with a nice 15-foot jumper, but not nearly enough post-up moves... Had best game against Philly: 17 points, 7-7 from field... Second-best game: March 15 against Milwaukee. Didn't play. Went instead to hospital for birth of twins... Born Oct. 31, 1968, in Oakland... Made $700,000 in 1994-95.

Year	Team	G	FG	FG Pct.	FT	FT Pct.	Reb.	Ast.	TP	Avg.
1993-94	Indiana	81	216	.508	194	.642	505	55	626	7.7
1994-95	Indiana	44	109	.445	117	.672	280	25	335	7.6
	Totals	125	325	.485	311	.653	785	80	961	7.7

HAYWOODE WORKMAN 29 6-3 180   Guard

Still can't shoot, which is why Pacers obtained Mark Jackson. But Larry Brown hustles him into the game when Jackson is getting lit up. Shot just 38 percent, 36 from outside the arc ... Did best work in November, when Jackson struggled with the system. Averaged 5.8 points and 4.1 assists in first 12 games... Has been called a poor man's Terry Porter, and that about covers it... The strong, silent type, with a great attitude and solid work habits... Took a while to find a niche. Second-round pick by Hawks, out of Oral Roberts, in 1989... Appeared in just six games, then joined Bullets for 73 in 1990-91... Signed with Pacers in 1993 after two years in Italy... Born Jan. 23, 1966, in Charlotte... Made $400,000 in 1994-95.

Year	Team	G	FG	FG Pct.	FT	FT Pct.	Reb.	Ast.	TP	Avg.
1989-90	Atlanta	6	2	.667	2	1.000	3	2	6	1.0
1990-91	Washington	73	234	.454	101	.759	242	353	581	8.0
1993-94	Indiana	65	195	.424	93	.802	204	404	501	7.7
1994-95	Indiana	69	101	.375	55	.743	111	194	292	4.2
	Totals	213	532	.427	251	.772	560	953	1380	6.5

DERRICK McKEY 29 6-10 225   Forward

Nothing new here. Continues to tease with size, skill and versatility... Defense is the only constant, which is fine by Larry Brown, his biggest fan... Led Pacers with 125 steals, three times getting five in a game... Averaged 13.3 points, up from 12.0... Ended streak that saw his average drop for five straight seasons ... Again second on the team in assists, with 3.5... Logged 2,805 minutes, most on team... Delivered in Game 7 against Knicks, getting 14 points and seven assists in 39 minutes... Came to Pacers in November 1993 with Gerald Paddio for Detlef Schrempf, a favorite among Pacers' fans... Born Oct. 10, 1966, in Meridian, Miss.... Was drafted ninth, by Seattle, in '87... Played at Alabama... Made $2.8 million in 1994-95.

Year	Team	G	FG	FG Pct.	FT	FT Pct.	Reb.	Ast.	TP	Avg.
1987-88	Seattle	82	255	.491	173	.772	328	107	694	8.5
1988-89	Seattle	82	487	.502	301	.803	464	219	1305	15.9
1989-90	Seattle	80	468	.493	315	.782	489	187	1254	15.7
1990-91	Seattle	73	438	.517	235	.845	423	169	1115	15.3
1991-92	Seattle	52	285	.472	188	.847	268	120	777	14.9
1992-93	Seattle	77	387	.496	220	.741	327	197	1034	13.4
1993-94	Indiana	76	355	.500	192	.756	402	327	911	12.0
1994-95	Indiana	81	411	.493	221	.744	394	276	1075	13.3
	Totals	603	3086	.497	1845	.785	3095	1602	8165	13.5

SCOTT HASKIN 25 6-11 250   Forward-Center

Still waiting... Recovered from knee problems, then back acted up. Underwent surgery, shelving him for season... Limited to 27 games and 186 minutes as a rookie, the result of a ruptured Achilles tendon... As they say, looks good in airport... Larry Brown likes his size and work habits, worries about heart... If he ever gets healthy, could be competent backup... Born Sept. 19, 1970, in Riverside, Cal.... Was 14th pick, out of Oregon State, in '93... Made $1.07 million in 1994-95.

Year	Team	G	FG	FG Pct.	FT	FT Pct.	Reb.	Ast.	TP	Avg.
1993-94	Indiana	27	21	.467	13	.684	55	6	55	2.0
1994-95	Indiana					Injured				
	Totals	27	21	.467	13	.684	55	6	55	2.0

SAM MITCHELL 32 6-7 210   Forward

There might not be a better ninth man in the league... Too small to play power forward, but does it anyway... Strengths are defense and rebounding, but isn't afraid to shoot, even from the perimeter. Shot a career-best .487... Sparked Pacers' comeback in Game 4 against Knicks with 11 points... Best stretch came early in 1993-94, when Pacers went 11-7 with him subbing for injured starter Dale Davis... Came to Pacers with Pooh Richardson from Minnesota for Chuck Person on Sept. 8, 1992... Was third-round pick, out of Mercer, by Houston in 1985. Never played game for Rockets... Played in CBA and France for four years before signing free-agent pact with expansion Wolves in July 1989... Born Sept. 1, 1963, in Columbus, Ga.... Made $850,000 in 1994-95.

Year	Team	G	FG	FG Pct.	FT	FT Pct.	Reb.	Ast.	TP	Avg.
1989-90	Minnesota	80	372	.446	268	.768	462	89	1012	12.7
1990-91	Minnesota	82	445	.441	307	.775	520	133	1197	14.6
1991-92	Minnesota	82	307	.423	209	.786	473	94	825	10.1
1992-93	Indiana	81	215	.445	150	.811	248	76	584	7.2
1993-94	Indiana	75	140	.458	82	.745	190	65	362	4.8
1994-95	Indiana	81	201	.487	126	.724	243	61	529	6.5
	Totals	481	1680	.446	1142	.772	2136	518	4509	9.4

DUANE FERRELL 30 6-7 215   Forward

Got off to a slow start, and never gained the confidence of Larry Brown... Averaged just 2.5 points and shot 32 percent the first two months of the season, some of which can be blamed on training-camp injuries... Picked it up the last 41 games, averaging 4.7 points and shooting 52 percent. But season high was just 11 points... Used to rely solely on slashing. Can now pull up and shoot it—in practice... Played six seasons with Hawks, topping out at 12.7 points per in 1991-92. Became expendable when Ken Norman arrived... Did some time in CBA before and after joining Hawks... Undrafted out of Georgia Tech in 1988... Born Feb. 28, 1965, in Baltimore... Made $650,000 in 1994-95.

Year	Team	G	FG	FG Pct.	FT	FT Pct.	Reb.	Ast.	TP	Avg.
1988-89	Atlanta	41	35	.422	30	.682	41	10	100	2.4
1989-90	Atlanta	14	5	.357	2	.333	7	2	12	0.9
1990-91	Atlanta	78	174	.489	125	.801	179	55	475	6.1
1991-92	Atlanta	66	331	.524	166	.761	210	92	839	12.7
1992-93	Atlanta	82	327	.470	176	.779	191	132	839	10.2
1993-94	Atlanta	72	184	.485	144	.783	129	65	513	7.1
1994-95	Indiana	56	83	.480	64	.753	88	31	231	4.1
	Totals	409	1139	.488	707	.769	845	387	3009	7.4

LaSALLE THOMPSON 34 6-10 260   Forward-Center

Season ended Feb. 18 with surgery for rotator-cuff tear of right shoulder. Could be the end of the road... Played just 453 minutes in 38 games, averaging 2.9 points and 2.3 rebounds. Had season highs of 13 points and six rebounds... Limited to 30 games in 1993-94 because of soreness in knees... Acquired with Randy Wittman from Sacramento for Wayman

INDIANA PACERS • 213

Tisdale and a second-rounder on Feb. 20, 1989 ... Born July 23, 1961, in Cincinnati ... Was fifth pick, out of Texas, in 1982 by Kings ... Made $2 million in 1994-95.

Year	Team	G	FG	FG Pct.	FT	FT Pct.	Reb.	Ast.	TP	Avg.
1982-83	Kansas City	71	147	.512	89	.650	375	33	383	5.4
1983-84	Kansas City	80	333	.523	160	.717	709	86	826	10.3
1984-85	Kansas City	82	369	.531	227	.721	854	130	965	11.8
1985-86	Sacramento	80	411	.518	202	.732	770	168	1024	12.8
1986-87	Sacramento	82	362	.481	188	.737	687	122	912	11.1
1987-88	Sacramento	69	215	.471	118	.720	427	68	550	8.0
1988-89	Sac.-Indiana	76	416	.489	227	.808	718	81	1059	13.9
1989-90	Indiana	82	223	.473	107	.799	630	106	554	6.8
1990-91	Indiana	82	276	.488	72	.692	563	147	625	7.6
1991-92	Indiana	80	168	.468	58	.817	381	102	394	4.9
1992-93	Indiana	63	104	.488	29	.744	178	34	237	3.8
1993-94	Indiana	30	27	.351	16	.533	75	16	70	2.3
1994-95	Indiana	38	49	.415	14	.875	89	18	112	2.9
	Totals	915	3100	.494	1507	.737	6456	1111	7711	8.4

DAMON BAILEY 24 6-3 201   Guard

All of Indiana waits, hoping Larry Brown will someday run the picket fence for this Hoosier prep legend ... Had surgery on both knees, missed entire season ... No room for him anyway, not with Reggie Miller and Byron Scott at shooting guard ... Losing Scott to the expansion draft creates opportunity, but that doesn't change the fact that he's probably too small and too slow ... Indiana's fifth all-time scorer, second in assists ... All-Big Ten ... Selected 44th in '94, much to the delight of Hoosier Dome crowd ... Born Oct. 21, 1971, in Bedford, Ind. ... Made $150,000 in 1994-95.

THE ROOKIES

TRAVIS BEST 23 5-11 182   Guard

Will battle Haywoode Workman for minutes behind Mark Jackson ... Drafted 23rd ... Joined Phil Ford as only ACC players to get more than 2,000 points and 600 assists in career ... Three-time All-ACC pick ... Career-high 32 points against East Carolina ... Averaged 20.2 points in senior season ... Born July 12, 1972, in Springfield, Mass.

FRED HOIBERG 23 6-4 203   Guard

Has toughest job of any rookie. If he succeeds, he'll take roster spot of Indiana legend Damon Bailey... Drafted No. 52, out of Iowa State. Folks in Ames call him "The Mayor"... Destroyed Colorado with 41 points. Until senior season, shot well over 50 percent... Made school-record 34 straight free throws... Born Oct. 15, 1972, in Lincoln, Neb. .

COACH LARRY BROWN: No happy feet yet, not after back-to-back trips to the Eastern Conference finals... Says next job will be in high school, when youngest son reaches that level... Remains one of the best teachers in the game, a fanatic for preparation and hard work. Trouble is, new rules have made the game too simple. Get a double-team in the post, swing it to one of the four players positioned around the three-point line... Opened with 47 wins, improved to 52 and the Pacers' first title—Central Division crown—since their ABA days... Happy as a lark with buddy Donnie Walsh, Pacer GM... Replaced Bob Hill after 1992-93 season... Made sense of the Clippers before that, going 64-53... Also a winner with San Antonio and New Jersey in the NBA, and Carolina and Denver in the ABA... Got his college teams to the Final Four three times, winning national championship with Kansas in '88... In 23 seasons, has had just one losing campaign... Pro record, including ABA, is 762-514... Was 177-61 in college, which included an improbable trip to the NCAA title game with UCLA... Played five years in ABA after leaving North Carolina... 1964 Olympic gold medalist... Born Sept. 14, 1940, in Brooklyn, N.Y.

GREATEST FIND

Without Antonio Davis, the Pacers don't go from pretender to contender. They don't take the New York Knicks to a seventh game in the '94 Eastern Conference finals, and they don't do it again last season, this time against the Orlando Magic.

Forty-four players went ahead of Davis, a 6-9 power forward, in the '90 draft. None of those 44 went to Europe for three sea-

INDIANA PACERS • 215

sons and returned a monster—as Davis did, much to the surprise of Pacers GM Donnie Walsh and coach Larry Brown.

Davis added strength, tenacity and the framework of an offensive game. He was the perfect complement to Dale Davis, able to fill in a power forward and center, when Rik Smits got in foul trouble. He averaged 7.7 points and 6.2 rebounds in his first season, and appeared in the NBA's first Rookie All-Star Game.

And had Davis not missed 37 games with a back injury last season, the Pacers may have been a 60-win team.

ALL-TIME PACER LEADERS

SEASON

Points: George McGinnis, 2,353, 1974–75 (ABA)
Billy Knight, 2,075, 1976–77
Assists: Don Buse, 689, 1975–76 (ABA)
Don Buse, 685, 1976–77
Rebounds: Mel Daniels, 1,475, 1970–71 (ABA)
Clark Kellogg, 860, 1982–83

GAME

Points: George McGinnis, 58 vs. Dallas, 11/28/72 (ABA)
Reggie Miller, 57 vs. Charlotte, 11/28/92
Assists: Don Buse, 20 vs. Denver, 3/26/76 (ABA)
Vern Fleming, 18 vs. Houston, 11/23/90
Micheal Williams, 18 vs. New York 11/13/91
Rebounds: George McGinnis, 37 vs. Carolina, 1/12/71 (ABA)
Herb Williams, 29 vs. Denver, 1/23/89

CAREER

Points: Billy Knight, 10,780, 1974–83 (ABA and NBA)
Reggie Miller, 12,467, 1987–95
Assists: Vern Fleming, 4,038, 1984–95
Don Buse, 2,747, 1972–77, 1980–82 (ABA)
Rebounds: Mel Daniels, 7,622, 1968–74 (ABA)
Herb Williams, 4,494, 1981–89

MILWAUKEE BUCKS

TEAM DIRECTORY: Pres.: Herb Kohl; VP-Bus. Oper.: John Steinmiller; VP-Basketball Oper./Head Coach: Mike Dunleavy; VP-Player Personnel: Lee Rose; Dir. Pub. Rel.: Bill King II; Asst. Coaches: Frank Hamblen, Jim Eyen, Butch Carter. Arena: Bradley Center (18,633). Colors: Hunter green, purple and silver.

SCOUTING REPORT

SHOOTING: Heaven help the Central Division this season, and everybody else in the NBA in the near future. The Bucks added the perfect accessory to a team featuring frontcourt threats Vin Baker and Glenn (Big Dog) Robinson with the acquisition of Michigan State rookie Shawn Respert, considered by many the best pure shooter coming out of college.

So if you're going to double up on Baker or Robinson, be prepared to surrender more than a few three-point jumpers to Respert or point guard Eric Murdock, who led the Bucks in scoring in 1993-94, Baker's rookie season. Arkansas products Todd Day and Lee Mayberry also have three-point range.

Robinson prefers taking players off the dribble or pulling up for jumpers, but he can play with his back to the basket. The same goes for Baker and top reserve Marty Conlon, who deserved Most Improved Player consideration and may make a run for the Sixth Man award.

Veteran Johnny Newman can also fill it up.

PLAYMAKING: If there is a problem with the Bucks, this will probably be it. Murdock has had trouble shaking his scorer's mentality. That forced coach Mike Dunleavy to take a closer look at Mayberry, a smaller version of Murdock.

If things don't improve, Dunleavy might try Respert at the point. Respert played there in high school, but that was five years ago. Respert thinks he can make the transition, and his ball-handling seems good enough. But like Murdock, Respert would probably put shooting ahead of creating.

REBOUNDING: Baker is a solid rebounder (10.3, 12th in the league), but he's hardly a banger. He does it with size and finesse and uncommon hustle, so there's no complaints there. If only he were big and mean and nasty, in the mold of a Charles Oakley, Dale Davis or Tyrone Hill.

Milwaukee's finest, Vin Baker has the right stuff.

Baker will have to do until the Bucks find a force in the middle. Right now, they have to settle for aging veteran Alton Lister and two projects—Eric Mobley, a first-rounder in 1994, and Wisconsin rookie Rashard Griffith, their second-round pick this season.

BUCK ROSTER

No.	Veterans	Pos.	Ht.	Wt.	Age	Yrs. Pro	College
42	Vin Baker	F	6-11	234	23	2	Hartford
R-17	Jon Barry	G	6-5	195	26	3	Georgia Tech
U-30	Marty Conlon	F	6-11	245	27	4	Providence
10	Todd Day	G-F	6-6	200	25	3	Arkansas
–	Andrei Fetisov	F	6-10	225	23	0	Russia
U-12	Tate George	G	6-5	208	27	4	Connecticut
–	Roy Hinson	F-C	6-9	215	34	12	Rutgers
–	Voshon Lenard	G	6-4	205	22	0	Minnesota
U-53	Alton Lister	C	7-0	255	37	13	Arizona State
R-11	Lee Mayberry	G	6-1	175	25	3	Arkansas
52	Eric Mobley	C	6-10	250	25	1	Pittsburgh
R-5	Eric Murdock	G	6-1	190	27	4	Providence
U-22	Johnny Newman	F	6-7	205	31	9	Richmond
13	Glenn Robinson	F	6-7	225	22	1	Purdue

R-restricted free agent
U-unrestricted free agent

Rd.	Rookies	Sel.No.	Pos.	Ht.	Wt.	College
1	Shawn Respert	8	G	6-3	195	Michigan State
2	Rashard Griffith	31	C	6-11	270	Wisconsin
2	Eurelejus Zukauskas	54	C	7-1	220	Lithuania

Mobley averaged just 3.3 rebounds, but 5.1 in 26 starts. That was still a lower average than Conlon (5.2). Griffith led the Big Ten in rebounding last season, but he might be too young, too slow and too overweight to keep up.

DEFENSE: Lots of work is needed here. The Bucks surrendered 103.7 points a game, and opponents shot a hefty .493 from the field. Opponents didn't get to the line that often, but that's because there wasn't that much resistance. Mobley arrived with the reputation as a shot-blocker but got only 27 in 46 appearances.

Newman might be the Bucks' best one-on-one defender, but he's a bit undersized—as is Respert, who is listed at 6-3 but is closer to 6-1. Murdock and Mayberry also get pushed around, but there's no problem with Day's size (6-6). It's his attitude and intensity that need work.

OUTLOOK: Respert and Griffith fill two major needs, but they don't improve the Bucks defensively. And until the Bucks upgrade their defense, they won't be championship contenders. They could use a few more players like Newman—solid veterans who could set good examples for their young superstars.

BUCK PROFILES

VIN BAKER 23 6-11 234   Forward

Was thought to be too skinny, too frail, too meek... Didn't they say the same thing about George Gervin?... Took all of 1½ years to play in All-Star Game. Should be a regular for about the next 10 years... Great instincts, touch and attitude. A load at both ends of the court... Among the top 30 in scoring (17.7, 30th), rebounds (10.3, 12) and blocks (1.41, 21). Second among Bucks in assists (3.6), fourth in steals (1.05)... Was first Buck since Jack Sikma to average a double-double... Got first Bucks' triple-double (12 points, 12 rebounds, 12 assists vs. Hornets) since Alvin Robertson did it in 1990-91... New career highs: 31 points, 18 rebounds... Was eighth pick, out of Hartford, in '93. Went after, among others, Isaiah Rider, Calbert Cheaney and Bobby Hurley... Born Nov. 23, 1971, in Lake Wales, Fla.... Made $1.06 million in 1994-95.

Year	Team	G	FG	FG Pct.	FT	FT Pct.	Reb.	Ast.	TP	Avg.
1993-94	Milwaukee	82	435	.501	234	.569	621	163	1105	13.5
1994-95	Milwaukee	82	594	.483	256	.593	846	296	1451	17.7
	Totals	164	1029	.490	490	.581	1467	459	2556	15.6

GLENN ROBINSON 22 6-7 225   Forward

Should have had a piece of Rookie of the Year, but spent season insulting voters and grousing about all the attention Grant Hill was getting... Mistake, especially after his agent asks for $100 million... So instead of dwelling on the positive—21.9 scoring, 6.4 rebounds, 1.44 steals—much is made of his negative, 3.9 turnovers... Born to score, from any distance... After slow start—due to holdout—claimed Rookie of the Month honors in December and April... Took just 49 games to score 1,000 points. Only Kareem Abdul-Jabbar did it quicker (35) in Bucks history... Scored 21 points in Rookie All-Star Game, but MVP went to Eddie Jones. Moped about that, too... Was first player taken, out of Purdue, in '94... Led nation in scoring (30.3) as junior... Fifteenth player in NCAA history to score

1,000 points in single season... Born Jan. 10, 1973, in Gary, Ind. ... Made $2.9 million in 1994-95.

Year	Team	G	FG	FG Pct.	FT	FT Pct.	Reb.	Ast.	TP	Avg.
1994-95	Milwaukee	80	636	.451	397	.796	513	197	1755	21.9

TODD DAY 25 6-6 200   Guard

Should change last name to Night. Is completely in the dark... At one point complained about not being a bigger part of the offense. Hasn't dawned on him that Glenn Robinson and Vin Baker are pretty good... Bucks would love to move him, but there's not a big market for knuckleheads... Numbers looked good, though—16.0 points, 3.9 rebounds and 1.27 steals. Launched 418 three-point jumpers, shot a respectable .390... Likes to talk trash to everybody, but seldom gets within shouting distance on defense... Left Arkansas as Razorbacks' all-time scorer (2,395), passing former Bucks great Sidney Moncrief... Born Jan. 7, 1970, in Memphis, Tenn.... Was eighth pick in '92... Made $2.12 million in 1994-95.

Year	Team	G	FG	FG Pct.	FT	FT Pct.	Reb.	Ast.	TP	Avg.
1992-93	Milwaukee	71	358	.432	213	.717	291	117	983	13.8
1993-94	Milwaukee	76	351	.415	231	.698	310	138	966	12.7
1994-95	Milwaukee	82	445	.424	257	.754	322	134	1310	16.0
	Totals	229	1154	.424	701	.723	923	389	3259	14.2

ERIC MURDOCK 27 6-1 190   Guard

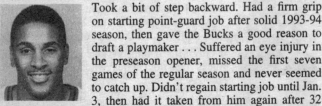

Took a bit of step backward. Had a firm grip on starting point-guard job after solid 1993-94 season, then gave the Bucks a good reason to draft a playmaker... Suffered an eye injury in the preseason opener, missed the first seven games of the regular season and never seemed to catch up. Didn't regain starting job until Jan. 3, then had it taken from him again after 32 games...Was Bucks' leading scorer in 1993-94, and had a hard time shaking shooter's mentality... Also lost his zip on defense, dropping from 197 to 113 steals... Rescued from shadow of John Stockton on June 24, 1992. Bucks got him and Blue Edwards from Utah for Jay Humphries and Larry Krystkowiak...

Was Jazz's 21st pick, out of Providence, in '91 . . . Born June 14, 1968, in Somerville, N.J. . . . Made $1 million in 1994-95.

Year	Team	G	FG	FG Pct.	FT	FT Pct.	Reb.	Ast.	TP	Avg.
1991-92	Utah	50	76	.415	46	.754	54	92	203	4.1
1992-93	Milwaukee	79	438	.468	231	.780	284	603	1138	14.4
1993-94	Milwaukee	82	477	.468	234	.813	261	546	1257	15.3
1994-95	Milwaukee	75	338	.415	211	.790	214	482	977	13.0
	Totals	286	1329	.450	722	.792	813	1723	3575	12.5

LEE MAYBERRY 25 6-1 175 — Guard

Cut into Eric Murdock's minutes by improving his defense and three-point shooting (from 35 to 40 percent) . . . Still gets knocked around by bigger and stronger point guards, of which there are many . . . Kept Murdock on the bench with two solid November performances: 14 points and 10 assists on the 18th, a career-high 22 points on the 19th . . . Persistent, patient and durable. Hasn't missed a game in three seasons, a streak of 246 games. That's the seventh-longest current streak in NBA . . . Managed to leave Arkansas with head on straight, despite playing with Todd Day and Oliver Miller . . . Left school as all-time assists leader . . . Was 23rd pick in '92 . . . Born June 12, 1970, in Tulsa, Okla. . . . Made $820,000 in 1994-95.

Year	Team	G	FG	FG Pct.	FT	FT Pct.	Reb.	Ast.	TP	Avg.
1992-93	Milwaukee	82	171	.456	39	.574	118	273	424	5.2
1993-94	Milwaukee	82	167	.415	58	.690	101	215	433	5.3
1994-95	Milwaukee	82	172	.422	58	.699	82	276	474	5.8
	Totals	246	510	.430	155	.660	301	764	1331	5.4

JON BARRY 26 6-5 195 — Guard

If only Mike Dunleavy loved him as much as Bucks' fans do. Dunleavy not impressed by his reckless abandon, as evidenced by 30 DNP-CDs . . . Only Bucks guard truly interested in passing. Got 10 of his 85 assists against the Lakers in November . . . Obviously didn't win any brownie points as a kid, when rebounding for Dunleavy during practice sessions in Houston . . . Father, Rick, is a Hall of Famer. Three brothers have played Division I hoops . . . Born July 25, 1969, in Oakland . . .

Was 21st pick, out of Georgia Tech, by Celtics in '92. Held out and was traded with second-rounder to Bucks for forward Alaa Abdelnaby, Dec. 4, 1992... Made $800,000 in 1994-95.

Year	Team	G	FG	FG Pct.	FT	FT Pct.	Reb.	Ast.	TP	Avg.
1992-93	Milwaukee	47	76	.369	33	.673	43	68	206	4.4
1993-94	Milwaukee	72	158	.414	97	.795	146	168	445	6.2
1994-95	Milwaukee	52	57	.425	61	.763	49	85	191	3.7
	Totals	171	291	.403	191	.761	238	321	842	4.9

MARTY CONLON 27 6-11 245   Forward

Should make the cover of CBA media guide, as one of the league's more improbable success stories... If improvement continues, will be Sixth Man candidate this year or next... Did everything well, especially the hustle part... Established career bests in scoring (9.9) and rebounding (5.2), and shot .532... Career-best 22 points vs. Pistons... Stuck with Bucks after stops in Charlotte, Washington, Sacramento and Seattle. Also played parts of two seasons in CBA, setting up a return to the big league with a 20-point scoring average in 21 games with Rockford in 1993-94... Born Jan. 19, 1968, in the Bronx, N.Y. ... Played at Providence, undrafted in '90... Made $182,500 in 1994-95.

Year	Team	G	FG	FG Pct.	FT	FT Pct.	Reb.	Ast.	TP	Avg.
1991-92	Seattle	45	48	.475	24	.750	69	12	120	2.7
1992-93	Sacramento	46	81	.474	57	.704	123	37	219	4.8
1993-94	Char.-Wash.	30	95	.576	43	.811	139	34	233	7.8
1994-95	Milwaukee	82	344	.532	119	.613	426	110	815	9.9
	Totals	203	568	.524	243	.675	757	193	1387	6.8

ALTON LISTER 37 7-0 255   Center

It is alive... Decided to play again after almost two years off. Why not? Makes just as much sense as Tree Rollins splitting time between assistant coach and player... Besides, had scheduled a June wedding and needed the dough to impress new wife... Played more games (60) than in 1991-92 and 1992-93 combined (46)... Did OK, averaging 2.8 points and 3.9 rebounds in 12.9 minutes... Twice scored 10 points in a game, and had 13 rebounds against Philly... Good influence on young Bucks... Was 21st pick, out of Arizona State, by

Bucks ... Thirteen-year career included stops in Seattle and Golden State. Had best season with Sonics, averaging 11.6 points and 9.4 rebounds in 1986-87 ... Born Oct. 1, 1958, in Dallas ... Made $160,000 in 1994-95.

Year	Team	G	FG	FG Pct.	FT	FT Pct.	Reb.	Ast.	TP	Avg.
1981-82	Milwaukee	80	149	.519	64	.520	387	84	362	4.5
1982-83	Milwaukee	80	272	.529	130	.537	568	111	674	8.4
1983-84	Milwaukee	82	256	.500	114	.626	603	110	626	7.6
1984-85	Milwaukee	81	322	.538	154	.588	647	127	798	9.9
1985-86	Milwaukee	81	318	.551	160	.602	592	101	796	9.8
1986-87	Seattle	75	346	.504	179	.675	705	110	871	11.6
1987-88	Seattle	82	173	.504	114	.606	627	58	461	5.6
1988-89	Seattle	82	271	.499	115	.646	545	54	657	8.0
1989-90	Golden State	3	4	.500	4	.571	8	2	12	4.0
1990-91	Golden State	77	188	.478	115	.569	483	93	491	6.4
1991-92	Golden State	26	44	.557	14	.424	92	14	102	3.9
1992-93	Golden State	20	19	.452	7	.538	44	5	45	2.3
1994-95	Milwaukee	60	66	.493	35	.500	236	12	167	2.8
	Totals	829	2428	.515	1205	.593	5537	881	6062	7.3

JOHNNY NEWMAN 31 6-7 205   Forward-Guard

Played a bigger role than expected, considering his original assignment was backing up Glenn Robinson. If Big Dog doesn't get in foul trouble, that's an eight-minute job ... Ended up making a spare part of shooting guard Jon Barry ... Hasn't lost any of his explosiveness, but size is sometimes a problem at small forward ... Consistent scorer, competent defender ... Closer line makes him a three-point option, though not a main one ... Played in all 82, averaging 7.7 points—lowest since rookie season with Cavs (5.0) ... Led Bucks in steals 11 times ... Born Nov. 28, 1963, in Danville, Va. ... Second-round pick, out of Richmond, by Cavs in '86 ... Signed as free agent by Knicks in '87, by Hornets in '90 ... Made $300,000 in 1994-95.

Year	Team	G	FG	FG Pct.	FT	FT Pct.	Reb.	Ast.	TP	Avg.
1986-87	Cleveland	59	113	.411	66	.868	70	27	293	5.0
1987-88	New York	77	270	.435	207	.841	159	62	773	10.0
1988-89	New York	81	455	.475	286	.815	206	162	1293	16.0
1989-90	New York	80	374	.476	239	.799	191	180	1032	12.9
1990-91	Charlotte	81	478	.470	385	.809	254	188	1371	16.9
1991-92	Charlotte	55	295	.477	236	.766	179	146	839	15.3
1992-93	Charlotte	64	279	.522	194	.808	143	117	764	11.9
1993-94	Char.-N.J.	81	313	.471	182	.809	180	72	832	10.3
1994-95	Milwaukee	82	226	.463	137	.801	173	91	634	7.7
	Totals	660	2803	.470	1932	.808	1555	1045	7831	11.9

Portland nailed Michigan State's Shawn Respert (No. 8).

ERIC MOBLEY 25 6-10 250   Center

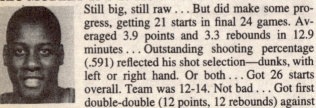

Still big, still raw... But did make some progress, getting 21 starts in final 24 games. Averaged 3.9 points and 3.3 rebounds in 12.9 minutes... Outstanding shooting percentage (.591) reflected his shot selection—dunks, with left or right hand. Or both... Got 26 starts overall. Team was 12-14. Not bad... Got first double-double (12 points, 12 rebounds) against Bullets... Came in with rep as shot-blocker, but got only 27... Had 73 rejects as senior at Pittsburgh, earning him third-team All-Big East... Born Feb. 1, 1970, in the Bronx, N.Y.... Made $620,000 in 1994-95.

Year	Team	G	FG	FG Pct.	FT	FT Pct.	Reb.	Ast.	TP	Avg.
1994-95	Milwaukee	46	78	.591	22	.489	153	21	180	3.9

THE ROOKIES

SHAWN RESPERT 23 6-3 195 Guard
Drafted eighth by Portland, traded to Bucks for 11th pick Gary Trent... Big Ten Player of the Year at Michigan State after averaging 25.6 points... Considered the best pure shooter in the draft... Recovered from knee injury that limited him to one game in 1990-91... Listed at 6-3, not much taller than 6-1... Born Feb. 6, 1972, in Detroit.

RASHARD GRIFFITH 21 6-11 270 Center
Left after sophomore season at Wisconsin... Led Big Ten in rebounding and blocks, but scouts had their doubts... Needs work on conditioning, quickness and work habits... Two-year averages: 15.6 points, 9.7 rebounds... Went in second round, at 31... Nailed Purdue with 29 points and 16 rebounds... Born Oct. 8, 1974, in Chicago.

COACH MIKE DUNLEAVY: Honeymoon can't be over...  Four years remain on eight-year deal that also includes VP of basketball operations title... Bucks jumped from 20 to 34 victories, and should make a run at a playoff spot in weak East... Biggest accomplishments: getting Vin Baker with the eighth pick of '93 draft, signing CBA refugee Marty Conlon... Good with a chalkboard... Left Bucks in '90 to coach the Lakers. Not a bad move. Guided them to 58-win season and a Finals matchup against Michael Jordan's Bulls... Fell to 43-39 the following season, but without Magic. Parlayed that into megadeal with Bucks... Played nine seasons in NBA, plus two more as player-assistant. Basically a journeyman, with an 8.0 scoring average... Most notable accomplishment: led NBA in three-point shooting in '83... Was sixth-round pick, out of South Carolina, by Sixers in '76... Born March 21, 1954, in Brooklyn, N.Y.

GREATEST FIND

Flip a coin.

It's either Bob Dandridge or Jon McGlocklin, key members of Milwaukee's 1970-71 championship team—the only title team in Bucks history, the one with Kareem Abdul-Jabbar in the middle.

That team won 66 games, then breezed through the playoffs. After eliminating San Francisco and Los Angeles in five games, the Bucks swept Baltimore in four straight—with Dandridge averaging 19.2 points and McGlocklin averaging 14.9.

With the 13th pick in the 1968 expansion draft, they nabbed McGlocklin from San Diego, originally a third-round pick from Cincinnati. Dandridge was the Bucks' fourth-round pick in '69, behind Abdul-Jabbar, Rutgers' Bob Greacen and East Tennessee State's Harley Swift.

Dandridge averaged 18.6 points in nine seasons, McGlocklin 12.6 in eight seasons.

Edge: Dandridge.

ALL-TIME BUCK LEADERS

SEASON

Points: Kareem Abdul-Jabbar, 2,822, 1971-72
Assists: Oscar Robertson, 668, 1970-71
Rebounds: Kareem Abdul-Jabbar, 1,346, 1971-72

GAME

Points: Kareem Abdul-Jabbar, 55 vs. Boston, 12/10/71
Assists: Guy Rodgers, 22 vs. Detroit, 10/31/68
Rebounds: Swen Nater, 33 vs. Atlanta, 12/19/76

CAREER

Points: Kareem Abdul-Jabbar, 14,211, 1969-75
Assists: Paul Pressey, 3,272, 1982-90
Rebounds: Kareem Abdul-Jabbar, 7,161, 1969-75

TORONTO RAPTORS

TEAM DIRECTORY: Pres.: John Bitove; Exec. VP-Basketball: Isiah Thomas; Exec. Dir. Communications: John Lashway; Communications Mgr.: Elaine McKeracher; Coach: Brendan Malone; Asst. Coaches: John Shumate, Darrell Walker, Bob Zuffelato. Arena: SkyDome (22,911). Colors: Red, purple, black and silver.

SCOUTING REPORT

SHOOTING: Raptors general manager Isiah Thomas drafted point guard Damon Stoudamire for his ability to create for others, but the Arizona product may have to carry the scoring load for a while. Of the players the Raptors obtained in the expansion and

Ex-Bull B.J. Armstrong: First pick in expansion draft.

college drafts, and trades, the only sure thing appears to be Jerome Kersey and B.J. Armstrong (provided he's not traded).

But Kersey, a long-time star with Portland, shot just 42 percent from the field last season. If he doesn't have one good season left in him, the Raptors might have to rely on unknowns for perimeter scoring—Stoudamire, former Sixers point guard B.J. Tyler, former Warriors guard Keith Jennings and their second-round pick, Michigan's Jimmy King.

They might have more success inside, with the likes of former Pistons John Salley and Oliver Miller, though coach Brendan Malone says Miller probably won't play until December or January—after he gets his weight under control. Former Mav Doug Smith might respond to new scenery, and Malone is itching to work with ex-Sonic Dontonio Wingfield.

PLAYMAKING: Thomas sees a lot of himself in Stoudamire, who led the Wildcats to a pair of Pac-10 titles and a trip to the 1994 Final Four. That means Stoudamire is quick and fearless, a player Thomas said will make those around him much better.

There are questions about Stoudamire's size—5-10, 171 pounds—but he's a giant compared to the 5-7, 160-pound Jennings, who finished 10th in the league in assist-to-turnover ratio. Tyler has better skills, but not the instincts of Jennings. Armstrong is better known for his shooting than his passing.

As for the big men, Salley and Miller are probably the best passers. But Miller will start the season in a fat farm and Salley may be traded after owners and players settle on a collective bargaining agreement.

REBOUNDING: There shouldn't be a shortage of candidates, even if Miller and Salley don't play. Warriors big man Victor Alexander, another weight problem, and Carlos Rogers are said to be on the trading block.

The best of the group might be 6-9 Tony Massenburg, who last season made 30 starts for the Clippers. If he doesn't start at center, the job could go to Celtic bust Acie Earl, Bucks retread Ed Pinckney or two projects—6-10 Andres Guibert, formerly of the Wolves, or 7-0 Zan Tabak, who can show his teammates what the Houston Rockets' championship rings look like.

DEFENSE: It should be OK on the perimeter, with speedsters Stoudamire and Jennings. King shows promise as a defender, and 6-8 Willie Anderson, the former Spur, can be a pain if he's healthy—but he never seems to be healthy. Anderson recovered

RAPTOR ROSTER

No.	Veterans	Pos.	Ht.	Wt.	Age	Yrs. Pro	College
—	Willie Anderson	G	6-8	200	28	7	Georgia
—	B.J. Armstrong	G	6-2	185	28	6	Iowa
—	Acie Earl	C	6-10	240	25	2	Iowa
—	Andres Guibert	F	6-10	242	27	2	Cuba
U-	Keith Jennings	G	5-7	160	26	3	East Tennessee State
	Jerome Kersey	F	6-7	225	33	11	Longwood
—	Tony Massenburg	F	6-9	245	28	3	Maryland
—	Oliver Miller	C	6-9	280	25	3	Arkansas
—	Ed Pinckney	F	6-9	240	32	10	Villanova
—	John Salley	F-C	6-11	255	31	9	Georgia Tech
U-	Doug Smith	F	6-10	220	26	4	Missouri
—	Zan Tabak	C	7-0	245	25	1	Croatia
—	B.J. Tyler	G	6-1	185	24	1	Texas
U-	Dontonio Wingfield	F	6-8	256	21	1	Cincinnati

U-unrestricted free agent

Rd.	Rookies	Sel.No.	Pos.	Ht.	Wt.	College
1	Damon Stoudamire	7	G	5-10	171	Arizona
2	Jimmy King	35	G	6-5	210	Michigan

from leg injuries, then lost his starting job after suffering an elbow injury.

Salley was once one of the league's better shot-blockers, but he added bulk after leaving the Pistons and it didn't help. Wingfield and Smith have the bulk for banging, but there's no guarantee they'll throw their weight around.

The same goes for Pinckney, whose knees are no longer capable of sustained banging. Earl, Guibert and Tabak are statues, leaving Alexander and Rogers as the best low-post defenders next to Salley.

OUTLOOK: It doesn't figure to be pretty. The best the Raptors can hope for is a winning record against their expansion brethren, the Vancouver Grizzlies. If not that, then something a little better than the 0-17 start of the expansion Miami Heat in 1988-89.

This much is certain: Malone will have his hands full. Keeping Thomas happy might be the toughest job of all. His association with Malone dates to 1988, but that friendship will be tested. Thomas was never a good loser, and he always seemed to lash out at somebody when it happened. Malone is now that somebody.

RAPTOR PROFILES

B.J. ARMSTRONG 28 6-2 185 — Guard

Victim of the Bulls' quest to find a Horace Grant clone... Bulls figured to entice the Knicks' Anthony Mason with Armstrong's $2.8-million salary slot... Raptors took him with the idea of moving to four in the draft and taking Chicago prep phenom Kevin Garnett, but deal never materialized... Getting picked first by Raptors ends Armstrong's consecutive-game streak in Chicago at 445... Remained one of the league's best stationary shooters outside the three-point arc (108-253, .427), but Phil Jackson noticed that offense sometimes ran smoother with Steve Kerr at the controls... Defense, mobility slipped... No. 18, out of Iowa, in '89 draft... Left as Hawkeyes' all-time assist leader... Born Sept. 9, 1967, in Detroit.

Year	Team	G	FG	FG Pct.	FT	FT Pct.	Reb.	Ast.	TP	Avg.
1989-90	Chicago	81	190	.485	69	.885	102	199	452	5.6
1990-91	Chicago	82	304	.481	97	.874	149	301	720	8.8
1991-92	Chicago	82	335	.481	104	.806	145	266	809	9.9
1992-93	Chicago	82	408	.499	130	.861	149	330	1009	12.3
1993-94	Chicago	82	479	.476	194	.855	170	323	1212	14.8
1994-95	Chicago	82	418	.468	206	.884	186	244	1150	14.0
	Totals	491	2134	.481	800	.861	901	1663	5352	10.9

TONY MASSENBURG 28 6-9 245 — Center-Forward

Raptors' second expansion pick... With Clippers last season, he stepped into the void created by the losses of Stanley Roberts and Elmore Spencer and sometimes held his own despite being one of the smallest centers in the league... Out of position but made 30 starts there... In the opening lineup 20 other times at power forward... Clippers liked his toughness... Signed as a free agent after playing a season in Spain... Originally a second-round choice by San Antonio in 1990, out of Maryland... Born July 31, 1967, in Sussex, Va.... Made $422,500 last season.

Year	Team	G	FG	FG Pct.	FT	FT Pct.	Reb.	Ast.	TP	Avg.
1990-91	San Antonio	35	27	.450	28	.622	58	4	82	2.3
1991-92	S.A.-Char.-Bos.-G.S.	18	10	.400	9	.600	25	0	29	1.6
1994-95	L.A. Clippers	80	282	.469	177	.753	455	67	741	9.3
	Totals	133	319	.465	214	.725	538	71	852	6.4

ANDRES GUIBERT 27 6-10 242 — Center

Raptors' thrid pick in expansion draft is a project in waiting... Former Timberwolf handles the ball well for a big man and runs the court... Aggressive defender... But raw... Defected from native Cuba to Puerto Rico in the summer of 1993... Timberwolves signed him as a free agent before last season, making him the first Cuban to play in the NBA... He may have to go to Europe to get much-needed playing time... Averaged only 9.8 minutes... Name is pronounced ON-draz Ge-BEART... Born Oct. 28, 1968, in Havana... Earned $175,000 last season.

Year	Team	G	FG	FG Pct.	FT	FT Pct.	Reb.	Ast.	TP	Avg.
1993-94	Minnesota	5	6	.300	3	.500	16	2	15	3.0
1994-95	Minnesota	17	16	.340	13	.684	45	10	45	2.6
	Totals	22	22	.328	16	.640	61	12	60	2.7

DONTONIO WINGFIELD 21 6-8 256 — Forward

The youngest player in the NBA last season was taken by Raptors as their fifth pick in expansion draft after one year with Seattle... Left Cincinnati after his freshman year... Sonics took him as a project at No. 37... Cost himself big bucks because another couple years of school could have meant a jump into the first round... Then again, it also would have meant more of that annoying distraction known as going to class... Give him an incomplete for the rookie season... Great Midwest Conference Newcomer of the Year in one and only college campaign... Second-team all-conference... Born June 23, 1974, in Albany, Ga.... Made $150,000 last season.

Year	Team	G	FG	FG Pct.	FT	FT Pct.	Reb.	Ast.	TP	Avg.
1994-95	Seattle	20	18	.353	8	.800	30	3	46	2.3

KEITH JENNINGS 26 5-7 160 — Guard

Gets fresh start in Toronto after Warriors exposed him to expansion draft... He was Raptors' fourth pick... Playing time decreased big time after Bob Lanier replaced Don Nelson, at least until Tim Hardaway went out... Started 24 times, including 17 of the last 20 following Hardaway's surgery... Led Warriors in games played... Finished 10th in the league in assist-to-turnover ratio (3.1-to-1) and free throw percentage (87.6)... Born Nov. 2, 1968, in Culpepper, Va., so he turns 27 the week the season begins... Nickname is "Mister Jennings"... Shortest player in Warriors' history... Won the Francis Pomeroy Award as the best college player under 6 feet in 1992 while attending East Tennessee State... Also was Southern Conference Player of the Year... Undrafted, so Golden State signed him as a free agent... Made $350,000 last season.

Year	Team	G	FG	FG Pct.	FT	FT Pct.	Reb.	Ast.	TP	Avg.
1992-93	Golden State	8	25	.595	14	.778	11	23	69	8.6
1993-94	Golden State	76	138	.404	100	.833	89	218	432	5.7
1994-95	Golden State	80	190	.447	134	.876	148	373	589	7.4
	Totals	164	353	.436	248	.852	248	614	1090	6.6

DOUG SMITH 26 6-10 238 Forward

A disappointment in Dallas, he hopes to turn career around in Toronto... Raptors took him with their sixth pick in expansion draft... Established career lows in most every category... Never developed after being picked sixth in 1991... Last season he, Donald Hodge and Terry Davis were the only remaining Mavericks from that season... He, Donald Hodge and Terry Davis were all players from that season that the Mavericks had little or no use for... Born Sept. 17, 1969, in Detroit, and played college ball at Missouri... Made $1.95 million last season.

Year	Team	G	FG	FG Pct.	FT	FT Pct.	Reb.	Ast.	TP	Avg.
1991-92	Dallas	76	291	.415	89	.736	391	129	671	8.8
1992-93	Dallas	61	289	.434	56	.757	328	104	634	10.4
1993-94	Dallas	79	295	.435	106	.835	349	119	698	8.8
1994-95	Dallas	63	131	.417	57	.760	144	44	320	5.1
	Totals	279	1006	.426	308	.776	1212	396	2323	8.3

JEROME KERSEY 33 6-7 225 Forward

Raptors gambled, picking him and his $3.6-million salary with their seventh pick of expansion draft... A long-time Trail Blazer... Time has taken a toll on his athletic ability... Couldn't compensate, shooting just 41.5 percent... At least his scoring average didn't drop for a sixth straight year... Reached 10,000-point plateau and is third on the all-

TORONTO RAPTORS • 233

time franchise list... Second only to Clyde Drexler in rebounds by a Blazer... Also No. 2 in games... Longwood College product was major component of Portland's two appearances in the Finals... Second-round pick in 1984... Born June 26, 1962, in Clarksville, Va.

Year	Team	G	FG	FG Pct.	FT	FT Pct.	Reb.	Ast.	TP	Avg.
1984-85	Portland	77	178	.478	117	.646	206	63	473	6.1
1985-86	Portland	79	258	.549	156	.681	293	83	672	8.5
1986-87	Portland	82	373	.509	262	.720	496	194	1009	12.3
1987-88	Portland	79	611	.499	291	.735	657	243	1516	19.2
1988-89	Portland	76	533	.469	258	.694	629	243	1330	17.5
1989-90	Portland	82	519	.478	269	.690	690	188	1310	16.0
1990-91	Portland	73	424	.478	232	.709	481	227	1084	14.8
1991-92	Portland	77	398	.467	174	.664	633	243	971	12.6
1992-93	Portland	65	281	.438	116	.634	406	121	686	10.6
1993-94	Portland	78	203	.433	101	.748	331	75	508	6.5
1994-95	Portland	63	203	.415	95	.766	256	82	508	8.1
	Totals	831	3981	.476	2071	.699	5078	1762	10067	12.1

ZAN TABAK 25 7-0 245   Center-Forward

Raptors' eighth pick in expansion draft... How do you say "scrub" in Croatian?... This guy was a second-round draft pick while in the womb... His father is 6-7, his mother 6-2, so it's not surprising he turned out to be a big guy... The rest is up to him... No. 51 pick in 1991 stayed in Europe for a couple of years before coming to the Rockets before last season... Played more than 15 minutes only once... It's easy to see why no center gets many opportunities behind Hakeem Olajuwon, but he couldn't beat out Charles Jones... Made $500,000... Born June 15, 1970, in Split, Croatia, and played on the country's national team in 1992... Wife also played in the first division. Get in line for their kids now.

Year	Team	G	FG	FG Pct.	FT	FT Pct.	Reb.	Ast.	TP	Avg.
1994-95	Houston	37	24	.453	27	.614	57	4	75	2.0

WILLIE ANDERSON 28 6-8 205   Guard

Time for another comeback, but this time in Toronto instead of San Antonio... Raptors' ninth pick in expansion draft...... Returned from a series of leg injuries a few years ago ... Now needs to return again... Starting shooting guard started the first 11 games, missed the next 14 with a strained right elbow and never got the job back... He sat while

234 • THE COMPLETE HANDBOOK OF PRO BASKETBALL

Vinny Del Negro took the spot in the opening lineup... Averaged just 14.6 minutes an outing... Spurs took him 10th in 1988 ... Played at Georgia and then on the '88 Olympic team... First-team all-rookie from there... Born Jan. 8, 1967, in Greenville, S.C.... Earns an average of $2.075 million on his contract.

Year	Team	G	FG	FG Pct.	FT	FT Pct.	Reb.	Ast.	TP	Avg.
1988-89	San Antonio	81	640	.498	224	.775	417	372	1508	18.6
1989-90	San Antonio	82	532	.492	217	.748	372	364	1288	15.7
1990-91	San Antonio	75	453	.457	170	.798	351	358	1083	14.4
1991-92	San Antonio	57	312	.455	107	.775	300	302	744	13.1
1992-93	San Antonio	38	80	.430	22	.786	57	79	183	4.8
1993-94	San Antonio	80	394	.471	145	.848	242	347	955	11.9
1994-95	San Antonio	38	76	.469	30	.732	55	52	185	4.9
	Totals	451	2487	.476	915	.782	1794	1874	5946	13.2

ACIE EARL 25 6-10 265   Center-Forward

Was the 11th player picked by Toronto in expansion draft... Now the Raptors can agonize over trying to get him to learn some basic defense. Little things, like moving the feet... One Boston scribe referred to him as "American Tourister"—simply excess baggage... Started the first three games of the season. Those were his last starts... Injury-list stint with sprained wrist... Simply plopped underneath defensively and then never moved... If opposing centers stepped out, he never followed. If opposing guards drove, he didn't step up... Left Iowa in '93 as school's all-time leader in blocked shots... Celts took him No. 19 on first round in '93... Paid him $845,000 last year... Born June 23, 1970, in Peoria, Ill.

Year	Team	G	FG	FG Pct.	FT	FT Pct.	Reb.	Ast.	TP	Avg.
1993-94	Boston	74	151	.406	108	.675	247	12	410	5.5
1994-95	Boston	30	26	.382	14	.483	45	2	66	2.2
	Totals	104	177	.402	122	.646	292	14	476	4.6

ED PINCKNEY 32 6-9 215   Forward

Right knee no longer wobbles, but skills are a distant memory... Established 10-year low in scoring (2.3) and a high in DNP-CDs (20)... Did get 17 starts, in which averages were 4.4 points and 7.6 rebounds. Bucks were 7-10 in those games... Good guy to have in the locker room, even when not playing... Was traded by Boston to Bucks with second-round

TORONTO RAPTORS • 235

pick on June 30, 1994, for Derek Strong and Blue Edwards... Also had stops in Sacramento and Phoenix... Only twice did scoring average get into double-digits. Much more was expected from 1985 Collegiate Player of the Year, the central figure in Villanova's stunning upset of Patrick Ewing and Georgetown in NCAA Finals... Was 10th pick, by Suns, in '85... Born March 27, 1963, in the Bronx, N.Y.... Made $1.48 million in 1994-95.

Year	Team	G	FG	FG Pct.	FT	FT Pct.	Reb.	Ast.	TP	Avg.
1985-86	Phoenix	80	255	.558	171	.673	308	90	681	8.5
1986-87	Phoenix	80	290	.584	257	.739	580	116	837	10.5
1987-88	Sacramento	79	179	.522	133	.747	230	66	491	6.2
1988-89	Sac.-Bos.	80	319	.513	280	.800	449	118	918	11.5
1989-90	Boston	77	135	.542	92	.773	225	68	362	4.7
1990-91	Boston	70	131	.539	104	.897	341	45	366	5.2
1991-92	Boston	81	203	.537	207	.812	564	62	613	7.6
1992-93	Boston	7	10	.417	12	.923	43	1	32	4.6
1993-94	Boston	76	151	.522	92	.736	478	62	394	5.2
1994-95	Milwaukee	62	48	.495	44	.710	211	21	140	2.3
	Totals	692	1721	.538	1392	.765	3429	649	4834	7.0

B. J. TYLER 24 6-1 185　　　　　　　　　　Guard

Sixers' biggest disappointment last year... All the speed and quickness he showed at DePaul and then Texas didn't do him a bit of good when he had no clue about how to run the offense... Shot 38 percent, which didn't endear him to Sixers, who had made him the No. 20 pick on the first round out of Texas and then were so disgusted, they gladly offered him up to expansion... Toronto made him the second B.J. point guard they selected, along with Armstrong... Maybe Isiah Thomas can teach him a thing or 12... Born April 30, 1971, in Galveston, Tex.... Made $715,000 in 1994-95.

Year	Team	G	FG	FG Pct.	FT	FT Pct.	Reb.	Ast.	TP	Avg.
1994-95	Philadelphia	55	72	.381	35	.700	62	174	195	3.5

JOHN SALLEY 31 6-11 250　　　　　Forward-Center

Reunited with old Bad Boy buddy Isiah Thomas... Well, at least he's closer to Detroit in Toronto than he was in Miami... Taken as Raptors' next-to-last pick in expansion draft after three generally disappointing years with Heat... Helped Detroit to two championships... Tried to do more with Heat last season, proved less effective than ever... Decent backup center who demanded starting minutes. Barely got backup numbers (7.3 points, 4.5 rebounds) despite career-best 50 starts ... Hand-checking rules severely crippled his interior defense. Couldn't get away with all the tricks of earlier seasons ... Runs floor well, but age has taken toll ... Stand-up comic type ... Georgia Tech, Class of '86 ... Pistons took him at No. 11 ... Traded to Miami for a first-rounder and draft rights to Isaiah Morris Sept. 8, 1992 ... Born May 16, 1964, in Brooklyn, N.Y. ... 1994-95 salary: $2.652 million.

Year	Team	G	FG	FG Pct.	FT	FT Pct.	Reb.	Ast.	TP	Avg.
1986-87	Detroit	82	163	.562	105	.614	296	54	431	5.3
1987-88	Detroit	82	258	.566	185	.709	402	113	701	8.5
1988-89	Detroit	67	166	.498	135	.692	335	75	467	7.0
1989-90	Detroit	82	209	.512	174	.713	439	67	593	7.2
1990-91	Detroit	74	179	.475	186	.727	327	70	544	7.4
1991-92	Detroit	72	249	.512	186	.715	296	116	684	9.5
1992-93	Miami	51	154	.502	115	.799	313	83	423	8.3
1993-94	Miami	76	208	.477	164	.729	407	135	582	7.7
1994-95	Miami	75	197	.499	153	.739	336	123	547	7.3
	Totals	661	1783	.511	1403	.715	3151	836	4972	7.5

OLIVER MILLER 25 6-9 330 Center

Greatest gift is his ability to rig scales ... Did it in Phoenix and Detroit. After it happened in Detroit—he went from 315 to 335 after scales were corrected—Pistons exposed him to the expansion draft and he was grabbed by Toronto as its last pick ... Even when not eating, opening mouth is a problem. Ripped Charles Barkley upon leaving Phoenix, then reportedly said something in a local bar that instigated a fight. Result was a broken right hand and too much spare time with a fork ... Best line from fan: "Hey, Oliver, who's in there with you?" ... Still averaged 8.5 points and 7.4 rebounds, but shooting percentage dipped from .609 to .555 ... Started 22 of 64 appearances ... Made three treys in Pistons' season-ending loss at Miami ... Arkansas product was born April 6, 1970, in Fort Worth, Tex. ... The 22nd pick of the 1992 draft ... Signed offer sheet with Pistons in 1994; Suns decided against matching ... Made $1.6 million in first year of five-year, $10-million pact.

Year	Team	G	FG	FG Pct.	FT	FT Pct.	Reb.	Ast.	TP	Avg.
1992-93	Phoenix	56	121	.475	71	.710	275	118	313	5.6
1993-94	Phoenix	69	277	.609	80	.584	476	244	636	9.2
1994-95	Detroit	64	232	.555	78	.629	475	93	545	8.5
	Totals	189	630	.559	229	.634	1226	455	1494	7.9

THE ROOKIES

DAMON STOUDAMIRE 22 5-10 171　　　　　　　**Guard**
Most projected him as 10-15 pick, but Raptors GM Isiah Thomas liked him at No. 7 . . . Zeke knows his point guards . . . Pac-10's Co-Player of the Year with UCLA's Ed O'Bannon . . . Has great range, loves to compete . . . Led league in scoring (22.8) and assists (7.3) as senior . . . Only Arizona player to twice score 40 points . . . Born Sept. 3, 1973, in Portland, Ore.

JIMMY KING 22 6-5 210　　　　　　　　　　**Guard**
Last of Michigan's Fab Five to get drafted. Chris Webber, Juwan Howard and Jalen Rose preceeded him. Only Ray Jackson got shut out . . . Hit double figures in 28 of 30 games as senior . . . Good defender, terrific finisher. Needs to work on his jumper . . . Drafted 35th . . . Born Aug. 9, 1973, South Bend, Ind.

COACH BRENDAN MALONE: Should give lessons to cats about landing on your feet after a tough fall . . . Hired as first Raptors' coach less than two months after getting the boot with Don Chaney and K.C. Jones in Detroit, where he had worked since the fall of 1988 . . . Nearly accepted Toronto front-office offer from former Piston Isiah Thomas before 1994-95 season . . . Hard worker, personable, great with players 8 through 12 on the roster . . . Worked under Chaney, Ron Rothstein and Chuck Daly in Detroit. Worked his way from scout to lead assistant . . . Came to Pistons from the Knicks. Was scout and assistant coach under Hubie Brown for two seasons . . . Before that, spent two seasons as head coach at Rhode Island . . . Top recruiter for Syracuse's Jim Boeheim. During his stay there, the Orangemen were 134-52 . . . Began coaching career at New York's Power Memorial Academy, the high school of Kareem Abdul-Jabbar (then Lew Alcindor). Teams won two city championships. Three times was New York City Coach of the Year . . . Inducted into New York's Catholic Hall of Fame . . . Played at Iowa . . . Has master's degree from NYU . . . Born April 21, 1942, in New York City.

DALLAS MAVERICKS

TEAM DIRECTORY: Owner/Pres.: Donald Carter; Chief Oper. Off./GM: Norm Sonju; Dir. Player Personnel: Keith Grant; Dir. Media Services: Kevin Sullivan; Coach: Dick Motta; Asst. Coaches: Brad Davis, Kip Motta. Arena: Reunion Arena (17,502). Colors: Blue and green.

SCOUTING REPORT

SHOOTING: Jamal Mashburn. Jim Jackson. Jason Kidd running the offense. So what's not to like? Well, there is this little matter: the Mavericks can't shoot. They were last in three-point percentage and beat out only New Jersey for overall accuracy. It's not good to miss so many opportunities, go just 10-9 in games decided by three points or less and then miss the playoffs in the final couple of weeks of the season.

On the other hand, the Mavericks of 1994-95 took 208 more shots than anybody in the league—giving them about an extra 2½ games on offense than the next-closest team—which served as testimony to the work on the offensive boards and to Kidd. That compensated enough for the terrible shooting. Dallas averaged 103.2 points a game, good for No. 9, its highest output since 1988-89, and a jump from the last-place finish of 95.1 the season before.

Mashburn was fifth in the league in scoring and second among all forwards (only Karl Malone did better) and still will be just 23 in late November. He shoots from the outside or uses dribble penetration, but mostly he just makes a lot of people look bad. Jackson, meanwhile, presents similar two-pronged problems for opposing shooting guards. This all sets the stage for the Mavericks to have two players average 27 or 28 points sometime soon.

PLAYMAKING: Watch the Mavericks closely as they start a fastbreak, but ignore Kidd with the ball. Just pay attention to the other four players. They're the ones who will look like sprinters getting into the starting block. Then, when the point guard gets control, it's like a track meet, everyone charging to the other end and waiting for a pass.

And you thought Kidd's rookie numbers were impressive—ninth in assists, first in triple-doubles. Indeed, the most telling sign of his impact, and impending greatness, is the way teammates

DALLAS MAVERICKS • 239

Jason Kidd made it as co-Rookie of the Year.

react. They love playing with him, knowing the ball will always be in the right place for a score.

REBOUNDING: The point guard crashes the boards. Doesn't that say something? Led by the underrated Popeye Jones, the Mavericks made a huge jump in this category, from middle of the pack by percentage in 1993-94 to second-best last season behind the Trail Blazers. And nobody was better on the offensive end, invaluable in providing second-chance baskets amidst the shooting struggles.

Little-known Jones finished ninth overall by average and first

MAVERICK ROSTER

No.	Veterans	Pos.	Ht.	Wt.	Age	Yrs. Pro	College
1	Scott Brooks	G	5-11	165	30	7	Cal-Irvine
43	Terry Davis	F-C	6-10	250	28	6	Virginia Union
7	Tony Dumas	G	6-6	190	23	1	Missouri-KC
30	Lucious Harris	G	6-5	190	24	2	Long Beach State
35	Donald Hodge	C	7-0	233	26	4	Temple
24	Jim Jackson	G	6-6	220	25	3	Ohio State
54	Popeye Jones	F	6-8	250	25	2	Murray State
5	Jason Kidd	G	6-4	212	22	1	California
32	Jamal Mashburn	F	6-8	240	22	2	Kentucky
U-21	George McCloud	F-G	6-8	215	28	5	Florida State
42	Roy Tarpley	C-F	7-0	245	30	6	Michigan
R-44	Lorenzo Williams	F	6-9	200	26	3	Stetson

R-restricted free agent
U-unrestricted free agent

Rd.	Rookies	Sel.No.	Pos.	Ht.	Wt.	College
1	Cherokee Parks	12	C-F	6-11	235	Duke
1	Loren Meyer	24	C	6-10	257	Iowa State

in total offensive boards, not too bad for a guy just 6-8 who was acquired two years ago for the forgettable Eric Riley. Now add to that two more first-round picks, Cherokee Parks and Loren Meyer. Anything from Roy Tarpley becomes gravy.

DEFENSE: The two rookies may both challenge for playing time at center, but Lorenzo Williams won't be pushed out easily because he provides a shot-blocking presence. That's a big deal around here since it has been lacking as the Mavericks search for deterrents inside—they were third-worst in shooting percentage-against. Size has obviously been a factor, with Williams just 6-9 at center and Jones 6-8 at power forward.

OUTLOOK: The forecast is for bright days ahead for Dick Motta's youth brigade. The average age of the regular starting five last season (Kidd, Jackson, Mashburn, Jones, Williams) was 23.4 years old, making them the youngest of any first five in the league. Three of those could become superstars at the same time, and a fourth, Jones, has already accomplished more than most would have expected. So give them time to improve the defense, time to really learn to play together, and then prepare to get out of the way. It's much safer than getting run over.

MAVERICK PROFILES

JIM JACKSON 25 6-6 220   Guard

Not just an all-star in waiting. A superstar in waiting... Was top non-scoring center in the NBA at 25.7 points when he suffered a badly sprained left ankle Feb. 24... That ended his season... Missed the final 31 games and finished 91 points shy of qualifying among the league scoring leaders... Lost time was first games he had missed since coming to the pros as the No. 4 pick in 1992... Few guards are stronger, so teams have trouble keeping him from getting inside... Some even put a small forward on him... Only Dana Barros and Scott Burrell made bigger jumps in scoring average from 1993-94 to last season... Making big strides to improve shooting percentage, and should be better still than the 47.2 of 1994-95... "What is there not to like about him?" Hawks coach Lenny Wilkens says. "He can go outside or inside, he pushes the ball, he can defend."... Born Oct. 14, 1970, in Toledo, Ohio, and stayed close to home to attend Ohio State... Made $2.7 million last season.

Year	Team	G	FG	FG Pct.	FT	FT Pct.	Reb.	Ast.	TP	Avg.
1992-93	Dallas	28	184	.395	68	.739	122	131	457	16.3
1993-94	Dallas	82	637	.445	285	.821	388	374	1576	19.2
1994-95	Dallas	51	484	.472	306	.805	260	191	1309	25.7
	Totals	161	1305	.446	659	.805	770	696	3342	20.8

JAMAL MASHBURN 22 6-8 240   Forward

Speaking of superstars in the making... In only his second season, he finished No. 5 in the league in scoring and No. 2 among forwards, behind only Karl Malone... Youngest player among the top nine scorers... First Maverick to finish in the top five since Mark Aguirre in 1983-84... So tough because he can shoot outside or put the ball on the floor... Handles the ball well... His 1,926 points was the most by a Maverick since Aguirre (1,932) in 1987-88... His 19.2 points per game in 1993-94 was tops among all rookies, just after Mavericks made him No. 4 pick... Born Nov. 29, 1972, in New York, and starred at Kentucky... Made $2,633,300 in '94-95.

Year	Team	G	FG	FG Pct.	FT	FT Pct.	Reb.	Ast.	TP	Avg.
1993-94	Dallas	79	561	.406	306	.699	353	266	1513	19.2
1994-95	Dallas	80	683	.436	447	.739	331	298	1926	24.1
	Totals	159	1244	.422	753	.722	684	564	3439	21.6

JASON KIDD 22 6-4 212   Guard

Kidd's play. Definitely not kid's play... Co-Rookie of the Year along with Grant Hill... Led NBA with four triple-doubles, and they all came in a 16-day span in April... Finishing one rebound shy of a triple-double in his first pro game should have been a clue... Terrific instincts... Needs to improve his outside shot so teams won't continue to play off him. Or as teammate Jim Jackson says: "His shooting just has to catch up to the rest of his game. But that's just a matter of time."... Beyond that, he was everything Mavericks could have hoped for after drafting him second overall... Has strength and speed... You can see teammates love playing with him because he is so good at distributing the ball on the break... Get open, he'll get it to you... Set team rookie record with 607 assists... Finished No. 7 in the league in steals and No. 9 in assists... City of Dallas fell in love with former Cal superstar... Born March 23, 1973, in San Francisco... Made $2,770,800 last season.

Year	Team	G	FG	FG Pct.	FT	FT Pct.	Reb.	Ast.	TP	Avg.
1994-95	Dallas	79	330	.385	192	.698	430	607	922	11.7

RON (POPEYE) JONES 25 6-8 250   Forward

Increased his strength, then increased his value... A good prospect from 1993-94 became a valuable contributor in 1994-95... Also a candidate for league's Most Improved Player... Makes good use of upper-body strength to push past opponents attempting to get offensive rebounds... Other asset is a big butt... Led NBA last season with 329 offensive boards, the second-most in team history... Tied for No. 9 in rebounds at 10.6 a game... Houston drafted him out of Murray State in 1992, but he didn't come to the NBA until Rockets traded him to Dallas for Eric Riley in the summer of '93 ... Deal was a yawner at the time, but it has worked out great for Mavs since ... Born June 17, 1970, in Martin, Tenn. ... 1994-95 salary: $769,000.

Year	Team	G	FG	FG Pct.	FT	FT Pct.	Reb.	Ast.	TP	Avg.
1993-94	Dallas	81	195	.479	78	.729	605	99	468	5.8
1994-95	Dallas	80	372	.443	80	.645	844	163	825	10.3
	Totals	161	567	.455	158	.684	1449	262	1293	8.0

LORENZO WILLIAMS 26 6-9 200 Center

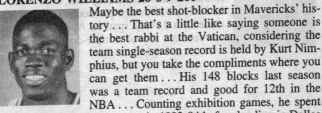

Maybe the best shot-blocker in Mavericks' history ... That's a little like saying someone is the best rabbi at the Vatican, considering the team single-season record is held by Kurt Nimphius, but you take the compliments where you can get them ... His 148 blocks last season was a team record and good for 12th in the NBA ... Counting exhibition games, he spent time with four different teams in 1993-94 before landing in Dallas on a pair of 10-day contracts ... Also passed through CBA, U.S. Basketball League and the Global Basketball Assn. since playing college ball at Stetson ... Parlayed opportunity with Dallas into 11 starts, then became The Guy at center last season ... Size is an obvious problem on defense, but compensates with jumping ability that leads to blocks ... Also has a good knack for timing his leaps ... Born July 15, 1969, in Ocala, Fla. ... Undrafted ... Made $200,000 last season.

Year	Team	G	FG	FG Pct.	FT	FT Pct.	Reb.	Ast.	TP	Avg.
1992-93	Char.-Orl.-Bos.	27	17	.472	2	.286	55	5	36	1.3
1993-94	Orl.-Char.-Dal.	38	49	.445	12	.429	217	25	110	2.9
1994-95	Dallas	82	145	.477	38	.376	690	124	328	4.0
	Totals	147	211	.469	52	.382	962	154	474	3.2

ROY TARPLEY 30 7-0 245 Forward-Center

"I think to myself and wonder, 'Why did I do those things?' " he said ... He's not the only one who wonders ... Returned to Mavericks after three-year absence because of drug problems ... Spent previous two seasons in Greece ... Too good a talent for Mavs to turn their back on, even though he could be a headache again ... Had a one-game suspension for conduct detrimental to the team... The difference this time is that he needs them more than they need him... Mavericks' elder statesman in 1994-95... Game became much more outside-oriented after return... Showed that he could still make a considerable contribution... Started once... Came into last season at 72.8 percent from the line, then proceeded to lead team by going 83.6 percent... Originally a No. 7 pick in 1986, out of Michigan... Born Nov. 28, 1964, in New York... 1994-95 salary: $3 million.

Year	Team	G	FG	FG Pct.	FT	FT Pct.	Reb.	Ast.	TP	Avg.
1986-87	Dallas	75	233	.467	94	.676	533	52	561	7.5
1987-88	Dallas	81	444	.500	205	.740	959	86	1093	13.5
1988-89	Dallas	19	131	.541	66	.688	218	17	328	17.3
1989-90	Dallas	45	314	.451	130	.756	589	67	758	16.8
1990-91	Dallas	5	43	.544	16	.889	55	12	102	20.4
1994-95	Dallas	55	292	.479	102	.836	449	58	691	12.6
	Totals	280	1457	.483	613	.744	2803	292	3533	12.6

TERRY DAVIS 28 6-10 250   Forward-Center

Nice comeback. Now sit down... Went from missing all but 15 games of 1993-94 while recovering from a shattered left elbow to playing in 46 last season... Flip side was that he was "DNP-CD" in 24 of final 31 outings... This is the same rebounding specialist who looked to have a nice future with the Mavericks after being signed as a free agent in the summer of 1991. And the same guy who got a five-year extension in December of '92... Done in by emergence of Popeye Jones at power forward... Finished last season in 10th place on Mavericks' all-time rebounding list at 1,603... Was not drafted out of Virginia Union in 1989... Heat signed him as a free agent... Born June 17, 1967, in South Boston, Va.... Made $1.56 million last season.

Year	Team	G	FG	FG Pct.	FT	FT Pct.	Reb.	Ast.	TP	Avg.
1989-90	Miami	63	122	.466	54	.621	229	25	298	4.7
1990-91	Miami	55	115	.487	69	.556	266	39	300	5.5
1991-92	Dallas	68	256	.482	181	.635	672	57	693	10.2
1992-93	Dallas	75	393	.455	167	.594	701	68	955	12.7
1993-94	Dallas	15	24	.407	8	.667	74	6	56	3.7
1994-95	Dallas	46	49	.434	42	.636	156	10	140	3.0
	Totals	322	959	.465	521	.609	2098	205	2442	7.6

SCOTT BROOKS 30 5-11 165 — Guard

Went from world champion to third-best team in the state, but became a major player again ... Played 28 games with Houston before being traded to Dallas on Feb. 23 for Morlon Wiley and a 1995 second-rounder ... Rockets were so in love with Wiley they cut him the next day ... Brooks, meanwhile, became the backup point guard after Jim Jackson went down and Lucious Harris moved from Jason Kidd's understudy to starting shooting guard ... Was No. 1 all-time in Houston history in three-point percentage when he left ... Scrappy ... His 530 regular-season appearances were the most on the team heading into the offseason ... He and Doc Rivers hold the NBA record of five consecutive seasons with more steals than turnovers ... Started college career at TCU before finishing at Cal-Irvine ... Born July 31, 1965, in French Camp, Cal. ... 1994-95 salary: $550,000.

Year	Team	G	FG	FG Pct.	FT	FT Pct.	Reb.	Ast.	TP	Avg.
1988-89	Philadelphia	82	156	.420	61	.884	94	306	428	5.2
1989-90	Philadelphia	72	119	.431	50	.877	64	207	319	4.4
1990-91	Minnesota	80	159	.430	61	.847	72	204	424	5.3
1991-92	Minnesota	82	167	.447	51	.810	99	205	417	5.1
1992-93	Houston	82	183	.475	112	.830	99	243	519	6.3
1993-94	Houston	73	142	.491	74	.871	102	149	381	5.2
1994-95	Hou.-Dal.	59	126	.458	64	.810	66	116	341	5.8
	Totals	530	1052	.450	473	.845	596	1430	2829	5.3

GEORGE McCLOUD 28 6-8 215 — Forward

Former first-round bust with Pacers tries to work his way back ... Has textbook stroke for spot-up shooter ... Just not always textbook accuracy ... Streaky ... That's one reason he was in the CBA (Rapid City) when Mavs came calling in January ... Signed to a pair of 10-day contracts, then for the rest of the season Feb. 22 ... Made a nice contribution ... If nothing else, it was a good reminder to other teams before he headed into the summer as an unrestricted free agent ... Started twice and responded with 16 points in one and a career-high 25 points in the other ... Metro Conference Player of the Year in 1989 at Florida State, just before Pacers took him No. 7 overall ... Averaged 5.5 points in four seasons with Pacers ... Next stop was Italy ... CBA all-star last season ... Born May 27, 1967, in Daytona Beach, Fla.

Year	Team	G	FG	FG Pct.	FT	FT Pct.	Reb.	Ast.	TP	Avg.
1989-90	Indiana	44	45	.313	15	.789	42	45	118	2.7
1990-91	Indiana	74	131	.373	38	.776	118	150	343	4.6
1991-92	Indiana	51	128	.409	50	.781	132	116	338	6.6
1992-93	Indiana	78	216	.411	75	.735	205	192	565	7.2
1994-95	Dallas	42	144	.439	80	.833	147	53	402	9.6
	Totals	289	664	.400	258	.782	644	556	1766	6.1

LUCIOUS HARRIS 24 6-5 190　　　　　　　　Guard

The supporting player became a starter during playoff stretch drive ... When Jim Jackson suffered a badly sprained ankle, he took over at shooting guard for 30 of the last 31 games ... Struggled from the field—the 43.9 percent was a drop from his mark as a reserve—but contributed 13.3 points ... That didn't fill Jackson's void, but wasn't bad for a 1993 second-round pick who still needs to get bigger ... His 38.7 accuracy on three-pointers was best on the Mavericks ... Had one fewer turnover last season than rookie season despite playing 530 more minutes ... Born Dec. 18, 1970, in Los Angeles, and played college ball at Long Beach State ... Made $455,000 last season.

Year	Team	G	FG	FG Pct.	FT	FT Pct.	Reb.	Ast.	TP	Avg.
1993-94	Dallas	77	162	.421	87	.731	157	106	418	5.4
1994-95	Dallas	79	280	.459	136	.800	220	132	751	9.5
	Totals	156	442	.444	223	.772	377	238	1169	7.5

DONALD HODGE 26 7-0 233　　　　　　　　Center

Went into summer as restricted free agent ... Please, don't everyone call his agent at once ... The next sign of upper-body strength will be his first ... Mavs' starting small forward weighs more, the shooting guard only a little less ... No need to ask why he can't defend the post against centers or power forwards ... Some people can survive in the league by compensating with offense, but he hasn't shown the ability to be one of them ... His shooting percentage has gone up and down from season to season since Mavericks took him in the second round, No. 33 overall, in the 1991 draft ... Played college ball at Temple

... Born Feb. 25, 1969, in Washington, D.C. ... 1994-95 salary: $1.005 million.

Year	Team	G	FG	FG Pct.	FT	FT Pct.	Reb.	Ast.	TP	Avg.
1991-92	Dallas	51	163	.497	100	.667	275	39	426	8.4
1992-93	Dallas	79	161	.403	71	.683	294	75	393	5.0
1993-94	Dallas	50	46	.455	44	.846	95	32	136	2.7
1994-95	Dallas	54	83	.407	39	.765	122	41	209	3.9
	Totals	234	453	.439	254	.711	786	187	1164	5.0

TONY DUMAS 23 6-6 190   Guard

Oh, well, it's not like the Mavericks needed him to play like a first-round choice... He came No. 19 overall, long after super-rookie Jason Kidd, then shot 38.4 percent, including starting the season at 17.9 percent on three-pointers before finishing at 30.1... Apparently didn't see his job title as shooting guard... Did rank No. 7 in the nation the year before at Missouri-Kansas City... Didn't make Rookie All-Star Game, but became the first Maverick to participate in slam-dunk contest at All-Star Weekend... Born Aug. 25, 1972, in Chicago... Got a four-year contract that started at $700,000.

Year	Team	G	FG	FG Pct.	FT	FT Pct.	Reb.	Ast.	TP	Avg.
1994-95	Dallas	58	96	.384	50	.649	62	57	264	4.6

THE ROOKIES

CHEROKEE PARKS 23 6-11 235   Center-Forward
Dallas becomes part of the Cherokee Nation... Looking to add size, Mavericks took him 12th overall... No. 2 all-time in blocked shots in Duke history... Member of the U.S. national team for the 1994 Goodwill Games... Improved his production in points, assists and rebounds in each of four seasons at Duke ... Honorable mention All-American as a senior... Born Oct. 11, 1972, in Huntington Beach, Cal.

LOREN MEYER 22 6-10 257   Center
Not a big name nationally—only honorable mention All-Big Eight Conference—but ended up a first-round pick... No. 24

overall... Good athlete for a big guy... Made a successful return last season after suffering a broken collarbone and playing only 15 games as a junior... Played at Iowa State, but switched to uniform No. 40 as a senior in memory of Iowa's Chris Street, who was killed in a car accident in 1993... Born Dec. 30, 1972, in Emmetsburg, Iowa.

COACH DICK MOTTA: Some perspective on his experience:
When he coached his first NBA game on Oct. 15, 1968, nine of the Mavericks on the 1994-95 roster hadn't even been born and the oldest of the three others was three years old... That kind of resume was a big reason Dallas hired him after the Quinn Buckner try-the-rookie-guy fiasco... Another reason was his track record with the franchise... Coached Mavericks their first seven years in the league... Has 23 seasons as a coach in all... Career record: 892-906... Only coach to ever guide two teams to four consecutive seasons of improved records... Guided 1977-78 Bullets to NBA title... Probably a little better coach than when he won the Idaho high-school title in 1959... His star player then was Phil Johnson, now an assistant with the Jazz... Spent six years at Weber State before joining the NBA with Bulls in 1968-69... Won Coach of the Year in third of his eight seasons in Chicago... With Bullets for four years before coming to Dallas as one of the architects of an expansion team that grew into one of the league's best... Tried to give the same boost to Sacramento Kings, but that ended in disappointment 25 games into his third season... Long-time favorite of Mavs' owner Donald Carter... Born Sept. 3, 1931, in Midvale, Utah... Utah State graduate who didn't play basketball.

GREATEST FIND

The Mavs didn't get a real return on what could have been the greatest find: Mark Price as a second-round pick in 1986. He quickly was traded to Cleveland for a No. 2 pick and future considerations.

Forced to look elsewhere, the decision is just as obvious. Guard Brad Davis, a disappointment for the Lakers as a No. 1

pick, had been waived and was playing with the Anchorage Northern Lights of the CBA when the Mavericks called in December of 1980.

What followed was 12 seasons, making Davis the final member of the charter team to retire. By the time he did, Davis was No. 1 in franchise history in games played and became the first Maverick to have his uniform retired.

ALL-TIME MAVERICK LEADERS

SEASON

Points: Mark Aguirre, 2,330, 1983–84
Assists: Derek Harper, 634, 1987–88
Rebounds: James Donaldson, 973, 1986–87

GAME

Points: Jamal Mashburn, 50 vs. Chicago, 11/12/94
Jim Jackson, 50 vs. Denver, 11/26/94
Assists: Derek Harper, 18 vs. Boston, 12/29/88
Rebounds: James Donaldson, 27 vs. Portland (3 OT), 12/29/89

CAREER

Points: Rolando Blackman, 16,643, 1981–92
Assists: Derek Harper, 4,790, 1983–84
Rebounds: James Donaldson, 4,589, 1985–92

DENVER NUGGETS

TEAM DIRECTORY: Owner: Comsat; Pres./Head Coach: Bernie Bickerstaff; Dir. Player Personnel: Mike Evans; Dir. Media Services: Tommy Sheppard; Asst. Coaches: Gene Littles, Tom Nissalke. Arena: McNichols Sports Arena (17,171). Colors: Gold, blue and red.

SCOUTING REPORT

SHOOTING: It's a long way down when you live a mile high, but the Nuggets could be facing a fall. They finished seventh in the league in shooting last season, an especially commendable mark considering few teams were as bad on three-pointers, then spent the summer either saying good-by or facing the possible departure of some of their most reliable shooters. Versatile Rodney Rogers (49.8 percent) was sent to the Clippers, Brian Williams (58.9) was expected to follow once the lockout was settled, and Tom Hammonds (53.5) was an unrestricted free agent.

The encouraging side for Denver was that only Rogers had a significant role in the offense. Besides, rookie Antonio McDyess proved accurate while at Alabama, and don't forget the return of LaPhonso Ellis, an NBA-proven weapon. Imagine the potential matchup problems for opponents if the Nuggets follow through on the notion to play Ellis at small forward, though it could come back to hurt them on defense. The challenge then would be to spread the court enough as to not have all three frontcourt players clogged around the lane at the same time.

PLAYMAKING: No playoff team had a worse assist-to-turnover ratio in 1994-95, so, yes, the problems of the past continue. There is, however, reason to be encouraged. It comes in the person of Jalen Rose, who was inconsistent as a shooter (hardly unusual for a rookie) but filled with talent as a ball-handler. That makes him equally dangerous in the open court or while passing out of a double-team on the post, which happens often when defenders are forced to contend with a 6-8 point guard.

If Rose continues to blossom, Mahmoud Abdul-Rauf will be the backup and also play shooting guard, which suits his game much better, even if his 6-1 frame does not. Robert Pack? He's still a terrific drive-and-dish penetrator, but, as a free agent, whether he is still a Nugget was up in the air at mid-summer.

Dikembe Mutombo again topped the NBA in blocked shots.

REBOUNDING: Speaking of encouraging...

Only six teams were better than the Nuggets by percentage last season, and that was without Ellis for all but 58 minutes off the bench because of a serious knee injury. Now he should be back, maybe as the 6-8 starting small forward, alongside McDyess, who is 6-9 with springs, and Dikembe Mutombo. The expected loss of Williams would hurt more in this area than Rogers' departure.

Mutombo was second in rebounds to Dennis Rodman in 1994-95, after finishing sixth, third and third the previous seasons. His career average is an impressive 12.5

NUGGET ROSTER

No.	Veteran	Pos.	Ht.	Wt.	Age	Yrs. Pro	College
1	Mahmoud Abdul-Rauf	G	6-1	150	26	5	LSU
3	Dale Ellis	G-F	6-7	215	35	12	Tennessee
20	LaPhonso Ellis	F	6-8	240	25	3	Notre Dame
9	Greg Grant	G	5-7	140	29	6	Trenton State
U-21	Tom Hammonds	F	6-9	223	28	6	Georgia Tech
53	Cliff Levingston	C-F	6-8	225	34	11	Wichita State
55	Dikembe Mutombo	C	7-2	250	29	4	Georgetown
14	Robert Pack	G	6-2	190	26	4	USC
42	Mark Randall	F	6-9	245	28	4	Kansas
5	Jalen Rose	G	6-8	210	22	2	Michigan
23	Bryant Stith	G	6-5	208	24	3	Virginia
8	Brian Williams	F	6-11	260	26	4	Arizona
34	Reggie Williams	F-G	6-7	195	31	8	Georgetown
—	Randy Woods	G	5-10	185	25	3	LaSalle

U-Unrestricted free agent

Rd.	Rookies	Sel.No.	Pos.	Ht.	Wt.	College
1	Antonio McDyess	2	F	6-9	220	Alabama
2	Anthony Pelle	44	C	7-0	260	Fresno State

DEFENSE: Previously respected, this may now become one of the most feared teams in this category because of size. Imagine a starting lineup with Rose and Bryant Stith in the backcourt and Ellis, McDyess and Mutombo across the front. That translates into, in order, 6-8, 6-5 (with good strength), 6-8, 6-9 (with great leaping ability) and 7-2. That practically makes them the third-tallest peak in the Rocky Mountain range.

Mutombo, of course, is the anchor, having led the NBA in blocks the last two seasons. Last season, he was .55 ahead of runnerup Hakeem Olajuwon, a considerable margin in this department. What Mutombo does not get his hands on, he often manages to alter just by his intimidating presence in the lane, deterring opponents from coming inside for easy baskets. In the end, the Nuggets finished eighth in shooting percentage-against, then added another shot-blocker in the draft, Anthony Pelle of Fresno State.

OUTLOOK: Ellis' knees are a big concern, but there are far more reasons to be optimstic about Bernie Bickerstaff's Nuggetts. If McDyess is as advertised, the up-and-coming team that lost its way (and mind) last season should be back on track.

NUGGET PROFILES

DIKEMBE MUTOMBO 29 7-2 250   Center

Always a defensive force, but his offensive game is getting better... Doesn't look nearly as clumsy on inside moves compared to a few years ago... Meanwhile, he has led the league in blocked shots the last two years and in 1994-95 finished second in rebounding... Got at least 20 boards on seven occasions... Has started 246 consecutive games, the third-longest active streak in the NBA... At 37.8, the only Nugget to average more than 30 minutes a game last season... Two-time all-star since coming to the NBA as the No. 4 pick in 1991... Big East Defensive Player of the Year at Georgetown as a senior... Dikembe Mutombo Mpolondo Mukamba Jean Jacque Wamutombo was born June 25, 1966, in Kinshasa, Zaire... Made $3.1 million last season.

Year	Team	G	FG	FG Pct.	FT	FT Pct.	Reb.	Ast.	TP	Avg.
1991-92	Denver	71	428	.493	321	.642	870	156	1177	16.6
1992-93	Denver	82	398	.510	335	.681	1070	147	1131	13.8
1993-94	Denver	82	365	.569	256	.583	971	127	986	12.0
1994-95	Denver	82	349	.556	248	.654	1029	113	946	11.5
	Totals	317	1540	.527	1160	.641	3940	543	4240	13.4

MAHMOUD ABDUL-RAUF 26 6-1 150   Guard

Scoring average has dropped each of the last two years, but every time it has been good enough to pace the team... Beat Chicago, Miami and Dallas with game-winning shots last season... Point-guard size with shooting-guard skills... Has more tenure in Denver uniform than any player on the roster, having come aboard as the No. 3 pick in 1990, out of LSU... Was known as Chris Jackson then... Entered the NBA after his sophomore year, then proceeded to shoot 41.3 and 42.1 percent the next two seasons. Started to pick it up in 1992-93, which would have been his rookie campaign had he stayed in school... Born March 9, 1969, in Gulfport, Miss.... 1994-95 salary: $2.2 million.

Year	Team	G	FG	FG Pct.	FT	FT Pct.	Reb.	Ast.	TP	Avg.
1990-91	Denver	67	417	.413	84	.857	121	206	942	14.1
1991-92	Denver	81	356	.421	94	.870	114	192	837	10.3
1992-93	Denver	81	633	.450	217	.935	225	344	1553	19.2
1993-94	Denver	80	588	.460	219	.956	168	362	1437	18.0
1994-95	Denver	73	472	.470	138	.885	137	263	1165	16.0
	Totals	382	2466	.445	752	.914	765	1367	5934	15.5

LaPHONSO ELLIS 25 6-8 240   Forward

You can't climb to the next level on a bad leg ... Hoped to show in third year that he belonged among the league's elite power forwards, but suffered a stress fracture to the right knee last Sept. 9 and missed almost all season ... Underwent surgery Nov. 22 and sat out the first 76 games ... Appeared in the final six games of regular season, then went back on injured list and was not on playoff roster ... Best showing was 12 points, seven rebounds, three blocks against Timberwolves ... Nice talent who should only get better with experience ... Denver got Notre Dame product No. 5 overall in 1992 ... From there, he became the first Nugget rookie to start all 82 games and was voted first-team all-rookie ... Born May 5, 1970, in East St. Louis, Ill. ... Made $2.73 million last season.

Year	Team	G	FG	FG Pct.	FT	FT Pct.	Reb.	Ast.	TP	Avg.
1992-93	Denver	82	483	.504	237	.748	744	151	1205	14.7
1993-94	Denver	79	483	.502	242	.674	682	167	1215	15.4
1994-95	Denver	6	9	.360	6	1.000	17	4	24	4.0
	Totals	167	975	.501	485	.711	1443	322	2444	14.6

REGGIE WILLIAMS 31 6-7 195   Guard-Forward

The captain went down with the ship, sort of ... Amidst all the upheaval surrounding Dan Issel's resignation as coach, he resigned as team captain ... Still a mediocre shooter, but he led team in steals and finished second in scoring and blocked shots ... Started in 70 of 74 appearances ... Was an unwanted free agent, having been cut by Cleveland and San

Antonio, when Denver signed him in Jan. 1991 ... No. 4 pick by the Clippers in 1987 after starring at Georgetown ... Member of Hoyas' 1984 NCAA title team and the all-time leading scorer in school history when he left ... Born March 5, 1964, in Baltimore ... 1994-95 salary: $1.567 million.

Year	Team	G	FG	FG Pct.	FT	FT Pct.	Reb.	Ast.	TP	Avg.
1987-88	L.A.Clippers	35	152	.356	48	.727	118	58	365	10.4
1988-89	L.A.Clippers	63	260	.438	92	.754	179	103	642	10.2
1989-90	LAC-Clev-S.A.	47	131	.388	52	.765	83	53	320	6.8
1990-91	S.A.-Den.	73	384	.449	166	.843	306	133	991	13.6
1991-92	Denver	81	601	.471	216	.803	405	235	1474	18.2
1992-93	Denver	79	535	.458	238	.804	428	295	1341	17.0
1993-94	Denver	82	418	.412	165	.733	392	300	1065	13.0
1994-95	Denver	74	388	.459	132	.759	329	231	993	13.4
	Totals	534	2869	.440	1109	.783	2240	1408	7191	13.5

JALEN ROSE 22 6-8 210 — Guard

Is heading into a nice pro career ... Started 37 times as a rookie, including every game after the all-star break ... Needs to become more consistent from the perimeter, but is still dangerous out to three-point range ... Probably the best passer on the team ... Nuggets have an advantage over most teams with someone of his size handling the ball ... Played in the Rookie All-Star Game ... Set team record for first-year players with 389 assists ... Part of the Fab Five that led Michigan to consecutive trips to the NCAA final ... Born Jan. 30, 1973, in Detroit ... Made $975,000 last season.

Year	Team	G	FG	FG Pct.	FT	FT Pct.	Reb.	Ast.	TP	Avg.
1994-95	Denver	81	227	.454	173	.739	217	389	663	8.2

BRYANT STITH 24 6-5 208 — Guard

Nuggets have to be encouraged that his shooting percentage continues to climb ... Still no threat beyond 18 feet, a glaring weakness for a shooting guard ... Only 20 three-pointers last season ... Then again, it was 18 more than his first two pro seasons combined ... Good strength, so he likes to go inside ... Named team captain Dec. 20 ... In the opening lineup

256 • **THE COMPLETE HANDBOOK OF PRO BASKETBALL**

51 times... Once had a string of 138 consecutive starts... Led Virginia to NIT championship as a senior in 1992, beating LaPhonso Ellis and Notre Dame in the title game... Nuggets took him 13th from there... Born Dec. 10, 1970, in Emporia, Va.... 1994-95 salary: $1.375 million.

Year	Team	G	FG	FG Pct.	FT	FT Pct.	Reb.	Ast.	TP	Avg.
1992-93	Denver	39	124	.446	99	.832	124	49	347	8.9
1993-94	Denver	82	365	.450	291	.829	349	199	1023	12.5
1994-95	Denver	81	312	.472	267	.824	268	153	911	11.2
	Totals	202	801	.458	657	.827	741	401	2281	11.3

ROBERT PACK 26 6-2 190   Guard

Plenty of teams regret at least not investing a second-round pick on him. Now we find out what they really think of speedy point guard... Headed into the summer as an unrestricted free agent... Great penetrator... Not much of an outside threat, although he finally posted a good three-point percentage, albeit with limited attempts... Didn't help that he missed the final 30 games due to injury... Started in 32 of 42 appearances... Played with Harold Miner in the backcourt at USC... Not only did he go undrafted, but he couldn't even get an invitation to summer league... Trail Blazers gave him a chance and never regretted it... They traded him to Denver in 1992 for a second-rounder... Born Feb. 3, 1969, in New Orleans... Made $1.059 million last season.

Year	Team	G	FG	FG Pct.	FT	FT Pct.	Reb.	Ast.	TP	Avg.
1991-92	Portland	72	115	.423	102	.803	97	140	332	4.6
1992-93	Denver	77	285	.470	239	.768	160	335	810	10.5
1993-94	Denver	66	223	.443	179	.758	123	356	631	9.6
1994-95	Denver	42	170	.430	137	.783	113	290	507	12.1
	Totals	257	793	.447	657	.774	493	1121	2280	8.9

BRIAN WILLIAMS 26 6-11 260   Forward

Orlando must hate him... Magic spent the No. 10 pick in 1991 to bring him in, only to get an up-and-down player and person... Then he developed into dependable reserve with the Nuggets after Denver dumped Todd Lichti and Anthony Cook on Magic in Aug. 1993... Still is young enough that he could make more strides, so this is an interesting package...

Started college career at Maryland, then transferred to Arizona ... Led Pacific-10 Conference in shooting as a junior ... Born April 6, 1969, in Fresno, Cal. ... 1994-95 salary: $2 million.

Year	Team	G	FG	FG Pct.	FT	FT Pct.	Reb.	Ast.	TP	Avg.
1991-92	Orlando	48	171	.528	95	.669	272	33	437	9.1
1992-93	Orlando	21	40	.513	16	.800	56	5	96	4.6
1993-94	Denver	80	251	.541	137	.649	446	50	639	8.0
1994-95	Denver	63	196	.589	106	.654	298	53	498	7.9
	Totals	212	658	.549	354	.662	1072	141	1670	7.9

TOM HAMMONDS 28 6-9 223 — Forward

Helped by athleticism, hindered by being a tweener ... It's especially crowded at power forward when LaPhonso Ellis is healthy, so he could become the odd man out ... Started five times ... Lottery bust as No. 9 pick by Washington in 1989 ... Nuggets got him as a free agent midway through 1992-93 ... Had his jersey No. 20 retired after starring at Georgia Tech ... No. 4 on the school's all-time scoring list ... Played for the U.S. team that won a gold medal at the 1986 world championships ... Races stock cars in the offseason ... Born March 27, 1967, in Crestview, Fla. ... Made $700,000 in 1994-95.

Year	Team	G	FG	FG Pct.	FT	FT Pct.	Reb.	Ast.	TP	Avg.
1989-90	Washington	61	129	.437	63	.643	168	51	321	5.3
1990-91	Washington	70	155	.461	57	.722	206	43	367	5.2
1991-92	Washington	37	195	.488	50	.610	185	36	440	11.9
1992-93	Char.-Den.	54	105	.475	38	.613	127	24	248	4.6
1993-94	Denver	74	115	.500	71	.683	199	34	301	4.1
1994-95	Denver	70	139	.535	132	.746	222	36	410	5.9
	Totals	366	838	.481	411	.683	1107	224	2087	5.7

DALE ELLIS 35 6-7 215 — Guard-Forward

Hired gun ... One of the all-time great long-range marksmen ... No. 1, in fact, in NBA history in three-pointers made (1,119) ... Led the Nuggets in scoring off the bench ... Started three games when Reggie Williams and Bryant Stith were hurt ... Originally was No. 9 pick overall by Dallas in 1983 ... It looked like he couldn't shoot, of all things, so Mavericks traded him to Seattle for Al Wood in an amazing swindle ... Named NBA's Most Improved Player in 1986-87 and was an all-star reserve in 1989 ... Played league-record 69 minutes Nov. 9, 1989, against Milwaukee ... Spent two years with Spurs before signing with Nuggets last season ... All-American at Tennessee ... Born Aug. 6, 1960, in Marietta, Ga. ... Earned $1.007 million in 1994-95.

Year	Team	G	FG	FG Pct.	FT	FT Pct.	Reb.	Ast.	TP	Avg.
1983-84	Dallas	67	225	.456	87	.719	250	56	549	8.2
1984-85	Dallas	72	274	.454	77	.740	238	56	667	9.3
1985-86	Dallas	72	193	.411	59	.720	168	37	508	7.1
1986-87	Seattle	82	785	.516	385	.787	447	238	2041	24.9
1987-88	Seattle	75	764	.503	303	.767	340	197	1938	25.8
1988-89	Seattle	82	857	.501	377	.816	342	164	2253	27.5
1989-90	Seattle	55	502	.497	193	.818	238	110	1293	23.5
1990-91	Sea.-Mil.	51	340	.474	120	.723	173	95	857	16.8
1991-92	Milwaukee	81	485	.469	164	.774	253	104	1272	15.7
1992-93	San Antonio	82	545	.499	157	.797	312	107	1366	16.7
1993-94	San Antonio	77	478	.494	83	.776	255	80	1170	15.2
1994-95	Denver	81	351	.453	110	.866	222	57	918	11.3
	Totals	877	5799	.487	2115	.784	3238	1301	14832	16.9

CLIFF LEVINGSTON 34 6-8 225   Forward-Center

The one they call "Good News" will be in for some bad news soon. His career is over ... Made 57 appearances last season, but at less than 10 minutes per ... And that was with LaPhonse Ellis out most of the season. Imagine if the starting power forward had been around ... Won a pair of championship rings with the Bulls, then spent the next two seasons in Spain and Italy, respectively ... Came back to the NBA when Denver signed him to a $650,000 free-agent deal on the opening day of training camp ... Wichita State star was No. 9 pick by Detroit in 1982 ... Led the Shockers in rebounding each of three seasons ... Born Jan. 4, 1961, in San Diego.

Year	Team	G	FG	FG Pct.	FT	FT Pct.	Reb.	Ast.	TP	Avg.
1982-83	Detroit	62	131	.485	84	.571	232	52	346	5.6
1983-84	Detroit	80	229	.525	125	.672	545	109	583	7.3
1984-85	Atlanta	74	291	.527	145	.653	566	104	727	9.8
1985-86	Atlanta	81	294	.534	164	.678	534	72	752	9.3
1986-87	Atlanta	82	251	.506	155	.731	533	40	657	8.0
1987-88	Atlanta	82	314	.557	190	.772	504	71	819	10.0
1988-89	Atlanta	80	300	.528	133	.696	498	75	734	9.2
1989-90	Atlanta	75	216	.509	83	.680	319	80	516	6.9
1990-91	Chicago	78	127	.450	59	.648	225	56	314	4.0
1991-92	Chicago	79	125	.498	60	.625	227	66	311	3.9
1994-95	Denver	57	55	.423	19	.422	124	27	129	2.3
	Totals	830	2333	.516	1217	.676	4307	752	5888	7.1

MARK RANDALL 28 6-9 245 Forward

Never strayed too far from home... A Nugget in 1993-94, he was with Rapid City of the CBA when Denver signed him again last season... This time, it was on a 10-day contract Feb. 23... Inked for the rest of the season on March 17... Went on the injured list about a week later... Will he be back this season? Probably not. But keep checking... Only Nugget to hail from Colorado, having starred at Cherry Creek High in Englewood... His coach there was Mack Calvin, the longtime NBA assistant who is now head coach with Mexico City of the CBA... Led Kansas to the NCAA title game as a senior in 1991, just before the Bulls took him with the 26th pick... Born Sept. 30, 1967, in Edina, Minn.

Year	Team	G	FG	FG Pct.	FT	FT Pct.	Reb.	Ast.	TP	Avg.
1991-92	Chi.-Minn.	54	68	.456	32	.744	71	33	171	3.2
1992-93	Minn.-Det.	37	40	.500	16	.615	55	11	97	2.6
1993-94	Denver	28	17	.340	22	.786	22	11	58	2.1
1994-95	Denver	8	3	.300	0	.000	12	1	6	0.8
	Totals	127	128	.443	70	.722	160	56	332	2.6

RANDY WOODS 25 5-10 185 Guard

Maybe the Clippers kept him around so no one would bring up the Bo Kimble draft pick any more... Came to Denver in offseason deal... His average of eight minutes a game last season was a team low... Started three times, and shot 25 percent in those games... Shooting guard through high school and college, even at 5-10, before Clippers took LaSalle product 16th in 1992 with the idea of converting him to point guard... Attended same high school, only a few years behind, as current teammate Pooh Richardson... Played college ball with Lionel Simmons... Born Sept. 23, 1970, in Philadelphia... 1994-95 salary: $800,000.

Year	Team	G	FG	FG Pct.	FT	FT Pct.	Reb.	Ast.	TP	Avg.
1992-93	L.A. Clippers	41	23	.348	19	.731	14	40	68	1.7
1993-94	L.A. Clippers	40	49	.368	20	.571	29	71	145	3.6
1994-95	L.A. Clippers	62	37	.316	28	.737	44	134	124	2.0
	Totals	143	109	.345	67	.677	87	245	337	2.4

GREG GRANT 29 5-7 140   Guard

Major stockholder of U-Haul... Denver was his third stop last season... Started with Orlando, but was on the injured list and never got in a game... Then went to Mexico City, where he averaged 16.8 points and a CBA-leading 9.9 assists... Nuggets signed him to a 10-day contract March 14, then for the rest of the season April 5... Played in each of the last 10 games and led Denver in assists in the final three... Not just a waterbug. That's his nickname, too... Wonder why... Smallest player in Nugget history... Led all Division III scorers as a senior at Trenton State (N.J.) in 1989, just before the Suns drafted him 52nd... Made $150,000 last season... Born Aug. 29, 1966, in Trenton, N.J.

Year	Team	G	FG	FG Pct.	FT	FT Pct.	Reb.	Ast.	TP	Avg.
1989-90	Phoenix	67	83	.384	39	.661	59	168	208	3.1
1990-91	New York	22	10	.370	5	.833	10	20	26	1.2
1991-92	Char.-Phil.	68	99	.440	20	.833	69	217	225	3.3
1992-93	Philadelphia	72	77	.350	20	.645	67	206	194	2.7
1994-95	Denver	14	10	.303	9	.750	9	43	31	2.2
	Totals	243	279	.387	93	.705	214	654	684	2.8

THE ROOKIES

ANTONIO McDYESS 21 6-9 220   Forward
Clippers took him second overall, then immediately traded Alabama product with Randy Woods to Denver for Rodney Rogers, and Brent Barry... If this guy is as promised, he'll become a steal for the Nuggets... Not just a good leaper, but very quick off the ground... Left school after sophomore season... His play in the NCAA tournament made a very favorable impression with the scouts... Born Sept. 7, 1974, in Quitman, Miss.

ANTHONY PELLE 22 7-0 260   Center
As if the team that has Dikembe Mutombo needs another potential force inside... Had 53 blocks in 26 games as a senior at Fresno State... Then showed the same skills at Portsmouth Invitational... Transferred to Fresno after spending first three seasons at Villanova, with little playing time... Born Dec. 1, 1972, in New York.

COACH BERNIE BICKERSTAFF:  You just couldn't stay away, could you?... Already the president and general manager when he took over as coach on Feb. 20... Directed a dramatic turnaround that got the once-flailing Nuggets into the playoffs for the second straight year... They were 21-29 and eight games out of the final postseason spot when he replaced interim coach Gene Littles, who had moved into the job when Dan Issel quit... Under Bickerstaff, Denver went 20-12, the seventh-best mark in the league for those final 32 games... Career record: 222-220 (50.2 percent)... Few realize it, but this will be his 24th season in the NBA... Only previous job as head coach was five years with the Sonics, from 1985-90... NBA Coach of the Year in 1986-87... Also served as No. 1 assistant with Washington from 1974-85, during which time the Bullets were in the Finals three times and won the championship in 1978... Quit there largely because of the stress that caused health concerns... Came to Denver to run the show from the front office, not the sidelines... Starred at the University of San Diego... Member of the USA Basketball committee that will select the coaching staff and players for the 1996 Olympics... Has a street dedicated in his honor—Bernard Bickerstaff Boulevard—in Benham, Ky., where he was born Nov. 2, 1943.

GREATEST FIND

A virtual unknown today, Byron Beck went from being a fifth-round pick in 1967 to spending 10 years with the franchise, beginning back when it was known as the Rockets.

In seven of those years, he averaged double-digit scoring, unspectacular but steady play that earned him the honor of having his uniform No. 40 retired.

Reggie Williams could make an argument for being the Nuggets' greatest find. Consider, after all, that he had been dumped in trade by the Clippers as a first-round washout, and then cut by both the Cavaliers and Spurs in close succession. He was signed Jan. 5, 1991, as an unwanted free agent and responded by averaging 18.2, 17 and 13 points his first three seasons while starting at small forward and shooting guard.

ALL-TIME NUGGET LEADERS

SEASON

Points: Spencer Haywood, 2,519, 1969–70 (ABA)
Alex English, 2,414, 1985–86
Assists: Michael Adams, 693, 1990–91
Rebounds: Spencer Haywood, 1,637, 1969–70 (ABA)
Dikembe Mutombo, 1,070, 1992–93

GAME

Points: David Thompson, 73 vs. Detroit, 4/9/78
Assists: Larry Brown, 23 vs. Pittsburgh, 2/20/72 (ABA)
Lafayette Lever, 23 vs. Golden State, 4/21/89
Rebounds: Spencer Haywood, 31 vs. Kentucky, 11/13/69 (ABA)
Jerome Lane, 25 vs. Houston, 4/21/91

CAREER

Points: Alex English, 21,645, 1979–90
Assists: Alex English, 3,679, 1979–90
Rebounds: Dan Issel, 6,630, 1975–85

HOUSTON ROCKETS

TEAM DIRECTORY: Owner: Les Alexander; VP-Basketball Oper.: Bob Weinhauer; VP-Bus. Oper.: John Thomas; Dir. Pub. Rel.: Kathy Frietsch; Coach: Rudy Tomjanovich; Asst. Coaches: Carroll Dawson, Bill Berry, Larry Smith. Arena: The Summit (16,279). Colors: Red and gold.

No debate on Hakeem Olajuwon's playoff MVP award.

SCOUTING REPORT

SHOOTING: Think they'll survive the loss of Vernon Maxwell? His release means the two-time champion Rockets may only take 100 more three-pointers than any other team. Last season, they had 155 more attempts from behind the arc, a remarkable state considering the dominating player, Hakeem Olajuwon, was inside and the complement, Clyde Drexler, loved to play on the run.

But that says a lot about this team. Everything happens in the flow. After all, Olajuwon watched all those bombs fly overhead and he still got about 300 more shots than any other Rocket in 1994-95, and this was while sitting out 10 games because of injury. Once the ball went into him, the options were limitless. Fall away. Spin-move into the lane. Jumper from 16 feet.

If Drexler continues to play like he's 33 going on 29, defenses get stretched even more. The additional years of experience have provided a much-needed maturity to his game; gone are the wild three-pointers he was known for in Portland. Meanwhile, he still runs the floor like a locomotive, sometimes even getting the defensive rebound to lead the break.

And then there's the interesting decision facing coach Rudy Tomjanovich: Keep Robert Horry at power forward, like in the late rounds of the '95 playoffs, or move him back to small forward? His skills as a three-point shooter make for a difficult matchup at the higher weight class.

PLAYMAKING: Kenny Cassell. Sam Smith. Interchangeable parts—known officially as Kenny Smith and Sam Cassell—that continue to work. Only people outside the organization still question the system's worth.

It works because both players are unselfish. Cassell could be emerging into a standout in another city, but here he goes about developing into one of the game's best backups at any position. Smith is a better shooter, finishing seventh in the NBA in three-point percentage last season, but Cassell had a better assist-to-turnover ratio.

REBOUNDING: Terrible. Now try telling them how that causes so many problems. Mention it as they're polishing those two rings.

It's Olajuwon against the world here. The Rockets finished 20th in the league by percentage en route to the first title, then a tie for 25th last season while finishing the encore. Only Detroit

ROCKET ROSTER

No.	Veterans	Pos.	Ht.	Wt.	Age	Yrs. Pro	College
52	Chucky Brown	F	6-8	215	27	6	North Carolina State
10	Sam Cassell	G	6-3	195	25	2	Florida State
32	Pete Chilcutt	F	6-11	235	27	4	North Carolina
22	Clyde Drexler	G	6-7	222	33	12	Houston
17	Mario Elie	F-G	6-5	210	31	5	American Int'l
7	Carl Herrera	F	6-9	225	28	4	Houston
25	Robert Horry	F	6-9	220	25	3	Alabama
27	Charles Jones	C	6-9	215	38	12	Albany State
34	Hakeem Olajuwon	C	7-0	255	32	11	Houston
30	Kenny Smith	G	6-3	170	30	8	North Carolina

Rd.	Rookie	Sel.No.	Pos.	Ht.	Wt.	College
2	Eric Meek	41	F-C	6-10	245	Duke

and Minnesota were worse. Strange company (though the tie was with Charlotte, another surprise considering the presence of Alonzo Mourning and Larry Johnson).

To think the Rockets are trying to make things even more challenging. They went into the lockout without a legitimate power forward and no backup center to be trusted over the long haul, which is why their lone draft pick, at No. 41, went to Duke big man Erik Meek. The counter is that Drexler has always been uncommonly good here for a guard.

DEFENSE: They don't force many turnovers, but few clubs play as good team defense. Two seasons ago, the third-best mark in the league in shooting percentage-against. Last season, a tie for second overall and No. 1 in the West.

Horry has a big impact as one of only a handful of small forwards, if he plays there, who blocks shots. And Drexler, though not many realized it, finished 11th in the league in 1994-95 in steals. Oh, yeah. That Olajuwon guy. Second in blocks, ninth in steals and guaranteed to be somewhere near the top in intimidations if those were tracked.

OUTLOOK: They've got no chance. Won't even get out of the first round. No, won't even get into the playoffs. So you know what that means. That's right. Another parade.

ROCKET PROFILES

HAKEEM OLAJUWON 32 7-0 255   Center

He's the Chicago of the NBA. The player with the big shoulders... That's two years in a row now he has carried an entire franchise across the finish line... What he did in the playoffs was nothing less than awesome... The only question is where it ranks among the all-time great showings... Named Finals MVP for the second straight season, joining Michael Jordan as the only player to ever do that... Rockets think his turnaround jumper from the left baseline is the most reliable weapon in the game. "I don't know how you stop that shot," coach Rudy Tomjanovich said. "It's an all-pro shot, a Hall of Fame shot."... From a future Hall of Fame player... Ten-time all-star... Born Jan. 21, 1963, in Lagos, Nigeria, and came to the United States as a skinny unknown at the University of Houston... Stayed in town when the Rockets picked him first overall in 1984... Earning an average of $3.169 million annually.

Year	Team	G	FG	FG Pct.	FT	FT Pct.	Reb.	Ast.	TP	Avg.
1984-85	Houston	82	677	.538	338	.613	974	111	1692	20.6
1985-86	Houston	68	625	.526	347	.645	781	137	1597	23.5
1986-87	Houston	75	677	.508	400	.702	858	220	1755	23.4
1987-88	Houston	79	712	.514	381	.695	959	163	1805	22.8
1988-89	Houston	82	790	.508	454	.696	1105	149	2034	24.8
1989-90	Houston	82	806	.501	382	.713	1149	234	1995	24.3
1990-91	Houston	56	487	.508	213	.769	770	131	1187	21.2
1991-92	Houston	70	591	.502	328	.766	845	157	1510	21.6
1992-93	Houston	82	848	.529	444	.779	1068	291	2140	26.1
1993-94	Houston	80	894	.528	388	.716	955	287	2184	27.3
1994-95	Houston	72	798	.517	406	.756	775	255	2005	27.8
	Totals	828	7905	.516	4081	.710	10239	2135	19904	24.0

CLYDE DREXLER 33 6-7 222   Guard

You mean all college reunions aren't like this?... Came back to Houston, his hometown, and back to a Phi Slama Jama teammate Hakeem Olajuwon, then finally won a championship ring... Reached the Finals twice before, but the Trail Blazers lost both times... The Valentine's Day trade that sent him from Portland to the Rockets along with Tracy Murray for

HOUSTON ROCKETS • 267

Otis Thorpe and the rights to Marcelo Nicola was the most controversial of last season . . . By the time the playoffs had ended, it was obviously also one of the best . . . Provided Houston with a second offensive weapon . . . And looked four years younger . . . Great in the Finals . . . "I coached Clyde Drexler his first three years in the NBA," Jack Ramsay said. "He's never played better basketball." . . . Underrated for his passing skills . . . Born June 22, 1962, in New Orleans . . . Trail Blazers drafted him 14th in 1983 . . . Made $1.578 million last season.

Year	Team	G	FG	FG Pct.	FT	FT Pct.	Reb.	Ast.	TP	Avg.
1983-84	Portland	82	252	.451	123	.728	235	153	628	7.7
1984-85	Portland	80	573	.494	223	.759	476	441	1377	17.2
1985-86	Portland	75	542	.475	293	.769	421	600	1389	18.5
1986-87	Portland	82	707	.502	357	.760	518	566	1782	21.7
1987-88	Portland	81	849	.506	476	.811	533	467	2185	27.0
1988-89	Portland	78	829	.496	438	.799	615	450	2123	27.2
1989-90	Portland	73	670	.494	333	.774	507	432	1703	23.3
1990-91	Portland	82	645	.482	416	.794	546	493	1767	21.5
1991-92	Portland	76	694	.470	401	.794	500	512	1903	25.0
1992-93	Portland	49	350	.429	245	.839	309	278	976	19.9
1993-94	Portland	68	473	.428	286	.777	445	333	1303	19.2
1994-95	Port.-Hou.	76	571	.461	364	.824	480	362	1653	21.8
Totals		902	7155	.479	3955	.789	5585	5087	18789	20.8

ROBERT HORRY 25 6-9 220   Forward

Horry, Horry, hallelujah . . . The starting small forward during the regular season and early rounds of the playoffs became the starting power forward and played a huge role against San Antonio and Orlando . . . Three-point range causes major matchup problems, and he didn't get killed on the boards . . . Terrific in the open court . . . Still has Pistons' jersey on the wall of his home as a reminder of the aborted trade to Detroit in 1993-94 . . . Teammates with Latrell Sprewell and James Robinson at Alabama . . . One of only two players in SEC history to block 100 shots in a season. The other is some guy named Shaquille O'Neal . . . No. 11 pick in 1992 . . . Born Aug. 25, 1970, in Andalusia, Ala. . . . 1994-95 salary: $1.499 million.

Year	Team	G	FG	FG Pct.	FT	FT Pct.	Reb.	Ast.	TP	Avg.
1992-93	Houston	79	323	.474	143	.715	392	191	801	10.1
1993-94	Houston	81	322	.459	115	.732	440	231	803	9.9
1994-95	Houston	64	240	.447	86	.761	324	216	652	10.2
Totals		224	885	.461	344	.732	1156	638	2256	10.1

KENNY SMITH 30 6-3 170   Guard

Still holding off the kid... Started in all 81 appearances last season, keeping Sam Cassell in a reserve role... But clearly not your typical point guard... Averaged just 4.0 assists a game, fourth on the team behind Cassell, Clyde Drexler and Vernon Maxwell... On the other hand, he was eighth in the NBA in three-point accuracy (42.9 percent) after finishing seventh in 1993-94... No. 1 in franchise history in career three-point percentage... All it took the Rockets to get him from Atlanta in Sept. 1990 was John Lucas and Tim McCormick... Lottery pick by Sacramento, No. 6 overall, in 1987 after starring at North Carolina... Born March 8, 1965, in Queens, N.Y.... 1994-95 salary: $2.633 million.

Year	Team	G	FG	FG Pct.	FT	FT Pct.	Reb.	Ast.	TP	Avg.
1987-88	Sacramento	61	331	.477	167	.819	138	434	841	13.8
1988-89	Sacramento	81	547	.462	263	.737	226	621	1403	17.3
1989-90	Sac.-Atl.	79	378	.466	161	.821	157	445	943	11.9
1990-91	Houston	78	522	.520	287	.844	163	554	1380	17.7
1991-92	Houston	81	432	.475	219	.866	177	562	1137	14.0
1992-93	Houston	82	387	.520	195	.878	160	446	1065	13.0
1993-94	Houston	78	341	.480	135	.871	138	327	906	11.6
1994-95	Houston	81	287	.484	126	.851	155	323	842	10.4
	Totals	621	3225	.485	1553	.828	1314	3712	8517	13.7

SAM CASSELL 25 6-3 195   Guard

Two years in the pros, two championship rings... Came up big in the playoffs both times... His role is as the backup point guard who often gets the minutes of a starter... The only Rocket to play all 82 games last season... No. 1 on the team in assists... Has the poise of a 10-year veteran... Another in the long line of products from Dunbar High in Baltimore... Later starred at Florida State, playing in the same backcourt with Charlie Ward... Left as the school record holder with 97 steals... Rockets got him with the 24th pick in 1993... Born Nov. 18, 1969, in Baltimore... Made $845,000 in 1994-95.

Year	Team	G	FG	FG Pct.	FT	FT Pct.	Reb.	Ast.	TP	Avg.
1993-94	Houston	66	162	.418	90	.841	134	192	440	6.7
1994-95	Houston	82	253	.427	214	.843	211	405	783	9.5
	Totals	148	415	.423	304	.842	345	597	1223	8.3

MARIO ELIE 31 6-5 210 — Guard-Forward

Always versatile, but never more valuable than during the championship drive... Baseline three-pointer in the closing seconds at Phoenix gave the Rockets a Game 7 victory and a trip to the Western Conference finals... Soon after, he went from being Clyde Drexler's backup at shooting guard to the starting small forward... Terrific in the Finals... Normally a sixth or seventh man... Started 13 times during the regular season... Rockets got him from Portland in the summer of 1993 for a second-round pick... Has been in the playoffs each of his five years in the league since Milwaukee took him with the 160th pick of the 1985 draft... American International product was born Nov. 26, 1963, in New York... Makes an average of $1.45 million a year.

Year	Team	G	FG	FG Pct.	FT	FT Pct.	Reb.	Ast.	TP	Avg.
1990-91	Phil.-G.S.	33	79	.497	75	.843	110	45	237	7.2
1991-92	Golden State	79	221	.521	155	.852	227	174	620	7.8
1992-93	Portland	82	240	.458	183	.855	216	177	708	8.6
1993-94	Houston	67	208	.446	154	.860	181	208	626	9.3
1994-95	Houston	81	243	.499	144	.842	196	189	710	8.8
	Totals	342	991	.481	711	.851	930	793	2901	8.5

CARL HERRERA 28 6-9 225 — Forward

Never got the chance to appreciate Otis Thorpe being traded... Would have become the starting power forward, but injuries nixed that... It was a hamstring in February and March, two dislocated shoulders in April and May... Made one appearance in the playoffs, then watched from the sidelines... Like current teammates Hakeem Olajuwon and Clyde Drexler, he attended the University of Houston... Second-round pick by Miami in 1990, then traded to the Rockets with Dave Jamerson for Alec Kessler... Played in Spain for a year, then returned to Houston... First player from Venezuela to make the NBA... 1992 Olympian for that country... Has climbed to No. 6 in Rockets' history in shooting (51.2 percent)... Born Dec. 14,

1966, in Trinidad . . . 1994-95 salary: $1.35 million.

Year	Team	G	FG	FG Pct.	FT	FT Pct.	Reb.	Ast.	TP	Avg.
1991-92	Houston	43	83	.516	25	.568	99	27	191	4.4
1992-93	Houston	81	240	.541	125	.710	454	61	605	7.5
1993-94	Houston	75	142	.458	69	.711	285	37	353	4.7
1994-95	Houston	61	171	.523	73	.624	278	44	415	6.8
	Totals	260	636	.512	292	.673	1116	169	1564	6.0

CHUCKY BROWN 27 6-8 215 Forward

Nice contributions last season from a 10-day guy . . . Hard worker and class act had stabilizing influence on the court during a lengthy stretch of starts at power forward . . . A natural small forward, so he was playing out of position . . . With Yakima of the CBA when the Rockets came calling in February . . . Not much of a scoring threat, but chooses his shots wisely . . . No. 2 on the all-time shooting percentage list at North Carolina State . . . Cavaliers took him 43rd overall in 1989 . . . It's been one long road trip since . . . Rockets were his fifth NBA team in six years . . . Also had one season in Italy . . . Clarence Brown was born Feb. 29, 1968, in New York.

Year	Team	G	FG	FG Pct.	FT	FT Pct.	Reb.	Ast.	TP	Avg.
1989-90	Cleveland	75	210	.470	125	.762	231	50	545	7.3
1990-91	Cleveland	74	263	.524	101	.701	213	80	627	8.5
1991-92	Clev.-LAL	42	60	.469	30	.612	82	26	150	3.6
1992-93	New Jersey	77	160	.483	71	.724	232	51	391	5.1
1993-94	Dallas	1	1	1.000	1	1.000	1	0	3	3.0
1994-95	Houston	41	105	.603	38	.613	189	30	249	6.1
	Totals	310	799	.505	366	.707	948	237	1965	6.3

PETE CHILCUTT 27 6-11 235 Forward

He couldn't cut it in Sacramento and Detroit, so what would happen in Houston? Of course. He became the starting power forward during much of the playoffs for a championship team . . . Wonder why we didn't see that coming . . . He earned job in the regular season after Otis Thorpe was traded and Carl Herrera went down with a shoulder injury . . . Went back to the bench late in playoffs when Rockets changed to a small lineup and put Robert Horry at power forward ... Signed as a free agent about a month into last season ... Sacramento made him the 17th pick of the 1991 draft after a standout career at North Carolina ... Tar Heels' teammates included J.R. Reid, Hubert Davis, Rick Fox and Scott Williams ... Born Sept. 14, 1968, in Sumter, S.C. ... Made $126,300 in 1994-95.

Year	Team	G	FG	FG Pct.	FT	FT Pct.	Reb.	Ast.	TP	Avg.
1991-92	Sacramento	69	113	.452	23	.821	187	38	251	3.5
1992-93	Sacramento	59	165	.485	32	.696	194	84	362	6.2
1993-94	Sac.-Det.	76	203	.453	41	.631	371	86	450	5.9
1994-95	Houston	68	146	.445	31	.738	317	66	358	5.3
	Totals	272	627	.459	127	.702	1069	254	1421	5.2

CHARLES JONES 38 6-9 215   Center

The only role he should have played last spring was *steam* rolled ... Instead, his play as Hakeem Olajuwon's backup against David Robinson and then Shaquille O'Neal in the final two rounds was a nice contribution to the title ... Used 12 years of NBA experience to compensate for difference in skills ... Nothing spectacular, but kept a body on his man all the time and did not concede anything ... All this came after he was signed to a 10-day contract in March and then eventually for the rest of the season, in time to make three appearances in the regular season ... Albany State product was originally an eighth-round pick by the Suns in 1979 ... Brothers Caldwell, Major and Wil all played in the NBA, and Caldwell and Major spent time with the Rockets ... Born April 3, 1957, in McGehee, Ark.

Year	Team	G	FG	FG Pct.	FT	FT Pct.	Reb.	Ast.	TP	Avg.
1983-84	Philadelphia	1	0	.000	1	.250	0	0	1	1.0
1984-85	Chi.-Wash.	31	67	.528	40	.690	184	26	174	5.6
1985-86	Washington	81	129	.508	54	.628	321	76	312	3.9
1986-87	Washington	79	118	.474	48	.632	356	80	284	3.6
1987-88	Washington	69	72	.407	53	.707	325	59	197	2.9
1988-89	Washington	53	60	.480	16	.640	257	42	136	2.6
1989-90	Washington	81	94	.508	68	.648	504	139	256	3.2
1990-91	Washington	62	67	.540	29	.580	359	48	163	2.6
1991-92	Washington	75	33	.367	20	.500	317	62	86	1.1
1992-93	Washington	67	33	.524	22	.579	277	42	88	1.3
1993-94	Detroit	42	36	.462	19	.559	235	29	91	2.2
1994-95	Houston	3	1	.333	1	.500	7	0	3	1.0
	Totals	644	710	.481	371	.626	3142	603	1791	2.8

THE ROOKIE

ERIK MEEK 22 6-10 245 **Forward-Center**
Averaged just 15.4 minutes and five points a game during Duke career, but his stock soared with postseason showings... MVP of the Portsmouth Invitational and earned a spot in the Desert Classic in Phoenix... Rockets, still looking for an emergency backup at center, took him 41st... Born Jan. 17, 1973, in San Diego.

COACH RUDY TOMJANOVICH: For his next number, he will find a cure for the common cold and in his spare time come up with a Middle East peace plan... Deserves as much credit as Hakeem Olajuwon or Clyde Drexler for Rockets' magical run last season... Made sure the team did not go into the tank during the regular season that included the then-questionable Otis Thorpe-Clyde Drexler trade, several injuries

and the suspension of Vernon Maxwell... Then, in the playoffs, he made a key personnel decision by moving Robert Horry from small forward to power forward... Horry made it work with his play, but Rudy T made it happen in the first place... Joins some of the biggest names of his coaching generation—Pat Riley, Chuck Daly, Phil Jackson—as people who have won back-to-back titles... The one drawback: the adulation and glowing praise. He hates that... Loves the winning, but wishes he could still remain anonymous in the process... To think he took over for Don Chaney for the final 30 games of 1991-92 on a test run, unsure if he even wanted to be a head coach because of the lack of job security and lack of personal time... Since then, he's 176-100 (63.8 percent)... Jackson is the only active coach with a better winning percentage in the playoffs... Heads into 26th consecutive season with the organization, a stretch that started when the San Diego Rockets picked him No. 2 overall in 1970... Went from being All-American at Michigan to an 11-year career and five trips to the All-Star Game... Later, he had his jersey No. 45 retired... Became a scout after retiring in 1981, then an assistant coach from 1983-92... Blue-collar kind of guy was born Nov. 24, 1948, in Hamtramck, Mich.

Robert Horry earned big chunk of championship trophy.

GREATEST FIND

Remember when he used to get all that attention for twirling batons? Calvin Murphy used that and his basketball skills to become one of the most recognizable names of his time. A second-round pick from Niagara in 1970, he became arguably the greatest player in team history—now second to Hakeem Olajuwon—on basketball skills alone.

Murphy spent his entire career (1970-71 to 1982-83) with the Rockets, who then retired his uniform number. He was inducted into the Hall of Fame in 1983.

ALL-TIME ROCKET LEADERS

SEASON

Points: Moses Malone, 2,520, 1980–81
Assists: John Lucas, 768, 1977–78
Rebounds: Moses Malone, 1,444, 1978–79

GAME

Points: Calvin Murphy, 57 vs. New Jersey, 3/18/78
Assists: Art Williams, 22 vs. San Francisco, 2/14/70
        Art Williams, 22 vs. Phoenix, 12/28/68
Rebounds: Moses Malone, 37 vs. New Orleans, 2/9/79

CAREER

Points: Hakeem Olajuwon, 19,904, 1984–95
Assists: Calvin Murphy, 4,402, 1970–83
Rebounds: Hakeem Olajuwon, 10,239, 1984–95

MINNESOTA TIMBERWOLVES

TEAM DIRECTORY: Owner: Glen Taylor; GM: Flip Saunders; VP Basketball Oper.: Kevin McHale; Dir. Media Rel.: Kent Wipf; Coach: Bill Blair; Asst. Coaches: Mike Schuler, Randy Wittman, Greg Ballard. Arena: Target Center (19,006). Colors: Blue, green and silver.

Slam-dunking J.R. Rider headed Wolves in scoring.

SCOUTING REPORT

SHOOTING: We have a pretty good idea why they can't get shots, as in why they finished last in the league in attempts in 1994-95 after finishing next-to-last the season before. That has a lot to do with the point guards that aren't generating the offense and the big men that aren't getting any rebounds. But more on both of those aspects later.

For now, we will dwell on the inability of all the players to convert the few opportunities they get. Christian Laettner, Isaiah Rider, Doug West, Tom Gugliotta. Say what you will about the antics of a couple of them, but they should constitute some offensive firepower. If they lost games, 120-110, we would understand a little better. But to average 94.2 points—a drop of 2½ from the season before—shoot 44.9 percent and not have a single regular break 49 percent? Brutal.

And here's a crazy thought. Make a three-pointer every homestand or so. No team had worse accuracy last season. Rider set the tone—he had more tries from behind the line than 16 of the top 20 finishers by percentage, but didn't finish in the top 40 himself. Ease off, J.R.

PLAYMAKING: No area of the team will more intriguing. In fact, part of this department will be one of the most-watched stories of the entire league.

Kevin Garnett, heading into his senior year of high school a year ago at this time, is no point guard. But of all the glowing praise heaped upon the prospect extraordinaire, so much is about his ball-handling and passing skills. A point forward at 6-10, and eventually 7-foot? Too early to tell. This much we do know now: The Timberwolves can use the help.

Only three teams had a worse assist-to-turnover ratio last season. Only two teams committed more turnovers, which would at least be easier to understand if this was a team that loved to run and score. But, as stated above, they don't score. And don't give us this bit about Micheal Williams missing all but one game because of a foot injury—he was the starter in 1993-94, when Minnesota was just as bad. Chris Smith hasn't proved to be the answer, either.

REBOUNDING: They were last by percentage among the 27 teams during 1994-95 in defensive rebounds, thus inhibiting the offense from even getting started, and last overall. There are reasons the Timberwolves are encouraged that things will turn

TIMBERWOLF ROSTER

No.	Veterans	Pos.	Ht.	Wt.	Age	Yrs. Pro	College
30	Pat Durham	G-F	6-7	210	28	2	Colorado State
44	Greg Foster	C-F	6-11	240	27	5	Texas-El Paso
22	Winston Garland	G	6-2	180	30	7	SW Missouri State
24	Tom Gugliotta	F	6-10	240	25	3	North Carolina State
32	Christian Laettner	F	6-11	235	26	3	Duke
15	Darrick Martin	G	5-11	170	24	1	UCLA
34	Isaiah Rider	G-F	6-5	215	24	2	UNLV
45	Sean Rooks	C-F	6-10	260	26	3	Arizona
3	Chris Smith	G	6-3	191	25	3	Connecticut
5	Doug West	G	6-6	200	28	6	Villanova
4	Micheal Williams	G	6-2	175	29	7	Baylor

Rd.	Rookies	Sel.No.	Pos.	Ht.	Wt.	College
1	Kevin Garnett	5	F	6-10	220	Farragut HS
2	Mark Davis	48	G-F	6-7	210	Texas Tech
2	Jerome Allen	49	G	6-4	184	Pennsylvania

around: 1) This is the only time of the year they have anything to be encouraged about, so why waste the chance? 2) They finished 16th overall the season before. 3) They have legitimate size.

Sean Rooks is nothing special at 6-10. But Minnesota has two good, young, proven power forwards, Laettner at 6-11 and Gugliotta 6-10, the drawback being that both seem comfortable off the blocks, so all it took to lead the team last season was the 7.6 by Laettner. Then consider the arrival of Garnett, who should get pushed around for a year or two and then add bulk as he fills out his now-slender frame.

DEFENSE: Coach Bill Blair was known as a defensive specialist when he served as an assistant, especially in his most recent stint with Larry Brown and the Pacers. Prove it.

Blair gets a break because he doesn't exactly have a roster full of Michael Coopers or Dennis Rodmans. But he doesn't get a free pass after this season.

OUTLOOK: The main addition to a team that won 21 games last season is a guy who would be a college freshman. Wake us after the next lottery.

TIMBERWOLF PROFILES

CHRISTIAN LAETTNER 26 6-11 235   Forward

What's this world coming to? He isn't the most talented player or the biggest problem child on the team anymore... But he is still good: his 16.3 points a game last season was second among Timberwolves to Isaiah Rider, while his 7.6 rebounds was tops on the team... Works very well on the perimeter for a big guy, so will probably never generate the kind of numbers on the boards most clubs want from a power forward... Finished 12th in the NBA in free-throw attempts... Passed Sam Mitchell in December to become No. 1 in franchise history in rebounds... Also first in turnovers, free throws made and attempted, and needs only 11 more blocked shots to overtake Felton Spencer for top of the heap in that category... Duke All-American was the only college player on the original Dream Team for the 1992 Olympics... Third pick overall in 1992... Born Aug. 17, 1969, in Buffalo, N.Y.... Timberwolves' highest-paid player last season at $3.36 million.

Year	Team	G	FG	FG Pct.	FT	FT Pct.	Reb.	Ast.	TP	Avg.
1992-93	Minnesota	81	503	.474	462	.835	708	223	1472	18.2
1993-94	Minnesota	70	396	.448	375	.783	602	307	1173	16.8
1994-95	Minnesota	81	450	.489	409	.818	613	234	1322	16.3
	Totals	232	1349	.471	1246	.813	1923	764	3967	17.1

ISAIAH (J.R.) RIDER 24 6-5 215   Guard

Can't we all just get along?... Flashes of talent are too often overshadowed by off-court run-ins... Led Timberwolves in scoring at 20.4 points a game... That was 19th overall in the NBA and eighth among all guards... Set team record for three-pointers attempted (396) and made (139)... Not a great percentage (.351), but not bad for someone whose real game is based on strength and speed... Runner and a jumper, so he's effective in transition game... Also has enough muscle to overpower most shooting guards on the post, then either get to the basket or fall away for a short jumper... Won the slam-dunk contest when All-Star Weekend was in Minnesota... Starred at

UNLV before Minnesota took him No. 5 in 1993 ... Born March 12, 1971, in Oakland ... Made $2.5 million last season.

Year	Team	G	FG	FG Pct.	FT	FT Pct.	Reb.	Ast.	TP	Avg.
1993-94	Minnesota	79	522	.468	215	.811	315	202	1313	16.6
1994-95	Minnesota	75	558	.447	277	.817	249	245	1532	20.4
	Totals	154	1080	.457	492	.815	564	447	2845	18.5

TOM GUGLIOTTA 25 6-10 240 Forward

Googs moves ... A Bullet since being drafted No. 6 out of North Carolina State in 1992, he went to Golden State early last season in the Chris Webber deal. Then, just after the all-star break, was shipped to Minnesota in exchange for Donyell Marshall ... Remember when Gugliotta was a hot young prospect? That was what, two years ago? ... Still a player, even if some people take the trades to mean he doesn't have much ... Had the option to get out of his contract after last season ... Started in 17 of 31 appearances with the Timberwolves ... Scottie Pippen was the only forward in the league to average more steals ... Born Dec. 19, 1969, in Huntington Station, N.Y.

Year	Team	G	FG	FG Pct.	FT	FT Pct.	Reb.	Ast.	TP	Avg.
1992-93	Washington	81	484	.426	181	.644	781	306	1187	14.7
1993-94	Washington	78	540	.466	213	.685	728	276	1333	17.1
1994-95	Wash.-G.S.-Minn.	77	371	.443	174	.690	572	279	976	12.7
	Totals	236	1395	.446	568	.673	2081	861	3496	14.8

DOUG WEST 28 6-6 200 Guard-Forward

The last of the original Timberwolves is hanging on amidst all the hotshot kids ... Still a solid talent, averaging 32.8 minutes per game ... Started in 65 of 71 games ... Flip side was 11 DNP-CDs ... Struggled with his shot much of the second half of the season ... Passed Tony Campbell on March 8 to become No. 1 in team history in scoring ... Already had the club record for career starts and minutes ... Minnesota got a great return on the No. 38 pick in the 1989 draft ... Standout at Villanova before that ... Nice athletic ability, used best in the open court... Born May 27, 1967, in Altoona, Pa.... 1994-95 salary: $1.275 million.

Year	Team	G	FG	FG Pct.	FT	FT Pct.	Reb.	Ast.	TP	Avg.
1989-90	Minnesota	52	53	.393	26	.813	70	18	135	2.6
1990-91	Minnesota	75	118	.480	58	.690	136	48	294	3.9
1991-92	Minnesota	80	463	.518	186	.805	257	281	1116	14.0
1992-93	Minnesota	80	646	.517	249	.841	247	235	1543	19.3
1993-94	Minnesota	72	434	.487	187	.810	231	172	1056	14.7
1994-95	Minnesota	71	351	.461	206	.837	227	185	919	12.9
	Totals	430	2065	.494	912	.814	1168	939	5063	11.8

SEAN ROOKS 26 6-10 260   Center

Great scams in history: Indians sell Manhattan for $24, Timberwolves give Dallas a first-round pick for Rooks... Not a bad player, but also not worth a likely lottery pick... Mavericks will cash in in one of the next three drafts... Timberwolves, meanwhile, will be hoping they have someone else starting at center by then... Could have a decent career, likely as a backup, especially for a second-round pick... That's where the Mavericks got him, No. 30 overall in 1992 after his career at Arizona... Set career high last season in minutes, breaking former mark of 2,087, set in 1992-93... Born Sept. 9, 1969, in New York... Made $600,000 last season.

Year	Team	G	FG	FG Pct.	FT	FT Pct.	Reb.	Ast.	TP	Avg.
1992-93	Dallas	72	368	.493	234	.602	536	95	970	13.5
1993-94	Dallas	47	193	.491	150	.714	259	49	536	11.4
1994-95	Minnesota	80	289	.470	290	.761	486	97	868	10.9
	Totals	199	850	.484	674	.688	1281	241	2374	11.9

MICHEAL WILLIAMS 29 6-2 175   Guard

Didn't give Bill Blair a chance to demote him... Played one game last season—28 minutes Nov. 8 at Detroit—before foot problems did him in... Went on the injured list three days later... Finally underwent surgery to repair a torn tendon in his left heel March 1... He was the starting point guard in 1993-94 when the Timberwolves led the league in turnovers, so the pressure figured to be on him to produce... Now he just needs to worry about getting healthy... Needs 99 steals to leap frog over Tony Campbell, Tyrone Corbin and Pooh Richardson for first place on the club's all-time list... Minnesota got the Baylor product with Chuck Person from Indiana in September 1992, for Richardson and Sam Mitchell... Born July 23, 1966, in Dallas... Made $2.175 million last season.

Year	Team	G	FG	FG Pct.	FT	FT Pct.	Reb.	Ast.	TP	Avg.
1988-89	Detroit	49	47	.364	31	.660	27	70	127	2.6
1989-90	Phoe.-Char.	28	60	.504	36	.783	32	81	156	5.6
1990-91	Indiana	73	261	.499	290	.879	176	348	813	11.1
1991-92	Indiana	79	404	.490	372	.871	282	647	1188	15.0
1992-93	Minnesota	76	353	.446	419	.907	273	661	1151	15.1
1993-94	Minnesota	71	314	.457	333	.839	221	512	971	13.7
1994-95	Minnesota	1	1	.250	4	.800	1	3	6	6.0
	Totals	377	1440	.468	1485	.866	1012	2322	4412	11.7

WINSTON GARLAND 30 6-2 180 Guard

Unspectacular. Even unwanted. But undeniably resilient... That and a professional approach and attitude has kept him in the league... Suns cut him in camp before last season in favor of keeping youngsters like Elliot Perry and Trevor Ruffin, so Garland became the starting point guard in Minnesota... Best suited as a third or fourth guard... Great clubhouse presence... In the opening lineup in 58 of his 73 appearances after being signed as a free agent to replace the injured Micheal Williams... Came into the NBA as a second-round pick by Milwaukee in the 1987 draft after a standout career at Southwest Missouri State... Born Dec. 19, 1964, in Gary, Ind. ... 1994-95 salary: $143,860.

Year	Team	G	FG	FG Pct.	FT	FT Pct.	Reb.	Ast.	TP	Avg.
1987-88	Golden State	67	340	.439	138	.879	227	429	831	12.4
1988-89	Golden State	79	466	.434	203	.809	328	505	1145	14.5
1989-90	G.S.-LAC	79	230	.401	102	.836	214	303	574	7.3
1990-91	L.A. Clippers	69	221	.426	118	.752	198	317	564	8.2
1991-92	Denver	78	333	.444	171	.859	190	411	846	10.8
1992-93	Houston	66	152	.443	81	.910	108	138	391	5.9
1994-95	Minnesota	73	170	.415	89	.795	168	318	448	6.1
	Totals	511	1912	.430	902	.830	1433	2421	4799	9.4

GREG FOSTER 27 6-11 240   Center-Forward

Five seasons, five teams... Doesn't exactly figure to be a lifer in the Twin Cities, either... And this was after he attended two colleges, first UCLA and then Texas-El Paso... Bullets took him from there in the second round in 1990... After stops with the Hawks and Bucks, he opened last season in Chicago... Averaged 6.1 points and 3.2 rebounds in 17 games before being waived Dec. 12... Minnesota signed him four days later... Averaged 4.6 points, 3.4 rebounds and 13.9 minutes in 61 appearances with the Timberwolves... Born Oct. 3, 1968, in Oakland... 1994-95 salary: $193,300.

Year	Team	G	FG	FG Pct.	FT	FT Pct.	Reb.	Ast.	TP	Avg.
1990-91	Washington	54	97	.460	42	.689	151	37	236	4.4
1991-92	Washington	49	89	.461	35	.714	145	35	213	4.3
1992-93	Wash.-Atl.	43	55	.458	15	.714	83	21	125	2.9
1993-94	Milwaukee	3	4	.571	2	1.000	3	0	10	3.3
1994-95	Chi.-Minn.	78	150	.472	78	.703	259	39	385	4.9
	Totals	227	395	.465	172	.705	641	132	969	4.3

CHRIS SMITH 25 6-3 191   Guard

Micheal Williams was hurt, and Smith still couldn't earn the starting job at point guard... That was supposed to be his chance... Turned out it was his chance to watch Winston Garland in the opening lineup... Started 17 times and averaged 7.9 points and 3.5 assists in 26.7 minutes... Had a much better assist-to-turnover ratio as a reserve (4.05-to-1) than as a starter (2.22-to-1)... In a shooting slump the last month of the season, but still finished eighth in the league in three-point percentage at 43.5... Born May 17, 1970, in Bridgeport, Conn., and stayed close to home to play for UConn... No. 34 pick of the 1992 draft... 1994-95 salary: $355,000.

Year	Team	G	FG	FG Pct.	FT	FT Pct.	Reb.	Ast.	TP	Avg.
1992-93	Minnesota	80	125	.433	95	.792	96	196	347	4.3
1993-94	Minnesota	80	184	.435	95	.674	122	285	473	5.9
1994-95	Minnesota	64	116	.439	41	.651	73	146	320	5.0
	Totals	224	425	.435	231	.713	291	627	1140	5.1

Christian Laettner has become solid contributor.

PAT DURHAM 28 6-7 210 — Guard-Forward

Just passing through... Late cut by Minnesota in camp, then brought back Nov. 24 after two games with CBA's Rapid City Thunder... This was after he spent part of 1993-94 in France, which came after a couple of 10-day contracts with Golden State, which came after being named MVP at the CBA All-Star Game, and so on... Originally a second-round pick by Dallas in 1989, out of Colorado State... Also had training-camp stints with Bucks and Cavaliers and played in Switzerland... Big moment of last season came when he hit the go-ahead three-pointer with 22 seconds left in a Dec. 26 win over the Clippers... Born March 10, 1967, in Dallas... 1994-95 salary: $126,000.

Year	Team	G	FG	FG Pct.	FT	FT Pct.	Reb.	Ast.	TP	Avg.
1992-93	Golden State	5	6	.240	9	.750	14	4	21	4.2
1994-95	Minnesota	59	117	.494	63	.656	94	53	302	5.1
	Totals	64	123	.469	72	.667	108	57	323	5.0

DARRICK MARTIN 24 5-11 170 — Guard

A chance, finally... UCLA product spent two years with Magic Johnson's touring team before the NBA called last spring... Signed a pair of 10-day contracts, then hooked on for the remainder of the season March 7... Quickly earned a significant role, averaging 23.6 minutes in 34 appearances... Started nine of the last 11 games... Needs to become a better shooter... Opened the season with Sioux Falls of the CBA and stayed for 37 games, long enough to get named to the All-Star Game... At 5-11, he ties Scott Brooks as the shortest player in team history... Born March 6, 1971, in Denver.

Year	Team	G	FG	FG Pct.	FT	FT Pct.	Reb.	Ast.	TP	Avg.
1994-95	Minnesota	34	95	.408	57	.877	64	133	254	7.5

THE ROOKIES

KEVIN GARNETT 19 6-10 220 — Forward

The first senior taken in the draft... OK, so he was a high-school senior... The Timberwolves took him fifth overall with the plan of being patient and waiting for him to develop... If he went to college, scouts figure he would have been the No. 1 pick in two years. That kind of talent... Great ball-handling and passing skills for a big man at any level... Many call him the best high-school player they've ever seen... Spent first three years in Mauldin, S.C., where he was born May 19, 1976, then transferred to Farragut Academy in Chicago for his senior year.

MARK DAVIS 22 6-7 210   Guard-Forward
Finished in the top 10 in the Southwest Conference in scoring, rebounding, blocks, steals, assists and shooting as a senior at Texas Tech... All-SWC and also on the all-conference defensive team... Played every position during two years with the Red Raiders, including point guard... No. 48 pick... Born April 26, 1973, in Thibodaux, La.

JEROME ALLEN 22 6-4 184   Guard
Two-time Ivy League Player of the Year and the first ever to do it as a sophomore... Also three-time all-conference... No. 1 in Penn history in assists and steals and No. 5 in points... Played on the U.S. team in the 1993 Goodwill Games... Drafted 49th... Who needs an agent? He majored in strategic management at the Wharton School of Business... Born Jan. 28, 1973, in Philadelphia.

COACH BILL BLAIR: Now understands the phrase, "Be careful what you wish for."... Got first shot at being NBA head coach after spending the previous 13 years as an assistant. One problem: It was with the Timberwolves... Rookie coach vs. Brat Pack seemed like a huge mismatch... Missed five games (April 7-16) after suffering a lower back injury while playing tennis during a trip to Dallas... Became fourth sideline boss in Timberwolves' history Aug. 29, 1994, not long after helping Larry Brown guide Pacers to Eastern Conference finals... Known as a defensive specialist, he was a factor in Indiana going from 106.1 points allowed in 1992-93 to 97.5 the next season... NBA resume also includes stops with Bullets (1986-92), Bulls (1983-85) and New Jersey (1981-83)... Served under Kevin Loughery in Washington and Chicago and Brown with the Nets and Pacers... Also was a scout with Pacers in mid-

80s... Played at VMI and then coached there from 1972-76... Was Keydets' captain as a senior in 1964 while earning all-conference honors and helping the team to the NCAA tournament ... Fourth-round pick by the St. Louis Hawks, but opted to play and coach for the Army in Korea and the U.S.... After coaching at his alma mater, he became sideline boss at Colorado from 1976-81... Born May 17, 1942, in Whitesburg, Ky.

GREATEST FIND

Look to West, young man.

Doug West was Minnesota's third pick of its inaugural draft of 1989, No. 38 overall, after Pooh Richardson and Gary Leonard. He has outlasted those two and everyone else from that first season and become one of the more underrated players in the game, an athletic small forward who showed he can average 19 points a game before the arrival of Isaiah Rider cut into his time and scoring opportunities.

That means that West, the leading scorer in team history, is also the No. 1 find. No one else is even close.

ALL-TIME TIMBERWOLF LEADERS

SEASON

Points: Tony Campbell, 1,903, 1989-90
Assists: Jerome Richardson, 734, 1990-91
Rebounds: Christian Laettner, 708, 1992-93

GAME

Points: Tony Campbell, 44 vs. Boston, 2/2/90
Assists: Sidney Lowe, 17 vs. Golden State, 3/20/90
      Pooh Richardson, 17 vs. Washington, 3/13/92
Rebounds: Todd Murphy, 20 vs. L.A. Clippers, 1/2/90

CAREER

Points: Doug West, 5,063, 1989-95
Assists: Jerome Richardson, 1,973, 1989-92
Rebounds: Christian Laettner, 1,923, 1992-95

Doug West is now Wolves' all-time scoring leader.

SAN ANTONIO SPURS

TEAM DIRECTORY: Chairman: Robert F. McDermott; Pres./CEO: John Diller; Exec.VP Basketball Oper./GM: Gregg Popovich; Exec. VP Business Oper.: Russ Bookbinder; Media Services Dir.: Tom James; Coach: Bob Hill; Asst. Coaches: Dave Cowens, Hank Egan, Paul Pressey. Arena: Alamodome (20,662). Colors: Metallic silver and black.

SCOUTING REPORT

SHOOTING: Maybe it was the arrival of Bob Hill as coach. Maybe it was the return of Avery Johnson as point guard. Or

All-around play made David Robinson the MVP.

maybe it was both. Whatever, the Spurs made a big jump in scoring, from 100 even in 1993-94 to 106.6 last season. The main factor was that they were fourth in percentage.

No, the main factor was David Robinson. An officer and a gentleman, he is also the reigning league MVP, a talent at both ends of the floor. On offense, he runs the floor in a way that few centers or power forwards can compare, can hit the medium-range jumper and has great quickness and agility. The only thing he really lacks is a polished post game, but that gets into nitpicking considering the guy somehow managed to get 27.6 points a game and shoot 53 percent.

Neither starting guard—Johnson or Vinny Del Negro—is much of a three-point threat, although Del Negro is fairly consistent when he does fire. Instead, the air cover for Robinson usually comes from the small forwards, Sean Elliott and Chuck Person. Yes, the same Sean Elliott who had all of 109 makes from behind the line his first five seasons. He had 133 last season alone.

PLAYMAKING: It's not just the underrated Johnson who makes a difference, though that is a very good place to start. Del Negro is a former point guard who still handles the ball and last season was second only to Charlotte's Muggsy Bogues in assist-to-turnover ratio.

There's more. Doc Rivers will contribute another steady, veteran hand if he returns after a summer as an unrestricted free agent. If not, his minutes will go to first-round pick Cory Alexander, the Virginia product. And, though we're changing positions, don't forget that Robinson is one of the best passing big men in the game, good enough to have led the Spurs in assists in 1993-94.

REBOUNDING: As if we have something new to say on the subject. Dennis Rodman is great on the boards, now more than ever since he has joined Moses Malone and Wilt Chamberlain as the only players to ever win four consecutive rebounding titles. But Rodman is a great big pain, now more than ever. You decide if he's worth it.

The Spurs may vote no before the end of the summer. If so, seeing as no one of the same magnitude will be coming in return, the fall from one of the best rebounding teams (No. 1 in 1993-94, No. 5 last season) may not be far behind. And this team does not generate enough shots on its own to score at the same pace

SPUR ROSTER

No.	Veterans	Pos.	Ht.	Wt.	Age	Yrs. Pro	College
U-34	Terry Cummings	F	6-9	245	34	13	DePaul
15	Vinny Del Negro	G	6-4	200	29	5	North Carolina State
U-32	Sean Elliott	F	6-8	215	27	6	Arizona
U-54	Jack Haley	C	6-10	250	31	7	UCLA
6	Avery Johnson	G	5-11	175	30	7	Southern
U-2	Moses Malone	C	6-10	260	40	21	Petersburg HS
00	Julius Nwosu	F	6-10	255	24	1	Liberty
45	Chuck Person	F	6-8	225	31	9	Auburn
7	J.R. Reid	F-C	6-9	265	27	6	North Carolina
U-25	Doc Rivers	G	6-4	210	34	12	Marquette
50	David Robinson	C	7-1	235	30	6	Navy
10	Dennis Rodman	F	6-8	210	34	9	SE Oklahoma State

U-unrestricted free agent

Rd.	Rookie	Sel.No.	Pos.	Ht.	Wt.	College
1	Cory Alexander	29	G	6-1	183	Virginia

without a healthy dose of offensive boards.

Few noticed, but Robinson averaged 10.8 a game en route to MVP.

DEFENSE: Rodman concentrates so much on rebounding these days that he isn't nearly the same defender he once was. That still makes him better than above 90 percent of the league, but he frustrates the Spurs with his freelancing away from his man. It always helps to have Robinson back there as the safety net—he finished fourth in blocked shots and is quick enough to slide across the lane on help defense.

In the end, they were still very good in this area. Only five teams held opponents to a lower shooting percentage and the 100.6 points allowed was nearly a full point below the league average.

OUTLOOK: Hard to believe that the biggest individual challenge is facing Robinson. Or were we the only ones who thought he looked intimidated, even scared, during the matchup against Hakeem Olajuwon in last spring's Western Conference finals? He either needs to be able to handle those situations better or the Spurs need to surround him with a lot of tough players. The next level—the championship—hangs in the balance.

SPUR PROFILES

DAVID ROBINSON 30 7-1 235 Center

An officer and a gentleman—and a Most Valuable Player... Easily won NBA's top individual award last season... Showed in the playoffs he still needs to get mentally tougher... Didn't have near the intensity of Hakeem Olajuwon in their matchup for the West crown... Finished third in the league in scoring, fourth in blocks, seventh in rebounding and 15th in shooting and steals... Great quickness and agility for a seven-footer... No. 1 in franchise history in blocks and rebounds, No. 2 in points... Rookie of the Year in 1990, Defensive Player of the Year in '92, six-time all-star... Represented his country in the military and in the 1988 and '92 Olympics... Starred at Navy before Spurs took him No. 1 overall in 1987... Born Aug. 6, 1965, in Key West, Fla.... 1994-95 salary: $7.3 million.

Year	Team	G	FG	FG Pct.	FT	FT Pct.	Reb.	Ast.	TP	Avg.
1989-90	San Antonio	82	690	.531	613	.732	983	164	1993	24.3
1990-91	San Antonio	82	754	.552	592	.762	1063	208	2101	25.6
1991-92	San Antonio	68	592	.551	393	.701	829	181	1578	23.2
1992-93	San Antonio	82	676	.501	561	.732	956	301	1916	23.4
1993-94	San Antonio	80	840	.507	693	.749	855	381	2383	29.8
1994-95	San Antonio	81	788	.530	656	.774	877	236	2238	27.6
	Totals	475	4340	.527	3508	.744	5563	1471	12209	25.7

DENNIS RODMAN 34 6-8 210 Forward

That's Chameleon Head to you... Our favorite hair: lime-jello green. It makes his head look like a Chia Pet... Needs to look in the mirror, and we don't mean to check the 'do... The more he says he does not tear teams apart, the more he does it... No one asks him to dress in a three-piece suit. But how hard is it to come to practice on time?... His antics frustrate teammates, no matter what he says... By the end of last season, there was a good chance the Spurs would try to unload him before the end of summer... Has led the league in rebounding four straight years... Moses Malone and Wilt Chamberlain are the only other players to ever accomplish that... First-team all-defense again, though he certainly isn't the same player of old in that area... Came to San Antonio along with Isaiah Morris in exchange for Sean Elliott and David Wood in Oct. 1993... Pistons drafted him in the second round in 1986, out of Southeastern Oklahoma State... Born May 13, 1961, in Trenton, N.J.... Made $2.5 million last season.

Year	Team	G	FG	FG Pct.	FT	FT Pct.	Reb.	Ast.	TP	Avg.
1986-87	Detroit	77	213	.545	74	.587	332	56	500	6.5
1987-88	Detroit	82	398	.561	152	.535	715	110	953	11.6
1988-89	Detroit	82	316	.595	97	.626	772	99	735	9.0
1989-90	Detroit	82	288	.581	142	.654	792	72	719	8.8
1990-91	Detroit	82	276	.493	111	.631	1026	85	669	8.2
1991-92	Detroit	82	342	.539	84	.600	1530	191	800	9.8
1992-93	Detroit	62	183	.427	87	.534	1132	102	468	7.5
1993-94	San Antonio	79	156	.534	53	.520	1367	184	370	4.7
1994-95	San Antonio	49	137	.571	75	.676	823	97	349	7.1
	Totals	677	2309	.539	875	.594	8489	996	5563	8.2

SEAN ELLIOTT 27 6-8 215　　　　　　　　Forward

Like he was never gone... Spurs brought familiar face back before last season, rescuing him from a lottery-bound team in Detroit... He repaid them with 18.1 points a game, a career high... Also hit 133 three-pointers in 81 games after getting 109 in 388 games his first five seasons... Emotional player... Sometimes lets those emotions get the best of him ... But at least he still had feelings after a tough year with the Pistons... Spurs got him back for Bill Curley and a 1996 second-round pick... They originally got him with the No. 3 pick in 1989... All-star in 1993... Born Feb. 2, 1968, in Tucson, Ariz., and stayed home to star at Arizona... 1994-95 salary: $1.35 million.

Year	Team	G	FG	FG Pct.	FT	FT Pct.	Reb.	Ast.	TP	Avg.
1989-90	San Antonio	81	311	.481	187	.866	297	154	810	10.0
1990-91	San Antonio	82	478	.490	325	.808	456	238	1301	15.9
1991-92	San Antonio	82	514	.494	285	.861	439	214	1338	16.3
1992-93	San Antonio	70	451	.491	268	.795	322	265	1207	17.2
1993-94	Detroit	73	360	.455	139	.803	263	197	885	12.1
1994-95	San Antonio	81	502	.468	326	.807	287	206	1466	18.1
	Totals	469	2616	.481	1530	.821	2064	1274	7007	14.9

AVERY JOHNSON 30 5-11 175 — Guard

Does he have the plague and only general managers and coaches know about it? ... How else to explain how a guy like this bounces around so much? ... Spurs don't get anywhere near 62 wins last season without him ... Gets down the lane against even the quickest point guards ... Very positive clubhouse influence ... Seventh in the league in assists and 19th in shooting ... Averaged 14.3 points to become just the fifth player in NBA history to improve in scoring in each of his first seven years as a pro. The company is pretty good: Alex English, Kevin McHale, Happy Hairston and Derek Harper ... Undrafted in 1988 out of Southern University before signing with Seattle as a free agent ... This is third stint with the Spurs, arriving each time as a free agent ... Born March 25, 1965, in New Orleans ... Made $650,000 last season.

Year	Team	G	FG	FG Pct.	FT	FT Pct.	Reb.	Ast.	TP	Avg.
1988-89	Seattle	43	29	.349	9	.563	24	73	68	1.6
1989-90	Seattle	53	55	.387	29	.725	43	162	140	2.6
1990-91	Den.-S.A.	68	130	.469	59	.678	77	230	320	4.7
1991-92	S.A.-Hou.	69	158	.479	66	.653	80	266	386	5.6
1992-93	San Antonio	75	256	.502	144	.791	146	561	656	8.7
1993-94	Golden State	82	356	.492	178	.704	176	433	890	10.9
1994-95	San Antonio	82	448	.519	202	.685	208	670	1101	13.4
	Totals	472	1432	.489	687	.705	754	2395	3561	7.5

J.R. REID 27 6-9 265 — Forward

The Spurs' safety net for having Dennis Rodman ... He and Terry Cummings came through last season when Dennis the Menace was injured/suspended/acting like Rodman ... The question is, can he do it regularly enough to start? ... Spurs no doubt were pondering that heading into the summer while contemplating Rodman's future ... Started 37 times and averaged 6.7 points, 5.5 rebounds and 22.4 minutes ... The 50.8 percent last season was a career best ... Hits the medium-range jumpers ... Played with current teammate David Robinson on the 1988 Olympic team ... No. 5 pick by Charlotte in 1989 and a local favorite after starring at North Carolina ... Traded by Hornets to Spurs on Dec. 9, 1992, for Sidney Green and two picks

...Born March 31, 1968, in Virginia Beach, Va....Made $2.215 million last season.

Year	Team	G	FG	FG Pct.	FT	FT Pct.	Reb.	Ast.	TP	Avg.
1989-90	Charlotte	82	358	.440	192	.664	691	101	908	11.1
1990-91	Charlotte	80	360	.466	182	.703	502	89	902	11.3
1991-92	Charlotte	51	213	.490	134	.705	317	81	560	11.0
1992-93	Char.-S.A.	83	283	.476	214	.764	456	80	780	9.4
1993-94	San Antonio	70	260	.491	107	.699	220	73	627	9.0
1994-95	San Antonio	81	201	.508	160	.687	393	55	563	7.0
	Totals	447	1675	.473	989	.704	2579	479	4340	9.7

VINNY DEL NEGRO 29 6-4 200   Guard

Finally becomes the regular shooting guard... That's his natural position, but he played mostly point guard in the first two seasons after the Spurs lured him back from Italy with a lucrative free-agent deal... Moved into the starting lineup Nov. 26 for an injured Willie Anderson, responded with 21 points and kept the job for the rest of the season... His 66 three-pointers were nothing for most shooting guards, but something for him, considering he had only 37 in 306 games heading into 1994-95... A teammate with Toni Kukoc overseas ... Second-round pick by Sacramento in 1988 after playing at North Carolina State... Born Aug. 9, 1966, in Springfield, Mass. ...Made $1.471 million in 1994-95.

Year	Team	G	FG	FG Pct.	FT	FT Pct.	Reb.	Ast.	TP	Avg.
1988-89	Sacramento	80	239	.475	85	.850	171	206	569	7.1
1989-90	Sacramento	76	297	.462	135	.871	198	250	739	9.7
1992-93	San Antonio	73	218	.507	101	.863	163	291	543	7.4
1993-94	San Antonio	77	309	.487	140	.824	161	320	773	10.0
1994-95	San Antonio	75	372	.486	128	.790	192	226	938	12.5
	Totals	381	1435	.482	589	.837	885	1293	3562	9.3

GLENN (DOC) RIVERS 34 6-4 210   Guard

Provided the backcourt depth the Spurs needed last season... Forget the 36 percent from the field. Ignore the fact that he had been waived by the Knicks in December and was a free-agent claimer... Made a big contribution to San Antonio's success... Attitude, toughness and leadership, for starters... That comes as no surprise... Played both guard spots off the bench... Played three games with New York, 60 with the Spurs

... Nice return after undergoing reconstructive knee surgery the season before ... Has a future in broadcasting ... No. 31 pick by Atlanta in 1983, out of Marquette ... Born Oct. 13, 1961, in Chicago ... 1994-95 salary: $1.4 million.

Year	Team	G	FG	FG Pct.	FT	FT Pct.	Reb.	Ast.	TP	Avg.
1983-84	Atlanta	81	250	.462	255	.785	220	314	757	9.3
1984-85	Atlanta	69	334	.476	291	.770	214	410	974	14.1
1985-86	Atlanta	53	220	.474	172	.608	162	443	612	11.5
1986-87	Atlanta	82	342	.451	365	.828	299	823	1053	12.8
1987-88	Atlanta	80	403	.453	319	.758	366	747	1134	14.2
1988-89	Atlanta	76	371	.455	247	.861	286	525	1032	13.6
1989-90	Atlanta	48	218	.454	138	.812	200	264	598	12.5
1990-91	Atlanta	79	444	.435	221	.844	253	340	1197	15.2
1991-92	L.A.Clippers	59	226	.424	163	.832	147	233	641	10.9
1992-93	New York	77	216	.437	133	.821	192	405	604	7.8
1993-94	New York	19	55	.433	14	.636	39	100	143	7.5
1994-95	N.Y.-S.A.	63	108	.358	60	.732	109	162	321	5.1
	Totals	786	3187	.447	2378	.785	2487	4766	9066	11.5

CHUCK PERSON 31 6-8 225   Forward

The air cover for the Navy battleship ... Joined Spurs as a free agent last summer, then immediately set a franchise record with 172 three-pointers in a season ... It was his personal best, 40 more than during 1991-92 with Indiana ... Third-best scorer off the bench in NBA, behind Dell Curry and Roy Tarpley ... Along with Dale Ellis, Danny Ainge, Michael Adams, Reggie Miller and Mark Price, the only players in NBA history to hit at least 800 three-pointers ... Starred at Auburn before the Pacers took him in the first round in 1986 ... Rookie of the Year in 1986-87 ... Younger brother Wesley plays with the Suns ... Born June 27, 1964, in Brantley, Ala. ... 1994-95 salary: $1.3 million.

Year	Team	G	FG	FG Pct.	FT	FT Pct.	Reb.	Ast.	TP	Avg.
1986-87	Indiana	82	635	.468	222	.747	677	295	1541	18.8
1987-88	Indiana	79	575	.459	132	.670	536	309	1341	17.0
1988-89	Indiana	80	711	.489	243	.792	516	289	1728	21.6
1989-90	Indiana	77	605	.487	211	.781	445	230	1515	19.7
1990-91	Indiana	80	620	.504	165	.721	417	238	1474	18.4
1991-92	Indiana	81	616	.480	133	.675	426	382	1497	18.5
1992-93	Minnesota	78	541	.433	109	.649	433	343	1309	16.8
1993-94	Minnesota	77	356	.422	82	.759	253	185	894	11.6
1994-95	San Antonio	81	317	.423	66	.647	258	106	872	10.8
	Totals	715	4976	.467	1363	.727	3961	2377	12171	17.0

TERRY CUMMINGS 34 6-9 245   Forward

Battling to the very end... Teamed with J.R. Reid to provide solid play in place of Dennis Rodman... Came through in last guaranteed season on his contract. Spurs can pick up option for this season at $2.14 million or go for buyout at $1.1 million... San Antonio or elsewhere, two-time all-star says he intends to play two or three more years if he can hook on with a contender... Has already written a script for a motion picture and is working on a second... A first-person story wouldn't be bad: All-American at DePaul enters NBA as No. 2 pick overall by San Diego Clippers in 1982, decides to stick with basketball in the face of heart problems, has a nice career... Came to Spurs from Milwaukee for Alvin Robertson and Greg Anderson in May 1989... Born March 15, 1961, in Chicago... Earns an average of $2.406 million annually.

Year	Team	G	FG	FG Pct.	FT	FT Pct.	Reb.	Ast.	TP	Avg.
1982-83	San Diego	70	684	.523	292	.709	744	177	1660	23.7
1983-84	San Diego	81	737	.494	380	.720	777	139	1854	22.9
1984-85	Milwaukee	79	759	.495	343	.741	716	228	1861	23.6
1985-86	Milwaukee	82	681	.474	265	.656	694	193	1627	19.8
1986-87	Milwaukee	82	729	.511	249	.662	700	229	1707	20.8
1987-88	Milwaukee	76	675	.485	270	.665	553	181	1621	21.3
1988-89	Milwaukee	80	730	.467	362	.787	650	198	1829	22.9
1989-90	San Antonio	81	728	.475	343	.780	677	219	1818	22.4
1990-91	San Antonio	67	503	.484	164	.683	521	157	1177	17.6
1991-92	San Antonio	70	514	.488	177	.711	631	102	1210	17.3
1992-93	San Antonio	8	11	.379	5	.500	19	4	27	3.4
1993-94	San Antonio	59	183	.428	63	.589	297	50	429	7.3
1994-95	San Antonio	76	224	.483	72	.585	378	59	520	6.8
	Totals	911	7158	.487	2985	.708	7357	1936	17340	19.0

JACK HALEY 31 6-10 250   Center

Most important 12th man in league history... He's the liaison between Dennis Rodman and the rest of the world... "People wonder how I get along with Dennis," Haley says. "Ask the guys on the team. They'll say I'm the crazy one."... Let's compromise: You're both crazy... Averaged just 3.8 minutes a game and broke 10 minutes only once, March 21 against the Clippers... "DNP-CD" 51 times... A practice player and cheerleader... Fourth-round pick by the Bulls in 1987, then soon began donating his salary to Michael Jordan via

poker games... Spurs got him as a free agent on Dec. 15, 1993
... Born Jan. 27, 1964, in Long Beach, Cal.... Made $150,000
in 1994-95.

Year	Team	G	FG	FG Pct.	FT	FT Pct.	Reb.	Ast.	TP	Avg.
1988-89	Chicago	51	37	.474	36	.783	71	10	110	2.2
1989-90	Chi.-N.J.	67	138	.398	85	.680	300	26	361	5.4
1990-91	New Jersey	78	161	.469	112	.619	356	31	434	5.6
1991-92	L.A. Lakers	49	31	.369	14	.483	95	7	76	1.6
1992-93	L.A. Lakers					Injured				
1993-94	San Antonio	28	21	.438	17	.810	24	1	59	2.1
1994-95	San Antonio	31	26	.426	21	.656	27	2	73	2.4
	Totals	304	414	.431	285	.657	873	77	1113	3.7

JULIUS NWOSU 24 6-10 255 — Forward

Uniform number: 00. Role on team: 0... Averaged just 3.7 minutes... Missed 46 games while on the injured list due to pain associated with a stress fracture in the right leg... Signed with the Spurs as a free agent after spending the previous season in Spain... Did not play any basketball while growing up in his native Nigeria... Was just 6-1, 150 pounds as a junior in high school... After graduating from high school, he was asked to play on the national team because he lived next door to the practice site... We aren't making this up (though someone else may have)... Was eventually spotted by a missionary who recommended him to Liberty University... Born May 1, 1971, in Nkwere, Nigeria... 1994-95 salary: $150,000.

Year	Team	G	FG	FG Pct.	FT	FT Pct.	Reb.	Ast.	TP	Avg.
1994-95	San Antonio	23	9	.321	13	.765	24	3	31	1.3

MOSES MALONE 40 6-10 260 — Center

Has played 21 seasons of pro ball—19 in the NBA and two in the ABA... Finished last season No. 1 among active players in career points, rebounds and minutes and No. 2 to Robert Parish in games... Played only 17 games with the Spurs before rupturing a tendon in his right leg... Has surgery Jan. 15 and missed the rest of the season... Not on the playoff roster... Record run of games without fouling out is now at 1,207... Three-time Most Valuable Player... Did not attend college; went right from Petersburg (Va.) High School to the Utah Stars of the ABA as a third-round pick in 1974... Two decades later, he came to the Spurs as a free agent... Born March 23, 1955, in Sugarland, Tex.... Made $468,750 last season.

Year	Team	G	FG	FG Pct.	FT	FT Pct.	Reb.	Ast.	TP	Avg.
1974-75	Utah (ABA)	83	591	.571	375	.635	1209	82	1557	18.8
1975-76	St. Louis (ABA)	43	251	.512	112	.612	413	58	614	14.3
1976-77	Buf.-Hou.	82	389	.480	305	.693	1072	89	1083	13.2
1977-78	Houston	59	413	.499	318	.718	886	31	1144	19.4
1978-79	Houston	82	716	.540	599	.739	1444	147	2031	24.8
1979-80	Houston	82	778	.502	563	.719	1190	147	2119	25.8
1980-81	Houston	80	806	.522	609	.757	1180	141	2222	27.8
1981-82	Houston	81	945	.519	630	.762	1188	142	2520	31.1
1982-83	Philadelphia	78	654	.501	600	.761	1194	101	1908	24.5
1983-84	Philadelphia	71	532	.483	545	.750	950	96	1609	22.7
1984-85	Philadelphia	79	602	.469	737	.815	1031	130	1941	24.6
1985-86	Philadelphia	74	571	.458	617	.787	872	90	1759	23.8
1986-87	Washington	73	595	.454	570	.824	824	120	1760	24.1
1987-88	Washington	79	531	.487	543	.788	884	112	1607	20.3
1988-89	Atlanta	81	538	.491	561	.789	956	112	1637	20.2
1989-90	Atlanta	81	517	.480	493	.781	812	130	1528	18.9
1990-91	Atlanta	82	280	.468	309	.831	667	68	869	10.6
1991-92	Milwaukee	82	440	.474	396	.786	744	93	1279	15.6
1992-93	Milwaukee	11	13	.310	24	.774	46	7	50	4.5
1993-94	Philadelphia	55	102	.440	90	.769	226	34	294	5.3
1994-95	San Antonio	17	13	.371	22	.688	46	6	49	2.9
	Totals	1455	10277	.495	9018	.760	17834	1936	29580	20.3

THE ROOKIE

CORY ALEXANDER 22 6-1 183   Guard
Some youth behind Avery Johnson at the point... The last pick of the first round, No. 29 overall... Broke his right ankle twice in as many years while playing at Virginia... First time was in the season-opener of his junior campaign, which caused him to miss the rest of the season... Had 20 appearances as a senior... Got a medical redshirt after the first one, so technically left school with a year of eligibility remaining... Second only to John Crotty in school history for assist average... Born June 22, 1973, in Waynesboro, Va.

COACH BOB HILL: Received some consideration for Coach  of the Year... Or were those just sympathy votes for his dealing with Dennis Rodman?... Deserves high marks for the job he did with Rodman and the Spurs as a whole... The 62 wins during the regular season was a league best and also a franchise record... Then earned his portion of the blame for team's loss in the Western Conference finals. Picked the wrong time to shake up the rotation, leaving players scratching their heads, and presided over a team that too many times was not mentally prepared for playoff games... In contrast to ex-coach John Lucas, he tried tough love with Rodman. Didn't go over big with the Worm, but making everyone follow the same rules earned him points with the rest of the players... Career mark: 195-174 (52.8 percent)... Previously coach of the Knicks and Pacers... Played basketball and baseball at Bowling Green and was even drafted by the San Diego Padres. After being released, he returned to his alma mater as an assistant basketball coach... Went to Pitt in 1975 to become an assistant, then on to Kansas from 1978-85... The NBA was the next stop, first on Hubie Brown's staff in New York. When Brown was fired after a 4-12 start to 1986-87, he took over and went 20-46 the rest of the way. Rick Pitino arrived after the season... Became a scout with the Hornets, a broadcaster with the Nets, coach of Topeka of the CBA for the final 17 games of 1987-88, and then coach of Vitrus Knorr in Italy... Returned to the NBA as an assistant with the Pacers. When Dick Versace was fired in Dec. 1990, Hill got the promotion and spent 2½ seasons on the sideline in Indiana ... Was an assistant with Orlando when the Spurs came calling last summer... Born Nov. 24, 1948, in Columbus, Ohio.

GREATEST FIND

It just took the Spurs a while to find him.

Avery Johnson was never drafted out of Southern University. But he had three stints with the Spurs, each time as a free agent, each time with a bigger role. He made significant contributions in 1992-93, left to join the Golden State Warriors, then returned before last season, better than ever.

Any team could have had the point guard. In his return to the Spurs, he improved his game, had more great chemistry with David Robinson and was an influence in the locker room.

ALL-TIME SPUR LEADERS

SEASON

Points: George Gervin, 2,585, 1979–80
Assists: Johnny Moore, 816, 1984–85
Rebounds: Swen Nater, 1,279, 1974–75 (ABA)
David Robinson, 1,063, 1990–91

GAME

Points: David Robinson, 71 vs. LA Clippers, 4/24/94
Assists: John Lucas, 24 vs. Denver, 4/15/84
Rebounds: Manny Leaks, 35 vs. Kentucky, 11/27/70 (ABA)
Edgar Jones, 25 vs. Dallas, 3/13/84
Artis Gilmore, 25 vs. Utah, 1/17/87

CAREER

Points: George Gervin, 23,602, 1974–85
Assists: Johnny Moore, 3,865, 1980–90
Rebounds: David Robinson, 5,563, 1989–95

UTAH JAZZ

TEAM DIRECTORY: Owner: Larry Miller; Pres.: Frank Layden; GM: R. Tim Howells; Dir. Basketball Oper.: Scott Layden; VP-Pub. Rel.: David Allred; Dir. Media Rel.: Kim Turner; Coach: Jerry Sloan; Asst. Coaches: Phil Johnson, David Fredman, Gordon Chiesa. Arena: Delta Center (19,911). Colors: Purple, gold and green.

John Stockton passed Magic Johnson in all-time assists.

SCOUTING REPORT

SHOOTING: The greatness of this team is that everyone knows what they're going to do a majority of the time—throw into Karl Malone on the blocks—and it still works, dozens of times a game, a hundred games a season, 10 seasons. It works, of course, because of Malone and John Stockton. But, secondly, also because the Jazz does not waste chances.

Utah finished first in the league in shooting last season at a sparkling 51.2 percent, making it one of just two teams to break 50. The Jazz also were third, behind only Phoenix and Orlando, in assist-to-turnover ratio. That's how you can average 106.4 points a game, five better than the league average, while taking the fourth-fewest shots. Intelligence and execution.

Stockton was 11th among individuals in percentage (first among guards) and fourth in three-point accuracy. Malone was 12th overall and continues to add to his range, regularly drifting out for mid-range jumpers and fallaways in addition to signature bull-in-a-china-shop moves on the post. The mistake would be to stop here and overlook Jeff Hornacek, who adds more range and consistency. In all, seven Jazz regulars shot better than 50 percent last season.

PLAYMAKING: John Stockton. Next topic.

All right, some analysis. The all-time assist leader, the eight-time assist champion, turns 34 in late March, but shows no sign of slowing down. If there were any, he would be the first to see it. People know all about his hands and toughness and stamina, but so much of his success comes because of great vision. He's a terrific ball-handler, but the other reason it is difficult to take advantage of his slight size is that he sees the court so well that the pass will be delivered before the trap comes.

Hornacek, the shooting guard who used to start at the point in Phoenix, is a great insurance policy. Unrestricted free agent John Crotty waits to pick up the minutes that fall between the cracks.

REBOUNDING: Center Felton Spencer, rehabilitating from a serious leg injury, is not expected back until at least Christmas, and maybe considerably later. That means trouble in this department. Squeeze another few months out of 38-year-old James Donaldson, an unrestricted free agent? Rely heavily on rookie Greg Ostertag, the No. 1 pick? Make Antonio Carr, an unrestricted free agent, wear five inches of socks?

So it goes when you try to make strides in this area. The Jazz

JAZZ ROSTER

No.	Veterans	Pos.	Ht.	Wt.	Age	Yrs. Pro	College
21	David Benoit	F	6-8	220	27	4	Alabama
U-55	Antoine Carr	F-C	6-9	225	34	11	Wichita State
U-25	John Crotty	G	6-1	185	26	3	Virginia
U-54	James Donaldson	C	7-2	275	38	14	Washington State
14	Jeff Hornacek	G	6-4	190	32	9	Iowa State
31	Adam Keefe	F	6-9	241	25	3	Stanford
32	Karl Malone	F	6-9	256	32	10	Louisiana Tech
34	Bryon Russell	F	6-7	225	24	2	Long Beach State
50	Felton Spencer	C	7-0	280	27	5	Louisville
12	John Stockton	G	6-1	175	33	11	Gonzaga
5	Andy Toolson	G-F	6-6	210	29	1	Brigham Young
15	Jamie Watson	F	6-7	190	23	1	South Carolina

U-unrestricted free agent

Rd.	Rookie	Sel.No.	Pos.	Ht.	Wt.	College
1	Greg Ostertag	28	C	7-2	279	Kansas

has responded to the need by trading/drafting/signing several big men the last few years, though most have been made for backup roles. Imagine how bad things would be were it not for Malone, who tied for ninth last season and can still be counted on for double-digit rebound production at age 32.

DEFENSE: Utah finished tied for second—and first in the conference—last season in stingiest shooting percentage-against. Impressive. Now consider that the Jazz did it without much of a shot-blocking presence (see: pursuit of size, above). More impressive.

Stockton finished fourth among individuals in steals as he now bears down on that career mark, too. It should fall sometime around midseason, dropping Maurice Cheeks to second. The Jazz, always known as a hard-working team, overcame a lack of quickness enough to finish tied for ninth in turnovers forced.

OUTLOOK: That sound you hear is the final grains of sand dropping through the hourglass. Time has not run out yet—not with Malone, Stockton and Hornacek still playing so well—but it's getting there.

JAZZ PROFILES

KARL MALONE 32 6-9 256 — Forward

Great and durable... Last season, he became the 19th player in NBA history to accumulate 20,000 points but was the fifth-fastest to do so. Only Wilt Chamberlain (499 games), Michael Jordan (621), Oscar Robertson (671) and Kareem Abdul-Jabbar (684) got there quicker... "The Mailman" needed 772 outings... No. 4 in the league in scoring and No. 9 in rebounding last season... Has played in 816 of a possible 820 games in the 10 years since Utah picked him 13th in the 1985 draft... Eight-time all-star... Still dominating from the low post... Good medium-range jumper forces defenders to step outside with him... Hardly slowing down... Born July 24, 1963, in Summerfield, La., and stayed close to home to star at Louisiana Tech... 1994-95 salary: $3.378 million.

Year	Team	G	FG	FG Pct.	FT	FT Pct.	Reb.	Ast.	TP	Avg.
1985-86	Utah	81	504	.496	195	.481	718	236	1203	14.9
1986-87	Utah	82	728	.512	323	.598	855	158	1779	21.7
1987-88	Utah	82	858	.520	552	.700	986	199	2268	27.7
1988-89	Utah	80	809	.519	703	.766	853	219	2326	29.1
1989-90	Utah	82	914	.562	696	.762	911	226	2540	31.0
1990-91	Utah	82	847	.527	684	.770	967	270	2382	29.0
1991-92	Utah	81	798	.526	673	.778	909	241	2272	28.0
1992-93	Utah	82	797	.552	619	.740	919	308	2217	27.0
1993-94	Utah	82	772	.497	511	.694	940	328	2063	25.2
1994-95	Utah	82	830	.536	516	.742	871	285	2187	26.7
	Totals	816	7857	.526	5472	.721	8929	2470	21237	26.0

JOHN STOCKTON 33 6-1 175 — Guard

Now, everyone is chasing him... Passed Magic Johnson on Feb. 1 to become No. 1 on the all-time assist list... He's at 10,394 and counting... Hometown scoring? Not likely. Last season, he averaged 12 at the Delta Center, 12.7 on the road... Won the assist title for the eighth straight year... That ties Bob Cousy for most ever in the category... The 12.3 average in 1994-95 was nearly three more than his closest pursuer... Also fourth in the league in steals, fifth in three-point shooting and 11th in overall accuracy... Needs 86 steals to pass

Maurice Cheeks for the career record there... Hasn't missed a game since 1989-90... The run of consecutive starts is at 444, longest active streak in the league... Gold medalist in 1992 Olympics... Born March 26, 1962, in Spokane, Wash.... Attended Gonzaga before Jazz got him with the 16th pick in 1984 ... Made $2.6 million last season.

Year	Team	G	FG	FG Pct.	FT	FT Pct.	Reb.	Ast.	TP	Avg.
1984-85	Utah	82	157	.471	142	.736	105	415	458	5.6
1985-86	Utah	82	228	.489	172	.839	179	610	630	7.7
1986-87	Utah	82	231	.499	179	.782	151	670	648	7.9
1987-88	Utah	82	454	.574	272	.840	237	1128	1204	14.7
1988-89	Utah	82	497	.538	390	.863	248	1118	1400	17.1
1989-90	Utah	78	472	.514	354	.819	206	1134	1345	17.2
1990-91	Utah	82	496	.507	363	.836	237	1164	1413	17.2
1991-92	Utah	82	453	.482	308	.842	270	1126	1297	15.8
1992-93	Utah	82	437	.486	293	.798	237	987	1239	15.1
1993-94	Utah	82	458	.528	272	.805	258	1031	1236	15.1
1994-95	Utah	82	429	.542	246	.804	251	1011	1206	14.7
Totals		898	4312	.515	2991	.820	2379	10394	12076	13.4

JEFF HORNACEK 32 6-4 190   Guard

Dependable and versatile, as always... Started at shooting guard in each of his 81 appearances ... Can also back up John Stockton at point guard, the kind of depth that makes the Jazz arguably the best passing team in the league ... Played the point during early years with Phoenix... Last season, he finished second on the team in scoring and assists... No. 9 in the league in free-throw accuracy... Set an NBA record Nov. 23 with eight straight three-pointers... All-star in 1992...Former walk-on at Iowa State, he became a star before he left as the No. 46 pick by the Suns in 1986... Came to Utah for Jeff Malone in Feb. 1994... Born May 3, 1963, in Elmhurst, Ill.... 1994-95 salary: $2.12 million.

Year	Team	G	FG	FG Pct.	FT	FT Pct.	Reb.	Ast.	TP	Avg.
1986-87	Phoenix	80	159	.454	94	.777	184	361	424	5.3
1987-88	Phoenix	82	306	.506	152	.822	262	540	781	9.5
1988-89	Phoenix	78	440	.495	147	.826	266	465	1054	13.5
1989-90	Phoenix	67	483	.536	173	.856	313	337	1179	17.6
1990-91	Phoenix	80	544	.518	201	.897	321	409	1350	16.9
1991-92	Phoenix	81	635	.512	279	.886	407	411	1632	20.1
1992-93	Philadelphia	79	582	.470	250	.865	342	548	1511	19.1
1993-94	Phil.-Utah	80	472	.470	260	.878	279	419	1274	15.9
1994-95	Utah	81	482	.514	284	.882	210	347	1337	16.5
Totals		708	4103	.499	1840	.863	2584	3837	10542	14.9

FELTON SPENCER 27 7-0 280   Center

Everyone has seen his improvement... Now to see his recovery... Missed final four months of 1994-95 after rupturing his right Achilles tendon Jan. 13 at Boston... Just as he was in the process of a second straight season of solid contributions... Never had such a role with Timberwolves after they picked him sixth in 1990... Minnesota traded him to Utah for Mike Brown in June 1993... It became a great deal for Jazz when he established career highs in points and rebounds in first season... Left Louisville as No. 1 all-time in shooting percentage... Born Jan. 15, 1968, in Louisville, Ky.... Made $1.88 million in 1994-95.

Year	Team	G	FG	FG Pct.	FT	FT Pct.	Reb.	Ast.	TP	Avg.
1990-91	Minnesota	81	195	.512	182	.722	641	25	572	7.1
1991-92	Minnesota	61	141	.426	123	.691	435	53	405	6.6
1992-93	Minnesota	71	105	.465	83	.654	324	17	293	4.1
1993-94	Utah	79	256	.505	165	.607	658	43	677	8.6
1994-95	Utah	34	105	.488	107	.793	260	17	317	9.3
	Totals	326	802	.483	660	.685	2318	155	2264	6.9

BRYON RUSSELL 24 6-7 225   Forward

Still trying to decide where he fits in: starting small forward or reserve... In the opening lineup 15 times last season and 48 as a rookie... But can't hold on to the job... Doesn't shoot well enough, and David Benoit is a better athlete at that position... Third season is always critical for players on the fence—a time to make a big move or see what it's like to have a team run out of patience... Then again, Jazz don't exactly have a major investment in the second-round pick, No. 45 overall, from the 1993 draft... He only made $265,000 in 1994-95... Played in inaugural rookie All-Star Game... Came out of Long Beach State as a relative unknown... Averaged 13.2 points and 6.7 rebounds as a senior, hardly numbers that get players drafted... Born Dec. 31, 1970, in San Bernardino, Cal.

Year	Team	G	FG	FG Pct.	FT	FT Pct.	Reb.	Ast.	TP	Avg.
1993-94	Utah	67	135	.484	62	.614	181	54	334	5.0
1994-95	Utah	63	104	.437	62	.667	141	34	283	4.5
	Totals	130	239	.462	124	.639	322	88	617	4.7

Karl Malone: The newest 20,000-point man.

DAVID BENOIT 27 6-8 220   Forward

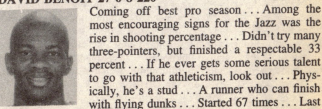

Coming off best pro season... Among the most encouraging signs for the Jazz was the rise in shooting percentage... Didn't try many three-pointers, but finished a respectable 33 percent... If he ever gets some serious talent to go with that athleticism, look out... Physically, he's a stud... A runner who can finish with flying dunks... Started 67 times... Last name is pronounced Ben-Wa, not Ben-OIT, as in Benjamin... Undrafted out of Alabama, where he was All-Southeastern Conference... Played a year in Spain before the Jazz signed him as a free agent... Born May 9, 1968, in Lafayette, La.... 1994-95 salary: $1 million.

Year	Team	G	FG	FG Pct.	FT	FT Pct.	Reb.	Ast.	TP	Avg.
1991-92	Utah	77	175	.467	81	.810	296	34	434	5.6
1992-93	Utah	82	258	.436	114	.750	392	43	664	8.1
1993-94	Utah	55	139	.385	68	.773	260	23	358	6.5
1994-95	Utah	71	285	.486	132	.841	368	58	740	10.4
	Totals	285	857	.448	395	.795	1316	158	2196	7.7

ADAM KEEFE 25 6-9 241   Forward

Jazz got a younger, bigger body in exchange for Tyrone Corbin, but where does he play? ... Time at small forward proved he wasn't quick enough for that position... Could become Karl Malone's backup at power forward, but there's not exactly a lot of minutes to be found in that line of work... Good shooter for his size... Terrific athlete who could have had a promising future in volleyball had he gone in that direction... Left Stanford as No. 5 scorer and No. 4 rebounder in Pacific-10 Conference history... Member of the Cardinal team that won the NIT title in 1991... Atlanta used its first pick, No. 10 overall, to draft him a year later... Hawks traded him to Utah for Corbin in Sept. 1994... Born Feb. 22, 1970, in Irvine, Cal.... 1994-95 salary: $1.5 million.

Year	Team	G	FG	FG Pct.	FT	FT Pct.	Reb.	Ast.	TP	Avg.
1992-93	Atlanta	82	188	.500	166	.700	432	80	542	6.6
1993-94	Atlanta	63	96	.451	81	.730	201	34	273	4.3
1994-95	Utah	75	172	.577	117	.676	327	30	461	6.1
	Totals	220	456	.514	364	.699	960	144	1276	5.8

ANTOINE CARR 34 6-9 225   Forward-Center

Now there's a Dog Pound in Salt Lake City ... Known as "Big Dog," he came to Utah before last season as a free agent and made a nice contribution... Provided depth behind Karl Malone and saw some action at center after Felton Spencer went down... In the opening lineup four times... Fifth on the team in scoring... Wore goggles the second half of the season, after having his left eye scratched Feb. 7... Fan favorite wherever he goes... Originally, that was Italy... No. 8 pick overall by Detroit in 1983 after starring at Wichita State, but spent first season in Europe... Best season was 1990-91 with Sacramento... Born July 23, 1961, in Oklahoma City... 1994-95 salary: $666,600.

Year	Team	G	FG	FG Pct.	FT	FT Pct.	Reb.	Ast.	TP	Avg.
1984-85	Atlanta	62	198	.528	101	.789	232	80	499	8.0
1985-86	Atlanta	17	49	.527	18	.667	52	14	116	6.8
1986-87	Atlanta	65	134	.506	73	.709	156	34	342	5.3
1987-88	Atlanta	80	281	.544	142	.780	289	103	705	8.8
1988-89	Atlanta	78	226	.480	130	.855	274	91	582	7.5
1989-90	Atl.-Sac.	77	356	.494	237	.795	322	119	949	12.3
1990-91	Sacramento	77	628	.511	295	.758	420	191	1551	20.1
1991-92	San Antonio	81	359	.490	162	.764	346	63	881	10.9
1992-93	San Antonio	71	379	.538	174	.777	388	97	932	13.1
1993-94	San Antonio	34	78	.488	42	.724	51	15	198	5.8
1994-95	Utah	78	290	.531	165	.821	265	67	746	9.6
	Totals	720	2978	.512	1539	.780	2795	874	7501	10.4

JAMIE WATSON 23 6-7 190   Forward

Utah's rookie class last season... Second-round pick, No. 47 overall, made 60 appearances, but his average of 11.2 minutes per was the least on the team... Guess that means he met expectations... What did you really want from a guy who wasn't even first-team all-conference in college?... Started once and got 14 points against the Knicks... Averaged just 6.0 and 7.5 points first two seasons at South Carolina before jumping to 14.7 as a junior and then 18.1... Second-team All-SEC both times... No. 3 in steals (152) and No. 7 in assists (296) by the time he left school... Born Feb. 23, 1972, in Elm City, N.C.... 1994-95 salary: $150,000.

Year	Team	G	FG	FG Pct.	FT	FT Pct.	Reb.	Ast.	TP	Avg.
1994-95	Utah	60	76	.500	38	.679	74	59	195	3.3

JOHN CROTTY 26 6-1 185   Guard

You wanted a chance? You got it... The 1,019 minutes last season were almost double his first two years in the NBA... Jazz like him, but it's rough being a young point guard on a team that has John Stockton and Jeff Hornacek... Good assist-to-turnover ratio, which will help... Needs to become a good enough shooter to at least keep the defenses honest...

Undrafted out of Virginia in 1991 and signed as a free agent before the 1992-93 season... Along with Phil Ford and Kenny Smith, one of only three players in ACC history to get at least 1,500 points and 600 assists... Set school record with 683 career assists and 179 career three-pointers... Born July 15, 1969, in Orange, N.J.... Made $250,000 last season.

Year	Team	G	FG	FG Pct.	FT	FT Pct.	Reb.	Ast.	TP	Avg.
1992-93	Utah	40	37	.514	26	.684	17	55	102	2.6
1993-94	Utah	45	45	.455	31	.861	31	77	132	2.9
1994-95	Utah	80	93	.403	98	.810	97	205	295	3.7
	Totals	165	175	.435	155	.795	145	337	529	3.2

JAMES DONALDSON 38 7-2 275   Center

When Felton Spencer went out last season, he came in... Signed to a 10-day contract Jan. 16, then to another and finally for the rest of the season Feb. 6... Started 40 of his 43 appearances at center... Always a high-percentage shooter... No. 1 in NBA in accuracy in 1984-85 while with the Clippers ... Was at 59.5 percent last season... Spent training camp with the 76ers before getting cut... Originally a fourth-round pick by Seattle in 1979... Had one stretch in the 1980s when he did not miss a game for six seasons... Played in Greece in 1993-94... Two expansion teams mean new opportunities for him to squeeze out one more NBA season... Born Aug. 16, 1957, in Meacham, England.

Year	Team	G	FG	FG Pct.	FT	FT Pct.	Reb.	Ast.	TP	Avg.
1980-81	Seattle	68	129	.542	101	.594	309	42	359	5.3
1981-82	Seattle	82	255	.609	151	.629	490	51	661	8.1
1982-83	Seattle	82	289	.583	150	.688	501	97	728	8.9
1983-84	San Diego	82	360	.596	249	.761	649	90	969	11.8
1984-85	L.A. Clippers	82	351	.637	227	.749	668	48	929	11.3
1985-86	LAC-Dal.	83	256	.558	204	.803	795	96	716	8.6
1986-87	Dallas	82	311	.586	267	.812	973	63	889	10.8
1987-88	Dallas	81	212	.558	147	.778	755	66	571	7.0
1988-89	Dallas	53	193	.573	95	.766	570	38	481	9.1
1989-90	Dallas	73	258	.539	149	.700	630	57	665	9.1
1990-91	Dallas	82	327	.532	165	.721	727	69	819	10.0
1991-92	Dal.-N.Y.	58	112	.457	61	.709	289	33	285	4.9
1992-93	Utah	6	8	.571	5	.556	29	1	21	3.5
1994-95	Utah	43	44	.595	22	.710	107	14	110	2.6
	Totals	957	3105	.571	1993	.732	7492	765	8203	8.6

THE ROOKIE

GREG OSTERTAG 22 7-2 279   Center

The search for help at center continues... It led Jazz to take him 28th, even though Kansas product has asthma that reduces his endurance... Should have a great opportunity early because Felton Spencer, the incumbent center, may not return until after Christmas because of a torn Achilles... Top shot-blocker in Big Eight Conference history... He and Danny Manning are the only Jayhawks to ever total 700 rebounds and 200 blocks in a career... Born March 6, 1973, in Dallas.

COACH JERRY SLOAN: No. 1 on coaches' tenure list with their current club... Heads into his eighth season with the Jazz... Winningest coach in team history at 364-193 (65.3 percent)... Has won two Midwest Division titles and at least 50 games in six of his seven full seasons since replacing Frank Layden... Directed Jazz to franchise-record 60 victories last season... Runnerup to Del Harris for Coach of the Year by *The Sporting News*, significant because that award is voted by peers, not the media... No. 7 on the win list among active coaches... Has twice coached Jazz to Western Conference finals... Career mark: 458-314 (59.3 percent)... That includes three seasons with Chicago, the team he is most identified with as a player... The first Bull to have his uniform number retired... Became a Chicago scout upon retiring in 1976 and took over as head coach in '79... Two-time all-star and six-time member of the all-defensive team during playing career with Baltimore and Chicago... Came to the NBA after leading Evansville to a pair of Division II titles... Intense as a player, to the point of maniacal... Joined Jazz as a scout, then became an assistant to Layden in 1984-85... Took over for Layden on Dec. 8, 1988... Jazz players immediately came to appreciate his straightforward approach... Born March 14, 1946, in Louisville, Ky.... Grew up in McLeansboro, Ill., and still has a home there.

GREATEST FIND

The argument can be made that getting arguably the best pure point guard in NBA history at No. 16 in the draft is a find. We counter that John Stockton was a first-round draft choice and the Jazz's top pick and, therefore, not a surprise.

No one, however, can argue about Mark Eaton. The 7-4 center lasted until the fourth round in 1982. That was, of course, not long before he turned into one of the biggest factors in the game—a giant in the lane who wreaked havoc on opponents for years.

Eaton was the league's Defensive Player of the Year twice, in 1984-85 and 1988-89. He was also first-team all-defense three times and made the second team two other seasons. That's first-round impact lasting until the fourth round.

ALL-TIME JAZZ LEADERS

SEASON

Points: Karl Malone, 2,540, 1989–90
Assists: John Stockton, 1,164, 1990–91
Rebounds: Len Robinson, 1,288, 1977–78

GAME

Points: Pete Maravich, 68 vs. New York, 2/25/77
Assists: John Stockton, 28 vs. San Antonio, 1/15/91
Rebounds: Len Robinson, 27 vs. Los Angeles, 11/11/77

CAREER

Points: Karl Malone, 21,237, 1985–95
Assists: John Stockton, 10,394, 1984–95
Rebounds: Karl Malone, 8,929, 1985–95

VANCOUVER GRIZZLIES

TEAM DIRECTORY: Chairman: Arthur Griffiths; Exec. VP: Tod Leiweke; VP-Basketball Oper./GM: Stu Jackson; Mgr. Basketball Oper.: Chuck Davisson; Dir. Scouting: Larry Riley; Dir. Media Rel.: Steve Frost; Head Coach: Brian Winters; Asst. Coach: Jimmy Powell. Arena: General Motors Place (20,004). Colors: Turquoise, bronze and red.

Grizzlies took Oklahoma State's Bryant Reeves as No. 6.

SCOUTING REPORT

SHOOTING: Get real. There weren't enough good offensive players out there for the established teams, let alone the newcomers in Canada. This is usually the area that suffers the most with expansion clubs, though there is at least reason to believe the Griz won't get shut out often.

Bryant Reeves of Oklahoma State, the first college draftee in franchise history, could develop into a solid offensive player on the post. He uses his big (country) body well to establish position and then move into the lane, then can finish with a hook. The other keeper is Blue Edwards, who shot 49.5 percent last season with the Jazz and averaged 16.9 points as recently as 1992-93 with the Bucks.

The rest is held together by tape and chewing gum, a contingent led by Byron Scott and Gerald Wilkins, both of whom could be traded before camp even starts to a contender looking for insurance. Among young players, Trevor Ruffin has range and scoring potential, though he didn't get to show it behind Elliot Perry and Kevin Johnson in Phoenix.

PLAYMAKING: There are worse people to run an expansion team than Greg Anthony, who has a history of taking questionable shots but has experience without being close to over the hill. The concern is his decision-making, especially on the fly. Derrick Phelps and Ruffin are the backups.

REBOUNDING: Big Country, you have the floor. The inclination might be to bring the first-round pick along slowly ... until you remember that the backup will probably be Benoit Benjamin. Everything, of course, will be a challenge for this team, except that in this case, it's much more localized—six of the top nine rebounders last season will be in the same division, the Midwest. Another, Shawn Kemp, is just down the road in Seattle.

Benjamin remains as he always has been. Antonio Harvey remains a what-may-be, a good athlete who can leap but is still very raw heading into his third season. Decent playing time for a change will decide his future, here and in the league. Reggie Slater is just 6-7, but he showed at Denver he can mix it up at power forward because of strength and toughness.

GRIZZLIES ROSTER

No.	Veterans	Pos.	Ht.	Wt.	Age	Yrs. Pro	College
—	Greg Anthony	G	6-2	185	27	4	UNLV
—	Benoit Benjamin	C	7-0	265	30	10	Creighton
U-	Rodney Dent	F	6-9	256	24	1	Kentucky
—	Blue Edwards	G	6-4	228	30	6	East Carolina
—	Doug Edwards	F	6-7	235	24	2	Florida State
—	Kenny Gattison	F	6-8	256	31	8	Old Dominion
—	Antonio Harvey	F	6-11	225	25	2	Pfeiffer
U-	Derrick Phelps	G	6-4	181	23	1	North Carolina
—	Kevin Pritchard	G	6-3	185	28	4	Kansas
U-	Trevor Ruffin	G	6-1	200	25	1	Hawaii
—	Byron Scott	G	6-4	200	34	12	Arizona State
U-	Reggie Slater	F	6-7	215	25	1	Wyoming
—	Larry Stewart	F	6-8	230	27	4	Coppin State
—	Gerald Wilkins	G	6-6	218	32	9	Tenn.-Chattanooga

U-unrestricted free agent

Rd.	Rookies	Sel.No.	Pos.	Ht.	Wt.	College
1	Bryant Reeves	6	C	7-0	292	Oklahoma State
2	Lawrence Moten	36	G	6-5	185	Syracuse

DEFENSE: Benjamin and Harvey can both be shot-blockers, Anthony is good in this department, and Edwards, though just 6-5, can be a strong body on a guard. After that, things get a little thin. A specific concern is how well Wilkins can move when trying to keep up with quick guards, now that he is 32 and coming off a blown season thanks to a blown Achilles tendon.

OUTLOOK: Not good, but no one expects anything else. The goal will not be measured in wins, but how well the players develop. Maybe the coach, too. Brian Winters, highly regarded as Lenny Wilkens' assistant in Cleveland and most recently Atlanta, moves into the hot seat for the first time.

Meanwhile, take a good look at the inaugural roster. A lot of these guys won't be here in a couple of years. Come to think of it, a lot of these guys won't be in the league in a couple of years.

GRIZZLIES PROFILES

GREG ANTHONY 27 6-2 185   Guard

Was fishing for large-mouthed bass in Vermont the day of expansion draft. Immediately began switching bait and lure tactics to land salmon... Second player selected overall, first by Grizzlies, in expansion draft... Should begin season as starting point guard... Always a good on-ball defender... Problems always have been with shot, shot selection and decisions on fast break... Usually was odd man out when Knicks tried to clear up their point-guard logjams during his four years... A DNP-coach's decision 20 times... Career lows in minutes, points, assists... Finished season strong and eventually had best shooting year (.437)... Future politician... Knicks' first-round pick, No. 12 overall, in 1991 after NCAA title season at UNLV... Born Nov. 15, 1967, in Las Vegas... Made $1.471 million in 1994-95.

Year	Team	G	FG	FG Pct.	FT	FT Pct.	Reb.	Ast.	TP	Avg.
1991-92	New York	82	161	.370	117	.741	136	314	447	5.5
1992-93	New York	70	174	.415	107	.673	170	398	459	6.6
1993-94	New York	80	225	.394	130	.774	189	365	628	7.9
1994-95	New York	61	128	.437	60	.789	64	160	372	6.1
	Totals	293	688	.400	414	.738	559	1237	1906	6.5

RODNEY DENT 24 6-9 255   Forward

Grizzlies took him with a promise of compensation from Magic in the expansion draft... Was Magic's second-round pick in '94 out of Kentucky... Blew out his left knee in college, Jan. 4, 1994. Torn anterior cruciate ligament... Spent the entire season rehabilitating knee. Placed on the injured list in November... Had NBA written all over his professionally-crafted frame before the injury... Born Christmas Day, Dec. 25, 1970, in Edison, Ga.... Made NBA minimum $150,000.

ANTONIO HARVEY 25 6-11 225 — Forward

Grizzlies grabbed him from Lakers in expansion draft... He's the kind of guy teams like to take a look at: young and athletic with some potential, all at a low monetary risk... But very raw... Trying to develop a perimeter game... Still not strong enough to play power forward on a regular basis, especially on defense... But leaping ability allows him to have an occasional impact as a shot-blocker... Fourth on the Lakers in that category despite just 9.7 minutes per game... Participated in slam-dunk contest during All-Star Weekend... Undrafted out of Pfeiffer College, an NAIA school in North Carolina... Lakers signed him as a rookie free agent... Started college career at Southern Illinois, then went to Georgia and finally Pfeiffer... Born July 9, 1970, in Pascagoula, Miss.... Made $325,000 in 1994-95.

Year	Team	G	FG	FG Pct.	FT	FT Pct.	Reb.	Ast.	TP	Avg.
1993-94	L.A. Lakers	27	29	.367	12	.462	59	5	70	2.6
1994-95	L.A. Lakers	59	77	.438	24	.533	102	23	179	3.0
	Totals	86	106	.416	36	.507	161	28	249	2.9

REGGIE SLATER 25 6-7 215 — Forward

Grizzlies' fourth pick in expansion draft... May be short for a power forward, but makes up for it with strength and toughness... First caught Nuggets' attention eye while playing with the Colorado Pro-Am All-Stars, earning an invitation to the Rocky Mountain Revue... He turned into a spot on the training-camp roster and then on the squad in the regular season... Played behind Brian Williams, Rodney Rogers, Tom Hammonds and sometimes Cliff Levingston, but still made contributions... Missed the final 32 games after tearing knee ligament... Raw... Spent two seasons in Europe after graduating from Wyoming... Born Aug. 27, 1970, in Houston... Made $150,000 last season.

Year	Team	G	FG	FG Pct.	FT	FT Pct.	Reb.	Ast.	TP	Avg.
1994-95	Denver	25	40	.494	40	.727	57	12	120	4.8

TREVOR RUFFIN 25 6-1 200 Guard

From Phoenix to Vancouver, the Grizzlies' fifth expansion pick... It was tough finding time behind Kevin Johnson, Elliot Perry and Danny Ainge at point, but he still got noticed because of scoring potential... Has the size of a point guard and the offensive game of a shooting guard... Versatility is one thing, but a team's primary ball-handler who doesn't handle the ball well enough tends to become a bit player, or worse... Began college career at Arizona Western, then transferred to Hawaii... Used to cut class to watch Laker practices during training camp... Next thing he knew, after L.A. signed undrafted rookie as a free agent, he was in those practices... One of the last cuts by Lakers, he returned home to Buffalo and was awaiting an overseas deal when the Suns called because of an injury to Kevin Johnson. Caught the first flight to Seattle the next morning, played that night against the Sonics and scored 17 points while making four of five three-pointers... Eventually named to Rookie All-Star Game... Born Sept. 26, 1970, in Buffalo... Made $143,860 in 1994-95.

Year	Team	G	FG	FG Pct.	FT	FT Pct.	Reb.	Ast.	TP	Avg.
1994-95	Phoenix	49	84	.426	27	.711	23	48	233	4.8

DERRICK PHELPS 23 6-4 181 Guard

He didn't originally make the '94 NBA draft, but he got picked in the '95 expansion draft, the Grizzlies' sixth choice... Plucked off the Sacramento roster... Vancouver brass must have watched him somewhere else—he played three games and five minutes with the Kings... Best known from college days as a key member of North Carolina teams... Spent most of his first pro season with Chicago Rockers of the CBA... All-Rookie in that league... Kings signed him around mid-season... Born July 31, 1972, in Queens, N.Y.

Year	Team	G	FG	FG Pct.	FT	FT Pct.	Reb.	Ast.	TP	Avg.
1994-95	Sacramento	3	0	.000	0	.000	0	1	0	0.0

VANCOUVER GRIZZLIES • 319

KENNY GATTISON 31 6-8 246   Forward-Center

Grizzlies' eighth pick (from Hornets) in expansion draft... Career seemed over after suffering spinal injury when hit by inadvertent elbow by Cleveland's Michael Cage on Nov. 15... Was at 16 points and eight rebounds at time of injury... Underwent surgery Jan. 20, amazingly returned to practice March 8... Played last 15 games, averaging 8.0 points and 3.7 rebounds in 21.3 minutes... Was almost the same player, a banger who worked hard and never complained... Came through when the Hornets needed him in 1993-94, averaging 10.5 points when Larry Johnson was shelved... Hornets' all-time leader in field-goal percentage (.522)... Was third-round pick, out of Old Dominion, in '86... Played 77 games as Suns rookie, missed entire 1987-88 season with knee injury... Went to CBA after cut by Suns, signed as free agent by Hornets December 1989... Born May 23, 1964, in Wilmington, N.C.... Made $1.25 million in 1994-95.

Year	Team	G	FG	FG Pct.	FT	FT Pct.	Reb.	Ast.	TP	Avg.
1986-87	Phoenix	77	148	.476	108	.632	270	36	404	5.2
1987-88	Phoenix					Injured				
1988-89	Phoenix	2	0	.000	1	.500	1	0	1	0.5
1989-90	Charlotte	63	148	.550	75	.682	197	39	372	5.9
1990-91	Charlotte	72	243	.532	164	.661	379	44	650	9.0
1991-92	Charlotte	82	423	.529	196	.688	580	131	1042	12.7
1992-93	Charlotte	75	203	.529	102	.604	353	68	508	6.8
1993-94	Charlotte	77	233	.524	126	.646	358	95	592	7.7
1994-95	Charlotte	21	47	.470	31	.608	75	17	125	6.0
	Totals	469	1445	.522	803	.652	2213	430	3694	7.9

LARRY STEWART 27 6-8 230   Forward

Vancouver's seventh pick in expansion draft... Unheralded, undrafted and unheard-of player out of mighty Coppin State (Class of '91) became a starter for Bullets in 1991-92 and was named to All-Rookie team... Had two steady, solid years and then twice broke foot. Also was shot in suburban home during apparent robbery... So-so 1994-95 season. Undersized against the mule forwards. He can be bowled over, making him defensive liability... Has a good knack for the ball around the basket and is a better-than-average passing four...

Born Aug. 21, 1968, in Philadelphia... Made $700,000 in 1994-95.

Year	Team	G	FG	FG Pct.	FT	FT Pct.	Reb.	Ast.	TP	Avg.
1991-92	Washington	76	303	.514	188	.807	449	120	794	10.4
1992-93	Washington	81	306	.543	184	.727	383	146	796	9.8
1993-94	Washington	3	3	.375	7	.700	7	2	13	4.3
1994-95	Washington	40	41	.461	20	.667	67	18	102	2.6
	Totals	200	653	.522	399	.759	906	286	1705	8.5

GERALD WILKINS 32 6-6 218   Guard-Forward

Grizzlies' 10th pick hopes to get healthy now that he's out of Cleveland... How's this for eerie? Achilles tendon snaps in preseason game against Celtics and older brother Dominique, whose Achilles snapped the previous season—while making a similar move, at almost the same location on the floor... Somebody call Tales from the Crypt... It figured, though. Previous season, he had played all 82 games... And played well, improving average from 11.1 to 14.3. That included 38-point strafing of Magic. Hit six treys in the game, a real accomplishment with the line at 23-9.... Not thought of as a great defender, but led Cavs with 105 steals in 1993-94... Can also play small forward... Dominique's rep didn't do him any good: second-round pick of the Knicks in '85 out of Tennessee-Chattanooga. Played out option after seven seasons in New York... Signed for $500,000 as free agent in 1992 and wound up with $2.5 million last season... Born Sept. 11, 1963, in Atlanta.

Year	Team	G	FG	FG Pct.	FT	FT Pct.	Reb.	Ast.	TP	Avg.
1985-86	New York	81	437	.468	132	.557	208	161	1013	12.5
1986-87	New York	80	633	.486	235	.701	294	354	1527	19.1
1987-88	New York	81	591	.446	191	.786	270	326	1412	17.4
1988-89	New York	81	462	.451	186	.756	244	274	1161	14.3
1989-90	New York	82	472	.457	208	.803	371	330	1191	14.5
1990-91	New York	68	380	.473	169	.820	207	275	938	13.8
1991-92	New York	82	431	.447	116	.730	206	219	1016	12.4
1992-93	Cleveland	80	361	.453	152	.840	214	183	890	11.1
1993-94	Cleveland	82	446	.457	194	.776	303	255	1170	14.3
1994-95	Cleveland					Injured				
	Totals	717	4213	.460	1583	.748	2317	2377	10318	14.4

BYRON SCOTT 34 6-4 200 — Guard

Was Grizzlies' seventh pick in expansion draft ... Basically duplicated numbers from first season (1993-94) with Pacers, but had nothing left for '95 playoffs ... Shot under 40 percent and missed 11 of his first 12 three-point attempts ... It was the complete opposite of his first playoffs with Pacers, which began with a game-winning triple in Game 1 of an opening-round sweep of Magic ... But even when it's not falling, it's still one of the prettiest jumpers on the planet ... Abandoned by Lakers, signed free-agent pact with Pacers on Dec. 7, 1993. Scored eight points in first game ... Key member of Lakers' glory teams, winning title rings in 1985, '87 and '88 ... Was fourth pick in 1983, out of Arizona State, by Clippers ... Born March 28, 1961, in Ogden, Utah ... Made $1.65 million in 1994-95.

Year	Team	G	FG	FG Pct.	FT	FT Pct.	Reb.	Ast.	TP	Avg.
1983-84	Los Angeles	74	334	.484	112	.806	164	177	788	10.6
1984-85	L.A. Lakers	81	541	.539	187	.820	210	244	1295	16.0
1985-86	L.A. Lakers	76	507	.513	138	.784	189	164	1174	15.4
1986-87	L.A. Lakers	82	554	.489	224	.892	286	281	1397	17.0
1987-88	L.A. Lakers	81	710	.527	272	.858	333	335	1754	21.7
1988-89	L.A. Lakers	74	588	.491	195	.863	302	231	1448	19.6
1989-90	L.A. Lakers	77	472	.470	160	.766	242	274	1197	15.5
1990-91	L.A. Lakers	82	501	.477	118	.797	246	177	1191	14.5
1991-92	L.A. Lakers	82	460	.458	244	.838	310	226	1218	14.9
1992-93	L.A. Lakers	58	296	.449	156	.848	134	157	792	13.7
1993-94	Indiana	67	256	.467	157	.805	110	133	696	10.4
1994-95	Indiana	80	265	.455	193	.850	151	108	802	10.0
	Totals	914	5484	.489	2156	.832	2677	2507	13752	15.0

BENOIT BENJAMIN 30 7-0 265 — Center

Benjy Finds Another Home ... Woof ... As lazy as he is tall ... Somehow, he'll blame the media ... Jayson Williams took him under his wing and tried to convince him to work hard with Nets. Fed him large quantities of ginseng. Was that a zany team, or what? ... Sad part is, this guy has ability. Good touch around basket. Can be a legit shot-blocker, even if it's against short guys ... Will even get inspired when playing elite centers ... Coaches keep taking the gamble because he is 7-0 ... With Nets trying to secure a playoff spot, he felt it was more important for him to leave team to visit his chiropractor in Texas ... Now, as team's 11th pick in expansion draft, he's Vancouver's problem.

Like he was Clippers' problem. And Seattle's problem. And Lakers' problem... Overpaid at $3.774 million. He'd be overpaid at six bucks an hour... Nets got him from Lakers for Sam Bowie and a second-rounder June 21, 1993... No. 3 pick by Clippers in 1985, out of Creighton... Sent to Sonics for Olden Polynice and draft picks Feb. 20, 1991... On to Lakers with Doug Christie for Sam Perkins Feb. 22, 1993... Born Nov. 22, 1964, in Monroe, La.

Year	Team	G	FG	FG Pct.	FT	FT Pct.	Reb.	Ast.	TP	Avg.
1985-86	L.A. Clippers	79	324	.490	229	.746	600	79	878	11.1
1986-87	L.A. Clippers	72	320	.449	188	.715	586	135	828	11.5
1987-88	L.A. Clippers	66	340	.491	180	.706	530	172	860	13.0
1988-89	L.A. Clippers	79	491	.541	317	.744	696	157	1299	16.4
1989-90	L.A. Clippers	71	362	.526	235	.732	657	159	959	13.5
1990-91	LAC-Sea.	70	386	.496	210	.712	723	119	982	14.0
1991-92	Seattle	63	354	.478	171	.687	513	76	879	14.0
1992-93	Sea.-LAL	59	133	.491	69	.663	209	22	335	5.7
1993-94	New Jersey	77	283	.480	152	.710	499	44	718	9.3
1994-95	New Jersey	61	271	.510	133	.760	440	38	675	11.1
	Totals	697	3264	.497	1884	.722	5453	1001	8413	12.1

THEODORE (BLUE) EDWARDS 30 6-4 228   G-F

A Blue Grizzlie, their last pick in expansion draft... Started his career with Jazz as the 21st player picked in the 1989 draft... Played three seasons in Utah before being traded to Milwaukee, which traded him to Boston... Bucks' leading scorer in 1992-93 at 16.9 points per outing, and didn't miss a game in two seasons there... Came back to Salt Lake City from Boston on Feb. 3, 1995, in exchange for Jay Humphries... Played 36 games with the Jazz; averaged 6.6 points and 1.8 rebounds and shot 49.5 percent... Provided depth in the backcourt or went to forward and allowed Jerry Sloan to use a small lineup... Colonial Athletic Assn. Player of the Year as a senior at East Carolina... Born Oct. 31, 1965, in Washington, D.C.... Made $1.7 million in 1994-95.

Year	Team	G	FG	FG Pct.	FT	FT Pct.	Reb.	Ast.	TP	Avg.
1989-90	Utah	82	286	.507	146	.719	251	145	727	8.9
1990-91	Utah	62	244	.526	82	.701	201	108	576	9.3
1991-92	Utah	81	433	.522	113	.774	298	137	1018	12.6
1992-93	Milwaukee	82	554	.512	237	.790	382	214	1382	16.9
1993-94	Milwaukee	82	382	.478	151	.799	329	171	953	11.6
1994-95	Bos.-Utah	67	181	.461	75	.833	130	77	459	6.9
	Totals	456	2080	.503	804	.769	1591	852	5115	11.2

DOUG EDWARDS 24 6-7 235 — Forward

Played a whopping 319 minutes in two seasons. Fortunate to play that much... Most famous for taking Keith Askins' sucker punch in '94 playoffs. Was slapped with two-game playoff ban and $10,000 fine. Wasn't missed... Seems to have a thing for the Pistons. In two games against them, he registered career highs in points (11), field goals (4), free throws attempted (6), assists (3) and minutes (16)... Missed first 19 games of 1993-94 season with calf injury... Drafted 15th, out of Florida State, where he became first Seminole to get 1,500 points, 700 rebounds and 200 assists... Born Jan. 21, 1971, in Miami... Made $845,000 in 1994-95.

Year	Team	G	FG	FG Pct.	FT	FT Pct.	Reb.	Ast.	TP	Avg.
1993-94	Atlanta	16	17	.347	9	.563	18	8	43	2.7
1994-95	Atlanta	38	22	.458	23	.719	48	13	67	1.8
	Totals	54	39	.402	32	.667	66	21	110	2.0

THE ROOKIES

BRYANT REEVES 22 7-0 292 — Center

Big Country heads to the NBA's new country... First college pick in Grizzlies' history, No. 6 overall... Big Eight Player of the Year as a senior at Oklahoma State... Joins Danny Manning, Wayman Tisdale, Byron Houston and Doug Smith as the only players in conference history with 2,000 points and 1,000 rebounds... Good shooting touch for a big guy... Needs to prove he can be equally effective on defense... Born June 8, 1973, in Fort Smith, Ark.

LAWRENCE MOTEN 23 6-5 185 — Guard

Left Syracuse as the leading scorer in Big East history, surpassing Terry Dehere... That means he's also No. 1 in the Syracuse record books, ahead of Derrick Coleman... First Orangeman since Hall of Famer Dave Bing to lead the team in scoring three straight years... Vancouver got him with the 36th pick... Born March 25, 1972, in Washington, D.C.

COACH BRIAN WINTERS: Their first coach and his first gig

as a head coach... Long regarded as one of the top young prospects while he was serving apprenticeship to Lenny Wilkens in Cleveland and Atlanta... Spent nine years in all with the league's all-time winningest coach... Nice guy, but hardly glamorous... Best known for his playing days... Starred at South Carolina before the Lakers drafted him 12th overall in 1974... Then became part of one of the biggest trades in sports history: to Milwaukee as part of the package that sent Kareem Abdul-Jabbar to Los Angeles... He missed out on Showtime, but still had a very nice career... All-Star in 1976 and '78... Spent eight seasons with the Bucks, then retired in September 1983... A month later, the franchise retired his jersey No. 32... Third-leading scorer in Bucks history... Spent two years as an assistant at Princeton before hooking up with Wilkens and the Cavaliers in 1986... Now, the next step... "I felt there would have to be a very special opportunity to break me away from my coaching partnership with Lenny and Dick Helm," Winters said. "I believe the Vancouver Grizzlies have presented this very opportunity."
... Born March 1, 1952, in Queens, N.Y.

GOLDEN STATE WARRIORS

TEAM DIRECTORY: Owner: Christopher Cohan; GM: Dave Twardzik; VP/Asst. GM: Al Attles; Dir. Player Personnel: Ed Gregory; Dir. Media Rel.: Julie Marvel; Head Coach: Rick Adelman; Asst. Coaches: Rod Higgins, George Irvine, John Wetzel. Arena: Oakland Coliseum Arena (15,025). Colors: Gold and blue.

SCOUTING REPORT

SHOOTING: The disaster of 1994-95 in a nutshell. The year before, they were the best in the league, and then, while all else

Warriors root for a full-bodied Tim Hardaway.

around them crumbled, the Warriors dropped to a tie for 11th.

Now to pull out of the nosedive. That means you, Latrell Sprewell, all the way down to 41.8 percent last season, complete with a funk. He's the team's best weapon, someone capable of hitting from the outside or driving the lane for a thunderous slam. Why Golden State has reason to be encouraged is that he's not alone.

Chris Mullin has shown that injuries are really the only thing that can stop him, especially from three-point range. The air cover gets even better if Ricky Pierce, who went into the summer as a free agent contemplating retirement, decides to stick around for one more season. Or if B.J. Armstrong was traded from Toronto to the Bay Area after the lockout. Inside, Rony Seikaly may not be the force the Warriors could of/should of had in Chris Webber, but he is at least a solid shooter. Now add the post moves of No. 1 draft pick Joe Smith of Maryland.

PLAYMAKING: Remember a year ago at this time? Uncertainty everywhere, what with Tim Hardaway coming off major knee surgery and Avery Johnson, his capable backup, having returned to San Antonio as a free agent. It's so different now.

Hardaway may be coming off another operation, but one much more minor, to his left wrist. He remains one of the game's most dangerous point guards, capable of nights with double-digit assists (he averaged 9.3 a game in 1994-95) or nights with 25 points. Not only that, but imagine the depth here if Armstrong joins the fold.

REBOUNDING: It says plenty that their first two picks in the draft—Smith at No. 1 overall and Andrew DeClercq at No. 34—are big men. Or maybe, more to the point, it actually says one thing: HELP!

Only seven teams were worse by percentage last season. The Webber fiasco, which took its biggest toll in the harmony department, obviously did its damage here as well. This season, a healthy Seikaly should probably get more than 28.8 minutes a game, so he will also get more than 7.4 boards. The X-Factor may be second-year man Donyell Marshall, whose contribution of 6.5 rebounds in 32 outings in 1994-95 after coming in trade from Minnesota shows he can make a big difference with an entire season in Oakland.

DEFENSE: See above. The top picks have to make an impact because, apparently, no one else will.

WARRIOR ROSTER

No.	Veterans	Pos.	Ht.	Wt.	Age	Yrs. Pro	College
52	Victor Alexander	F-C	6-10	265	26	4	Iowa State
25	Chris Gatling	F-C	6-10	230	28	4	Old Dominion
10	Tim Hardaway	G	6-0	195	29	6	Texas-El Paso
U-20	Tim Legler	G	6-4	210	28	6	LaSalle
R-9	Ryan Lorthridge	G	6-4	190	23	1	Jackson State
3	Donyell Marshall	F	6-9	218	22	1	Connecticut
R-50	Dwayne Morton	F-G	6-7	195	24	1	Louisville
17	Chris Mullin	F	6-7	215	32	10	St. John's
U-22	Ricky Pierce	G	6-4	215	36	13	Rice
34	Carlos Rogers	F-C	6-11	220	24	1	Tennessee State
44	Clifford Rozier	C-F	6-11	255	23	1	Louisville
4	Rony Seikaly	C	6-11	253	30	7	Syracuse
15	Latrell Sprewell	G	6-5	190	25	3	Alabama
U-12	David Wood	F	6-9	230	30	5	Nevada-Reno

R-restricted free agent
U-unrestricted free agent

Rd.	Rookies	Sel.No.	Pos.	Ht.	Wt.	College
1	Joe Smith	1	F	6-10	225	Maryland
2	Andrew DeClercq	34	F-C	6-10	230	Florida
2	Dwayne Whitfield	40	F	6-9	240	Jackson State
2	Martin Lewis	50	G	6-6		Seward County CC
2	Michael McDonald	55	C	6-10	232	New Orleans

Only three teams allowed opponents a higher shooting percentage. The Warriors don't block many shots and they don't force many turnovers. At least one of those has to change because they play in a division with a ton of quick point guards who love to come down the lane and then shoot or dish off—Rod Strickland, Kevin Johnson, Gary Payton, Nick Van Exel. There are 16 games against those guys alone, so you see how it can add up.

OUTLOOK: Here's the encouraging news: It can't get any worse than last season (though they may want that in writing). How much better it gets depends on a lot of things. The starting backcourt, Sprewell and Hardaway, must settle their feud and put the team first. Smith needs to at least show signs of what everyone thinks he can be with experience, even if those same people should remember this would only be his junior year in college. And all the players must mesh with the new coach, Rick Adelman.

This remains, as always, a very intriguing team. Hardaway, Sprewell, Armstrong, Smith, Mullin, Seikaly. That strikes fear. Just as long it doesn't strike out.

WARRIOR PROFILES

LATRELL SPREWELL 25 6-5 190   Guard

Part of the problem or part of the solution?... Big-time talent was overshadowed last season by antics... Was suspended twice for a total of three games for conduct detrimental to the team and for skipping a practice... OK, Latrell, we get the idea already. You're upset friends Chris Webber and Billy Owens were traded. Now stop writing their uniform numbers on your shoes and remember you're a part of the Warriors, like it or not... Led team in scoring second straight season and finished 17th in the league... Only player in the NBA to average at least 40 minutes in each of the last two years... All-Star Game starter for the first time... The year before, Western Conference coaches voted him in as a reserve, thus making him the first player to make the midseason classic without being on the ballot since Bill Laimbeer in 1983... Born Sept. 8, 1970, in Milwaukee... Made $890,000 last season.

Year	Team	G	FG	FG Pct.	FT	FT Pct.	Reb.	Ast.	TP	Avg.
1992-93	Golden State	77	449	.464	211	.746	271	295	1182	15.4
1993-94	Golden State	82	613	.433	353	.774	401	385	1720	21.0
1994-95	Golden State	69	490	.418	350	.781	256	279	1420	20.6
	Totals	228	1552	.436	914	.770	928	959	4322	19.0

TIM HARDAWAY 29 6-0 195   Guard

The knee held up; the rest of the body didn't... Came back after missing all of 1993-94 following reconstructive knee surgery and, slowly but surely, became the player of old... As the knee got stronger, his famed killer crossover was looking at least like an assault-and-battery crossover... "He has reestablished himself for this basketball team in everybody's eyes," then-coach Bob Lanier said... The return made him one of the few bright spots in the Warriors' season... Had to undergo season-ending surgery on his left wrist March 17... Ligament damage, just like the knee... Missed final 20 games... Still finished 10th in the league in three-pointers made with a team-record 168

... First-round pick out of Texas-El Paso in 1989 ... Missed just four of his first 312 outings ... Since then, has been sidelined 118 of a possible 180 games ... Born Sept. 1, 1966, in Chicago ... Made $3.7 million last season.

Year	Team	G	FG	FG Pct.	FT	FT Pct.	Reb.	Ast.	TP	Avg.
1989-90	Golden State	79	464	.471	211	.764	310	689	1162	14.7
1990-91	Golden State	82	739	.476	306	.803	332	793	1881	22.9
1991-92	Golden State	81	734	.461	298	.766	310	807	1893	23.4
1992-93	Golden State	66	522	.447	273	.744	263	699	1419	21.5
1993-94	Golden State					Injured				
1994-95	Golden State	62	430	.427	219	.760	190	578	1247	20.1
	Totals	370	2889	.458	1307	.768	1405	3566	7602	20.5

CHRIS MULLIN 32 6-7 215   Forward

He can still play; it's just that he doesn't get many chances anymore ... Again hampered by injuries, this time costing him 57 of the first 59 games ... The main problems were a chip fracture of the tibia, a sprained ligament in the knee and a strained hamstring, all in the left leg ... Once the latest black cloud passed, he averaged 19.7 points and 6.3 assists in April ... In all, his 19 points a game was third-best on the team, and his 35.6 minutes per game in his 25 outings sure didn't look like someone about to fall apart ... Also shot a career-best 45.2 percent on three-pointers ... In short, not the perennial all-star of the recent past, but still a factor ... Only Nate Thurmond, Paul Arizin and Rick Barry have logged more minutes in a Warrior uniform ... Golden State picked former St. John's star No. 7 in 1985 ... Born July 30, 1963, in Brooklyn, N.Y. ... Is making an average of $2.84 million annually on current contract.

Year	Team	G	FG	FG Pct.	FT	FT Pct.	Reb.	Ast.	TP	Avg.
1985-86	Golden State	55	287	.463	189	.896	115	105	768	14.0
1986-87	Golden State	82	477	.514	269	.825	181	261	1242	15.1
1987-88	Golden State	60	470	.508	239	.885	205	290	1213	20.2
1988-89	Golden State	82	830	.509	493	.892	483	415	2176	26.5
1989-90	Golden State	78	682	.536	505	.889	463	319	1956	25.1
1990-91	Golden State	82	777	.536	513	.884	443	329	2107	25.7
1991-92	Golden State	81	830	.524	350	.833	450	286	2074	25.6
1992-93	Golden State	46	474	.510	183	.810	232	166	1191	25.9
1993-94	Golden State	62	410	.472	165	.753	345	315	1040	16.8
1994-95	Golden State	25	170	.489	94	.879	115	125	476	19.0
	Totals	653	5407	.512	3000	.862	3032	2611	14243	21.8

RONY SEIKALY 30 6-11 253   Center

Do not adjust your TVs... Warriors really finally have a legitimate, first-rate center... Arrived from Miami just before the start of the 1994-95 regular season in exchange for Billy Owens and the rights to Predrag Danilovic... Hampered by tendinitis in his right ankle that forced him to miss 42 games... Shot a career-best 51.6 percent, but will need to bump up his rebounding average of 7.4... Had averaged a double-double each of the previous five seasons, one of only six players to do that with points and rebounds... Voted Most Improved Player for 1989-90, his second season as a pro... Along with Dennis Rodman, still owns the league's best rebounding game of the 1990s, the 34 he got against Washington on March 3, 1993... Former Syracuse star was born May 10, 1965, in Beirut, Lebanon... Heat took him ninth overall in 1988... 1994-95 salary: $3.29 million.

Year	Team	G	FG	FG Pct.	FT	FT Pct.	Reb.	Ast.	TP	Avg.
1988-89	Miami	78	333	.448	181	.511	549	55	848	10.9
1989-90	Miami	74	486	.502	256	.594	766	78	1228	16.6
1990-91	Miami	64	395	.481	258	.619	709	95	1050	16.4
1991-92	Miami	79	463	.489	370	.733	934	109	1296	16.4
1992-93	Miami	72	417	.480	397	.735	846	100	1232	17.1
1993-94	Miami	72	392	.488	304	.720	740	136	1088	15.1
1994-95	Golden State	36	162	.516	111	.694	266	45	435	12.1
	Totals	475	2648	.484	1877	.663	4810	618	7177	15.1

CHRIS GATLING 28 6-10 230   Forward-Center

Continues to make improvements, slowly but surely... Once an erratic role player known for sporadic bursts of energy, he became much more steady last season... Better yet, he became one of the few bright spots in the Warriors' season... Got extra minutes and took advantage... No. 1 in the NBA in shooting at 63.3 percent, the best in the league since James Donaldson's 63.7 in 1984-85... Broke Bernard King's franchise record of 58.8 percent... His 7.6 rebounds also led team... Has high sights set on winning Sixth Man Award some day... Free-throw shooting (.592) remains a glaring weakness for Old Dominion product... No. 16 pick in 1991 draft... Born Sept. 3,

1967, in Elizabeth City, N.C. ... Made $1.33 million last season.

Year	Team	G	FG	FG Pct.	FT	FT Pct.	Reb.	Ast.	TP	Avg.
1991-92	Golden State	54	117	.568	72	.661	182	16	306	5.7
1992-93	Golden State	70	249	.539	150	.725	320	40	648	9.3
1993-94	Golden State	82	271	.588	129	.620	397	41	671	8.2
1994-95	Golden State	58	324	.633	148	.592	443	51	796	13.7
	Totals	264	961	.586	499	.645	1342	148	2421	9.2

VICTOR ALEXANDER 26 6-10 265   Center-Forward

Role player... Emergence of Chris Gatling means fewer minutes... Got 24.7 an outing last season, more as the season went on, thanks to injuries to Gatling and Rony Seikaly... Starter in 29 of his final 39 appearances, only to be sidelined by a damaged knee ligament that cost him 18 of the last 22 games... One of only five players in team history to shoot better than 50 percent in each of his first four seasons with the team. The others are Gatling, Sarunas Marciulionis, Clifford Ray and Larry Smith... Born Aug. 31, 1969, in Detroit, and played at Iowa State... Warriors took him 17th in 1991... 1994-95 salary: $1.377 million.

Year	Team	G	FG	FG Pct.	FT	FT Pct.	Reb.	Ast.	TP	Avg.
1991-92	Golden State	80	243	.529	103	.691	336	32	589	7.4
1992-93	Golden State	72	344	.516	111	.685	420	93	809	11.2
1993-94	Golden State	69	266	.530	68	.527	308	66	602	8.7
1994-95	Golden State	50	230	.515	36	.600	291	60	502	10.0
	Totals	271	1083	.522	318	.636	1355	251	2502	9.2

DONYELL MARSHALL 22 6-9 218   Forward

Even before last midseason, opinion of coaches around the league included "too soft, already complains too much" and "has absolutely no idea how to play defense."... Needs to get tougher and/or quicker on defense... The flip side, from another: "The kid has a ton of talent and in the right situation he could still become a great player."... Which means Minnesota must have been the wrong situation—Timberwolves used the No. 4 pick last summer to draft him, then traded the former Connecticut star to Mavericks for Tom Gugliotta on Feb. 18... Averaged 10.8 points, 4.9 rebounds and 25.9 minutes with Wolves,

14.8 points, 6.5 rebounds and 32.8 minutes with Warriors ... Had to switch from usual No. 42, which he had worn since eighth grade, because Warriors retired it to honor Nate Thurmond ... Born May 18, 1973, in Reading, Pa. ... Great uncle is football Hall of Famer Lenny Moore ... Made $2.1 million last season.

Year	Team	G	FG	FG Pct.	FT	FT Pct.	Reb.	Ast.	TP	Avg.
1994-95	Minn.-G.S.	72	345	.394	147	.662	405	105	906	12.6

CARLOS ROGERS 24 5-11 220   Forward

Solid contributor as a rookie and could develop into more ... Much will depend on whether his body fills out ... Right now, it reminds some of Clifford Robinson, but not with the same ability ... Michael Smith of Sacramento and Boston's Eric Montross were the only first-year players with at least 1,000 minutes to shoot better last season ... And this was after a slow start, no doubt related to a training-camp holdout ... Scoring average went from 7.0 the first three months to 8.6 in February to 10.6 in March and 12.4 in April ... Played at small Tennessee State, but his stock shot up at the end ... Almost a Top 10 pick, the SuperSonics grabbed him at No. 11 ... Was packaged along with Ricky Pierce and sent to Golden State a few days later for Sarunas Marciulionis and Byron Houston ... Born Feb. 6, 1971, in Detroit ... Made $715,000 last season.

Year	Team	G	FG	FG Pct.	FT	FT Pct.	Reb.	Ast.	TP	Avg.
1994-95	Golden State	49	180	.529	76	.521	278	37	438	8.9

RICKY PIERCE 36 6-4 215   Guard

Contract was up after last season and Rice product said he would probably retire unless it's the right situation ... But there figures to be a lot of those situations for someone who's still a better shooter than a lot of starting guards ... Has range and smarts to use picks ... What championship contender looking for a final piece wouldn't at least be interested? ... Bothered much of 1994-95 with a foot injury and played a career-low 27 games ... Missed 54 of the last 61 outings ... Came into the league when Detroit made him the No. 18 pick in 1982 ... Warriors got him from Seattle along with Carlos Rogers

GOLDEN STATE WARRIORS • 333

and a couple of second-rounders for Sarunas Marciulionis and Byron Houston in the summer of '94... Born Aug. 19, 1959, in Dallas... 1994-95 salary: $2.5 million.

Year	Team	G	FG	FG Pct.	FT	FT Pct.	Reb.	Ast.	TP	Avg.
1982-83	Detroit	39	33	.375	18	.563	35	14	85	2.2
1983-84	San Diego	69	268	.470	149	.861	135	60	685	9.9
1984-85	Milwaukee	44	165	.537	102	.823	117	94	433	9.8
1985-86	Milwaukee	81	429	.538	266	.858	231	177	1127	13.9
1986-87	Milwaukee	79	575	.534	387	.880	266	144	1540	19.5
1987-88	Milwaukee	37	248	.510	107	.877	83	73	606	16.4
1988-89	Milwaukee	75	527	.518	255	.859	197	156	1317	17.6
1989-90	Milwaukee	59	503	.510	307	.839	167	133	1359	23.0
1990-91	Mil.-Sea.	78	561	.485	430	.913	191	168	1598	20.5
1991-92	Seattle	78	620	.475	417	.916	233	241	1690	21.7
1992-93	Seattle	77	524	.489	313	.889	192	220	1403	18.2
1993-94	Seattle	51	272	.471	189	.896	83	91	739	14.5
1994-95	Golden State	27	111	.437	93	.877	64	40	338	12.5
	Totals	794	4836	.499	3033	.877	1994	1611	12920	16.3

TIM LEGLER 28 6-4 210   Guard

Has shooting skills, will travel... Just not real good shooting skills, which is why he travels... Played in 79 games with Dallas in 1993-94, his busiest NBA season, only to be let go when Mavericks drafted a pair of guards, Jason Kidd and Tony Dumas, in the first round... Hit just 43.8 percent overall, although a respectable 37.4 on three-pointers... Was averaging 24.9 points for Omaha, No. 2 in the CBA, when Warriors signed him to a 10-day in early March... Is in fourth place all-time on the CBA scoring list... Joined Warriors for the rest of the season March 27... NBA resume also includes stops in Phoenix, Denver and Utah... Four-time CBA all-star, which ties a record... Some versatility to play small forward... Born Dec. 26, 1966, in Washington.

Year	Team	G	FG	FG Pct.	FT	FT Pct.	Reb.	Ast.	TP	Avg.
1989-90	Phoenix	11	11	.379	6	1.000	8	6	28	2.5
1990-91	Denver	10	25	.347	5	.833	18	12	58	5.8
1992-93	Utah-Dal.	33	105	.436	57	.803	59	46	289	8.8
1993-94	Dallas	79	231	.438	142	.840	128	120	656	8.3
1994-95	Golden State	24	60	.522	30	.882	40	27	176	7.3
	Totals	157	432	.439	240	.839	253	211	1207	7.7

CLIFFORD ROZIER 23 6-11 255 Center-Forward

Help for the inside... His 7.4 rebounds was fourth-best on the team, good production for someone getting just 22.6 minutes... No rookie averaged more boards after the all-star break... His 8.9 per outing in those 36 games was nice for newcomer or veteran... Averaged 10.1 rebounds and 8.2 points the final two months... His 13 offensive boards April 20 against Sacramento was the most by a Warrior since Larry Smith on March 23, 1986... In short, Warriors got good returns on the No. 16 pick... Played in Rookie All-Star Game... Signed a four-year contract coming out of Louisville in 1994, but has an option to become a restricted free agent after this season... Born Oct. 31, 1972, in Bradenton, Fla.... Made $650,000 last season.

Year	Team	G	FG	FG Pct.	FT	FT Pct.	Reb.	Ast.	TP	Avg.
1994-95	Golden State	66	189	.485	68	.447	486	45	448	6.8

RYAN LORTHRIDGE 23 6-4 190 Guard

That's right. Ryan Lorthridge... Warriors' fans learned his name in a hurry last season... He played in crunch time in NBA debut in January, then hit the winning basket against Denver in his second outing... Also made an impression with coach Bob Lanier. Just not always a good one... Lanier cut rookie's minutes after seeing bad work habits... There can't be a bigger crime for a CBA guy trying to stick... Needs to become a better shooter... Has some versatility to play both guard spots... Was final cut in camp with Nets, then headed to CBA... Was with Rockford when Warriors came calling... Played high-school ball with Pistons' Lindsey Hunter and Blazers' James Robinson, then was reunited with Hunter in college before becoming first-ever draft pick of CBA's Mexico City Aztecas... They traded him to Rockford... All-Southwestern Athletic Conference pick as a senior at Jackson State... Born July 27, 1972, in Nashville, Tenn.

Year	Team	G	FG	FG Pct.	FT	FT Pct.	Reb.	Ast.	TP	Avg.
1994-95	Golden State	37	106	.475	57	.648	71	101	272	7.4

DWAYNE MORTON 24 6-7 195   Forward-Guard

Ranked fourth in scoring and sixth in rebounding among rookie second-rounders... High-arcing shot... Just not a real accurate shot... Obviously needs to pick that up... Led Louisville in scoring as a junior and finished second to Clifford Rozier, his teammate then and now, in Metro Conference Player of the Year voting... But when scoring average and shooting percentage dropped senior season, pro scouts backed off... Fell all the way to No. 45 in the draft before Warriors grabbed him... Headed into the summer as a restricted free agent ... Born Aug. 10, 1971, in Louisville, Ky.... 1994-95 salary: $150,000.

Year	Team	G	FG	FG Pct.	FT	FT Pct.	Reb.	Ast.	TP	Avg.
1994-95	Golden State	41	50	.388	58	.682	58	18	167	4.1

DAVID WOOD 30 6-9 230   Forward

Everyone figured he would be the only Warrior to suit up for every game last season, right? ... Was "DNP-CD" four of the first 15 games, then played in each of the final 67 outings... Finished sixth on the team in minutes ... Dangerous three-point shooter... One-year free-agent signee at $150,000... This was actually his second stint with Golden State—sort of... Signed Dec. 7, 1991, and was in uniform that night, but did not play due to coach's decision against Sacramento ... Three days later, the NBA announced the contract had been nullified because Wood was a restricted free agent and subject to the right of first refusal by Houston... Eventually chose to play in Spain before resuming NBA career with San Antonio in 1992-93... Born Nov. 30, 1964, in Vancouver, Wash.

Year	Team	G	FG	FG Pct.	FT	FT Pct.	Reb.	Ast.	TP	Avg.
1988-89	Chicago	2	0	.000	0	.000	0	0	0	0.0
1990-91	Houston	82	148	.424	108	.812	246	94	432	5.3
1992-93	San Antonio	64	52	.444	46	.836	97	34	155	2.4
1993-94	Detroit	78	119	.459	62	.756	239	51	322	4.1
1994-95	Golden State	78	153	.469	91	.778	241	65	428	5.5
	Totals	304	472	.449	307	.793	823	244	1337	4.4

THE ROOKIES

JOE SMITH 20 6-10 225   Forward
The No. 1 pick in the draft... First team All-American by everyone, College Player of the Year by many... Already very refined... Needs to add weight to became a true force inside... Left Maryland after just two seasons... Joins David Thompson and Ralph Sampson as the only sophomores to ever be named Atlantic Coast Conference Player of the Year... Born July 26, 1975, in Norfolk, Va.

ANDREW DeCLERCQ 22 6-10 230   Forward-Center
Very active big man, almost to the point of, as one pro personnel guy says, "being hyper"... All-SEC as a senior at Florida... No. 34 pick from there... No. 2 in school history in blocked shots, No. 3 in rebounds... A starter since his freshman year, then went on to make the opening lineup 128 consecutive games, a Gator record... Born Feb. 1, 1973, in Detroit.

DWAYNE WHITFIELD 23 6-9 240   Forward
Blue-collar player... Played in the SWAC—where he was all-conference—but impressed against big-time competition at the Great Alaska Shootout... Set tournament record with 21 boards... "He works his butt off," said Spurs scout Ed Manning. "He's a lot like Dennis Rodman. He believes every rebound is his."... Jackson State standout went No. 40... Born Aug. 21, 1972, in Aberdeen, Miss.

MICHAEL McDONALD 26 6-10 232   Center
The senior citizen of the rookie class... Did not play high-school basketball, then played after enrolling at a community college as a 21-year-old... Transferred to New Orleans after one season and became a star... Left school as the career leader in average blocks... Ninth in the nation in that category as a senior... Also first-team All-Sun Belt Conference... Born Feb. 13, 1969, in Longview, Tex.

COACH RICK ADELMAN: A familiar face in a familiar situation... Got first opportunity as a head coach when he replaced Mike Schuler, disliked by many players, in Portland... Now comes in to replace Don Nelson, who fell out of favor with many of his charges... Officially, he is following Bob Lanier, who was interim coach after Nelson's departure... Coached the Trail Blazers to the Finals in 1990 and 1992, both eventual losses... Spent six seasons as the sideline boss there... Finished second in Coach of the Year voting in 1991 after Portland finished a league-best 63-19 and ended the Lakers' run of nine straight Pacific Division titles... Career mark is 291-154, which makes him No. 2 on the Blazers' win list, behind only Jack Ramsay... His winning percentage of 65.4 is the sixth-best in league history among coaches with at least 400 games... Also spent three years with the Trail Blazers as a player and five as an assistant coach... Originally made his mark in California, first as a player at Loyola University (now known as Loyola Marymount), then with San Diego as the 79th pick in the 1968 draft... Picked by Trail Blazers in the 1970 expansion draft... Later had stops in Chicago, New Orleans and Kansas City, lasting seven seasons in all before retiring in the summer of 1975... Upon returning to Portland in 1983 as an assistant to Ramsay, he worked with Dave Twardzik... Twardzik, now the Warrior GM, hired him as coach May 19... Born June 16, 1946, in Downey, Cal.... Has a master's degree in history.

GREATEST FIND

On Sept. 7, 1966, the Warriors traded guard Guy Rodgers to Chicago for cash, a draft choice and two players to be named later. Those two throw-ins turned out to be Jim King and Jeff Mullins.

King was a decent player, even an all-star once. Mullins, meanwhile, spent 10 years as a Warrior, averaging 17.6 points, and made three All-Star Game appearances. He had one string of four straight seasons scoring 20 points or more.

ALL-TIME WARRIOR LEADERS

SEASON

Points: Wilt Chamberlain, 4,029, 1961–62
Assists: Eric Floyd, 848, 1986–87
Rebounds: Wilt Chamberlain, 2,149, 1960–61

GAME

Points: Wilt Chamberlain, 100 vs. New York, 3/2/62
Assists: Guy Rodgers, 28 vs. St. Louis, 3/14/63
Rebounds: Wilt Chamberlain, 55 vs. Boston, 11/24/60

CAREER

Points: Wilt Chamberlain, 17,783, 1959–65
Assists: Guy Rodgers, 4,845, 1958–70
Rebounds: Nate Thurmond, 12,771, 1963–74

LOS ANGELES CLIPPERS

TEAM DIRECTORY: Owner: Donald Sterling; Exec. VP-Basketball Oper.: Elgin Baylor; Exec. VP: Andy Roeser; VP-Communications: Joe Safety; Coach: Bill Fitch; Asst. Coaches: Jim Brewer, Barry Hecker, Bob Ociepka. Arena: Los Angeles Sports Arena (16,005). Colors: Red, white and blue.

SCOUTING REPORT

SHOOTING: If that's what you want to call it.

Of all the Clippers' weak spots, this may be the most glaring, which is saying something. They finished 24th in the league in

Oregon State's Brent Barry was 15th draft pick.

shooting last season and averaged just 96.7 points a game, despite taking the sixth-most attempts. Only Minnesota was worse on three-pointers.

So what did they do in the draft? Pass on a potential scoring machine like Jerry Stackhouse to take Antonio McDyess at No. 2 overall and then trade McDyess to Denver for depth. What remains is a backcourt that can't shoot—Pooh Richardson was 39.4 percent in 1994-95 and Malik Sealy and Terry Dehere, who split the starting assignments at off guard, went 43.5 and 40.7, respectively. At least Sealy could call the season a success because he made a pretty good transition from small forward.

The points will probably come from the frontcourt. Loy Vaught still lacks reliable post moves, but is comfortable on the perimeter, must be respected out to 15 feet and has shot 50 percent in three consecutive seasons. Lamond Murray will only get better as he improves his shot selection, which in itself could push him to around 17 points a game. Rodney Rogers, who will challenge for playing time at both forward spots and may push Murray for the starting job, is versatile enough to hit a three-pointer or beat his man off the dribble to get inside.

PLAYMAKING: Richardson has struggled with his shot from the field and the line. That makes him less of a point guard because defenders play off him and wait for the pass, almost begging him to launch from the outside. If he drives, opponents just foul in the lane before he has the chance to dish off.

That makes it all the more creditable that he finished eighth in the league in assists, on such a low-scoring team at that. Gary Grant, a solid defender, will again be the backup, if he does not jump elsewhere as an unrestricted free agent. Either way, rookie Brent Barry, a good passer and versatile enough to play both guard spots, should provide another ball-handler.

REBOUNDING: The shooting guards and small forwards who used to crash the boards as well as anyone at their position, guys like Ron Harper and Danny Manning and Dominique Wilkins, are gone. So, too, are dependable centers, which is how the Clippers got in the position last season of playing 6-9 Tony Massenburg so much in the middle. Small wonder they didn't finish last in rebounding percentage.

Making a move to turn the tide, they brought in the two players for the frontline, Rogers and Brian Williams. Even the rookie guard, Barry, is 6-6. Bill Fitch can look ahead and see Vaught reaching double digits (he got 9.7 in 1994-95), Williams providing a lift and Stanley Roberts . . . maybe showing up. The 7-foot

CLIPPER ROSTER

No.	Veterans	Pos.	Ht.	Wt.	Age	Yrs. Pro	College
24	Terry Dehere	G	6-4	190	24	1	Seton Hall
30	Harold Ellis	G	6-5	200	25	2	Morehouse
23	Gary Grant	G	6-3	185	30	7	Michigan
7	Lamond Murray	F	6-7	236	22	1	California
45	Charles Outlaw	C-F	6-8	210	24	2	Houston
52	Eric Piatkowski	G-F	6-7	215	25	1	Nebraska
2	Pooh Richardson	G	6-1	180	29	6	UCLA
42	Eric Riley	C	7-0	245	25	2	Michigan
53	Stanley Roberts	C	7-0	295	25	4	Louisiana State
54	Rodney Rogers	F	6-7	260	25	2	Wake Forest
21	Malik Sealy	G	6-8	190	25	3	St. John's
4	Michael Smith	F	6-9	225	30	3	Brigham Young
27	Elmore Spencer	C	7-0	270	25	3	UNLV
35	Loy Vaught	F	6-9	240	27	5	Michigan

Rd.	Rookies	Sel.No.	Pos.	Ht.	Wt.	College
1	Brent Barry	15	G	6-6	185	Oregon State
2	Constantin Popa	53	C	7-3	235	Miami

center may not be the answer, but he at least can be part of the solution.

DEFENSE: The constant hustle that earned the respect of every opponent didn't show through in the standings, but it did in another area: the Clippers, without anyone who will be confused with an all-defensive selection, led the league in turnovers forced at 18.4 a game, about three or four more than many other teams. Imagine how much worse the offense could have been without those easy baskets.

Imagine how much better they should be with the added bulk inside. Countering the turnovers was the fact that opponents had a higher shooting percentage against the Clippers than any team. Are you listening, Stanley Roberts?

OUTLOOK: They won't be the worst team in the league, thanks to expansion; they should get into at least the mid-20s in wins and, if the stars are in alignment, maybe even push 30. Keep in mind that three significant pieces (Rogers, Williams, Barry) have been added, one possible starter (Roberts) may be back from injury, another starter (Murray) isn't a rookie anymore, and that the biggest loss from the 1994-95 roster may be Grant, and only if he leaves as a free agent. Then again, keep in mind it's the Clippers.

CLIPPER PROFILES

LOY VAUGHT 27 6-9 240 Forward

Not just the best player on the worst team; a talent on any team... A power forward who loves to do the dirty work... Most comfortable on offense facing the basket... Can hit consistently from the perimeter, as far out as 15 feet... That makes three straight seasons of better than 50 percent all the more impressive ... Finished sixth in the league in shooting in 1993-94 and 23rd last season... Emerged as a team leader after the Clippers lost veterans Danny Manning and Ron Harper... Has improved scoring in all five seasons as a pro since being drafted 13th in 1990... Overshadowed by bigger names at Michigan, but a key component of Wolverines' 1989 NCAA title... Born Feb. 27, 1968, in Grand Rapids, Mich.... Made $2.75 million in 1994-95.

Year	Team	G	FG	FG Pct.	FT	FT Pct.	Reb.	Ast.	TP	Avg.
1990-91	L.A. Clippers	73	175	.487	49	.662	349	40	399	5.5
1991-92	L.A. Clippers	79	271	.492	55	.797	512	71	601	7.6
1992-93	L.A. Clippers	79	313	.508	116	.748	492	54	743	9.4
1993-94	L.A. Clippers	75	373	.537	131	.720	656	74	877	11.7
1994-95	L.A. Clippers	80	609	.514	176	.710	772	139	1401	17.5
	Totals	386	1741	.511	527	.724	2781	378	4021	10.4

JEROME (POOH) RICHARDSON 29 6-1 180 Guard

Finally got the trade he had wanted for years ... Born (May 14, 1966) and raised in Philadelphia, but has considered Los Angeles home since starring at UCLA... Clippers got him from Pacers before last season along with Malik Sealy and Eric Piatkowski for Mark Jackson and Greg Minor... Inconsistent, but finished eighth in the league in assists... His 39.4 percent shooting was easily a career low... First draft pick in Minnesota history, No. 10 overall in 1989... First-team all-rookie... Grandmother gave him the nickname "Pooh" as a baby, based on the storybook character... No. 1 all-time in assists in Pacific-10 Conference history by the time he left UCLA ... 1994-95 salary: $2.12 million.

Year	Team	G	FG	FG Pct.	FT	FT Pct.	Reb.	Ast.	TP	Avg.
1989-90	Minnesota	82	426	.461	63	.589	217	554	938	11.4
1990-91	Minnesota	82	635	.470	89	.539	286	734	1401	17.1
1991-92	Minnesota	82	587	.466	123	.691	301	685	1350	16.5
1992-93	Indiana	74	337	.479	92	.742	267	573	769	10.4
1993-94	Indiana	37	160	.452	47	.610	110	237	370	10.0
1994-95	L.A. Clippers	80	353	.394	81	.648	261	632	874	10.9
	Totals	437	2498	.455	495	.638	1442	3415	5702	13.0

LAMOND MURRAY 22 6-7 236   Forward

Should break the Clippers' streak of bad draft picks ... Showed nice potential as a rookie ... Obviously needs to improve accuracy, which should come with better shot selection ... Also needs to work on his attitude—didn't always see eye to eye with Bill Fitch, culminating in his being sent home from a trip late in the season and earning a one-game suspension ... Good sign was that he put the ball on the floor to get to the basket, proving to be more aggressive than most rookies ... Cousin of former Rocket Tracy Murray ... Played in Rookie All–Star Game and scored the winning basket in overtime ... Passed Kevin Johnson to become all-time leading scorer in California history, then was No. 7 draft pick ... Born April 20, 1973, in Pasadena, Cal. ... Made $2 million in 1994-95.

Year	Team	G	FG	FG Pct.	FT	FT Pct.	Reb.	Ast.	TP	Avg.
1994-95	L.A. Clippers	81	439	.402	199	.754	354	133	1142	14.1

MALIK SEALY 25 6-8 190   Guard-Forward

Found a new home, and we don't mean Los Angeles ... After spending most of his first two years as a pro at small forward, he got an opportunity at shooting guard and didn't waste the chance ... Replaced incumbent Terry Dehere and started there 41 times ... Good size for the position ... But needs to become a better shooter ... In the end, he probably improved more than anyone on the team from training camp to the end of April ... Clippers got him with Pooh Richardson and Eric Piatkowski from Indiana in exchange for Mark Jackson and Greg

Minor... Pacers picked him No. 14 overall in 1992 after a standout career at St. John's... Born Feb. 1, 1970, in the Bronx, N.Y. ... 1994-95 salary: $1.26 million.

Year	Team	G	FG	FG Pct.	FT	FT Pct.	Reb.	Ast.	TP	Avg.
1992-93	Indiana	58	136	.426	51	.689	112	47	330	5.7
1993-94	Indiana	43	111	.405	59	.678	118	48	285	6.6
1994-95	L.A. Clippers	60	291	.435	174	.780	214	107	778	13.0
	Totals	161	538	.426	284	.740	444	202	1393	8.7

TERRY DEHERE 24 6-4 190   Guard

Insisted as a rookie he shot poorly because he did not get enough playing time to get in the flow... Needs a new excuse now... Inherited job as starting shooting guard from Ron Harper and went 40.7 percent... Then again, it was a significant increase from the 37.7 mark of 1993-94... Ended up losing the job to Malik Sealy, who previously had little experience at shooting guard... Started 28 times... Defense got better... Played high-school ball with Kings' Bobby Hurley in New Jersey before staying close to star at Seton Hall... Left in 1993 as the No. 13 pick, the all-time leading scorer in Big East history and three-time all-conference choice... Born Sept. 12, 1971, in New York... Made $1.365 million last season.

Year	Team	G	FG	FG Pct.	FT	FT Pct.	Reb.	Ast.	TP	Avg.
1993-94	L.A. Clippers	64	129	.377	61	.753	68	78	342	5.3
1994-95	L.A. Clippers	80	279	.407	229	.784	152	225	835	10.4
	Totals	144	408	.397	290	.777	220	303	1177	8.2

STANLEY ROBERTS 25 7-0 295   Center

And here we thought the biggest problem with his body was his stomach... Guess again... Blew out right Achilles tendon Dec. 4, 1993, after just 14 games... Returned for training camp last fall, only to rupture his left Achilles tendon in Oct. 26 preseason game... Missed the entire season... The injury problem is compounded by his weight problem... Needs to keep off the pounds to keep unnecessary stress off the feet... Has the talent to be a starting center... Post moves are getting better all the time... Anxious to learn and get better... Shaquille

O'Neal's teammate at LSU, he left school early and played in Spain before Magic used the 23rd pick in 1991 to get him into the NBA ... Became O'Neal's teammate again; therefore, he also became expendable ... Orlando traded him to L.A. in the summer of 1992 as part of the three-team trade that also included the Knicks, Charles Smith and Mark Jackson ... Born Feb. 7, 1970, in Hopkins, S.C. ... Made $3.496 million in 1994-95.

Year	Team	G	FG	FG Pct.	FT	FT Pct.	Reb.	Ast.	TP	Avg.
1991-92	Orlando	55	236	.529	101	.515	336	39	573	10.4
1992-93	L.A. Clippers	77	375	.527	120	.488	478	59	870	11.3
1993-94	L.A. Clippers	14	43	.430	18	.409	93	11	104	7.4
1994-95	L.A. Clippers					Injured				
	Totals	146	665	.520	239	.492	907	109	1547	10.6

ERIC PIATKOWSKI 25 6-7 215   Guard-Forward

Second-year player has the tools and versatility to make it ... Can run the floor in transition or shoot from the perimeter ... Nice combination ... A lot of teams liked him coming out of Nebraska in summer of '94 ... Stock shot up with postseason showings and then at pre-draft combines ... Indiana took him at No. 15, then traded him to L.A. as part of the Mark Jackson-Pooh Richardson deal ... His father, Walt, played for Bill Fitch at Bowling Green and then played four seasons in the ABA (1968-72) with Denver, the Floridians and Kentucky ... Had trouble getting into proper shape after missing much of training camp because of a training-camp holdout ... Born Sept. 30, 1970, in Steubenville, Ohio ... 1994-95 salary: $962,5000.

Year	Team	G	FG	FG Pct.	FT	FT Pct.	Reb.	Ast.	TP	Avg.
1994-95	L.A. Clippers	81	201	.441	90	.783	133	77	566	7.0

ELMORE SPENCER 25 7-0 270   Center

Missed 31 games after going on the injured list because of emotional and personal problems ... We think the Clippers are the ones with problems for giving this guy an extension during training camp ... They can only hope he develops into a dependable backup ... With Stanley Roberts around, he always has to be ready to start ... In the opening lineup eight times in 1994-95... Finished 14th in blocked shots the season before despite getting only 25.4 minutes a night, so he can do some damage... Proved last fall he can also walk out of training camp and make the three-mile stroll back to the hotel on foot... Clippers got UNLV product with 25th pick in 1992... Born Dec. 6, 1969, in Atlanta... Earned $700,000 last season.

Year	Team	G	FG	FG Pct.	FT	FT Pct.	Reb.	Ast.	TP	Avg.
1992-93	L.A. Clippers	44	44	.537	16	.500	62	8	104	2.4
1993-94	L.A. Clippers	76	288	.533	97	.599	415	75	673	8.9
1994-95	L.A. Clippers	19	52	.441	28	.560	65	25	132	6.9
	Totals	139	384	.519	141	.578	542	108	909	6.5

GARY GRANT 30 6-3 185   Guard

Seven years as a Clipper? That's only about four more than most people would have figured... Says he would like to finish his career with the only pro organization he has known... Went into the summer as an unrestricted free agent... Good defender... Former No. 1 at the point now plays both guard spots off the bench... Too erratic to be starting as the primary ball-handler... Until last season, he was not accurate enough to be starting at shooting guard... Then made a nice jump to 47 percent during injury-riddled campaign... Biggest problem was missing 29 games at the start after arthroscopic knee surgery in the offseason... Played with Clipper teammate Loy Vaught at Michigan... Seattle drafted him 15th in 1988, then immediately traded him to L.A. in three-team trade that also included Charles Smith, Hersey Hawkins, Michael Cage and the 76ers... Born April 21, 1965, in Canton, Ohio... 1994-95 salary: $1.1 million.

Year	Team	G	FG	FG Pct.	FT	FT Pct.	Reb.	Ast.	TP	Avg.
1988-89	L.A. Clippers	71	361	.435	119	.735	238	506	846	11.9
1989-90	L.A. Clippers	44	241	.466	88	.779	195	442	575	13.1
1990-91	L.A. Clippers	68	265	.451	51	.689	209	587	590	8.7
1991-92	L.A. Clippers	78	275	.462	44	.815	184	538	609	7.8
1992-93	L.A. Clippers	74	210	.441	55	.743	139	353	486	6.6
1993-94	L.A. Clippers	78	253	.449	65	.855	142	291	588	7.5
1994-95	L.A. Clippers	33	78	.470	45	.818	35	93	205	6.2
	Totals	446	1683	.451	467	.768	1142	2810	3899	8.7

CHARLES (BO) OUTLAW 24 6-8 210   Forward-Center

Another undersized center forced to step up in weight class after the loss of Stanley Roberts and Elmore Spencer... Able to compensate for height disadvantage with great leaping ability... Hard worker... Made impact as a shot-blocker... Good shooter, as long as it's within three feet. Has no real post moves seven or eight feet out... No real skills 15 feet out, either—49.5 percent from the line the last two seasons... That becomes a factor since those who make their living in the paint tend to get fouled a lot... Nicknamed "LW" by Bill Fitch because he always has to have the last word in a conversation... Clippers signed former University of Houston star as a free agent after he played with Grand Rapids of the CBA... Born April 13, 1971, in San Antonio... Made $250,000 in 1994-95.

Year	Team	G	FG	FG Pct.	FT	FT Pct.	Reb.	Ast.	TP	Avg.
1993-94	L.A. Clippers	37	98	.587	61	.592	212	36	257	6.9
1994-95	L.A. Clippers	81	170	.523	82	.441	313	84	422	5.2
	Totals	118	268	.545	143	.495	525	120	679	5.8

HAROLD ELLIS 25 6-5 200   Forward

Reality check... As midseason free-agent acquisition in 1993-94, he became a hit with then-coach Bob Weiss and fan favorite because of his hustle... Last season, he became attached to the bench, far down from Bill Fitch... Made 69 appearances, but at 9.5 minutes per... Only Randy Woods averaged less time... Started seven times... Spent more time at small forward, where he wasn't so overmatched physically... Needs to develop a shot... CBA all-star with Quad City just before getting the call from the Clippers... Division II Player of the Year at Morehouse College in 1992... Three-time All-American... Born Oct. 7, 1970, in Atlanta... Made $250,000 in 1994-95.

Year	Team	G	FG	FG Pct.	FT	FT Pct.	Reb.	Ast.	TP	Avg.
1993-94	L.A. Clippers	49	159	.545	106	.711	153	31	424	8.7
1994-95	L.A. Clippers	69	91	.481	69	.590	88	40	252	3.7
	Totals	118	250	.520	175	.658	241	71	676	5.7

RODNEY ROGERS 24 6-7 260   Forward

Sent to Clippers for Randy Woods in draft-day deal... Out of position at power forward last season as Nuggets tried to compensate for the loss of LaPhonso Ellis... Fireplug body doesn't look the part, but he's an athlete... Can score inside or hit from outside... That makes for often difficult matchups for defenders: he can post up small forwards and take power forwards to the perimeter... Third on the team in scoring... Turned pro in 1993 after being named Atlantic Coast Conference Player of the Year and second-team All-American as a junior at Wake Forest... Nuggets got him ninth overall... Born June 20, 1971, in Durham, N.C. ... Made $1.56 million in 1994-95.

Year	Team	G	FG	FG Pct.	FT	FT Pct.	Reb.	Ast.	TP	Avg.
1993-94	Denver	79	239	.439	127	.672	226	101	640	8.1
1994-95	Denver	80	375	.488	179	.651	385	161	979	12.2
	Totals	159	614	.467	306	.659	611	262	1619	10.2

ERIC RILEY 25 7-0 245   Center

After losing Stanley Roberts and Elmore Spencer, the Clippers wanted to get a talented big body... Instead, they just got a big body... Picked up after being waived by Rockets... Missed much of February after suffering multiple injuries in a car accident... Had the look of a disinterested player, but that may just be the same laid-back personality that earned him the nickname "Easy E"... High-school teammates in Cleveland with future Michigan football stars Elvis Grbac and Desmond Howard... He went to Ann Arbor for basketball and wound up a two-time honorable mention All-American... Mavericks took him No. 33 in 1993, then traded him to Rockets for Ron (Popeye) Jones... That became a steal of a deal for Dallas... Born June 2, 1970, in Cleveland... Made $305,000 last season.

Year	Team	G	FG	FG Pct.	FT	FT Pct.	Reb.	Ast.	TP	Avg.
1993-94	Houston	47	34	.486	20	.541	59	9	88	1.9
1994-95	L.A. Clippers	40	65	.448	47	.734	112	11	177	4.4
	Totals	87	99	.460	67	.663	171	20	265	3.0

MICHAEL SMITH 25 6-9 225 — Forward

Local kid makes good, sort of... One of the best high-school quarterbacks in California history returned when Clippers signed him to free-agent contract in February... Had been playing in Spain when they called... Became the designated shooter... Had a good percentage for someone who didn't get a lot of minutes... Most people need at least some time to get into the flow... Skills like that will keep a guy in the league... Good size for small forward... Red Auerbach is probably still lamenting taking him over Vlade Divac with 13th pick in 1989... Starred at BYU... Born May 19, 1970, in Rochester, N.Y.

Year	Team	G	FG	FG Pct.	FT	FT Pct.	Reb.	Ast.	TP	Avg.
1989-90	Boston	65	136	.476	53	.828	100	79	327	5.0
1990-91	Boston	47	95	.475	22	.815	56	43	218	4.6
1994-95	L.A. Clippers	29	63	.470	26	.867	56	20	153	5.3
	Totals	141	294	.474	101	.835	212	142	698	5.0

THE ROOKIES

BRENT BARRY 23 6-6 185 — Guard
Scouts say he's the best of the basketball-playing Barry boys... Son of Rick, brother of Milwaukee Bucks' Jon, Georgia Tech's Drew and former Kansas Jayhawks' Scooter... All-Pacific 10 Conference as a senior at Oregon State... Went 15th overall to Denver, then was traded before the end of the night to L.A. in the Rodney Rogers-Antonio McDyess deal... Clippers—and every team—love his versatility to play both spots in the backcourt... Born Dec. 31, 1971, in Hempstead, N.Y.

CONSTANTIN POPA 24 7-3 235 — Center
Member of the Romanian national team attended Fork Union Military Academy in Virginia, then stayed in the United States to play at Miami... Hurricanes' career leader in blocked shots... Third-team All-Big East Conference as a senior, when he led team in rebounds, blocks and shooting... Can shoot the hook with either hand... No. 53 pick... Born Feb. 18, 1971, in Bucharest, Romania.

COACH BILL FITCH:

Didn't get a single vote for 1994-95 Coach of the Year, but did one of the best coaching jobs... Squeezing 17 wins out of this group earned him rave reviews from everyone around the league... No. 1 in games coached in NBA history at 1,804... No. 5 in wins at 862... Reached 850 milestone Jan. 5 vs. Philadelphia... Chances are he won't get to the next milestone—900—this season... Only four coaches are ahead of him on the all-time list: Lenny Wilkens, Red Auerbach, Jack Ramsay and Dick Motta... Has 22 years experience as NBA head coach... Two-time Coach of the Year... Has 12 winning seasons and five division titles to his credit... Titles have come in the Central (Cleveland), Atlantic (Boston) and Midwest (Houston), so he's only missing the Pacific for the grand slam... Started coaching career at age 24 with 10 seasons at alma mater Coe College, then went to North Dakota... Next stop was Bowling Green, where one of his players was Walt Piatkowski, father of current Clipper Eric Piatkowski... Last college stop was Minnesota, before moving to the NBA with the Cavaliers... Went to the playoffs three times in nine seasons with Cleveland, then went to Boston... Coached the 1980-81 Celtics to the championship... Moved to Houston for 1983-84 and three years later had the Rockets in the Finals... They made the playoffs four of his five seasons... Coached Nets for two seasons, then figured he had retired for good... Master of the rebuilding projects came back for the challenge of all challenges: the Clippers... Born May 19, 1934, in Davenport, Iowa.

GREATEST FIND

It wasn't that no one expected him to be good. First-rounders are supposed to have a future. But as the Clippers' third pick of the draft?

So it came to be in 1987, when Reggie Williams was the fourth choice overall and Joe Wolf the 13th. That left Ken Norman, crushed over his "late" selection at No. 19.

It didn't take long before Norman left everyone in his dust. He spent six seasons there and became the all-time Los Angeles/San Diego Clipper leader in points before being passed by Danny

Manning. He was also No. 1 in games played before leaving as a free agent, allowing Gary Grant to move into the top spot in that department last season.

ALL-TIME CLIPPER LEADERS

SEASON

Points: Bob McAdoo, 2,831, 1974–75
Assists: Norm Nixon, 914, 1983–84
Rebounds: Swen Nater, 1,216, 1979–80

GAME

Points: Bob McAdoo, 52 vs. Boston, 2/22/74
Bob McAdoo, 52 vs. Seattle, 3/17/76
Charles Smith, 52 vs. Denver, 12/1/90
Assists: Ernie DiGregorio, 25 vs. Portland, 1/1/74
Rebounds: Swen Nater, 32 vs. Denver, 12/14/79

CAREER

Points: Randy Smith, 12,735, 1971–79, 1982–83
Assists: Randy Smith, 3,498, 1971–79, 1982–83
Rebounds: Bob McAdoo, 4,229, 1972–76

LOS ANGELES LAKERS

TEAM DIRECTORY: Owner: Jerry Buss; Exec. VP: Jerry West; GM: Mitch Kupchak; Dir. Pub. Rel.: John Black; Coach: Del Harris; Asst. Coaches: Bill Bertka, Larry Drew, Michael Cooper. Arena: The Great Western Forum (17,505). Colors: Royal purple and gold.

SCOUTING REPORT

SHOOTING: From Randy Pfund/Magic Johnson to Del Harris, one thing did not change. The Lakers are not hesitant. They also are not real accurate. Only Dallas and Portland had more attempts, but Los Angeles finished 15th by percentage. Only four teams tried more three-pointers, but the rank by percentage was 19th.

The Lakers are always dangerous, though, because of their versatility. Nick Van Exel continues to improve in breaking down the defense to get down the lane or will pull up for a three-pointer without hesitation, though he still needs to improve from 42 percent overall. Leading scorer Cedric Ceballos creates so many baskets on his own by getting offensive rebounds and garbage underneath and last season showed three-point range for the first time in his career. Vlade Divac lacks a traditional post game but makes up for it with quickness inside and skills on the perimeter.

Harris can find comfort in the notion that Ceballos is a mortal lock to shoot at least 50 percent every year. Divac has become consistent enough to hover around that level, and Eddie Jones, coming off a very encouraging rookie campaign, could make a run. If Van Exel ever gets to 46 or 48 percent, that should be worth several more points a night.

PLAYMAKING: When Van Exel came out of Cincinnati in the summer of 1993, the question was whether he could have an impact at this level. When he showed impressive flashes as a rookie, the question was whether he could do it at the next level, the playoffs. No one wonders anything any more. Especially in Seattle or San Antonio.

The Lakers finished fifth in assist-to-turnover ratio in 1994-95, a real positive considering they like to play uptempo, but proved in the postseason they need Sedale Threatt to be healthy, or for some other backup point guard to arrive. Jerry West thinks it could be Frankie King in time, but for now he is just a second-round pick from a small school with everything to prove in the

Nick Van Exel's playoff performance topped fine season.

NBA. Threatt can still do the job—he was fifth among individuals in assist-to-turnover ratio—but he will also be 34 by the time opening night comes.

REBOUNDING: We know now that rebounding isn't the end-all critical area it was once cracked up to be, what with the Houston Rockets having won consecutive NBA titles despite significant struggles in this area. Still, Harris in particular and the Lakers as a whole consider it imperative to improve.

Only five teams were worse by percentage last season, which just should not be. Ceballos is one of the best rebounding small forwards in the league and averaged eight a game last season.

LAKER ROSTER

No.	Veterans	Pos.	Ht.	Wt.	Age	Yrs. Pro	College
00	Corie Blount	F	6-10	242	26	2	Cincinnati
U-31	Sam Bowie	C	7-1	255	34	10	Kentucky
41	Elden Campbell	F-C	6-11	250	27	5	Clemson
23	Cedric Ceballos	F	6-7	225	26	5	Cal-Fullerton
12	Vlade Divac	C	7-1	250	27	6	Serbia
25	Eddie Jones	G-F	6-6	190	24	1	Temple
30	George Lynch	F	6-7	223	25	2	North Carolina
R-2	Anthony Miller	F	6-9	255	24	1	Michigan State
1	Anthony Peeler	G	6-4	212	25	3	Missouri
U-34	Tony Smith	G	6-4	205	27	5	Marquette
3	Sedale Threatt	G	6-2	185	34	12	West Virginia Tech
9	Nick Van Exel	G	6-1	170	23	2	Cincinnati

R-restricted free agent
U-unrestricted free agent

Rd.	Rookie	Sel.No.	Pos.	Ht.	Wt.	College
2	Frankie Jones	37	G	6-1	185	Western Carolina

Divac was 10th in the league. Problem is, there's no depth. Elden Campbell, the starting power forward, contributed just 6.1. Campbell will always be Campbell—loaded with physical skills, but too often lacking effort—so the Lakers went into the summer looking for help, either with a new starter through trade or the free-agent market, or with Anthony (Pig) Miller or newcomer Corie Blount emerging as solid backups.

DEFENSE: Led by Divac and Campbell, the Lakers can block a lot of shots. But a team that was strictly middle-of-the-road in shooting percentage-against in 1994-95 may take a further dip depending on what happened during the offseason. That is to say, two of their best defenders may be history: Tony Smith was an unrestricted free agent and probably headed elsewhere while Sam Bowie was an unrestricted free agent and probably headed to retirement.

OUTLOOK: Having spent 1994-95 shocking people, they now have to face the consequences: expectations. The Lakers should surpass 48 wins just by staying healthy, which would be a change, and by having a season together under their belts, even better that it included a couple of challenging playoff series. They certainly have the big shots worried.

LAKER PROFILES

NICK VAN EXEL 23 6-1 170   Guard

Nick at Nite... Star of the Lakers' playoff run with great showings against Seattle and San Antonio... At times, carried team against the Sonics... Most memorable outing: Hit one three-pointer with 10.2 seconds left to force overtime, then hit another, this time on the run, with 0.5 left in OT for the Game 5 win over Spurs... Latter probably was biggest shot the franchise had had since Magic Johnson's junior skyhook in the '87 Finals against Boston... Rookie campaign of 1993-94 made his drop to the second round seem like a steal for L.A.; last season made it look like the Brink's heist... Great quickness allows him to break down any defender and get into the lane... Still, a very streaky shooter... Set team single-season records for three-pointers made (183) and attempted (511)... Joined Nets' Kenny Anderson as one of only two players to average at least 16 points and eight assists... Played college ball at Cincinnati... Born Nov. 27, 1971, in Kenosha, Wisc.... 1994-95 salary: $1.9 million.

Year	Team	G	FG	FG Pct.	FT	FT Pct.	Reb.	Ast.	TP	Avg.
1993-94	L.A. Lakers	81	413	.394	150	.781	238	466	1099	13.6
1994-95	L.A. Lakers	80	465	.420	235	.783	223	660	1348	16.9
	Totals	161	878	.407	385	.783	461	1126	2447	15.2

CEDRIC CEBALLOS 26 6-7 225   Forward

Into the spotlight, finally... After years of playing in the shadows of Barkley, KJ and Majerle, he came home to Los Angeles... If the locals didn't know him before, they do now ... Became the first Laker to score 50 points since Gail Goodrich in March of '75... Picked by Western Conference coaches as an all-star reserve, although he didn't get to play because of thumb surgery... That injury cost him 22 games and a chance to meet the league qualifying standards for scoring... His 21.7 would have put him 12th... Scottie Pippen was the only small forward to average more rebounds... Showed himself to be much more of a three-point threat than he was with Suns... Ended up costing the Lakers the No. 21 pick in the draft in the deal with Phoenix... Born Aug. 2, 1969, in Maui, Hawaii...

Made $1.75 million in 1994-95.

Year	Team	G	FG	FG Pct.	FT	FT Pct.	Reb.	Ast.	TP	Avg.
1990-91	Phoenix	63	204	.487	110	.663	150	35	519	8.2
1991-92	Phoenix	64	176	.482	109	.736	152	50	462	7.2
1992-93	Phoenix	74	381	.576	187	.725	408	77	949	12.8
1993-94	Phoenix	53	425	.535	160	.724	344	91	1010	19.1
1994-95	L.A. Lakers	58	497	.509	209	.716	464	105	1261	21.7
	Totals	312	1683	.523	775	.714	1518	358	4201	13.5

VLADE DIVAC 27 7-1 250   Center

Better than ever... The 16 points and 2.18 blocked shots per game were career highs, the 10.4 rebounds a team high... That's two seasons in a row of being consistent after a very up-and-down start to his career... Was the only NBA player last season to record three 20-point, 20-rebound games... Even had back-to-back 20-20s, becoming the first Laker to do that since Kareem Abdul-Jabbar in December 1975... In short, the Lakers' patience has paid off... Feels more comfortable facing the basket, so game is more like that of a power forward... But handles the inside well on defense and forces tough matchups for opposing centers... Has a hook shot, but can't depend on it... Star in Yugoslavia before the Lakers drafted him 26th in 1989... Born Feb. 3, 1968, in Prijepolje, Yugoslavia... 1994-95 salary: $3.33 million.

Year	Team	G	FG	FG Pct.	FT	FT Pct.	Reb.	Ast.	TP	Avg.
1989-90	L.A. Lakers	82	274	.499	153	.708	512	75	701	8.5
1990-91	L.A. Lakers	82	360	.565	196	.703	666	92	921	11.2
1991-92	L.A. Lakers	36	157	.495	86	.768	247	60	405	11.3
1992-93	L.A. Lakers	82	397	.485	235	.689	729	232	1050	12.8
1993-94	L.A. Lakers	79	453	.506	208	.686	851	307	1123	14.2
1994-95	L.A. Lakers	80	485	.507	297	.777	829	329	1277	16.0
	Totals	441	2126	.509	1175	.720	3834	1095	5477	12.4

EDDIE JONES 24 6-6 190   Guard

Any more questions?... Jerry West raised some eyebrows when he used the Lakers' highest draft pick since 1982 on a shooting guard, the team's deepest position... Then Jones played, and everyone understood... Went right into the starting lineup at shooting guard... By the end of the season, coaches from around the league were so impressed they made him first-team all-rookie ... MVP at Rookie All-Star Game ... Driver, slasher, leaper ... But dangerous enough from the perimeter to keep defenses honest ... A good defender ... Assistant coach Michael Cooper, the former stopper, gives him high marks there ... Plays some small forward ... His 2.05 steals led the team and was sixth in the NBA ... Also had best steal-to-turnover ratio in the league (1.75-to-1) ... Temple product was born Oct. 20, 1971, in Toledo, Ohio ... Made $1.3 million last season.

Year	Team	G	FG	FG Pct.	FT	FT Pct.	Reb.	Ast.	TP	Avg.
1994-95	L.A. Lakers	64	342	.460	122	.722	249	128	897	14.0

ELDEN CAMPBELL 27 6-11 250   Forward

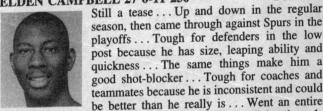

Still a tease ... Up and down in the regular season, then came through against Spurs in the playoffs ... Tough for defenders in the low post because he has size, leaping ability and quickness ... The same things make him a good shot-blocker ... Tough for coaches and teammates because he is inconsistent and could be better than he really is ... Went an entire month during 1994-95 without recording double-digit rebounds ... Finished 11th in the league in blocks ... Would have finished even higher if he got more than his 28.4 minutes ... Needs to be a more dependable rebounder ... Born July 23, 1968, in Inglewood, Cal. ... Played college ball at Clemson before Lakers took him No. 27 in 1990 ... 1994-95 salary: $2.1 million.

Year	Team	G	FG	FG Pct.	FT	FT Pct.	Reb.	Ast.	TP	Avg.
1990-91	L.A. Lakers	52	56	.455	32	.653	96	10	144	2.8
1991-92	L.A. Lakers	81	220	.448	138	.619	423	59	578	7.1
1992-93	L.A. Lakers	79	238	.458	130	.637	332	48	606	7.7
1993-94	L.A. Lakers	76	373	.462	188	.689	519	86	934	12.3
1994-95	L.A. Lakers	73	360	.459	193	.666	445	92	913	12.5
	Totals	361	1247	.457	681	.655	1815	295	3175	8.8

ANTHONY PEELER 25 6-4 212   Guard

The upside to the rash of Laker injuries ... Had a limited role before midseason, then emerged from the shadows to play a huge role and help keep the team afloat without Eddie Jones and Cedric Ceballos ... Averaged 17.3 points and 33.6 minutes while making 24 consecutive starts, his only ones of the season ... That sent his stock soaring again ... In the opening lineup for the playoffs... Opened the season deep on the bench after losing starting job to Jones... Averaged 17.1 points on the 25 occasions when he played at least 35 minutes ... Loves the transition game... Defense needs to improve... Big Eight Player of the Year at Missouri in 1991-92... Lakers picked him 15th from there... Born Nov. 25, 1969, in Kansas City, Mo.... Made $1.12 million in 1994-95.

Year	Team	G	FG	FG Pct.	FT	FT Pct.	Reb.	Ast.	TP	Avg.
1992-93	L.A. Lakers	77	297	.468	162	.786	179	166	802	10.4
1993-94	L.A. Lakers	30	176	.430	57	.803	109	94	423	14.1
1994-95	L.A. Lakers	73	285	.432	102	.797	168	122	756	10.4
	Totals	180	758	.445	321	.793	456	382	1981	11.0

SEDALE THREATT 34 6-2 185 Guard

He has one year left on his contract, more than that left on his body... Still makes a big contribution at his advanced age... Most useful the last two seasons as the Lakers' only true backup point guard behind Nick Van Exel... Has played that position for years, but his game is much better suited for shooting guard ... Missed 23 games due to injuries, making the 59 appearances his fewest since rookie season of 1983-84... A stress fracture of the right foot and a strained abdominal muscle did most of the damage... Came back from the stomach injury in time for the first game of the playoffs, hurt it again, and spent the rest of the Lakers' postseason run on the sidelines... Still finished second on the club in assists average... Originally a sixth-round pick by Philadelphia in 1983, out of West Virginia Tech... Born Sept. 10, 1961, in Atlanta... Made $2.4 million last season.

Year	Team	G	FG	FG Pct.	FT	FT Pct.	Reb.	Ast.	TP	Avg.
1983-84	Philadelphia	45	62	.419	23	.821	40	41	148	3.3
1984-85	Philadelphia	82	188	.452	66	.733	99	175	446	5.4
1985-86	Philadelphia	70	310	.453	75	.833	121	193	696	9.9
1986-87	Phil.-Chi	68	239	.448	95	.798	108	259	580	8.5
1987-88	Chi.-Sea.	71	216	.508	57	.803	88	160	492	6.9
1988-89	Seattle	63	235	.494	63	.818	117	238	544	8.6
1989-90	Seattle	65	303	.506	130	.828	115	216	744	11.4
1990-91	Seattle	80	433	.519	137	.792	99	273	1013	12.7
1991-92	L.A. Lakers	82	509	.489	202	.831	253	593	1240	15.1
1992-93	L.A. Lakers	82	522	.508	177	.823	273	564	1235	15.1
1993-94	L.A. Lakers	81	411	.482	138	.890	153	344	965	11.9
1994-95	L.A. Lakers	59	217	.497	88	.793	124	248	558	9.5
	Totals	848	3645	.488	1251	.818	1590	3304	8661	10.2

GEORGE LYNCH 25 6-7 223   Forward

No truth to the rumor he campaigned hard against the Cedric Ceballos trade... When Ceballos arrived, Lynch became a reserve small forward again... Averaged 17 minutes ... Got some time at power forward in the small lineup, but lost minutes to Eddie Jones when Lakers went with three guards... Started the first six games at power forward when Elden Campbell was, well, being Elden Campbell, but got killed on the boards... Missed 23 games with a stress fracture of the right foot, the first time he has been sidelined due to injury in college or the pros... Bone did not heal properly, so he played with pain in the playoffs... Looked like he would have off-season surgery to correct the problem... Played on North Carolina's 1993 NCAA championship team... Lakers got him with the 12th pick in 1993... Born Sept. 3, 1970, in Roanoke, Va. ... 1994-95 salary: $1.43 million.

Year	Team	G	FG	FG Pct.	FT	FT Pct.	Reb.	Ast.	TP	Avg.
1993-94	L.A. Lakers	71	291	.508	99	.596	410	96	681	9.6
1994-95	L.A. Lakers	56	138	.468	62	.721	184	62	341	6.1
	Totals	127	429	.494	161	.639	594	158	1022	8.0

ANTHONY (PIG) MILLER 24 6-9 255   Forward

No jokes about being in hog heaven or turning the Forum into a pig pen... He truly prefers being called Pig instead of Anthony... Has tattoo of a hog's head on his arm... Emerged as a crowd favorite for hard-hat work inside ... Could develop into dependable reserve... Doesn't have the height to compete for most rebounds, but has the attitude and the width... His one rebound every 3.5 minutes was second-best on the team, behind only Vlade Divac's 3.4... Started once... Golden State selected Michigan State standout in the second round in 1994, then traded him to L.A. a few days later for a No. 2 in 1995... Briefly considered going to Europe, but his agent, Fred Slaughter, encouraged him to try the Lakers and the NBA... Born Oct. 22, 1971, in Benton Harbor, Mich.... Made $150,000 last season.

Year	Team	G	FG	FG Pct.	FT	FT Pct.	Reb.	Ast.	TP	Avg.
1994-95	L.A. Lakers	46	70	.530	47	.618	152	35	189	4.1

SAM BOWIE 34 7-1 255   Center-Forward

Planning to walk away from the game while he still can... Went into the summer planning to retire... Also went into the summer planning to have minor knee surgery... Still has enough left to squeeze out a two-year contract, especially with two new teams coming in, but the body says enough is enough... Averages for scoring, rebounds and minutes were career lows, but his contributions were big-time... Played behind Vlade Divac at center and Elden Campbell at power forward... A better center than several playoff teams had in the starting lineup... Former Kentucky star is a great clubhouse influence... Broke into NBA as No. 2 pick overall by Portland in 1984... Class act... Born March 7, 1961, in Lebanon, Pa.... Made $3.2 million in 1994-95.

Year	Team	G	FG	FG Pct.	FT	FT Pct.	Reb.	Ast.	TP	Avg.
1984-85	Portland	76	299	.537	160	.711	656	215	758	10.0
1985-86	Portland	38	167	.484	114	.708	327	99	448	11.8
1986-87	Portland	5	30	.455	20	.667	33	9	80	16.0
1987-88	Portland					Injured				
1988-89	Portland	20	69	.451	28	.571	106	36	171	8.6
1989-90	New Jersey	68	347	.416	294	.776	690	91	998	14.7
1990-91	New Jersey	62	314	.434	169	.732	480	147	801	12.9
1991-92	New Jersey	71	421	.445	212	.757	578	186	1062	15.0
1992-93	New Jersey	79	287	.450	141	.779	556	127	717	9.1
1993-94	L.A. Lakers	25	75	.436	72	.867	131	47	223	8.9
1994-95	L.A. Lakers	67	118	.442	68	.764	288	118	306	4.6
	Totals	511	2127	.452	1278	.748	3845	1075	5564	10.9

TONY SMITH 27 6-4 205   Guard

Defensive specialist... Able to check small forwards at just 6-4 because of great strength and athleticism... That gave him a role when Del Harris went with a three-guard lineup... Also was the emergency backup point guard... Hardly his best position, but he played it at Marquette and as a rookie after the Lakers took him in the second round (No. 51) in 1990... Hit one of their biggest shots of 1994-95, a buzzer-beater against Cleveland at home in the ninth game of the season that in some ways set the tone for what would follow... Never known for his offense, but set a club record with five three-pointers in one quarter, accomplished Nov. 12 at Golden State... Went into the summer as an unrestricted free agent... Born June 14, 1968, in Wauwatosa, Wisc.... 1994-95 salary: $1.05 million.

Year	Team	G	FG	FG Pct.	FT	FT Pct.	Reb.	Ast.	TP	Avg.
1990-91	L.A. Lakers	64	97	.441	40	.702	71	135	234	3.7
1991-92	L.A. Lakers	63	113	.399	49	.653	76	109	275	4.4
1992-93	L.A. Lakers	55	133	.484	62	.756	87	63	330	6.0
1993-94	L.A. Lakers	73	272	.441	85	.714	195	148	645	8.8
1994-95	L.A. Lakers	61	132	.427	44	.698	107	102	340	5.6
	Totals	316	747	.438	280	.707	536	557	1824	5.8

CORIE BLOUNT 26 6-10 242　　　　　　　Forward

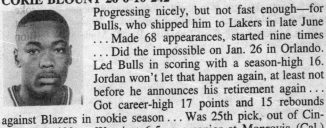

Progressing nicely, but not fast enough—for Bulls, who shipped him to Lakers in late June... Made 68 appearances, started nine times... Did the impossible on Jan. 26 in Orlando. Led Bulls in scoring with a season-high 16. Jordan won't let that happen again, at least not before he announces his retirement again... Got career-high 17 points and 15 rebounds against Blazers in rookie season... Was 25th pick, out of Cincinnati, in '93... Was just 6-5 as a senior at Monrovia (Cal.) High School... Born Jan. 4, 1969, in Monrovia... Middle name is Kasoun... Made $845,000 in 1994-95.

Year	Team	G	FG	FG Pct.	FT	FT Pct.	Reb.	Ast.	TP	Avg.
1993-94	Chicago	67	76	.437	46	.613	194	56	198	3.0
1994-95	Chicago	68	100	.476	38	.567	240	60	238	3.5
	Totals	135	176	.458	84	.592	434	116	436	3.2

THE ROOKIE

FRANKIE KING 23 6-1 185　　　　　　　Guard

Rip Van Winkle wasn't this much of a sleeper... Not invited to Chicago or Phoenix postseason all-star tournaments... Didn't even expect to get drafted... But he was the guy Jerry West wanted at this spot... Went 37th... Played mostly shooting guard at Western Carolina, but best chance with the Lakers will come as a reserve point guard... No. 2 in the nation in scoring as a senior... Born June 6, 1972, in Baxley, Ga.

COACH DEL HARRIS:  Everyone had him tabbed as the preseason favorite for Coach of the Year, right? ... Few people even had him down as a candidate for the Laker job heading into summer of '94 ... Got that gig and so much more ... No one ever questioned his knowledge and teaching skills ... The big question coming in was how he would relate to the young players, but he did a great job ... Persuaded them to conform to his system, not his personality ... In the end, he was the runaway winner for Coach of the Year ... Has done great coaching jobs before—taking Houston to the Finals in 1980-81 after a 40-42 regular season, holding an aging Milwaukee team together—but this was the first time he got the honor ... Later, getting a similar award from *The Sporting News* had special meaning since it was voted upon by his peers ... Makes longtime friend Jerry West look better than ever for making the hire ... Proven veteran was certainly a change for the franchise that previously had Pat Riley, Mike Dunleavy and Randy Pfund on the sidelines ... This big a change: he's a former ordained minister who played semi-pro baseball into his 30s ... Spent eight seasons with Milwaukee and Houston before coming to Los Angeles ... Has also been a consultant with Sacramento ... Best season was 1980-81, when he guided the Rockets to the Western Conference title ... Took over Bucks in the summer of 1987 and made the playoffs in all four years ... Son, Larry, is a scout/video coordinator with Bucks ... Born June 18, 1937, in Orleans, Ind.

GREATEST FIND

This could become Nick Van Exel, the No. 37 pick in 1993 and an all-star in the making, although the Lakers liked him enough to consider taking him with their first-round pick. He's still not good enough to top Michael Cooper, though.

Cooper was a third-round pick, No. 60 overall, in 1978 out of New Mexico, after the Lakers had already taken Ron Carter and Lew Massey. Cooper became the lethal defensive weapon of Showtime, the designated stopper of Larry Bird in the Finals.

He played 12 years in the NBA. He made first-team all-defense five times and was named Defensive Player of the Year in 1986-87.

ALL-TIME LAKER LEADERS

SEASON

Points: Elgin Baylor, 2,719, 1962–63
Assists: Earvin (Magic) Johnson, 989, 1990–91
Rebounds: Wilt Chamberlain, 1,712, 1968–69

GAME

Points: Elgin Baylor, 71 vs. New York, 11/15/60
Assists: Earvin (Magic) Johnson, 24 vs. Denver, 11/17/89
Earvin (Magic) Johnson, 24 vs. Phoenix, 1/9/90
Rebounds: Wilt Chamberlain, 42 vs. Boston, 3/7/69

CAREER

Points: Jerry West, 25,192, 1960–74
Assists: Earvin (Magic) Johnson, 9,921, 1980–91
Rebounds: Elgin Baylor, 11,463, 1958–72

PHOENIX SUNS

TEAM DIRECTORY: Pres./CEO: Jerry Colangelo; Senior VP: Cotton Fitzsimmons; VP-Dir. Player Personnel: Dick Van Arsdale; VP-Dir. Pub. Rel.: Tom Ambrose; Dir. Media Rel.: Julie Fie; Coach: Paul Westphal; Asst. Coaches: Paul Silas, Donn Nelson. Arena: America West (19,000). Colors: Purple, orange and copper.

SCOUTING REPORT

SHOOTING: It's not like this is an area of concern or anything; the Suns, after all, finished second in the league in scoring last season, just three-tenths of a point behind Orlando for No. 1, and fifth in field-goal percentage. On the other hand . . .

Charles Barkley must prove that his 48.6 percent of last season was a fluke and not the start of a significant slide. That is not terrible, but worth keeping an eye on this season considering he is third among all active players in shooting and 10th all-time. The Suns could suffer another blow if Elliot Perry, once a question mark in this category but all the way up to 52 percent last season, leaves as an unrestricted free agent.

Either way, this team is loaded with weapons. They took the third-most shots in the league last season and the third-most three-pointers, led in the latter department by Wesley Person, seventh among individuals. He should be even better as a second-year player. The sometimes-problem remains Dan Majerle, a dangerous threat because he was No. 2 in attempts and makes from behind the line, but only 39th in the NBA by percentage. That's when it is time to ease off.

PLAYMAKING: The Suns led the league last season in assist-to-turnover ratio, but Kevin Johnson is still shoot first, ask questions later, hardly the ideal game for a point guard. They can compensate, though, because, of all things, their frontline. Barkley is very good at drawing the double-and-triple teams to himself on the post and then whipping the ball out to a teammate spotted up near the three-point line. And Danny Manning, attempting the second comeback of his career from major knee surgery, handles the ball well for a big man and can even play some point forward.

Whether there is similar depth at point guard, however, remains to be seen. The summer lockout held things up even more than they hoped, what with Perry's status as a free agent, suddenly

Suns are happy about not-so-retiring Charles Barkley.

highly coveted at that. The Suns wanted him back. And, Danny Ainge, the emergency point, was contemplating retirement.

REBOUNDING: We said last year at this time that no one considers this a problem area anymore. We lied.

After climbing all the way from 15th in the league by per-

SUN ROSTER

No. Veterans	Pos.	Ht.	Wt.	Age	Yrs. Pro	College
U-22 Danny Ainge	G	6-5	185	36	14	Brigham Young
34 Charles Barkley	F	6-5	252	32	11	Auburn
45 A.C. Green	F	6-9	225	32	10	Oregon State
7 Kevin Johnson	G	6-1	190	29	8	California
35 Joe Kleine	C	7-0	271	33	10	Arkansas
21 Antonio Lang	G-F	6-8	205	23	1	Duke
9 Dan Majerle	G-F	6-6	220	30	7	Central Michigan
U-15 Danny Manning	F-C	6-10	234	29	7	Kansas
2 Elliot Perry	G	6-0	160	26	3	Memphis State
11 Wesley Person	G	6-6	195	24	1	Auburn
— Stefano Rusconi	F-C	6-10	240	27	0	Italy
24 Dan Schayes	C	6-11	276	36	14	Syracuse
U-23 Wayman Tisdale	C-F	6-9	260	31	10	Oklahoma

U-unrestricted free agent

Rd. Rookies	Sel.No.	Pos.	Ht.	Wt.	College
1 Michael Finley	21	F-G	6-7	215	Wisconsin
1 Mario Bennett	27	F	6-9	235	Arizona State
2 Chris Carr	56	F	6-6	200	Southern Illinois

centage to a tie for fourth in three seasons, the Suns dropped back down to a tie for 15th in 1994-95. The loss of Cedric Ceballos, underrated in this category, hurt. So did Barkley missing 14 games with injuries, seeing as he would have finished fourth if he had met the qualifying standards. Hmmm. Bet those centers had something to do with the decline—neither Joe Kleine, Danny Schayes or Wayman Tisdale averaged more than 3.5 boards.

DEFENSE: What's that? Yes, six other teams had a worse shooting percentage-against. It's just that only one of those, Boston, made the playoffs, and the Celtics were the last entrant from the weak Eastern Conference. Clubs like the Suns that consider themselves title contenders don't like to be mentioned in the same breath with the lowly Clippers, Bucks, Bullets, Warriors and the mediocre Mavericks and Celtics.

OUTLOOK: You don't need a star center to win the championship, just someone solid, as long as there is dependable help on defense close by. Paul Westphal's Suns don't have much defense of any kind, so this looks like another team that's good, but not good enough. The bigger question is, do they have the heart of a champion? Time will tell ... if it hasn't already.

SUN PROFILES

CHARLES BARKLEY 32 6-5 252 Forward

Talked retirement again, even after another huge season... Even after playing better the second half of 1994-95... The one exception was a drop in shooting to 48.6 percent, a career low, to fall from second to third among active players in that department (only Mark West and Otis Thorpe are better)... No. 10 all-time in shooting... Finished seventh in scoring and would have been fourth in rebounding but did not meet qualifying standards... Voted all-star starter for seventh straight year and made his ninth appearance in a row in All-Star Game... Became one of 12 players in NBA history to score 19,000 points... Underrated for his defense... Auburn product was an Olympian in 1992, MVP in 1992-93... Came in June 1992 trade from Philadelphia for Jeff Hornacek, Andrew Lang and Tim Perry... Born Feb. 20, 1963, in Leeds, Ala.... Earned $4.03 million last season.

Year	Team	G	FG	FG Pct.	FT	FT Pct.	Reb.	Ast.	TP	Avg.
1984-85	Philadelphia	82	427	.545	293	.733	703	155	1148	14.0
1985-86	Philadelphia	80	595	.572	396	.685	1026	312	1603	20.0
1986-87	Philadelphia	68	557	.594	429	.761	994	331	1564	23.0
1987-88	Philadelphia	80	753	.587	714	.751	951	254	2264	28.3
1988-89	Philadelphia	79	700	.579	602	.753	986	325	2037	25.8
1989-90	Philadelphia	79	706	.600	557	.749	909	307	1989	25.2
1990-91	Philadelphia	67	665	.570	475	.722	680	284	1849	27.6
1991-92	Philadelphia	75	622	.552	454	.695	830	308	1730	23.1
1992-93	Phoenix	76	716	.520	445	.765	928	385	1944	25.6
1993-94	Phoenix	65	518	.495	318	.704	727	296	1402	21.6
1994-95	Phoenix	68	554	.486	379	.748	756	276	1561	23.0
	Totals	819	6813	.555	5062	.735	9490	3233	19091	23.3

KEVIN JOHNSON 29 6-1 190 Guard

Coming off another injury-filled season, only this one was also marked by internal conflicts with Charles Barkley... Had lowest point and assist totals of career... But was big-time in the playoffs again... Suns' all-time assist leader and No. 14 on NBA list... Member of Dream Team II that won a gold medal at 1994 world championships in Toronto... Can penetrate or shoot from the outside, but sometimes fails into trap of becoming too much of a scorer instead of distributor... Good enough in baseball at Cal to be drafted by the Oakland A's in 1986... Even better in basketball—he was a first-round pick by Cleveland in 1987... Suns got him from Cavaliers midway through rookie season along with Mark West, Tyrone Corbin and picks for Larry Nance, Mike Sanders and a pick... Born March 4, 1966, in Sacramento, Cal.... Made $2.75 million last season.

Year	Team	G	FG	FG Pct.	FT	FT Pct.	Reb.	Ast.	TP	Avg.
1987-88	Clev.-Phoe.	80	275	.461	177	.839	191	437	732	9.2
1988-89	Phoenix	81	570	.505	508	.882	340	991	1650	20.4
1989-90	Phoenix	74	578	.499	501	.838	270	846	1665	22.5
1990-91	Phoenix	77	591	.516	519	.843	271	781	1710	22.2
1991-92	Phoenix	78	539	.479	448	.807	292	836	1536	19.7
1992-93	Phoenix	49	282	.499	226	.819	104	384	791	16.1
1993-94	Phoenix	67	477	.487	380	.819	167	637	1340	20.0
1994-95	Phoenix	47	246	.470	234	.810	115	360	730	15.5
	Totals	553	3558	.493	2993	.835	1750	5272	10154	18.4

DAN MAJERLE 30 6-6 220   Guard-Forward

Do not adjust your TV. He really was the leading vote-getter among all guards for the 1995 All-Star Game... In fact, he was the first reserve to start in the game since fan voting began in 1975... Wildly popular in the Valley of the Sun... Other people obviously think he can play. He was on Dream Team II and the 1988 Olympic team... Versatility is an asset—he started 25 times at guard and 25 times at forward... No. 2 in the league in three-pointers attempted (548) and made (199), even though he was only tied for 39th in percentage... But don't let that stop you, Dan... Born Sept. 9, 1965, in Traverse City, Mich., and stayed close to attend Central Michigan... Suns took him 14th in 1988... 1994-95 salary: $3 million.

Year	Team	G	FG	FG Pct.	FT	FT Pct.	Reb.	Ast.	TP	Avg.
1988-89	Phoenix	54	181	.419	78	.614	209	130	467	8.6
1989-90	Phoenix	73	296	.424	198	.762	430	188	809	11.1
1990-91	Phoenix	77	397	.484	227	.762	418	216	1051	13.6
1991-92	Phoenix	82	551	.478	229	.756	483	274	1418	17.3
1992-93	Phoenix	82	509	.464	203	.778	383	311	1388	16.9
1993-94	Phoenix	80	476	.418	176	.739	349	275	1320	16.5
1994-95	Phoenix	82	438	.425	206	.730	375	340	1281	15.6
	Totals	530	2848	.447	1317	.744	2647	1734	7734	14.6

DANNY MANNING 29 6-10 234   Forward

His knee is his Achilles heel... Suffered a torn anterior cruciate ligament in the left knee during a Feb. 6 practice, underwent reconstructive surgery and missed the rest of the season... If that sounds familiar, it should. The same thing happened to the right knee when he was a Clipper rookie in 1988... The difference this time is, he was working on a one-year contract at the bargain basement price of $1 million and had no contract beyond that. He took that slot because he wanted to sign with the Suns and that's all they had available... Has already said he will stay in Phoenix and they have already said they will pay him big money with a new contract... If there is a bright side to this, at least he has the mental preparation to know what the comeback entails... Was on pace to challenge for an all-star spot and Sixth Man of the Year award when the injury struck... Started in 19 of his 46 games, including two at center... College Player of the Year in 1988 while at Kansas and went on to become the No. 1 pick overall later that year... One problem: it was with the Clippers... Born May 17, 1966, in Hattiesburg, Miss.

Year	Team	G	FG	FG Pct.	FT	FT Pct.	Reb.	Ast.	TP	Avg.
1988-89	L.A. Clippers	26	177	.494	79	.767	171	81	434	16.7
1989-90	L.A. Clippers	71	440	.533	274	.741	422	187	1154	16.3
1990-91	L.A. Clippers	73	470	.519	219	.716	426	196	1159	15.9
1991-92	L.A. Clippers	82	650	.542	279	.725	564	285	1579	19.3
1992-93	L.A. Clippers	79	702	.509	388	.802	520	207	1800	22.8
1993-94	LAC-Atl.	68	586	.488	228	.669	465	261	1403	20.6
1994-95	Phoenix	46	340	.547	136	.673	276	154	822	17.9
	Totals	445	3365	.518	1603	.732	2844	1371	8351	18.8

A.C. GREEN 32 6-9 225   Forward

Has gone eight straight seasons without missing a game... The streak is at 731 consecutive regular-season games, good for No. 3 on the all-time list... Will need to go into 1996-97 to catch Johnny Kerr (844), even farther to pass Randy Smith (906)... Has missed only three games since coming to the NBA from Oregon State, all on coaches' decisions... Made 52 starts, one at center... Does the dirty work inside, but last season developed as something of a three-point threat... Finished a respectable 33.9 percent from behind the arc... Initials

A.C. do not stand for anything... Born Oct. 4, 1963, in Portland, Ore.... Lakers took him in the first round in 1985 and he became integral part of Showtime... Made four trips to Finals and won rings in 1987 and '88... In the middle of five-year, $25-million contract.

Year	Team	G	FG	FG Pct.	FT	FT Pct.	Reb.	Ast.	TP	Avg.
1985-86	L.A. Lakers	82	209	.539	102	.611	381	54	521	6.4
1986-87	L.A. Lakers	79	316	.538	220	.780	615	84	852	10.8
1987-88	L.A. Lakers	82	322	.503	293	.773	710	93	937	11.4
1988-89	L.A. Lakers	82	401	.529	282	.786	739	103	1088	13.3
1989-90	L.A. Lakers	82	385	.478	278	.751	712	90	1061	12.9
1990-91	L.A. Lakers	82	258	.476	223	.738	516	71	750	9.1
1991-92	L.A. Lakers	82	382	.476	340	.744	762	117	1116	13.6
1992-93	L.A. Lakers	82	379	.537	277	.739	711	116	1051	12.8
1993-94	Phoenix	82	465	.502	266	.735	753	137	1204	14.7
1994-95	Phoenix	82	311	.504	251	.732	669	127	916	11.2
	Totals	817	3428	.506	2532	.746	6568	992	9496	11.6

WAYMAN TISDALE 31 6-9 260   Forward-Center

Suns tried him as starting center, and that didn't work... Then they paired him with Charles Barkley at forward, and he didn't like it... Grew to prefer role coming off the bench... Had a tough time settling in because of injuries and Paul Westphal juggling the lineup... Started 13 times... A bargain at any position... So anxious to join Suns that he turned down multi-million dollar deals with other teams to sign as a free agent for one year at $850,000... That meant he was unrestricted again heading into the offseason... Still a handful for defenders on the low post... Bass player in Fifth Quarter, a band that has recorded two singles and played at the last three All-Star Weekends... Pacers made the former Oklahoma star the No. 2 pick overall in 1985... Born June 9, 1964, in Tulsa, Okla.

Year	Team	G	FG	FG Pct.	FT	FT Pct.	Reb.	Ast.	TP	Avg.
1985-86	Indiana	81	516	.515	160	.684	584	79	1192	14.7
1986-87	Indiana	81	458	.513	258	.709	475	117	1174	14.5
1987-88	Indiana	79	511	.512	246	.783	491	103	1268	16.1
1988-89	Ind.-Sac.	79	532	.514	317	.773	609	128	1381	17.5
1989-90	Sacramento	79	726	.525	306	.783	595	108	1758	22.3
1990-91	Sacramento	33	262	.483	136	.800	253	66	660	20.0
1991-92	Sacramento	72	522	.500	151	.763	469	106	1195	16.6
1992-93	Sacramento	76	544	.509	175	.758	500	108	1263	16.6
1993-94	Sacramento	79	552	.501	215	.808	560	139	1319	16.7
1994-95	Phoenix	65	278	.484	94	.770	247	45	650	10.0
	Totals	714	4901	.508	2058	.762	4783	999	11860	16.4

DANNY AINGE 36 6-5 185   Guard

Proved last season he can still provide depth in the backcourt... The only question now is, where will he provide it?... Went into summer as an unrestricted free agent... Would like to get at least one more year out of a career that started when Boston took the BYU star in the second round in 1981... That shouldn't be a problem unless he sets monetary demands too high... Does so much for a team besides 15-19 minutes a game at both guard spots and hitting the outside shot... Has a winning attitude and approach that can be an influence on any team... With Dale Ellis and Reggie Miller, the only players in league history to make 1,000 three-pointers... No. 4 all-time in three-point attempts... Has made six trips to Finals, winning in 1984 and '86 with the Celtics... Born March 17, 1959, in Eugene, Ore.... 1994-95 salary: $2.08 million.

Year	Team	G	FG	FG Pct.	FT	FT Pct.	Reb.	Ast.	TP	Avg.
1981-82	Boston	53	79	.357	56	.862	56	87	219	4.1
1982-83	Boston	80	357	.496	72	.742	214	251	791	9.9
1983-84	Boston	71	166	.460	46	.821	116	162	384	5.4
1984-85	Boston	75	419	.529	118	.868	268	399	971	12.9
1985-86	Boston	80	353	.504	123	.904	235	405	855	10.7
1986-87	Boston	71	410	.486	148	.897	242	400	1053	14.8
1987-88	Boston	81	482	.491	158	.878	249	503	1270	15.7
1988-89	Bos.-Sac.	73	480	.457	205	.854	255	402	1281	17.5
1989-90	Sacramento	75	506	.438	222	.831	326	453	1342	17.9
1990-91	Portland	80	337	.472	114	.826	205	285	890	11.1
1991-92	Portland	81	299	.442	108	.824	148	202	784	9.7
1992-93	Phoenix	80	337	.462	123	.848	214	260	947	11.8
1993-94	Phoenix	68	224	.417	78	.830	131	180	606	8.9
1994-95	Phoenix	74	194	.460	105	.808	109	210	571	7.7
Totals		1042	4643	.469	1676	.846	2768	4199	11964	11.5

WESLEY PERSON 24 6-6 195   Guard

The Pistolman... Younger brother of Chuck, the Rifleman... Played in Rookie All-Star Game... Started in 56 of 78 games, but averaged only 23.1 minutes because he often would give way to a defensive replacement after Suns built a lead... Handled the role with poise, making an impression all season as a rookie with maturity... Soft-spoken... Finished No. 7 in the league in three-point shooting... His 116 makes from behind the arc were the most ever by a Phoenix

rookie... Honorable mention All-American as a senior at Auburn
... Four-year starter with the Tigers before leaving as No. 3 all-
time scorer, behind only his brother Chuck and Mike Mitchell...
Born March 28, 1971, in Crenshaw, Ala.... Made $650,000 last
season.

Year	Team	G	FG	FG Pct.	FT	FT Pct.	Reb.	Ast.	TP	Avg.
1994-95	Phoenix	78	309	.484	80	.792	201	105	814	10.4

ELLIOT PERRY 26 6-0 160   Guard

Doesn't need the calf-high socks—or, like in college, the goggles—to draw attention now ... Had just a $25,000 guarantee when he went to camp before last season, then beat out Winston Garland, Duane Cooper and Anthony Goldwire for final backcourt job ... Then became one of the success stories of the NBA ... Finished second to Dana Barros for Most Improved Player ... Eighth in the league in steals ... Outside shooting used to be a weakness, but he's getting better ... He has emphasized that in offseason workouts ... After going 38 and 37.2 percent from the field the previous two years, he jumped to 52 percent in 1994-95 ... Suns were 38-13 when he started at point guard ... Charles Barkley wore high socks in the All-Star Game in Phoenix to honor him ... Crowd favorite ... Was in the CBA when the Suns brought him in on a 10-day contract in the spring of '94 ... Born March 28, 1969, in Memphis, Tenn., and stayed home to star at Memphis State before the Clippers drafted him in the second round in 1991 ... 1994-95 salary: $250,000.

Year	Team	G	FG	FG Pct.	FT	FT Pct.	Reb.	Ast.	TP	Avg.
1991-92	LAC-Char.	50	49	.380	27	.659	39	78	126	2.5
1993-94	Phoenix	27	42	.372	21	.750	39	125	105	3.9
1994-95	Phoenix	82	306	.520	158	.810	151	394	795	9.7
	Totals	159	397	.478	206	.780	229	597	1026	6.5

DAN SCHAYES 36 6-11 276   Center

The hell with pride, he wanted a job ... He and agent Herb Rudoy called Suns and asked for a tryout when team was searching for help at center ... Parlayed that into a free-agent contract and 69 games, his second-most since 1990-91 ... Had 27 starts while combining with Joe Kleine to hold down center spot ... Can shoot from the perimeter and pass well, which allowed him to play outside and draw defending centers away from Charles Barkley and Wayman Tisdale on the post... Son of Hall of Famer Dolph Schayes... Ballboy for the expansion Buffalo Braves in 1970... Starred at Syracuse before becoming a first-round pick with Utah in 1980... Married to former U.S. Olympic diver Wendy Lucero... Born May 10, 1959, in Syracuse, N.Y.... Made $672,000 last season.

Year	Team	G	FG	FG Pct.	FT	FT Pct.	Reb.	Ast.	TP	Avg.
1981-82	Utah	82	252	.481	140	.757	427	146	644	7.9
1982-83	Utah-Den.	82	342	.457	228	.773	635	205	912	11.1
1983-84	Denver	82	183	.493	215	.790	433	91	581	7.1
1984-85	Denver	56	60	.465	79	.814	144	38	199	3.6
1985-86	Denver	80	221	.502	216	.777	439	79	658	8.2
1986-87	Denver	76	210	.519	229	.779	380	85	649	8.5
1987-88	Denver	81	361	.540	407	.836	662	106	1129	13.9
1988-89	Denver	76	317	.522	332	.826	500	105	969	12.8
1989-90	Denver	53	163	.494	225	.852	342	61	551	10.4
1990-91	Milwaukee	82	298	.499	274	.835	535	98	870	10.6
1991-92	Milwaukee	43	83	.417	74	.771	168	34	240	5.6
1992-93	Milwaukee	70	105	.399	112	.818	249	78	322	4.6
1993-94	Mil.-LAL	36	28	.333	29	.906	79	13	85	2.4
1994-95	Phoenix	69	126	.508	50	.725	208	89	303	4.4
	Totals	968	2749	.490	2610	.807	5201	1228	8112	8.4

ANTONIO LANG 23 6-8 205 — Forward

Got limited action as a rookie because of two separate injuries... Missed the first 42 games because of back spasms and the last 15 with a sprained left knee... Eventually underwent arthroscopic surgery on the knee April 25... So much for the cynics who thought the Suns were stashing him with a bogus injury... Left off the playoff roster... Second-round pick in 1994... Member of NCAA title teams at Duke in 1991 and '92 and also reached the championship game in 1994... Teammates there with future NBA players Grant Hill, Bobby Hurley, Brian Davis and Christian Laettner... Valedictorian of high-school class in Mobile, Ala.... Born May 15, 1972, in Columbia, S.C. ... 1994 salary: $325,000.

Year	Team	G	FG	FG Pct.	FT	FT Pct.	Reb.	Ast.	TP	Avg.
1994-95	Phoenix	12	4	.400	3	.750	4	1	11	0.9

JOE KLEINE 33 7-0 271 Center

Playing time didn't jump much last season from the previous campaign, but his role did... Went from playing behind Mark West and Oliver Miller in 1993-94 to starting 42 games while joining forces with Dan Schayes at center... Combination known as "Schleine," though he jokingly preferred "Klayes" so that he gets top billing... 1984 Olympian... Can hit the jumper from 10 or 12 feet... That's why he is solid from the line... Born Jan. 4, 1962, in Colorado Springs, Colo., and played college with Alvin Robertson, Scott Hastings and Darrell Walker at Arkansas... Sacramento took him in the first round in 1985... Son, Daniel, was born the day he was traded to Boston... Suns got him as a free agent... 1994-95 salary: $845,000.

Year	Team	G	FG	FG Pct.	FT	FT Pct.	Reb.	Ast.	TP	Avg.
1985-86	Sacramento	80	160	.465	94	.723	373	46	414	5.2
1986-87	Sacramento	79	256	.471	110	.786	483	71	622	7.9
1987-88	Sacramento	82	324	.472	153	.814	579	93	801	9.8
1988-89	Sac.-Boston	75	175	.405	134	.882	378	67	484	6.5
1989-90	Boston	81	176	.480	83	.830	355	46	435	5.4
1990-91	Boston	72	102	.468	54	.783	244	21	258	3.6
1991-92	Boston	70	144	.491	34	.708	296	32	326	4.7
1992-93	Boston	78	108	.404	41	.707	346	39	257	3.3
1993-94	Phoenix	74	125	.488	30	.769	193	45	285	3.9
1994-95	Phoenix	75	119	.449	42	.857	259	39	280	3.7
	Totals	766	1689	.460	775	.797	3506	499	4162	5.4

THE ROOKIES

MICHAEL FINLEY 22 6-7 215 Forward-Guard
Suns either got another late find at No. 21 or someone on a downward spiral... Went from an impressive first three seasons at Wisconsin to a horrible senior year, shooting just 37.9 percent... Honorable mention All-American three straight years... Wisconsin's all-time leading scorer... College teammates with Bucks rookie Rashard Griffith and was coached by Grizzlies VP of basketball operations Stu Jackson until his senior season... Born March 6, 1973, in Melrose Park, Ill.

MARIO BENNETT 22 6-9 235 Forward
Surprise, surprise... Didn't expect to end up here, and he wasn't

alone... Suns publicly questioned his attitude before the draft; he responded by ripping them back... Then he went 27th. So it goes with the benefit of multiple picks in the first round... Left after three seasons across town at Arizona State... No. 1 in Sun Devils' history in blocks and shooting... Born Aug. 1, 1973, in Denton, Tex.

CHRIS CARR 21 6-6 200   Forward

Missouri Valley Conference Player of the Year before leaving school after his junior season... Scored 26 points against Syracuse in the NCAA tournament... Started 62 consecutive games for Southern Illinois... Average jumped from 3.9 points a game as a freshman to 22 as a junior... No. 56 pick... Born March 12, 1974, in Ironton, Mo.

COACH PAUL WESTPHAL: A great won-loss percentage may not be enough... Another early playoff exit won't do much for his standing with the critics... Some see him as too laid-back. He jokes he'll get a tattoo... Used 25 different starting lineups last season, switching sometimes because of injuries... Needed just 140 games to get 100 wins. Red Auerbach, Pat Riley and Bill Russell are the only coaches to get there faster... Second-fastest to 150 victories, behind only Phil Jackson... That doesn't count the 2-0 record as All-Star Game coach, including last season... Career record: 177-69 (.720)... Led Suns to franchise-record 62 wins his first season... That's also the NBA mark for first-year coaches... Joined Ed Macauley (1951), Billy Cunningham (1978), Pat Riley (1982) and Chris Ford (1991) as one of only five rookie coaches in All-Star Game ... Such success should have been expected... Had well-decorated 12-year NBA career... First-round selection by Celtics in 1972 and spent three seasons in Boston... Traded to Suns, where he played the next five years... Led team in scoring every season, topped by the 25.2 in 1977-78, and made the all-star team four times... Finished career with Seattle and New York... Suns retired his uniform No. 44 in 1989... Began coaching career with one year at Southwestern College and one at Grand Canyon College, both in Phoenix, before joining Cotton Fitzsimmons' staff... Was an assistant for four seasons before getting the promotion... Born Nov. 30, 1950, in Torrance, Cal.... Starred nearby at USC.

GREATEST FIND

There is a theory that you are only supposed to get other people's leftovers in the expansion draft. And then there were the Phoenix Suns.

They began to stock players on May 6, 1968, choosing players other teams did not protect. One of those was Dick Van Arsdale of the New York Knicks. The first year, he scored 21 points a game, and that was followed with averages of 21.3 and 21.9.

In the end, all Van Arsdale did was play nine years with the Suns, average 17.6 points and make the All-Star Game three times. Jeff Hornacek, who went from being a fourth-round pick in 1986 to become a key part of some of the best teams in franchise history, was a great find, but Van Arsdale was the greatest.

ALL-TIME SUN LEADERS

SEASON

Points: Tom Chambers, 2,201, 1989–90
Assists: Kevin Johnson, 991, 1988–89
Rebounds: Paul Silas, 1,015, 1970–71

GAME

Points: Tom Chambers, 60 vs. Seattle, 3/24/90
Assists: Gail Goodrich, 19 vs. Philadelphia, 10/22/69
Rebounds: Paul Silas, 27 vs. Cincinnati, 1/18/71

CAREER

Points: Walter Davis, 15,666, 1977–88
Assists: Kevin Johnson, 5,079, 1987–95
Rebounds: Alvan Adams, 6,937, 1975–88

PORTLAND TRAIL BLAZERS

TEAM DIRECTORY: Governor: Paul Allen; Pres.-GM: Bob Whitsitt; Dir. Sports Communications: John Christensen; Coach: P.J. Carlesimo; Asst. Coaches: Rick Carlisle, Dick Harter, Johnny Davis. Arena: Rose Garden (22,000). Colors: Red, black and white.

Clifford Robinson missed first game in six years.

SCOUTING REPORT

SHOOTING: It's about quantity, not quality. Has been for a while. Two years ago, the Trail Blazers took 111 more shots than any other team, but were only 20th in the league in accuracy. Last season, they were second to only Dallas in attempts and again finished 20th. So they are like buckshot—plentiful enough that some hit the target.

Buck Williams is the only returning regular who broke 50 percent last season, and he is a rebound-first power forward who was seventh on the team in shots. What the Trail Blazers do have, however, is Rod Strickland, a point guard who does a great job of getting down the lane to create, and Clifford Robinson, versatile enough to cause matchup problems by being too big for most small forwards to handle and too quick for centers.

PLAYMAKING: Few names came up more than Strickland's in the offseason trade rumors. The reason was two-fold: a) The Trail Blazers, looking to the future, hoped to get a lot of good young talent in return; and b) A lot of teams out there like him. Yes, the same guy who was dumped in trade by the Knicks and let go for nothing by the Spurs as a free agent.

He turns 30 before midseason, though increasing age hasn't affected his play so far—he finished fourth in the NBA in assists in 1994-95. Terry Porter, about to become his former backup, will almost certainly not be re-signed as a free agent. That responsibility is expected to fall to rookie Randolph Childress, drafted by the Pistons at No. 19 and reportedly ticketed to Portland as soon as salary-cap constraints are resolved.

REBOUNDING: All you need to know: Strickland, the point guard, averaged 3.8 boards a game, more than Joe Kleine, a sometimes starting center at Phoenix. Otis Thorpe contributed 6.9 an outing—as the backup power forward. Any more questions why this remains a strength for the Trail Blazers?

As long as Williams, who turns 36 not long after the All-Star break, continues to produce (8.2 rebounds in just 29.5 minutes last season), they will be in good shape. And that's even with Thorpe expected to land in Detroit in the Childress deal and the first full season without Clyde Drexler, long underrated for his impact on the offensive boards. The Trail Blazers finished No. 1 in rebounding percentage in 1994-95 and won't fall far, if at all.

TRAIL BLAZER ROSTER

No. Veterans	Pos.	Ht.	Wt.	Age	Yrs. Pro	College
U-2 Mark Bryant	F	6-9	246	30	7	Seton Hall
24 Chris Dudley	C	6-11	240	30	8	Yale
U-53 James Edwards	C	7-1	252	39	18	Washington
44 Harvey Grant	F	6-9	225	30	7	Oklahoma
12 Steve Henson	G	6-1	180	27	5	Kansas State
23 Aaron McKie	G	6-5	209	23	1	Temple
U-30 Terry Porter	G	6-3	195	32	10	Wisc.-Stevens Point
3 Clifford Robinson	F	6-10	225	28	6	Connecticut
26 James Robinson	G	6-2	180	25	2	Alabama
1 Rod Strickland	G	6-3	185	29	7	DePaul
33 Otis Thorpe	F	6-10	246	33	12	Providence
52 Buck Williams	F	6-8	225	35	14	Maryland

U-unrestricted free agent

Rd. Rookie	Sel.No.	Pos.	Ht.	Wt.	College
1 Gary Trent	11	F	6-8	240	Ohio

DEFENSE: Maybe it's the impact of coach P.J. Carlesimo. Or maybe it's having a full season with Chris Dudley inside. Whatever the reason, the Trail Blazers made their first improvement in shooting percentage-against after three years of decline. They were at 45.6 percent, a tie for eighth and a significant step forward.

This area is of particular importance because the Blazers don't run as well as the Portland teams that a few years ago regularly challenged for the Western Conference title. But if these players defend well, especially in creating turnovers, they can still get out.

OUTLOOK: The tracks have officially been changed. Clyde Drexler is gone and the veteran who came in return, Thorpe, should be in Detroit by now. The two best players, Strickland and Robinson, have both been mentioned in trade rumors.

With Sacramento and Dallas pushing for a playoff berth, someone has to drop out. This may be the team. Last season, the Trail Blazers finished five games ahead of the fast-charging Kings, who missed the postseason on the last day of the regular season. Consider the target in range.

TRAIL BLAZER PROFILES

ROD STRICKLAND 29 6-3 185   Guard

Can break down any defender to get to the basket... Arguably the best in the game at penetrating to dish off or create a shot for himself... An even better tribute comes from Mavericks' coach Dick Motta: "He makes a lot of their good people great people."... Very good rebounder for a point guard... Already No. 5 on Trail Blazers' all-time assist list after just three seasons... Last season, he led team in assists, steals and minutes... Elected Portland MVP two years in a row in a vote of teammates... Fourth in NBA in assists at 8.8 a game... Born July 11, 1966, in the Bronx, N.Y., and began pro career with Knicks as No. 19 pick in 1988 draft... Starred at DePaul... When San Antonio let him go as an unrestricted free agent, Trail Blazers got a steal to pick up a player this good without having to trade... Made $1.92 million last season.

Year	Team	G	FG	FG Pct.	FT	FT Pct.	Reb.	Ast.	TP	Avg.
1988-89	New York	81	265	.467	172	.745	160	319	721	8.9
1989-90	N.Y.-S.A.	82	343	.454	174	.626	259	468	868	10.6
1990-91	San Antonio	58	314	.482	161	.763	219	463	800	13.8
1991-92	San Antonio	57	300	.455	182	.687	265	491	787	13.8
1992-93	Portland	78	396	.485	273	.717	337	559	1069	13.7
1993-94	Portland	82	528	.483	353	.749	370	740	1411	17.2
1994-95	Portland	64	441	.466	283	.745	317	562	1211	18.9
	Totals	502	2587	.471	1598	.721	1927	3602	6867	13.7

CLIFFORD ROBINSON 28 6-10 225   Forward

The package gets even bigger... After making 51 three-pointers first five seasons, he had 142 last season, and at a respectable 37.1 percent... The mistake comes when he relies on the long-distance shot too much instead of inside moves... Versatile enough to play all three spots on the frontcourt... But the return of Chris Dudley meant he didn't have to play as much center... When he sat out the Utah game Feb. 24 with a sprained ankle, it broke a streak of 461 consecutive appearances, a franchise record and the third-longest active run in the league

... Before that, had taken part in all 527 games, regular season and playoffs, since the Trail Blazers picked him 36th, out of Connecticut, in 1989 ... Sixth Man of the Year in 1992-93 ... Born Dec. 16, 1966, in Albion, N.Y. ... 1994-95 salary: $2.72 million.

Year	Team	G	FG	FG Pct.	FT	FT Pct.	Reb.	Ast.	TP	Avg.
1989-90	Portland	82	298	.397	138	.550	308	72	746	9.1
1990-91	Portland	82	373	.463	205	.653	349	151	957	11.7
1991-92	Portland	82	398	.466	219	.664	416	137	1016	12.4
1992-93	Portland	82	632	.473	287	.690	542	182	1570	19.1
1993-94	Portland	82	641	.457	352	.765	550	159	1647	20.1
1994-95	Portland	75	597	.452	265	.694	423	198	1601	21.3
	Totals	485	2939	.454	1466	.681	2588	899	7537	15.5

BUCK WILLIAMS 35 6-8 225   Forward

Still a factor when most contemporaries have retired ... Started all 82 games and averaged a solid 8.2 rebounds in just 29.5 minutes ... The arrival of Otis Thorpe in trade for Clyde Drexler cut into his playing time ... But Drexler's departure also made him team captain ... One of only eight players in NBA history to have 12,000 rebounds and 15,000 points ... Heads into the final year of his contract ... Has missed just five out of a possible 492 games since coming from New Jersey to the Trail Blazers in the summer of 1989 for Sam Bowie and a first-round pick ... Great locker-room guy ... Starred at Maryland before Nets picked him with No. 3 choice in 1981 ... Impact guy from the start: third in the league in rebounding, fourth in shooting, all-star and Rookie of the Year ... Born March 8, 1960, in Rocky Mount, N.C. ... Made $3.2 million in 1994-95.

Year	Team	G	FG	FG Pct.	FT	FT Pct.	Reb.	Ast.	TP	Avg.
1981-82	New Jersey	82	513	.582	242	.624	1005	107	1268	15.5
1982-83	New Jersey	82	536	.588	324	.620	1027	125	1396	17.0
1983-84	New Jersey	81	495	.535	284	.570	1000	130	1274	15.7
1984-85	New Jersey	82	577	.530	336	.625	1005	167	1491	18.2
1985-86	New Jersey	82	500	.523	301	.676	986	131	1301	15.9
1986-87	New Jersey	82	521	.557	430	.731	1023	129	1472	18.0
1987-88	New Jersey	70	466	.560	346	.668	834	109	1279	18.3
1988-89	New Jersey	74	373	.531	213	.666	696	78	959	13.0
1989-90	Portland	82	413	.548	288	.706	800	116	1114	13.6
1990-91	Portland	80	358	.602	217	.705	751	97	933	11.7
1991-92	Portland	80	340	.604	221	.754	704	108	901	11.3
1992-93	Portland	82	270	.511	138	.645	690	75	678	8.3
1993-94	Portland	81	291	.555	201	.679	843	80	783	9.7
1994-95	Portland	82	309	.512	138	.673	669	78	757	9.2
	Totals	1122	5962	.552	3679	.664	12033	1530	15606	13.9

OTIS THORPE 33 6-10 246   Forward

Name a better backup power forward... He didn't start out that way, of course... Started the season in the Rockets' opening lineup, then got traded to Portland for Clyde Drexler and Tracy Murray on Valentine's Day... Trail Blazers stayed with Buck Williams at that spot... In other words, they didn't go with the youth movement... Still had a prominent role, playing 26.7 minutes per game... Nice combination of speed and ability to run the floor... Finished fourth in the league in shooting, which was no surprise. He was third and fifth the two seasons before... All-star in 1991-92... Originally a first-round pick by Kansas City in 1984 after starring at Providence... Born Aug. 5, 1962, in Boynton Beach, Fla.... 1994-95 salary: $2.578 million.

Year	Team	G	FG	FG Pct.	FT	FT Pct.	Reb.	Ast.	TP	Avg.
1984-85	Kansas City	82	411	.600	230	.620	556	111	1052	12.8
1985-86	Sacramento	75	289	.587	164	.661	420	84	742	9.9
1986-87	Sacramento	82	567	.540	413	.761	819	201	1547	18.9
1987-88	Sacramento	82	622	.507	460	.755	837	266	1704	20.8
1988-89	Houston	82	521	.542	328	.729	787	202	1370	16.7
1989-90	Houston	82	547	.548	307	.688	734	261	1401	17.1
1990-91	Houston	82	549	.556	334	.696	846	197	1435	17.5
1991-92	Houston	82	558	.592	304	.657	862	250	1420	17.3
1992-93	Houston	72	385	.558	153	.598	589	181	923	12.8
1993-94	Houston	82	449	.561	251	.657	870	189	1149	14.0
1994-95	Hou.-Port.	70	385	.565	167	.594	558	112	937	13.4
	Totals	873	5283	.555	3111	.687	7878	2054	13680	15.7

HARVEY GRANT 30 6-9 225   Forward

Moved into the backcourt late last season... Why not? He wasn't helping at small forward... P.J. Carlesimo wanted to counter teams posting up Terry Porter and James Robinson, so he moved him to shooting guard... First time he had been anything but a forward as a pro... Can handle enough of the guards on defense, but doesn't handle the ball well enough... Especially struggles in the open court... Always had the shooting range of a guard... Favorite spot is the baseline... Horace's twin brother... Came to Trail Blazers from Bullets in exchange for Kevin Duckworth in the summer of 1993... Washington used the No. 12 pick to get him in the 1988 draft... Born

July 4, 1965, in Augusta, Ga., and played at Oklahoma ... 1994-95 salary: $2.99 million.

Year	Team	G	FG	FG Pct.	FT	FT Pct.	Reb.	Ast.	TP	Avg.
1988-89	Washington	71	181	.464	34	.596	163	79	396	5.6
1989-90	Washington	81	284	.473	96	.701	342	131	664	8.2
1990-91	Washington	77	609	.498	185	.743	557	204	1405	18.2
1991-92	Washington	64	489	.478	176	.800	432	170	1155	18.0
1992-93	Washington	72	560	.487	218	.727	412	205	1339	18.6
1993-94	Portland	77	356	.460	84	.641	351	107	798	10.4
1994-95	Portland	75	286	.461	103	.705	284	82	683	9.1
		517	2765	.478	896	.723	2541	978	6440	12.5

TERRY PORTER 32 6-3 195   Guard

The end of last season also probably meant the end of his time with the Trail Blazers ... Went into the summer as an unrestricted free agent ... Missed the first 47 games after undergoing ankle surgery Oct. 26 ... Plays both backcourt spots ... Former all-star ... No. 8 in NBA history in three-pointers made (773) and attempted (2,004); both are Portland franchise records ... No. 1 in team history in assists, No. 2 in scoring and minutes and No. 3 in games ... Won J. Walter Kennedy Award in 1993 for community service ... Born April 8, 1963, in Milwaukee and stayed close to home to play at Wisconsin-Stevens Point ... A relative unknown before surviving until the final cut in the 1984 Olympic trials ... Trail Blazers took him No. 24 in 1985 ... Made $2.6 million last season.

Year	Team	G	FG	FG Pct.	FT	FT Pct.	Reb.	Ast.	TP	Avg.
1985-86	Portland	79	212	.474	125	.806	117	198	562	7.1
1986-87	Portland	80	376	.488	280	.838	337	715	1045	13.1
1987-88	Portland	82	462	.519	274	.846	378	831	1222	14.9
1988-89	Portland	81	540	.471	272	.840	367	770	1431	17.7
1989-90	Portland	80	448	.462	421	.892	272	726	1406	17.6
1990-91	Portland	81	486	.515	279	.823	282	649	1381	17.0
1991-92	Portland	82	521	.461	315	.856	255	477	1485	18.1
1992-93	Portland	81	503	.454	327	.843	316	419	1476	18.2
1993-94	Portland	77	348	.416	204	.872	215	401	1010	13.1
1994-95	Portland	35	105	.393	58	.707	81	133	312	8.9
	Totals	758	4001	.470	2555	.846	2620	5319	11330	14.9

MARK BRYANT 30 6-9 246　　　　　　　　Forward-Center

Can hit the mid-range jumper and runs the floor well for a big man... Maybe just not for the Trail Blazers anymore... The 49 appearances last season were a career low... Not even in the rotation after Otis Thorpe arrived ... Played in only 11 of the final 42 games... Headed into the summer as a free agent... Best-suited as a power forward... No. 21 pick in 1988 after leading Seton Hall to its first spot in NCAA tournament... All-Big East as a senior... Older brother, Spencer, also played at the Hall... Became one of seven Portland players ever to go right from college into opening-night starting lineup ... Born April 25, 1965, in Glen Ridge, N.J. ... 1994-95 salary: $1.4 million.

Year	Team	G	FG	FG Pct.	FT	FT Pct.	Reb.	Ast.	TP	Avg.
1988-89	Portland	56	120	.486	40	.580	179	33	280	5.0
1989-90	Portland	58	70	.458	28	.560	146	13	168	2.9
1990-91	Portland	53	99	.488	74	.733	190	27	272	5.1
1991-92	Portland	56	95	.480	40	.667	201	41	230	4.1
1992-93	Portland	80	186	.503	104	.703	324	41	476	6.0
1993-94	Portland	79	185	.482	72	.692	315	37	442	5.6
1994-95	Portland	49	101	.526	41	.651	161	28	244	5.0
	Totals	431	856	.490	399	.671	1516	220	2112	4.9

CHRIS DUDLEY 30 6-11 240　　　　　　　　　　　Center

The best rebounder on one of the best rebounding teams... Offensive boards a specialty... Averaged 9.3 boards in just 27.4 minutes... Imagine the production if he had played the 35 minutes many starters get... Of course, that would also mean more times he might have to shoot the ball, an act that should be discouraged whenever possible... Notorious for his troubles from the line... Oh, for the good old days of 1987-88, when he went 56.3 percent on free throws as a rookie... That was his career high... Trail Blazers signed him as a free agent Aug. 3, 1993... Yale product joined the NBA as a fourth-round pick of Cleveland in 1987... First three-time All-Ivy League choice in school history... Born Feb. 22, 1965, in Stamford,

Conn.... Made $3.5 million in 1994-95.

Year	Team	G	FG	FG Pct.	FT	FT Pct.	Reb.	Ast.	TP	Avg.
1987-88	Cleveland	55	65	.474	40	.563	144	23	170	3.1
1988-89	Cleveland	61	73	.435	39	.364	157	21	185	3.0
1989-90	Clev.-N.J.	64	146	.411	58	.319	423	39	350	5.5
1990-91	New Jersey	61	170	.408	94	.534	511	37	434	7.1
1991-92	New Jersey	82	190	.403	80	.468	739	58	460	5.6
1992-93	New Jersey	71	94	.353	57	.518	513	16	245	3.5
1993-94	Portland	6	6	.240	2	.500	24	5	14	2.3
1994-95	Portland	82	181	.406	85	.464	764	34	447	5.5
	Totals	482	925	.405	455	.453	3275	233	2305	4.8

AARON McKIE 23 6-5 209   Guard

For the longest time, it was about who he played with... In high school, Rasheed Wallace... At Temple, eight blocks from where he grew up, Eddie Jones... With the Trail Blazers, Clyde Drexler... But by the end of his first NBA season, Drexler was gone and McKie started to make a name for himself... Became the starting shooting guard... His 24 points and 10 rebounds March 9 at Miami was the first 20-10 by a Portland rookie since Sam Bowie 10 years earlier... Good defender, smart player, solid fundamentals... Trail Blazers used the No. 17 pick in the 1994 draft to take him... Born Oct. 2, 1972, in Philadelphia... 1994-95 salary: $650,000.

Year	Team	G	FG	FG Pct.	FT	FT Pct.	Reb.	Ast.	TP	Avg.
1994-95	Portland	45	116	.444	50	.685	129	89	293	6.5

JAMES ROBINSON 25 6-2 180   Guard

Shooting guards have to be able to shoot... But he's at 36.5 percent and 40.9 in the two seasons since Portland took him with the 21st pick in 1993... Got an opportunity when the position was unsettled following the Clyde Drexler trade... Started 25 times... Great leaping skills... In 1993, he participated in the slam-dunk contest at All-Star Weekend... Nickname: "Hollywood"... All-SEC and Alabama's scoring leader for three straight seasons when he came out after his junior year... Before that, he was 1989 high-school Player of the Year in Mississippi... Born Aug. 31, 1970, in Jackson, Miss.... Made $845,000 last season.

Year	Team	G	FG	FG Pct.	FT	FT Pct.	Reb.	Ast.	TP	Avg.
1993-94	Portland	58	104	.365	45	.672	78	68	276	4.8
1994-95	Portland	71	255	.409	65	.591	132	180	651	9.2
	Totals	129	359	.395	110	.621	210	248	927	7.2

STEVE HENSON 27 6-1 180 Guard

Have crewcut, will travel... Portland was his fourth NBA team in as many years... That doesn't count the one game with the Mexico City Aztecas before signing with the Trail Blazers on Nov. 20... Averaged 10.3 minutes per outing... A hard-working guy for practice ... Good athlete who finished third in the Big Eight decathlon in 1989, winning the high jump (6-9 ¾) and the javelin in the process... Four-year starter at Kansas State, where he was teammates with Mitch Richmond ... Bucks took him in the second round, No. 44 overall, in 1990 ... Born Feb. 2, 1968, in Junction City, Kan.

Year	Team	G	FG	FG Pct.	FT	FT Pct.	Reb.	Ast.	TP	Avg.
1990-91	Milwaukee	68	79	.418	38	.905	51	131	214	3.1
1991-92	Milwaukee	50	52	.361	23	.793	41	82	150	3.0
1992-93	Atlanta	53	71	.390	34	.850	55	155	213	4.0
1993-94	Charlotte	3	1	.500	0	.000	1	5	3	1.0
1994-95	Portland	37	37	.430	22	.880	26	85	119	3.2
	Totals	211	240	.398	117	.860	174	458	699	3.3

JAMES EDWARDS 39 7-1 252 Center

And you thought it was impossible for someone so big to be invisible... Signed one-year, free-agent contract with Trail Blazers, then played a career-low 266 minutes... Played double-digit minutes only 13 times... His signature fallaway jumper is still tough to stop... Don't be surprised if he's back for another season, albeit somewhere else... Third among active players in games played and ninth all-time... Also fourth in fouls and sixth in disqualifications... A Bad Boy, but a nice guy... Best known for his four seasons with the Pistons, which included two titles... Began pro career in 1977-78, after

PORTLAND TRAIL BLAZERS • 387

the Lakers drafted him in the third round out of Washington ...
Born Nov. 22, 1955, in Seattle ... 1994-95 salary: $325,000.

Year	Team	G	FG	FG Pct.	FT	FT Pct.	Reb.	Ast.	TP	Avg.
1977-78	L.A.-Ind.	83	495	.453	272	.646	615	85	1252	15.2
1978-79	Indiana	82	534	.501	298	.676	693	92	1366	16.7
1979-80	Indiana	82	528	.512	231	.681	578	127	1287	15.7
1980-81	Indiana	81	511	.509	244	.703	571	212	1266	15.6
1981-82	Cleveland	77	528	.511	232	.684	581	123	1288	16.7
1982-83	Clev.-Phoe.	31	128	.487	69	.639	155	40	325	10.5
1983-84	Phoenix	72	438	.536	183	.720	348	184	1059	14.7
1984-85	Phoenix	70	384	.501	276	.746	387	153	1044	14.9
1985-86	Phoenix	52	318	.542	212	.702	301	74	848	16.3
1986-87	Phoenix	14	57	.518	54	.771	60	19	168	12.0
1987-88	Phoe.-Det.	69	302	.470	210	.654	412	78	814	11.8
1988-89	Detroit	76	211	.500	133	.686	231	49	555	7.3
1989-90	Detroit	82	462	.498	265	.749	345	63	1189	14.5
1990-91	Detroit	72	383	.484	215	.729	277	65	982	13.6
1991-92	L.A. Clippers	72	250	.465	198	.731	202	53	698	9.7
1992-93	L.A. Lakers	52	122	.452	84	.712	100	41	328	6.3
1993-94	L.A. Lakers	45	78	.464	54	.684	65	22	210	4.7
1994-95	Portland	28	32	.386	11	.647	43	8	75	2.7
	Totals	1140	5761	.496	3241	.698	5964	1488	14764	13.0

THE ROOKIE

GARY TRENT 21 6-8 240   Forward

"The Shaq of the MAC" while starring at Ohio University ...
No. 8 pick, by Milwaukee, then traded before the end of the night
to the Trail Blazers for Shawn Respert and a 1996 first-rounder
... Three-time Mid-American Conference Player of the Year ...
Left school after junior season ... "He is an outstanding offensive player who has medium-range perimeter, but is also very tough around the basket," Bullets GM John Nash says ... Born Sept. 22, 1974, in Columbus, Ohio.

COACH P.J. CARLESIMO: Welcome to the NBA. P.S.—

Your best player hates you ... Left Seton Hall after 12 seasons and much praise ... Came to Portland and went through the usual growing pains as most who make the same jump ... The difference with him, he had to get his temperament in check ... A screamer in college ... That doesn't go over well in the NBA, especially with star guard Rod Strickland ...
Went 212-166 (56.1 percent) with the Pirates ... His 44-38 record

Rod Strickland was fourth in NBA in assists.

with the Trail Blazers made him the first coach in 25 years to go directly from college to the pros and post a winning mark... Cotton Fitzsimmons, who went from Kansas State to the Suns, was the last to accomplish that... Only the second coach in Seton Hall history to break 200 wins, joining Hall of Famer John (Honey) Russell... Had five 20-win seasons and six trips to the NCAA tournament... Best year was 1989, when Seton Hall reached the championship game before losing to Michigan... Got start as a head coach at New Hampshire College in 1975, then left after one year for Wagner College... From there, Seton Hall... Assistant coach on Chuck Daly's staff for the 1992 Olympic Dream Team... That was just one step for someone very involved in USA Basketball... The oldest of 10 children, he was a four-year letterman at Fordham... Born May 30, 1949, in Scranton, Pa.

GREATEST FIND

Dave Twardzik was drafted 26th and ended up having his uniform retired. Larry Steele went 37th and eventually got the same honor, although he averaged only 8.2 points a game.

Clifford Robinson, however, is a star. Whether his uniform No. 3 ends up in the rafters in Portland remains to be seen. What is certain, however, is that the versatile forward was a steal at No. 36 in 1989, even after the Trail Blazers had used their first-round pick on Byron Irvin.

Irvin and many other of the first 35 picks are long gone. Robinson, meanwhile, has developed into an all-star, with some of his best years still ahead.

ALL-TIME TRAIL BLAZER LEADERS

SEASON

Points: Clyde Drexler, 2,185, 1987–88
Assists: Terry Porter, 831, 1987–88
Rebounds: Lloyd Neal, 967, 1972–73

GAME

Points: Geoff Petrie, 51 vs. Houston, 1/20/73
Geoff Petrie, 51 vs. Houston, 3/16/73
Assists: Rod Strickland, 20 vs. Phoenix, 4/4/94
Rebounds: Sidney Wicks, 27 vs. Los Angeles, 2/26/75

CAREER

Points: Clyde Drexler, 18,040, 1984–95
Assists: Terry Porter, 5,319 1985–95
Rebounds: Clyde Drexler, 5,339 1984–95

SACRAMENTO KINGS

TEAM DIRECTORY: Managing General Partner: Jim Thomas; Pres.: Rick Benner; VP-Basketball Oper.: Geoff Petrie; Dir. Basketball Services: Wayne Cooper; Dir. Player Personnel: Jerry Reynolds; Dir. Media Rel.: Travis Stanley; Coach: Garry St. Jean; Asst. Coaches: Eddie Jordan, Mike Bratz. Arena: ARCO Arena (17,317). Colors: Purple, silver and black.

SCOUTING REPORT

SHOOTING: This has not just become a pretty good team, but a pretty good shooting team. Imagine that. From tied for fifth-worst in 1993-94 to tied for 11th-best last season, even after losing dependable Wayman Tisdale. They got more defensive-minded, eased off the gas pedal a bit, and flourished. Now to prove it can last.

The two starting big men, Olden Polynice at center and Brian Grant at power forward, are hardly the focal points of the offense, but they are dependable, at 54.4 and 51.1 percent, respectively. That was good for 10th in the league for Polynice, and good news for the Kings that Grant, now heading into just his second season, can contribute in areas besides rebounding and defense. Meanwhile, their backups, Michael Smith and Duane Causwell, also broke 50 percent.

As always, Mitch Richmond is the first option. He doesn't overwhelm by percentage (a mediocre 44.6 last campaign), but by options. At 6-5 and 215 pounds, he is strong enough to post up or back in most shooting guards. He is also consistent from the outside, sometimes even dangerous, even out past the three-point line. It's no mystery why he finished eighth in the league in scoring and first among all guards.

PLAYMAKING: The Kings are either gutsy or crazy. By trading Spud Webb back to Atlanta in the offseason, they made a commitment to two unproven, largely inexperienced players at a time when the franchise is ready to finally push its way into the playoffs. Bobby Hurley and Tyus Edney—here are the keys to the offense.

Hurley, of course, was supposed to get the job anyway. But that was when Sacramento picked him in the lottery of 1993 after a record-filled career at Duke that included the NCAA career-assist mark, and before the near-fatal car crash. He hasn't been

Mitch Richmond added All-Star Game MVP to his resume.

anything but a reserve. Edney, meanwhile, hasn't been anything but a college player, a little battler at UCLA, and a late second-round pick at that.

REBOUNDING: They're nothing spectacular—just 18th by percentage last season—but it's a step in the right direction for what in the past has been a woeful area. Polynice has finished 18th and fifth in average the last two seasons, and Grant, who should only get better, contributed 7.5. Now, the first-round pick of the '95 draft was used on a widebody, although a bit undersized, Corliss Williamson.

The big problem for the team was the defensive boards. That may be a matter of leaking out too soon for the offense, in which case it can be corrected.

KING ROSTER

No.	Veterans	Pos.	Ht.	Wt.	Age	Yrs. Pro	College
43	Frank Brickowski	F-C	6-9	248	36	11	Penn State
3	Randy Brown	G	6-3	190	27	4	New Mexico State
31	Duane Causwell	C	7-0	240	27	5	Temple
—	Tyrone Corbin	F	6-6	225	33	10	DePaul
33	Brian Grant	F	6-9	254	23	1	Xavier
7	Bobby Hurley	G	6-0	165	24	2	Duke
20	Doug Lee	G	6-6	210	31	3	Purdue
0	Olden Polynice	F-C	7-0	250	30	8	Virginia
2	Mitch Richmond	G	6-5	215	30	7	Kansas State
22	Lionel Simmons	F	6-7	210	26	5	LaSalle
34	Michael Smith	F	6-8	230	23	1	Providence
9	Henry Turner	G-F	6-7	200	29	2	Cal-Fullerton
42	Walt Williams	F-G	6-8	230	25	3	Maryland

Rd.	Rookies	Sel.No.	Pos.	Ht.	Wt.	College
1	Corliss Williamson	13	F	6-7	245	Arkansas
2	Tyus Edney	47	G	5-10	152	UCLA
2	Dejan Bodiroga	51	F	6-8	217	Serbia

DEFENSE: Who kidnapped the Kings and replaced them with these imposters? These guys play defense, and everyone knows the Kings don't. At least they didn't before. Credit coach Garry St. Jean, a Don Nelson disciple who wanted to bring the same kind of game to Sacramento, for deciding to adjust when it became apparent his team didn't have the kind of weapons to win a machine-gun battle.

So they emphasized stopping the ball and shot all the way up to a tie for No. 2—that is not a misprint—in the league in shooting percentage-against, behind only the Knicks, for whom this kind of thing was expected. That means a season after beating out only Dallas, Milwaukee and Washington, the Kings are the best in the West in this critical category.

OUTLOOK: They were on the front porch, having stayed alive until the last game of 1994-95 before being eliminated from the playoffs. Time to kick the door down? Not so fast. Sacramento will be better again, but so should the Mavericks, Nuggets and Warriors. Only one team in the West seems to be slipping, the Trail Blazers. Don't count the Kings in just yet. But don't count them out either.

KING PROFILES

MITCH RICHMOND 30 6-5 215   Guard

Continues to handle the responsibility of carrying the offense... That is, if you consider finishing No. 1 among guards and No. 8 overall in scoring handling it... Also improved his defense... Everybody in the league knows him as a big-time weapon, but whatever anonymity may have existed among fans probably disappeared when he was named All-Star Game MVP... Generally consistent from the outside and always able to operate inside, which makes him such a tough matchup... Team captain has received some criticism for lack of leadership skills, but the respect is there... Rookie of the Year in 1988-89 after Golden State got Kansas State product with the No. 5 pick... Part of potent but short-lived "Run TMC" with Warriors before being traded to Sacramento for Billy Owens... Born June 30, 1965, in Ft. Lauderdale, Fla.... 1994-95 salary: $3 million.

Year	Team	G	FG	FG Pct.	FT	FT Pct.	Reb.	Ast.	TP	Avg.
1988-89	Golden State	79	649	.468	410	.810	468	334	1741	22.0
1989-90	Golden State	78	640	.497	406	.866	360	223	1720	22.1
1990-91	Golden State	77	703	.494	394	.847	452	238	1840	23.9
1991-92	Sacramento	80	685	.468	330	.813	319	411	1803	22.5
1992-93	Sacramento	45	371	.474	197	.845	154	221	987	21.9
1993-94	Sacramento	78	635	.445	426	.834	286	313	1823	23.4
1994-95	Sacramento	82	668	.446	375	.843	357	311	1867	22.8
	Totals	519	4351	.469	2538	.836	2396	2051	11781	22.7

WALT WILLIAMS 25 6-8 230   Forward-Guard

Something of the X Factor: When he plays well, the Kings usually play well... Made big strides to improve his defense, but still needs to become a better ball-handler... Shot selection also needs some work... Led Kings in steals and finished second in scoring and assists... Versatile enough to play some point guard when the Kings go big, but all his 77 appearances were as the starter at small forward... Now has to become at least a respectable shooter... He's a career 42.9 percent from the field since the Kings picked him No. 7 overall out of Maryland in 1992... Second-team all-rookie... Set Terrapins' record as a senior by averaging 26.8 points... Born April

16, 1970, in Washington, D.C. . . . Made $2.04 million in 1994-95.

Year	Team	G	FG	FG Pct.	FT	FT Pct.	Reb.	Ast.	TP	Avg.
1992-93	Sacramento	59	358	.435	224	.742	265	178	1001	17.0
1993-94	Sacramento	57	226	.390	148	.635	235	132	638	11.2
1994-95	Sacramento	77	445	.446	266	.731	345	316	1259	16.4
	Totals	193	1029	.429	638	.710	845	626	2898	15.0

OLDEN POLYNICE 30 7-0 250   Center

"I'm not saying everything is smooth sailing," front-office executive Jerry Reynolds says. "He's not the most conforming person in a game that needs conformity. But I think with all the trades, he seems to have found a home." . . . Apparently he was just renting with SuperSonics, Clippers and Pistons . . . Just had a hotel reservation with Bulls, who used the eighth pick to draft him out of Virginia in 1987 and then immediately traded him to Seattle . . . Kings got him from Detroit for Pete Chilcutt and a second-round pick Feb. 20, 1994 . . . Emotional player, which can be good and bad . . . Finished 10th in the league in shooting (54.4 percent) and 18th in rebounding (9.0) . . . The season before, he was fifth in rebounds and 13th in shooting . . . Bad hands . . . Born Nov. 21, 1964, in Port-au-Prince, Haiti . . . 1994-95 salary: $1.9 million.

Year	Team	G	FG	FG Pct.	FT	FT Pct.	Reb.	Ast.	TP	Avg.
1987-88	Seattle	82	118	.465	101	.639	330	33	337	4.1
1988-89	Seattle	80	91	.506	51	.593	206	21	233	2.9
1989-90	Seattle	79	156	.540	47	.475	300	15	360	4.6
1990-91	Sea.-LAC	79	316	.560	146	.579	553	42	778	9.8
1991-92	L.A.Clippers	76	244	.519	125	.622	536	46	613	8.1
1992-93	Detroit	67	210	.490	66	.609	418	29	486	7.3
1993-94	Det.-Sac.	68	346	.523	97	.508	809	41	789	11.6
1994-95	Sacramento	81	376	.544	124	.639	725	62	877	10.8
	Totals	612	1857	.525	757	.572	3877	289	4473	7.3

BRIAN GRANT 23 6-9 254   Forward

Just what the Kings needed at power forward . . . Has strength, quickness, athleticism . . . Oh, yeah. And a bright future . . . Player personnel director Jerry Reynolds says, "He is the real deal. When we drafted him, I made the statement that I kind of compared him somewhere between an A.C. Green and an Otis Thorpe, and I believe I undersold him." . . .

No. 8 pick in 1994, then named first-team all-rookie in a vote by coaches ... His 7.5 rebounds was second on the team to Olden Polynice and second among all rookies ... Led all first-year players in blocks per game ... Started 59 times ... Solid shooter because he knows his range ... In the opening lineup for the Rookie All-Star Game ... Led Xavier in rebounding all four years, joining Tyrone Hill as the only players in school history to do that ... Two-time Midwestern Collegiate Conference Player of the Year ... Born March 5, 1972, in Columbus, Ohio ... 1994-95 salary: $808,000.

Year	Team	G	FG	FG Pct.	FT	FT Pct.	Reb.	Ast.	TP	Avg.
1994-95	Sacramento	80	413	.511	231	.636	598	99	1058	13.2

MICHAEL SMITH 23 6-8 230   Forward

As if getting Brian Grant in the 1994 draft wasn't enough ... Getting this guy in the second round, all the way at No. 35, was a steal ... Has shown he can rebound and defend, further solidifying the frontline ... And he doesn't make stupid mistakes, always a plus for a young player ... Should work on his offense, like adding a short jumper ... Sticking with high-percentage shots, he would have finished 11th in the NBA and first among all rookies in shooting percentage but he fell 80 baskets shy of qualifying ... Also needs to get better from the line ... First Kings rookie to play in all 82 games since another power forward, Otis Thorpe, in 1984-85 ... Played in the Rookie All-Star Game ... Led Big East Conference in rebounding all three years at Providence ... No. 2 in conference history in career boards ... Born March 28, 1972, in Washington, D.C. ... A steal at $150,000 last season.

Year	Team	G	FG	FG Pct.	FT	FT Pct.	Reb.	Ast.	TP	Avg.
1994-95	Sacramento	82	220	.542	127	.485	486	67	567	6.9

LIONEL SIMMONS 26 6-7 210   Forward

Weren't you once somebody? ... Had a difficult 1994-95, then was left unprotected in the expansion draft ... Returning from arthroscopic knee surgery proved tough ... Missed training camp and the first 19 games while rehabilitating ... It didn't help that he also had to adjust to being a reserve for the first time in his pro career ... Good rebounder for a small forward and a competent defender... Lacks great athleticism and speed... Was third-leading scorer in NCAA history, behind only Pete Maravich and Freeman Williams, when he left LaSalle as the No. 7 pick in 1990... Since then, he has become the Kings' Sacramento-era leader in steals while second in rebounds, minutes and games... Runnerup to Derrick Coleman for Rookie of the Year in 1991... Born Oct. 14, 1968, in Philadelphia... 1994-95 salary: $2.181 million.

Year	Team	G	FG	FG Pct.	FT	FT Pct.	Reb.	Ast.	TP	Avg.
1990-91	Sacramento	79	549	.422	320	.736	697	315	1421	18.0
1991-92	Sacramento	78	527	.454	281	.770	634	337	1336	17.1
1992-93	Sacramento	69	468	.444	298	.819	495	312	1235	17.9
1993-94	Sacramento	75	436	.438	251	.777	562	305	1129	15.1
1994-95	Sacramento	58	131	.420	59	.702	196	89	327	5.6
	Totals	359	2111	.437	1209	.770	2584	1358	5448	15.2

TYRONE CORBIN 32 6-6 225   Forward

Journeyman went from one-year Hawk to King in summer trade for Spud Webb... With Hawks last season he made it possible for coach Lenny Wilkens to bury Ken Norman at season's end... Starter in final three games, averaged 10.3 over the final 11... Wilkens was responsible for the ending of Corbin's consecutive-game streak at 415—at Sacramento on Nov. 12, via a DNP-CD... Solid pro who's just a little bit too small to excel at small forward... Came to Hawks from Utah in deal for Adam Keefe... Also stops in Minnesota, Phoenix, Cleveland and San Antonio... Drafted in second round, out of DePaul, by Spurs in '85... Dealt to Jazz for Minnesota forward Thurl Bailey in '92... Born Dec. 31, 1962, in Columbia, S.C.... Made $1.6 million in 1994-95.

Year	Team	G	FG	FG Pct.	FT	FT Pct.	Reb.	Ast.	TP	Avg.
1985-86	San Antonio	16	27	.422	10	.714	25	11	64	4.0
1986-87	S.A.-Clev.	63	156	.409	91	.734	215	97	404	6.4
1987-88	Clev.-Phoe.	84	257	.490	110	.797	350	115	625	7.4
1988-89	Phoenix	77	245	.540	141	.788	398	118	631	8.2
1989-90	Minnesota	82	521	.481	161	.770	604	216	1203	14.7
1990-91	Minnesota	82	587	.448	296	.798	589	347	1472	18.0
1991-92	Minn.-Utah	80	303	.481	174	.866	472	140	780	9.8
1992-93	Utah	82	385	.503	180	.826	519	173	950	11.6
1993-94	Utah	82	268	.456	117	.813	389	122	659	8.0
1994-95	Atlanta	81	205	.442	78	.684	262	67	502	6.2
	Totals	729	2954	.471	1358	.792	3823	1406	7290	10.0

SACRAMENTO KINGS • 397

RANDY BROWN 27 6-3 190   Guard

One of the team's best defenders... Second to only Walt Williams in steals despite only 16.2 minutes a game... Would have been 27th in the league in steals average, but came up four games shy of qualifying... Long arms and quick hands... They just can't point the ball to the basket very well... It's tough enough to find time playing behind all-star Mitch Richmond, but his 44.9 shooting hurts his case even more... Has played some point guard... High-school teammates with Walter Bond... Kings got the two-time All-Big West selection from New Mexico State as the No. 31 pick in 1991... Started his college career at Houston before transferring... Born May 22, 1968, in Chicago... Made $700,000 last season.

Year	Team	G	FG	FG Pct.	FT	FT Pct.	Reb.	Ast.	TP	Avg.
1991-92	Sacramento	56	77	.456	38	.655	69	59	192	3.4
1992-93	Sacramento	75	225	.463	115	.732	212	196	567	7.6
1993-94	Sacramento	61	110	.438	53	.609	112	133	273	4.5
1994-95	Sacramento	67	124	.432	55	.671	108	133	317	4.7
	Totals	259	536	.449	261	.680	501	521	1349	5.2

DUANE CAUSWELL 27 7-0 240   Center

Helped by having former long-time center Wayne Cooper as a Kings' assistant coach... Hindered by having worse hands than most clocks... He and Brian Grant were the team's only legitimate shot-blockers... Started in 24 of 58 appearances... Was DNP-CD 19 times for the Kings, who got him with the No. 18 pick in 1990... Arrival of Olden Polynice and use of Grant and Michael Smith at backup center greatly reduced his playing time... Third in franchise history with 579 career blocks. Only LaSalle Thompson (697) and Sam Lacey (1,098) have more... Also second in shooting and third in games in the Sacramento era... Teammates with Tim Perry, Mark Macon and Donald Hodge at Temple... Born May 31, 1968, in Queens Village, N.Y.... 1994-95 salary: $1.545 million.

Year	Team	G	FG	FG Pct.	FT	FT Pct.	Reb.	Ast.	TP	Avg.
1990-91	Sacramento	76	210	.508	105	.636	391	69	525	6.9
1991-92	Sacramento	80	250	.549	136	.613	580	59	636	8.0
1992-93	Sacramento	55	175	.545	103	.624	303	35	453	8.2
1993-94	Sacramento	41	71	.518	40	.588	186	11	182	4.4
1994-95	Sacramento	58	76	.517	57	.582	174	15	209	3.6
	Totals	310	782	.531	441	.614	1634	189	2005	6.5

BOBBY HURLEY 24 6-0 165 Guard

Could be a sparkplug off the bench... Or could be a what-could-have-been... His main accomplishment last season was just playing... Had near-fatal car crash Dec. 12, 1993, not far from Arco Arena, and almost did not recover... Needed eight hours of surgery that night and suffered a torn trachea from the main airway to his left lung, a torn ligament in right knee, multiple rib fractures, a fractured left shoulder and a small compression fracture in the mid-portion of his back... Most serious injury last season was a lower back strain that caused him to miss the final four games... Fan favorite wherever he went because of the inspirational comeback... Won a pair of national championships at Duke and left as the NCAA's career assists leader... Kings took him No. 7 in 1993... Born June 28, 1971, in Jersey City, N.J.... 1994-95 salary: $2.1 million.

Year	Team	G	FG	FG Pct.	FT	FT Pct.	Reb.	Ast.	TP	Avg.
1993-94	Sacramento	19	54	.370	24	.800	34	115	134	7.1
1994-95	Sacramento	68	103	.363	58	.763	70	226	285	4.2
	Totals	87	157	.365	82	.774	104	341	419	4.8

DOUG LEE 31 6-6 210 Guard

Born Oct. 24, 1964, in Peoria, Ill.... Wonder if he would even play there?... The challenge is not to do well in games, but just to get in games... Averaged microscopic 3.4 minutes an outing last season... Biggest moment was being fouled on a three-pointer with 0.3 left and then making all three free throws to force overtime April 8 against the Clippers... Purdue product was a second-round pick by Houston in 1987... Waived by the Rockets before the season began and proceeded to bounce from the AAU to the CBA to France to Israel before making the NBA with New Jersey... Moves well without the ball, but doesn't create much for other players... Signed a one-year contract with the Kings before last season at $150,000.

Year	Team	G	FG	FG Pct.	FT	FT Pct.	Reb.	Ast.	TP	Avg.
1991-92	New Jersey	46	50	.431	10	.526	35	22	120	2.6
1992-93	New Jersey	5	2	.286	0	.000	2	5	5	1.0
1994-95	Sacramento	22	9	.360	18	.857	5	5	43	2.0
	Totals	73	61	.412	28	.700	42	32	168	2.3

FRANK BRICKOWSKI 36 6-9 248   Forward-Center

The King who wasn't... Veteran big man came to Sacramento as a free agent, then suffered a dislocated right shoulder five minutes into the fifth preseason game... Never recovered to play during the regular season... Underwent surgery on the joint Jan. 24... Expected to be healthy in time for the second installment on his two-year contract that paid $2.333 million last season... Originally a third-round pick, No. 57 overall, by the Knicks in 1981... Played the first three seasons in Europe—Italy, France and Israel—before returning to the U.S. with the SuperSonics... Coached by current NBA assistants John Bach and Dick Harter while at Penn State... Father played for the Pittsburgh Steelers... Born Aug. 14, 1959, in Bayville, N.Y.

Year	Team	G	FG	FG Pct.	FT	FT Pct.	Reb.	Ast.	TP	Avg.
1984-85	Seattle	78	150	.492	85	.669	260	100	385	4.9
1985-86	Seattle	40	30	.517	18	.667	54	21	78	2.0
1986-87	LAL-S.A.	44	63	.508	50	.714	116	17	176	4.0
1987-88	San Antonio	70	425	.528	268	.768	483	266	1119	16.0
1988-89	San Antonio	64	337	.515	201	.715	406	131	875	13.7
1989-90	San Antonio	78	211	.545	95	.674	327	105	517	6.6
1990-91	Milwaukee	75	372	.527	198	.798	426	131	942	12.6
1991-92	Milwaukee	65	306	.524	125	.767	344	122	740	11.4
1992-93	Milwaukee	66	456	.545	195	.728	405	196	1115	16.9
1993-94	Mil.-Char.	71	368	.488	195	.768	404	222	935	13.2
1994-95	Sacramento				Injured					
	Totals	651	2718	.521	1430	.742	3225	1311	6882	10.6

HENRY TURNER 29 6-7 200   Guard-Forward

Second go-round with the Kings was even less memorable than the first, which is saying something... Got a two-year contract to sign as a free agent, then averaged only five minutes per game in 30 outings as a swingman... Played three seasons with three different teams in Italy between stints in Sacramento and another in Greece... Left Cal-Fullerton as No. 3 on the career rebounding list and No. 4 in scoring, then went right to Rochester of the CBA... Born Aug. 18, 1966, in Oakland... 1994-95 salary: $180,000.

Year	Team	G	FG	FG Pct.	FT	FT Pct.	Reb.	Ast.	TP	Avg.
1989-90	Sacramento	36	58	.475	40	.615	50	22	156	4.3
1994-95	Sacramento	30	23	.404	20	.571	28	7	68	2.3
	Totals	66	81	.453	60	.600	78	29	224	3.4

THE ROOKIES

CORLISS WILLIAMSON 21 6-7 245   Forward
Can he play power forward in the pros at 6-7?... The Kings don't need to know right away because they already have Brian Grant and Michael Smith... No. 13 pick... Great strength and solid fundamentals... Decent touch on offense... SEC Player of the Year as a junior before declaring early... Led Arkansas to 1994 NCAA title and the championship game in '95... Born Dec. 4, 1973, in Russellville, Ark.

TYUS EDNEY 22 5-10 152   Guard
Went later than many expected—No. 47—then caught a break when Kings traded Spud Webb soon after... Barring a late-summer trade, the competition to become the starting point guard is just between him and Bobby Hurley... Teams worried about a string of nagging injuries... Member of UCLA's national championship team and scored the memorable coast-to-coast driving basket to beat Missouri in the tournament... Won 1995 Francis Pomeroy Naismith Award as the top college player under six feet... Born Feb. 14, 1973, in Gardena, Cal.

DEJAN BODIROGA 22 6-8 217   Forward
Has size and range... Native of Serbia... Member of the former Yugoslavian national team... Played for Serbia in the 1995 European championships... That was taking place on the same day he was drafted 51st... Spent the last three seasons in Italy... Born March 2, 1973, in Zrenjanin, Bosnia.

COACH GARRY ST. JEAN: His three-year plan to make the playoffs fell just short, but last season was still a success... He got a healthy team and the chance to show how good a coach he can be, then he got a new contract at the end of the season... Had been in a tenuous position heading into 1994-95, the final installment on a three-year deal... When the Kings improved by 11 games, the fourth-best jump in the league, he was in good shape... Besides, if Sacramento didn't want him, other teams would have had interest... Went 39-43 and missed the playoffs by losing to Denver on the last day of the season... The 39 victories were the most for the franchise since the 1982-83 Kansas City Kings went 45-37... The season before, he coached the Kings out of last place in the Pacific Division for the first time since 1988-89... Winningest coach in Sacramento history... NBA assistant for 12 years, 10 on Don Nelson's staff, before Sacramento gave him first chance to be head coach... The other two years were spent with Nets... Also has front-office experience as assistant director of player personnel at New Jersey and Milwaukee... Born Feb. 10, 1950, in Chicopee, Mass., and became a high-school star there in basketball and soccer... Attended Springfield College.

GREATEST FIND

"Tiny" was big for the Kansas City Kings. Six years of service, 25.2 points a game, including 34.0 in 1972-73. No. 3 all-time in franchise history in assists and points.

To think the Kings got Nate Archibald out of Texas-El Paso with a second-round pick in 1970, after they had already taken center Sam Lacey. Archibald turned out to be one of the best players in the history of the organization.

He even contributed a few steals here and there. They weren't much compared to the Kings' steal, though.

ALL-TIME KING LEADERS

SEASON

Points: Nate Archibald, 2,719, 1972–73
Assists: Nate Archibald, 910, 1972–73
Rebounds: Jerry Lucas, 1,688, 1965–66

GAME

Points: Jack Twyman, 59 vs. Minneapolis, 1/15/60
Assists: Phil Ford, 22 vs. Milwaukee, 2/21/79
        Oscar Robertson, 22 vs. New York, 3/5/66
        Oscar Robertson, 22 vs. Syracuse, 10/29/61
Rebounds: Jerry Lucas, 40 vs. Philadelphia, 2/29/64

CAREER

Points: Oscar Robertson, 22,009, 1960–70
Assists: Oscar Robertson, 7,721, 1960–70
Rebounds: Sam Lacey, 9,353, 1971–82

SEATTLE SUPERSONICS

TEAM DIRECTORY: Owner: Barry Ackerley; Pres./GM: Wally Walker; VP-Basketball Oper.: Billy McKinney; Dir. Pub. Rel.: Cheri White; Coach: George Karl; Asst. Coaches: Bob Weiss, Terry Stotts, Dwane Casey. Arena: Key Arena (17,100). Colors: Green, red, yellow and bronze.

SCOUTING REPORT

SHOOTING: A strength, as always. Two years ago, the Sonics tied for fourth-best in the league in accuracy and last season moved up to third, behind only Utah and Orlando, while also finishing third in scoring. Three starters—Shawn Kemp (54.7) Detlef Schrempf (52.3) and Gary Payton (50.9)—shot better than 50 percent in 1994-95.

OK, so why? A couple of reasons.

For one thing, the trapping, pressing, switching defense creates so many easy baskets, and they have just the runners to convert, even with a 6-10 power forward. The same quickness that forces turnovers also gets them to the hoop in transition. That explains the opposing point guards who are back on their heels even as they bring the ball upcourt.

For another, there is the unconventional style. The point guard, Payton, took 348 more shots than any other Sonic last season, though his added consistency from the outside is one of the reasons he has developed into one of the best in the game at his position. Schrempf is 6-10, but finished second in the league behind Chicago's Steve Kerr in three-point shooting. A center-power forward who mostly comes off the bench, Sam Perkins, led the team in attempts from behind the line.

It all adds up to difficult matchups for most teams. And problems.

PLAYMAKING: Payton finished 15th in the league in assists last season at an unimpressive 7.1 a game, but somehow, no one sees this as a problem area. The Sonics placed sixth in assist-to-turnover ratio because they have so many others who handle the ball well.

Two small forwards, Schrempf and Nate McMillan, the latter also a sometimes-point guard, are very comfortable with the ball. Opponents can at least take come comfort in that Kendall Gill, the shooting guard who had played the point before, was traded

Gary Payton headed Sonics in scoring, assists, steals.

back to the Charlotte Hornets (for Hersey Hawkins and David Wingate).

REBOUNDING: There was reason to be concerned last season. The Sonics had dropped from fifth in the league by percentage from 1992-93 to 10th in 1993-94, and then, a few months later, lost Michael Cage to Cleveland as a free agent. What fate awaited them?

The same, it turned out. Or just about the same: a tie for 10th, even though no rebound specialist had arrived in place. That made it something of an accomplishment, or proof that Seattle could

SUPERSONIC ROSTER

No.	Veterans	Pos.	Ht.	Wt.	Age	Yrs. Pro	College
2	Vincent Askew	G-F	6-6	235	29	6	Memphis State
33	Hersey Hawkins	G	6-3	190	29	7	Bradley
21	Byron Houston	F	6-5	250	25	3	Oklahoma State
50	Ervin Johnson	C	6-11	245	27	2	New Orleans
40	Shawn Kemp	F	6-10	245	25	6	Trinity J.C.
R-45	Rich King	C	7-2	265	26	4	Nebraska
30	Sarunas Marciulionis	G	6-5	215	31	6	Lithuania
10	Nate McMillan	G-F	6-5	200	31	9	North Carolina State
20	Gary Payton	G	6-4	190	27	5	Oregon State
14	Sam Perkins	F-C	6-9	245	34	11	North Carolina
U-55	Steve Scheffler	C	6-9	250	28	5	Purdue
11	Detlef Schrempf	F	6-10	230	32	10	Washington
—	David Wingate	G-F	6-5	185	31	9	Georgetown

R-restricted free agent
U-unrestricted free agent

Rd.	Rookies	Sel.No.	Pos.	Ht.	Wt.	College
1	Sherell Ford	26	F	6-7	210	Illinois-Chicago
2	Eric Snow	43	G	6-3	190	Michigan State

still hold its own. Kemp, of course, is the force, No. 6 among individuals in 1994-95 at 10.9 boards an outing. Getting 6.2 per game from the small forward, Schrempf, helps too.

DEFENSE: No. 1 in steal-to-turnover ratio. No. 1 in steals, an impressive 120 more than any other team. Tied for No. 2 in turnovers forced. No. 4 in shooting percentage against. Payton, No. 3 among individuals in steals. McMillan, No. 5. Yeah, they do all right.

This is where the Sonics win so many of their games, with a team that has size and quickness and is well-drilled in the art of defense. There is, however, room for improvement. They undoubtedly would have led all teams last season in turnovers forced if not for finishing in a tie for 16th in blocked shots, an obvious area of weakness. That deficiency is why Ervin Johnson was moved into the starting lineup, but he still doesn't get a ton of minutes.

OUTLOOK: Like we know. Like anyone knows. A team loaded with talent goes into 1995-96 facing even more questions than last season, which is saying something. That's what consecutive first-round losses to lower-seeded opponents gets you.

SUPERSONIC PROFILES

SHAWN KEMP 25 6-10 245 — Forward

The Reign Man of the rain country... All-star the last three seasons, twice in the opening lineup... That means fans look upon him as one of the superstars... With skills like this, no wonder... Great athlete who can run the floor and even handle the ball... And just let him catch the ball deep on the blocks. One spin move and it's all over... Except for his scream as the exclamation point, that is... He says that's genuine playfulness. Others say it should be toned down... Finished among league leaders in shooting, rebounds and blocks... Big numbers came despite just 32.6 minutes per game... Passed Jack Sikma to become Sonics' all-time leading shot-blocker... Second on club's career rebounding list... Dream Team II member did not play in college, but was still drafted No. 17, technically out of Trinity Valley JC in Texas, in 1989... Entered the NBA at age 19... Born Nov. 26, 1969, in Elkhart, Ind.... 1994-95 salary: $1 million.

Year	Team	G	FG	FG Pct.	FT	FT Pct.	Reb.	Ast.	TP	Avg.
1989-90	Seattle	81	203	.479	117	.736	346	26	525	6.5
1990-91	Seattle	81	462	.508	288	.661	679	144	1214	15.0
1991-92	Seattle	64	362	.504	270	.748	665	86	994	15.5
1992-93	Seattle	78	515	.492	358	.712	833	155	1388	17.8
1993-94	Seattle	79	533	.538	364	.741	851	207	1431	18.1
1994-95	Seattle	82	545	.547	438	.749	893	149	1530	18.7
	Totals	465	2620	.515	1835	.724	4267	767	7082	15.2

GARY PAYTON 27 6-4 190 — Guard

The future is here... Only question that remains is where he ranks among the best point guards in the league... OK, that and why opposing point guards have hurt the Sonics so much in the playoffs two years in a row... Led Seattle in scoring, assists and steals... Two-time all-star... His 50.9 percent from the field was fifth-best among all point guards... Had been No. 1 year before, a major reason for his jump from "maybe one day" to reaching the elite... That had been a weakness since he came out of Oregon State as the No. 2 pick in 1990

... One of the best defenders in the backcourt... Has missed only one game in five seasons as a pro... Named college Player of the Year by *Sports Illustrated* as a senior... No. 2 in steals in NCAA history by the time he left school... Selected to Pacific-10 Conference all-decade team... Born July 23, 1968, in Oakland... Made $2.583 million in 1994-95.

Year	Team	G	FG	FG Pct.	FT	FT Pct.	Reb.	Ast.	TP	Avg.
1990-91	Seattle	82	259	.450	69	.711	243	528	588	7.2
1991-92	Seattle	81	331	.451	99	.669	295	506	764	9.4
1992-93	Seattle	82	476	.494	151	.770	281	399	1110	13.5
1993-94	Seattle	82	584	.504	166	.595	269	494	1349	16.5
1994-95	Seattle	82	685	.509	249	.716	281	583	1689	20.6
	Totals	409	2335	.489	734	.687	1369	2510	5500	13.4

DETLEF SCHREMPF 32 6-10 230 Forward

One of the oldest Sonics still hangs out with the kids... Last season, his 10th as a pro, may have been his best... All-star selection for the second time overall and his first since going from Indiana to Seattle for Derrick McKey and Gerald Paddio in Nov. 1993... His 19.2 points per game was a career best... Finished second in the league in three-point shooting and had a one-month stretch where he went 38 of 55 from long distance... On top of that, he has great size for a small forward, so he can also go inside... Has played power forward... Sixth Man of the Year in 1991 and '92 as a Pacer... Two-time Olympian for Germany... Born Jan. 21, 1963, in Leverkusen, Germany... Came to the United States to attend high school in the Seattle area, then attended Washington before Dallas took him No. 8 in 1985... Highest-paid Sonic last season at $5 million.

Year	Team	G	FG	FG Pct.	FT	FT Pct.	Reb.	Ast.	TP	Avg.
1985-86	Dallas	64	142	.451	110	.724	198	88	397	6.2
1986-87	Dallas	81	265	.472	193	.742	303	161	756	9.3
1987-88	Dallas	82	246	.456	201	.756	279	159	698	8.5
1988-89	Dal.-Indiana	69	274	.474	273	.780	395	179	828	12.0
1989-90	Indiana	78	424	.516	402	.820	620	247	1267	16.2
1990-91	Indiana	82	432	.520	441	.818	660	301	1320	16.1
1991-92	Indiana	80	496	.536	365	.828	770	312	1380	17.3
1992-93	Indiana	82	517	.476	525	.804	780	493	1567	19.1
1993-94	Seattle	81	445	.493	300	.769	454	275	1212	15.0
1994-95	Seattle	82	521	.523	437	.839	508	310	1572	19.2
	Totals	781	3762	.498	3247	.799	4967	2525	10997	14.1

HERSEY HAWKINS 29 6-3 190 — Guard

Never found a niche with the Hornets. Passing game was mystifying, and it was never easy being the third option behind Larry Johnson and Alonzo Mourning... Isn't as athletic as Kendall Gill, and was reminded of that almost daily... And now Gill is back in Charlotte, traded for Hawkins and David Wingate... Triples jumped from 78 to 131, but scoring average (14.3) was almost identical to first season in Charlotte (14.4)... Needs help creating a shot... Durable, dependable. Missed only seven games in seven seasons... Holds Hornets' club record with 37 straight FTs... Was sixth pick, out of Bradley, by Clippers in '88. Went to Philly in three-team, draft-night deal... Sixers sent him to Hornets for Dana Barros, Sidney Green and Greg Graham in '93... Born Sept. 29, 1966, in Chicago... Made $2.5 million in 1994-95.

Year	Team	G	FG	FG Pct.	FT	FT Pct.	Reb.	Ast.	TP	Avg.
1988-89	Philadelphia	79	442	.455	241	.831	225	239	1196	15.1
1989-90	Philadelphia	82	522	.460	387	.888	304	261	1515	18.5
1990-91	Philadelphia	80	590	.472	479	.871	310	299	1767	22.1
1991-92	Philadelphia	81	521	.462	403	.874	271	248	1536	19.0
1992-93	Philadelphia	81	551	.470	419	.860	346	317	1643	20.3
1993-94	Charlotte	82	395	.460	312	.862	377	216	1180	14.4
1994-95	Charlotte	82	390	.482	261	.867	314	262	1172	14.3
	Totals	567	3411	.466	2502	.867	2147	1842	10009	17.7

NATE McMILLAN 31 6-5 200 — Guard-Forward

Rarely does someone who shoots so poorly make such a big impact... No. 5 in the league in steals, and did it while averaging just 25.9 minutes... Not only that, he did it while playing small forward, shooting guard and point guard, proving he can defend all three positions... Versatility has long been a strength ... A solid clubhouse influence on a team that can use some... Sonics' all-time leader in steals and assists... His 25 assists in a 1986-87 game is still a team record and, along with Ernie DiGregorio, the best ever in the NBA by a rookie...

Third in franchise history in games, behind only Fred Brown and Jack Sikma... Born Aug. 3, 1964, in Raleigh, N.C., and stayed at home to attend North Carolina State... Sonics took him 30th in 1986... Made $1.06 million last season.

Year	Team	G	FG	FG Pct.	FT	FT Pct.	Reb.	Ast.	TP	Avg.
1986-87	Seattle	71	143	.475	87	.617	331	583	373	5.3
1987-88	Seattle	82	235	.474	145	.707	338	702	624	7.6
1988-89	Seattle	75	199	.410	119	.630	388	696	532	7.1
1989-90	Seattle	82	207	.473	98	.641	403	598	523	6.4
1990-91	Seattle	78	132	.433	57	.613	251	371	338	4.3
1991-92	Seattle	72	177	.437	54	.643	252	359	435	6.0
1992-93	Seattle	73	213	.464	95	.709	306	384	546	7.5
1993-94	Seattle	73	177	.447	31	.564	283	387	437	6.0
1994-95	Seattle	80	166	.418	34	.586	302	421	419	5.2
	Totals	686	1649	.448	720	.647	2854	4501	4227	6.2

SAM PERKINS 34 6-9 245   Center-Forward

The most encouraging sign was that his shooting percentage pulled out of a nosedive... Loves to shoot the three-pointer, even while playing center... That forces opposition's big man to come outside with him... Already fourth in Sonic history from behind the arc, just 2½ seasons after coming in trade from the Lakers for Doug Christie and Benoit Benjamin ... The flip side is that he can also post up... That versatility makes him extra valuable... Co-captain of the 1984 Olympic team that won a gold medal... Three-time All-American at North Carolina before Dallas made him the No. 4 pick in the 1984 draft ... Born June 14, 1961, in New York City... 1994-95 salary: $4.126 million.

Year	Team	G	FG	FG Pct.	FT	FT Pct.	Reb.	Ast.	TP	Avg.
1984-85	Dallas	82	347	.471	200	.820	605	135	903	11.0
1985-86	Dallas	80	458	.503	307	.814	685	153	1234	15.4
1986-87	Dallas	80	461	.482	245	.828	616	146	1186	14.8
1987-88	Dallas	75	394	.450	273	.822	601	118	1066	14.2
1988-89	Dallas	78	445	.464	274	.833	688	127	1171	15.0
1989-90	Dallas	76	435	.493	330	.778	572	175	1206	15.9
1990-91	L.A. Lakers	73	368	.495	229	.821	538	108	983	13.5
1991-92	L.A. Lakers	63	361	.450	304	.817	556	141	1041	16.5
1992-93	L.A. Lakers-Sea.	79	381	.477	250	.820	524	156	1036	13.1
1993-94	Seattle	81	341	.438	218	.801	366	111	999	12.3
1994-95	Seattle	82	346	.466	215	.799	398	135	1043	12.7
	Totals	849	4337	.472	2845	.813	6149	1505	11868	14.0

VINCENT ASKEW 29 6-6 235   Guard-Forward

Defensive specialist had career bests last season in minutes and scoring average... Can check guards and forwards and wear both down... That makes him a perfect fit for versatile Sonics... Not bad for a former player in Italy and the CBA who was once cut by Philadelphia... Played for George Karl with Albany Patroons, where he became the first player in league history to be named back-to-back MVP... The Sonics' original investment was sending a second-round pick to Sacramento Nov. 25, 1992... It's gotten bigger since then—he made $1.46 million in 1994-95 as the first installment on a new contract... Former Golden State Warrior wears No. 17 as a tribute to Chris Mullin... Born Feb. 28, 1966, in Memphis, Tenn., and played at Memphis State.

Year	Team	G	FG	FG Pct.	FT	FT Pct.	Reb.	Ast.	TP	Avg.
1987-88	Philadelphia	14	22	.297	8	.727	22	33	52	3.7
1990-91	Golden State	7	12	.480	9	.818	11	13	33	4.7
1991-92	Golden State	80	193	.509	111	.694	233	188	498	6.2
1992-93	Sac.-Sea.	73	152	.492	105	.705	161	122	411	5.6
1993-94	Seattle	80	273	.481	175	.829	184	194	727	9.1
1994-95	Seattle	71	248	.492	176	.739	181	176	703	9.9
	Totals	325	900	.484	584	.749	792	726	2424	7.5

DAVID WINGATE 31 6-5 185   Guard-Forward

Hornets traded him with Hersey Hawkins for Kendall Gill in June... Heart is strong, knees are weak... Played 52 games last season, and that's about the limit... Posted a career-low in points (2.3), but that's OK. Strength is defense, something he picked up at Georgetown... Did average 6.3 points and shoot 48 percent in nine starts, most of which came after Scott Burrell suffered season-ending Achilles tendon injury... Second-round pick, by Sixers, in '86... Traded to Spurs, in Maurice Cheeks-Johnny Dawkins deal, on Aug. 28, 1989... Dumped by Spurs, spent season with Bullets... Signed with Hornets, Nov. 18, 1992 ... Played at Baltimore's Dunbar High with, among others,

Muggsy Bogues ... Born Dec. 15, 1963, in Baltimore ... Made $570,000 in 1994-95.

Year	Team	G	FG	FG Pct.	FT	FT Pct.	Reb.	Ast.	TP	Avg.
1986-87	Philadelphia	77	259	.430	149	.741	156	155	680	8.8
1987-88	Philadelphia	61	218	.400	99	.750	101	119	545	8.9
1988-89	Philadelphia	33	54	.470	27	.794	37	73	137	4.2
1989-90	San Antonio	78	220	.448	87	.777	195	208	527	6.8
1990-91	San Antonio	25	53	.384	29	.707	75	46	136	5.4
1991-92	Washington	81	266	.465	105	.719	269	247	638	7.9
1992-93	Charlotte	72	180	.536	79	.738	174	183	440	6.1
1993-94	Charlotte	50	136	.481	34	.667	134	104	310	6.2
1994-95	Charlotte	52	50	.410	18	.750	60	56	122	2.3
	Totals	529	1436	.448	627	.739	1201	1191	3535	6.7

SARUNAS MARCIULIONIS 31 6-5 215   Guard

Has overcome a series of knee, leg and foot injuries ... Still very aggressive on offense, putting the ball on the floor to drive to the basket ... Good enough on three-pointers to keep defenses honest, but not really much of a threat out there ... Increased shooting range would help ... Owns the Hotel Sarunas, a 27-room Vilnius, Lithuania, inn ... Just in case you happen to be in the neighborhood ... First player from the Soviet Union to play in the NBA ... Won bronze medal with 1992 Lithuanian Olympic team ... Golden State lured him to the U.S. with a free-agent contract ... Finished as top-scoring reserve in the NBA with the Warriors in 1991-92 ... They traded him to Seattle in 1994 along with Byron Houston for Ricky Pierce, Carlos Rogers and a couple of second-rounders ... Born June 13, 1964, in Kanuas, U.S.S.R. ... 1994-95 salary: $2.1 million.

Year	Team	G	FG	FG Pct.	FT	FT Pct.	Reb.	Ast.	TP	Avg.
1989-90	Golden State	75	289	.519	317	.787	221	121	905	12.1
1990-91	Golden State	50	183	.501	178	.724	118	85	545	10.9
1991-92	Golden State	72	491	.538	376	.788	208	243	1361	18.9
1992-93	Golden State	30	178	.543	162	.761	97	105	521	17.4
1993-94	Golden State					Injured				
1994-95	Seattle	66	216	.473	145	.732	68	110	612	9.3
	Totals	293	1357	.518	1178	.766	712	664	3944	13.5

ERVIN JOHNSON 27 6-11 245   Center

Rode shot-blocking ability, one thing the Sonics lack on defense, into the starting lineup... Got career-high five blocks in just 25 minutes April 6 at Denver... Jumped from 6.2 minutes as a rookie out of New Orleans to 14.2 last season... A lot of backups get as much playing time, but he's headed in the right direction... Physically mature when Sonics picked him at No. 23 because he worked at a supermarket for 2½ years before beginning college... He was older before making pro debut than teammate Shawn Kemp was after five years in the NBA... Didn't play high-school ball, but developed enough at New Orleans to be named Sun Belt Conference Player of the Year and third-team All-American by UPI as a senior... Born Dec. 21, 1967, in New Orleans... 1994-95 salary: $716,600.

Year	Team	G	FG	FG Pct.	FT	FT Pct.	Reb.	Ast.	TP	Avg.
1993-94	Seattle	45	44	.415	29	.630	118	7	117	2.6
1994-95	Seattle	64	85	.443	29	.630	289	16	199	3.1
	Totals	109	129	.433	58	.630	407	23	316	2.9

BYRON HOUSTON 25 6-5 250   Forward

Classic tweener—too small to play power forward, too slow and not offensive enough to play small forward... Besides, there's nothing small about a forward at 250 pounds on a 6-5 frame... 84-inch wingspan is a defensive weapon few can match... Seattle got him as a throw-in on the Carlos Rogers-Sarunas Marciulionis/Ricky Pierce trade in the summer of 1994... Oklahoma hero after leading high-school team to state championship and then playing for Oklahoma State... Bulls drafted him with the last pick in the first round of 1992... Traded to Golden State before rookie season and led the Warriors in games played... Search parties and private investigators have been looking for him ever since... Born Nov. 22, 1969, in Watonga, Kan.... Made $700,000 in 1994-95.

Year	Team	G	FG	FG Pct.	FT	FT Pct.	Reb.	Ast.	TP	Avg.
1992-93	Golden State	79	145	.446	129	.665	315	69	421	5.3
1993-94	Golden State	71	81	.458	33	.611	194	32	196	2.8
1994-95	Seattle	39	49	.458	28	.737	55	6	132	3.4
	Totals	189	275	.452	190	.664	564	107	749	4.0

RICH KING 26 7-2 265   Center

The goal used to be modest: maybe he can develop into a solid backup center... Now it's more like: maybe he can get in a game... On the active roster for only eight games last season, the last of his contract, and was "DNP-CD" in six of those... Missed 74 games with knee injuries, most after undergoing arthroscopic surgery... Hasn't played more than seven minutes in a game the last two seasons... Not on the playoff roster for the third straight year... Made 1992 playoff roster but didn't play... So much for returns on the No. 14 pick in 1991... Starred at Nebraska before that... No. 1 in school history in blocked shots, No. 3 in rebounding and No. 4 in scoring... Born April 4, 1969, in Omaha, Neb.... 1994-95 salary: $800,000.

Year	Team	G	FG	FG Pct.	FT	FT Pct.	Reb.	Ast.	TP	Avg.
1991-92	Seattle	40	27	.380	34	.756	49	12	88	2.2
1992-93	Seattle	3	2	.400	2	1.000	5	1	6	2.0
1993-94	Seattle	27	15	.441	11	.500	20	8	41	1.5
1994-95	Seattle	2	0	.000	0	.000	0	0	0	0.0
	Totals	72	44	.393	47	.662	74	21	135	1.9

STEVE SCHEFFLER 28 6-9 250   Forward-Center

Were this hockey, he would be the enforcer... Not a dirty player, but very physical... Has the strength of a big-time center... Now if he could only get the skills of a decent player at any position... Contributes with hard work in practice and cheerleading in games... Second-round pick, No. 39 overall, by Charlotte in 1990 after being named the Big Ten Player of the Year while at Purdue... Part of Boilermaker teams that won back-to-back conference titles... Also has a stint with CBA's Quad City on his resume, in addition to NBA travels... Sonics signed him as a free agent... Brother, Tom, played with Portland in 1984-85... Born Sept. 3, 1967, in Grand Rapids, Mich.... 1994-95 salary: $275,000.

Year	Team	G	FG	FG Pct.	FT	FT Pct.	Reb.	Ast.	TP	Avg.
1990-91	Charlotte	39	20	.513	19	.905	45	9	59	1.5
1991-92	Sac.-Den.	11	6	.667	9	.750	14	0	21	1.9
1992-93	Seattle	29	25	.521	16	.667	36	5	66	2.3
1993-94	Seattle	35	28	.609	19	.950	26	6	75	2.1
1994-95	Seattle	18	12	.522	15	.833	23	4	39	2.2
	Totals	132	91	.552	78	.821	144	24	260	2.0

THE ROOKIES

SHERELL FORD 23 6-7 210   Forward
He can score. Hope he can also be patient... Doesn't figure to get a ton of minutes on a team that starts Detlef Schrempf... Scoring potential will get him noticed, though... No. 26 selection... Averaged 26.2 points as a senior and 24.3 as a junior at Illinois-Chicago... Midwestern Conference Player of the Year last season... High-school teammates with another first-round pick, Michael Finley, at Proviso East in Maywood, Ill.... Born Aug. 26, 1972, in Baton Rouge, La.

ERIC SNOW 22 6-3 190   Guard
A true pass-first, shoot-second point guard... Played in same backcourt at Michigan State with Bucks rookie Shawn Respert... Went 43rd to Milwaukee and then they traded him to Sonics for Eurelejas Zukauskas... Fourth in nation in assists as a senior... Second on all-time school list behind Scott Skiles... Born April 24, 1973, in Canton, Ohio.

COACH GEORGE KARL: Dodged the ax... So much for significant accomplishments last spring... He guided Sonics to a third straight 50-win season, then right out of the playoffs in the first round... That's happened two years in a row now, both times against teams with worse records... As if anyone needs reminding around the Puget Sound... Speculation that he would quickly be fired proved false... Does any coach go into 1995-96 with more pressure?... Joined the Sonics midway through 1991-92 and has gone 202-86 since then... His 70.1 rate is the best winning percentage in franchise history... Seattle has never lost more than three in a row on his watch... The 63-19 record in his second full season is the best mark in team history... Career: 321-262 (55.1)... Former point guard at North Carolina and San Antonio... Broke into coaching with the Spurs in 1978 as an assistant to Doug Moe... Became head coach for the first time with Montana of the CBA, where he spent three years and was Coach of the Year in two of those... Returned to the NBA as director of player acquisition for the Cavaliers in 1983 and a year later became coach. Fired late in 1985-86 ... Warriors hired him from there to be their sideline boss. That lasted two seasons... Next came stops with Albany of the CBA and Real Madrid of the Spanish League before the Sonics called ... Born May 12, 1951, in Penn Hills, Pa.

GREATEST FIND

It was supposed to be a roll of the dice in the 1989 draft: Shawn Kemp, one year removed from high school, who had never played in college, with the 17th pick.

It helped that it was the Sonics' second pick of the first round, allowing them the luxury to gamble a bit after having already taken guard Dana Barros. But no one was sure if Kemp, loaded with potential, would turn out or wash out. Six years later, of course, we know.

Kemp has become one of the best forwards of his generation, the combination of speed and power. Players like that aren't supposed to last until No. 17.

ALL-TIME SUPERSONIC LEADERS

SEASON

Points: Dale Ellis, 2,253, 1988–89
Assists: Lenny Wilkens, 766, 1971–72
Rebounds: Jack Sikma, 1,038, 1981–82

GAME

Points: Fred Brown, 58 vs. Golden State, 3/23/74
Assists: Nate McMillan, 25 vs. L.A. Clippers, 2/23/87
Rebounds: Jim Fox, 30 vs. L.A. Lakers, 12/26/73

CAREER

Points Fred Brown, 14,018, 1971–84
Assists: Nate McMillan, 4,501, 1986–95
Rebounds: Jack Sikma, 7,729, 1977–86

Shawn Kemp topped Sonics' three 50-pct. shooters.

1994 NBA COLLEGE DRAFT

FIRST ROUND

Sel. No.	Team	Name	College	Ht.
1.	Golden State	Joe Smith	Maryland	6-10
2.	a-L.A. Clippers	Antonio McDyess	Alabama	6-9
3.	Philadelphia	Jerry Stackhouse	North Carolina	6-6

Alabama's Antonio McDyess wound up a Nugget as No. 2.

Sixers chose North Carolina's Jerry Stackhouse (No. 3).

Sel. No.	Team	Name	College	Ht.
4.	Washington	Rasheed Wallace	North Carolina	6-10
5.	Minnesota	Kevin Garnett	Farragut Academy	6-10
6.	Vancouver	Bryant Reeves	Oklahoma State	7-0
7.	Toronto	Damon Stoudamire	Arizona	5-10
8.	b-Portland	Shawn Respert	Michigan State	6-3
9.	New Jersey	Ed O'Bannon	UCLA	6-8
10.	Miami	Kurt Thomas	Texas Christian	6-9

a-Traded to Denver
b-Traded to Milwaukee

North Carolina's Rasheed Wallace (No. 4) is a Bullet.

Sel. No.	Team	Name	College	Ht.
11.	c-Milwaukee	Gary Trent	Ohio University	6-8
12.	Dallas	Cherokee Parks	Duke	6-11
13.	Sacramento	Corliss Williamson	Arkansas	6-7
14.	Boston	Eric Williams	Providence	6-8
15.	d-Denver	Brent Barry	Oregon State	6-6
16.	Atlanta	Alan Henderson	Indiana	6-9
17.	Cleveland	Bob Sura	Florida State	6-5

c-Traded to Portland
d-Traded to L.A. Clippers

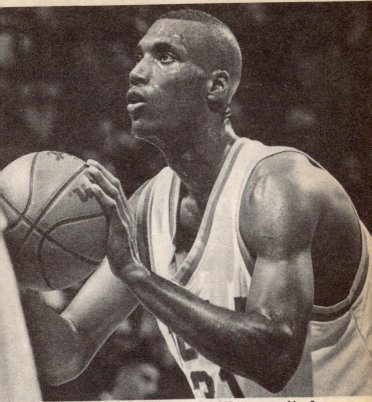

Nets opted for UCLA's Ed O'Bannon as No. 9.

Sel. No.	Team	Name	College	Ht.
18.	Detroit	Theo Ratliff	Wyoming	6-10
19.	Detroit	Randolph Childress	Wake Forest	6-1
20.	Chicago	Jason Caffey	Alabama	6-8
21.	Phoenix	Michael Finley	Wisconsin	6-7
22.	Charlotte	George Zidek	UCLA	7-0
23.	Indiana	Travis Best	Georgia Tech	5-11
24.	Dallas	Loren Meyer	Iowa State	6-10
25.	Orlando	David Vaughn	Memphis	6-10
26.	Seattle	Sherell Ford	Illinois-Chicago	6-7
27.	Phoenix	Mario Bennett	Arizona State	6-9

Ohio's Gary Trent (No. 11) landed in Portland.

Arizona's Damon Stoudamire (No. 7) joins Raptors.

Mavs selected Duke's Cherokee Parks as No. 12.

Celtics went to Providence for Eric Williams (No. 14).

Arkansas' Corliss Williamson is a King as No. 13.

Wyoming's Theo Ratliff: No. 18 to Pistons.

Sel. No.	Team	Name	College	Ht.
28.	Utah	Greg Ostertag	Kansas	7-2
29.	San Antonio	Cory Alexander	Virginia	6-1

SECOND ROUND

30.	Detroit	Lou Roe	Massachusetts	6-7
31.	Chicago	Dragan Tarlac	Greece	6-10
32.	e-Washington	Terrence Rencher	Texas	6-3
33.	Boston	Junior Burrough	Virginia	6-8

e-Traded to Miami

424 • **THE COMPLETE HANDBOOK OF PRO BASKETBALL**

Pacers made 23rd call with Georgia Tech's Travis Best.

Sel. No.	Team	Name	College	Ht.
34.	Golden State	Andrew DeClerq	Florida	6-10
35.	Toronto	Jimmy King	Michigan	6-5
36.	Vancouver	Lawrence Moten	Syracuse	6-5
37.	L.A. Lakers	Frankie King	Western Carolina	6-1
38.	Milwaukee	Rashard Griffith	Wisconsin	6-11
39.	Cleveland	Donny Marshall	Connecticut	6-7
40.	Golden State	Dwayne Whitfield	Jackson State	6-9
41.	Houston	Erik Meek	Duke	6-10
42.	Atlanta	Donnie Boyce	Colorado	6-5
43.	f-Milwaukee	Eric Snow	Michigan State	6-3
44.	Denver	Anthony Pelle	Fresno State	7-0
45.	Atlanta	Troy Brown	Providence	6-8
46.	Miami	George Banks	Texas-El Paso	6-7
47.	Sacramento	Tyus Edney	UCLA	5-10

COLLEGE DRAFT • 425

Memphis' David Vaughn goes to world of Magic as No. 25.

Sel. No.	Team	Name	College	Ht.
48.	Minnesota	Mark Davis	Texas Tech	6-7
49.	Minnesota	Jerome Allen	Pennsylvania	6-4
50.	Golden State	Martin Lewis	Seward County CC	6-6
51.	Sacramento	Dejan Bodiroga	Italy	6-8
52.	Indiana	Fred Holberg	Iowa State	6-4
53.	L.A. Clippers	Constantin Popa	Miami	7-3
54.	g-Seattle	Eurelejus Zukaukas	Lithuania	7-1
55.	Golden State	Michael McDonald	New Orleans	6-10
56.	Phoenix	Chris Carr	Southern Illinois	6-6
57.	Atlanta	Cuonzo Martin	Purdue	6-6
58.	Detroit	Don Reid	Georgetown	6-8

f-Traded to Seattle
g-Traded to Milwaukee

1994-95
NATIONAL BASKETBALL ASSOCIATION

FINAL STANDINGS

EASTERN CONFERENCE

Atlantic Division	Won	Lost	Pct.
Orlando	57	25	.695
New York	55	27	.671
Boston	35	47	.427
Miami	32	50	.390
New Jersey	30	52	.366
Philadelphia	24	58	.293
Washington	21	61	.256

Central Division	Won	Lost	Pct.
Indiana	52	30	.634
Charlotte	50	32	.610
Chicago	47	35	.573
Cleveland	43	39	.524
Atlanta	42	40	.512
Milwaukee	34	48	.415
Detroit	28	54	.341

WESTERN CONFERENCE

Midwest Division	Won	Lost	Pct.
San Antonio	62	20	.756
Utah	60	22	.732
Houston	47	35	.573
Denver	41	41	.500
Dallas	36	46	.439
Minnesota	21	61	.256

Pacific Division	Won	Lost	Pct.
Phoenix	59	23	.720
Seattle	57	25	.695
L.A. Lakers	48	34	.585
Portland	44	38	.537
Sacramento	39	43	.476
Golden State	26	56	.317
L.A. Clippers	17	65	.207

PLAYOFFS

EASTERN CONFERENCE
First Round
Orlando defeated Boston (3-1)
Chicago defeated Charlotte (3-1)
Indiana defeated Atlanta (3-0)
New York defeated Cleveland (3-1)
Semifinals
Orlando defeated Chicago (4-2)
Indiana defeated New York (4-3)
Finals
Orlando defeated Indiana (4-3)

WESTERN CONFERENCE
First Round
San Antonio defeated Denver (3-0)
L.A. Lakers defeated Seattle (3-1)
Phoenix defeated Portland (3-0)
Houston defeated Utah (3-2)
Semifinals
San Antonio defeated L.A. Lakers (4-2)
Houston defeated Phoenix (4-3)
Finals
Houston defeated San Antonio (4-2)

CHAMPIONSHIP
Houston defeated Orlando (4-0)

1994-95 NBA INDIVIDUAL HIGHS

Most Minutes Played, Season: 3,361, Baker, Milwaukee
Most Minutes Played, Game: 58, Vaught, L.A. Clippers vs. Boston, 2/17 (2 OT)
48, 40 times, most recently by Mills, Cleveland vs. Chicago, 4/9
Most Points, Game: 56, Rice, Miami, vs. Orlando, 4/15
Most Field Goals Made, Game: 21, four times, most recently by Jordan, Chicago, at New York, 3/28
Most Field Goal Attempts, Game: 37, Mashburn, Dallas, at Houston, 4/11 (2 OT); Jordan, Chicago, at New York, 3/28
Most 3-Pt. Field Goals Made, Game: 10, Dumars, Detroit, vs. Minnesota, 11/8
Most 3-Pt. Field Goal Attempts, Game: 18, Dumars, Detroit, vs. Minnesota, 11/8
Most Free Throws Made, Game: 24, Burton, Philadelphia, vs. Miami, 12/13
Most Free Throw Attempts, Game: 28, Burton, Philadelphia, vs. Miami, 12/13
Most Rebounds, Game: 30, Rodman, San Antonio, at Houston, 2/21
Most Offensive Rebounds, Game: 14, O'Neal, Orlando, at Charlotte, 11/9 (OT)
Rodman, San Antonio, at Indiana, 1/22
Rodman, San Antonio, at Chicago, 1/24 (OT)
Most Defensive Rebounds, Game: 21, Ewing, New York, at Indiana, 2/8
Most Offensive Rebounds, Season: 329, Jones, Dallas
Most Defensive Rebounds, Season: 715, Malone, Utah
Most Assists, Game: 22, Hardaway, Golden State, vs. Orlando, 12/16 (OT)
20, Stockton, Utah, vs. Philadelphia, 1/7
Most Blocked Shots, Game: 11, Mutombo, Denver, at Dallas, 11/8
Most Steals, Game: 8, 3 times, most recently by Sprewell, Golden State, at Orlando, 3/26
Most Personal Fouls, Season: 338, Bradley, Philadelphia
Most Games Disqualified, Season: 18, Bradley, Philadelphia

INDIVIDUAL SCORING LEADERS
Minimum 70 games or 1,400 points

	G	FG	FT	Pts.	Avg.
O'Neal, Orlando	79	930	455	2315	29.3
Olajuwon, Houston	72	798	406	2005	27.8
Robinson, San Antonio	81	788	656	2238	27.6
Malone, Utah	82	830	516	2187	26.7
Mashburn, Dallas	80	683	447	1926	24.1
Ewing, New York	79	730	420	1886	23.9
Barkley, Phoenix	68	554	379	1561	23.0
Richmond, Sacramento	82	668	375	1867	22.8
Rice, Miami	82	667	312	1831	22.3
Robinson, Milwaukee	80	636	397	1755	21.9
Drexler, Port.-Hou.	76	571	364	1653	21.8
Pippen, Chicago	79	634	315	1692	21.4
C. Robinson, Portland	75	597	265	1601	21.3
Mourning, Charlotte	77	571	490	1643	21.3
Hardaway, Orlando	77	585	356	1613	20.9
Payton, Seattle	82	685	249	1689	20.6
Sprewell, Golden State	69	490	350	1420	20.6
Barros, Philadelphia	82	571	347	1686	20.6
Rider, Minnesota	75	558	277	1532	20.4
Hill, Detroit	70	508	374	1394	19.9

REBOUND LEADERS
Minimum 70 games or 800 rebounds

	G	Off.	Def.	Tot.	Avg.
Rodman, San Antonio	49	274	549	823	16.8
Mutombo, Denver	82	319	710	1029	12.5
O'Neal, Orlando	79	328	573	901	11.4
Ewing, New York	79	157	710	867	11.0
Hill, Cleveland	70	269	496	765	10.9
Kemp, Seattle	82	318	575	893	10.9
Robinson, San Antonio	81	234	643	877	10.8
Olajuwon, Houston	72	172	603	775	10.8
Malone, Utah	82	156	715	871	10.6
Jones, Dallas	80	329	515	844	10.6
Divac, L.A. Lakers	80	261	568	829	10.4
Baker, Milwaukee	82	289	557	846	10.3
Mourning, Charlotte	77	200	561	761	9.9
Grant, Orlando	74	223	492	715	9.7
Vaught, L.A. Clippers	80	261	511	772	9.7
D. Davis, Indiana	74	259	437	696	9.4
Dudley, Portland	82	325	439	764	9.3
Polynice, Sacramento	81	277	448	725	9.0
Mason, New York	77	182	468	650	8.4
Williams, Dallas	82	291	399	690	8.4

FIELD-GOAL LEADERS
Minimum 300 FG Made

	FG	FGA	Pct.
Gatling, Golden State	324	512	.633
O'Neal, Orlando	930	1594	.583
Grant, Orlando	401	707	.567
Thorpe, Hou.-Port.	385	681	.565
D. Davis, Indiana	324	576	.563
Muresan, Washington	303	541	.560
Mutombo, Denver	349	628	.556
Kemp, Seattle	545	997	.547
Manning, Phoenix	340	622	.547
Polynice, Sacramento	376	691	.544
Stockton, Utah	429	791	.542
Malone, Utah	830	1548	.536
Montross, Boston	307	575	.534
Conlon, Milwaukee	344	647	.532
Robinson, San Antonio	788	1487	.530
Smits, Indiana	558	1060	.526
Schrempf, Seattle	521	997	.523
Perry, Phoenix	306	588	.520
Johnson, San Antonio	448	863	.519
Mourning, Charlotte	571	1101	.519

3-POINT FIELD-GOAL LEADERS
Minimum 82 Made

	FG	FGA	Pct.
Kerr, Chicago	89	170	.524
Schrempf, Seattle	93	181	.514
Barros, Philadelphia	197	425	.464
Davis, New York	131	288	.455
Stockton, Utah	102	227	.449
Hawkins, Charlotte	131	298	.440
Person, Phoenix	116	266	.436
Smith, Houston	142	331	.429
Armstrong, Chicago	108	253	.427
Curry, Charlotte	154	361	.427
Scott, Orlando	150	352	.426
Houston, Detroit	158	373	.424
Skiles, Washington	96	228	.421
Anderson, Orlando	179	431	.415
Miller, Indiana	195	470	.415
Rice, Miami	185	451	.410
Burrell, Charlotte	96	235	.409
Elliott, San Antonio	136	333	.408
Price, Cleveland	103	253	.407
Hornacek, Utah	89	219	.406

FREE-THROW LEADERS
Minimum 125 FT Made

	FT	FTA	Pct.
Webb, Sacramento	226	242	.934
Price, Cleveland	148	162	.914
Barros, Philadelphia	347	386	.899
Miller, Indiana	383	427	.897
Hornacek, Utah	284	322	.882
Jennings, Golden State	134	153	.876
Hawkins, Charlotte	261	301	.867
Chapman, Washington	137	159	.862
Houston, Detroit	142	171	.860
Brandon, Cleveland	159	186	.855
Rice, Miami	312	365	.855
Brown, Boston	236	277	.852
Smith, Houston	126	148	.851
Scott, Indiana	193	227	.850
Richmond, Sacramento	375	445	.843
Cassell, Houston	214	254	.843

ASSISTS LEADERS
Minimum 70 games or 400 assists

	G	A	Avg.
Stockton, Utah	82	1011	12.3
Anderson, New Jersey	72	680	9.4
Hardaway, Golden State	62	578	9.3
Strickland, Portland	64	562	8.8
Blaylock, Atlanta	80	616	7.7
Kidd, Dallas	79	607	7.7
Barros, Philadelphia	82	619	7.5
Jackson, Indiana	82	616	7.5
Skiles, Washington	62	452	7.3
Hardaway, Orlando	77	551	7.2
Payton, Seattle	82	583	7.1
Douglas, Boston	65	446	6.9
Murdock, Milwaukee	75	482	6.4
Webb, Sacramento	76	468	6.2
Coles, Miami	68	416	6.1
Harper, New York	80	458	5.7

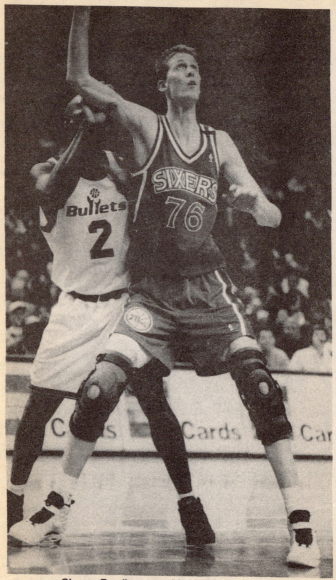

Shawn Bradley was third in blocked shots.

STEALS LEADERS
Minimum 70 games or 125 steals

	G	St.	Avg.
Pippen, Chicago	79	232	2.94
Blaylock, Atlanta	80	200	2.50
Payton, Seattle	82	204	2.49
Stockton, Utah	82	194	2.37
McMillan, Seattle	80	165	2.06
Jones, L.A. Lakers	64	131	2.05
Kidd, Dallas	79	151	1.91
Perry, Phoenix	82	156	1.90
Olajuwon, Houston	72	133	1.85
Barros, Philadelphia	82	149	1.82
Drexler, Port.-Hou.	76	136	1.79
Hill, Detroit	70	124	1.77
Gugliotta, Wash.-G.S.-Minn.	77	132	1.71
Hardaway, Orlando	77	130	1.69
Robinson, San Antonio	81	134	1.65
Anderson, Orlando	76	125	1.64
Richardson, L.A. Clippers	80	129	1.61
Gill, Seattle	73	117	1.60
Williams, Sacramento	77	123	1.60
Hornacek, Utah	81	129	1.59

BLOCKED-SHOTS LEADERS
Minimum 70 games or 100 blocked shots

	G	Blk.	Avg.
Mutombo, Denver	82	321	3.91
Olajuwon, Houston	72	242	3.36
Bradley, Philadelphia	82	274	3.34
Robinson, San Antonio	81	262	3.23
Mourning, Charlotte	77	225	2.92
O'Neal, Orlando	79	192	2.43
Divac, L.A. Lakers	80	174	2.18
Ewing, New York	79	159	2.01
Outlaw, L.A. Clippers	81	151	1.86
Miller, Detroit	64	116	1.81
Campbell, L.A. Lakers	73	132	1.81
Williams, Dallas	82	148	1.80
Lang, Atlanta	82	144	1.76
Muresan, Washington	73	127	1.74
Brown, New Jersey	80	135	1.69
D. Davis, Indiana	74	116	1.57
Dudley, Portland	82	126	1.54
West, Detroit	67	102	1.52
Kemp, Seattle	82	122	1.49
Grant, Sacramento	80	116	1.45

1994-95 ALL-NBA TEAM

FIRST

Pos.	Player, Team
F	Scottie Pippen, Bulls
F	Karl Malone, Jazz
C	David Robinson, Spurs
G	John Stockton, Jazz
G	Anfernee Hardaway, Magic

SECOND

Pos.	Player, Team
F	Shawn Kemp, Sonics
F	Charles Barkley, Suns
C	Shaquille O'Neal, Magic
G	Mitch Richmond, Kings
G	Gary Payton, Sonics

THIRD

Pos.	Player, Team
F	Detlef Schrempf, Sonics
F	Dennis Rodman, Spurs
C	Hakeem Olajuwon, Rockets
G	Reggie Miller, Pacers
G	Clyde Drexler, Rockets

*1994-95 NBA ALL-ROOKIE TEAM

FIRST
Player, Team
Jason Kidd, Mavericks
Grant Hill, Pistons
Glenn Robinson, Bucks
Eddie Jones, Lakers
Brian Grant, Kings

SECOND
Player, Team
Juwan Howard, Bullets
Eric Montross, Celtics
Wesley Person, Suns
Jalen Rose, Nuggets
Donyell Marshall, Warriors (tie)
Sharone Wright, 76ers (tie)

*Chosen without regard to position

1994-95 NBA ALL-DEFENSIVE TEAM

FIRST

Pos.	Player, Team
F	Scottie Pippen, Bulls
F	Dennis Rodman, Spurs
C	David Robinson, Spurs
G	Gary Payton, Sonics
G	Mookie Blaylock, Hawks

SECOND

Pos.	Player, Team
F	Horace Grant, Magic
F	Derrick McKey, Pacers
C	Dikembe Mutombo, Nuggets
G	John Stockton, Jazz
G	Nate McMillan, Sonics

MOST VALUABLE PLAYER

1955–56	Bob Pettit, St. Louis
1956–57	Bob Cousy, Boston
1957–58	Bill Russell, Boston
1958–59	Bob Pettit, St. Louis
1959–60	Wilt Chamberlain, Philadelphia
1960–61	Bill Russell, Boston
1961–62	Bill Russell, Boston
1962–63	Bill Russell, Boston
1963–64	Oscar Robertson, Cincinnati
1964–65	Bill Russell, Boston
1965–66	Wilt Chamberlain, Philadelphia
1966–67	Wilt Chamberlain, Philadelphia
1967–68	Wilt Chamberlain, Philadelphia
1968–69	Wes Unseld, Baltimore
1969–70	Willis Reed, New York
1970–71	Lew Alcindor, Milwaukee
1971–72	Kareem Abdul-Jabbar, Milwaukee
1972–73	Dave Cowens, Boston
1973–74	Kareem Abdul-Jabbar, Milwaukee
1974–75	Bob McAdoo, Buffalo
1975–76	Kareem Abdul-Jabbar, L.A.
1976–77	Kareem Abdul-Jabbar, L.A.
1977–78	Bill Walton, Portland
1978–79	Moses Malone, Houston
1979–80	Kareem Abdul-Jabbar, L.A.
1980–81	Julius Erving, Philadelphia
1981–82	Moses Malone, Houston
1982–83	Moses Malone, Philadelphia
1983–84	Larry Bird, Boston
1984–85	Larry Bird, Boston
1985–86	Larry Bird, Boston
1986–87	Magic Johnson, L.A. Lakers
1987–88	Michael Jordan, Chicago
1988–89	Magic Johnson, L.A. Lakers
1989–90	Magic Johnson, L.A. Lakers
1990–91	Michael Jordan, Chicago
1991–92	Michael Jordan, Chicago
1992–93	Charles Barkley, Phoenix
1993–94	Hakeem Olajuwon, Houston
1994–95	David Robinson, San Antonio

ROOKIE OF THE YEAR

1952–53	Don Meineke, Fort Wayne
1953–54	Ray Felix, Baltimore
1954–55	Bob Pettit, Milwaukee
1955–56	Maurice Stokes, Rochester
1956–57	Tom Heinsohn, Boston
1957–58	Woody Sauldsberry, Philadelphia
1958–59	Elgin Baylor, Minneapolis
1959–60	Wilt Chamberlain, Philadelphia
1960–61	Oscar Robertson, Cincinnati
1961–62	Walt Bellamy, Chicago
1962–63	Terry Dischinger, Chicago
1963–64	Jerry Lucas, Cincinnati
1964–65	Willis Reed, New York
1965–66	Rick Barry, San Francisco
1966–67	Dave Bing, Detroit
1967–68	Earl Monroe, Baltimore
1968–69	Wes Unseld, Baltimore
1969–70	Lew Alcindor, Milwaukee
1970–71	Dave Cowens, Boston
	Geoff Petrie, Portland
1971–72	Sidney Wicks, Portland
1972–73	Bob McAdoo, Buffalo
1973–74	Ernie DiGregorio, Buffalo
1974–75	Keith Wilkes, Golden State
1975–76	Alvan Adams, Phoenix
1976–77	Adrian Dantley, Buffalo
1977–78	Walter Davis, Pheonix
1978–79	Phil Ford, Kansas City
1979–80	Larry Bird, Boston
1980–81	Darrell Griffith, Utah
1981–82	Buck Williams, New Jersey
1982–83	Terry Cummings, San Diego
1983–84	Ralph Sampson, Houston
1984–85	Michael Jordan, Chicago
1985–86	Patrick Ewing, New York
1986–87	Chuck Person, Indiana
1987–88	Mark Jackson, New York
1988–89	Mitch Richmond, Golden State
1989–90	David Robinson, San Antonio
1990–91	Derrick Coleman, New Jersey
1991–92	Larry Johnson, Charlotte
1992–93	Shaquille O'Neal, Orlando
1993–94	Chris Webber, Golden State
1994–95	Grant Hill, Detroit
	Jason Kidd, Dallas

FINALS MVP AWARD

1969	Jerry West, Los Angeles	1983	Moses Malone, Philadelphia
1970	Willis Reed, New York	1984	Larry Bird, Boston
1971	Kareem-Abdul-Jabbar, Milwaukee	1985	K. Abdul-Jabbar, L.A. Lakers
1972	Wilt Chamberlain, Los Angeles	1986	Larry Bird, Boston
1973	Willis Reed, New York	1987	Magic Johnson, L.A. Lakers
1974	John Havlicek, Boston	1988	James Worthy, L.A. Lakers
1975	Rick Barry, Golden State	1989	Joe Dumars, Detroit
1976	Jo Jo White, Boston	1990	Isiah Thomas, Detroit
1977	Bill Walton, Portland	1991	Michael Jordan, Chicago
1978	Wes Unseld, Washington	1992	Michael Jordan, Chicago
1979	Dennis Johnson, Seattle	1993	Michael Jordan, Chicago
1980	Magic Johnson, Los Angeles	1994	Hakeem Olajuwon, Houston
1981	Cedric Maxwell, Boston	1995	Hakeem Olajuwon, Houston
1982	Magic Johnson, Los Angeles		

DEFENSIVE PLAYER OF THE YEAR

1982–83	Sidney Moncrief, Milwaukee	1989–90	Dennis Rodman, Detroit
1983–84	Sidney Moncrief, Milwaukee	1990–91	Dennis Rodman, Detroit
1984–85	Mark Eaton, Utah	1991–92	David Robinson, San Antonio
1985–86	Alvin Robertson, San Antonio	1992–93	Hakeem Olajuwon, Houston
1986–87	Michael Cooper, L.A. Lakers	1993–94	Hakeem Olajuwon, Houston
1987–88	Michael Jordan, Chicago	1994–95	Dikembe Mutombo, Denver
1988–89	Mark Eaton, Utah		

SIXTH MAN AWARD

1982–83	Bobby Jones, Philadelphia	1989–90	Ricky Pierce, Milwaukee
1983–84	Kevin McHale, Boston	1990–91	Detlef Schrempf, Indiana
1984–85	Kevin McHale, Boston	1991–92	Detlef Schrempf, Indiana
1985–86	Bill Walton, Boston	1992–93	Cliff Robinson, Portland
1986–87	Ricky Pierce, Milwaukee	1993–94	Dell Curry, Charlotte
1987–88	Roy Tarpley, Dallas	1994–95	Anthony Mason, New York
1988–89	Eddie Johnson, Phoenix		

MOST IMPROVED PLAYER

1985–86	Alvin Robertson, San Antonio	1990–91	Scott Skiles, Orlando
1986–87	Dale Ellis, Seattle	1991–92	Pervis Ellison, Washington
1987–88	Kevin Duckworth, Portland	1992–93	Chris Jackson, Denver
1988–89	Kevin Johnson, Phoenix	1993–94	Don MacLean, Washington
1989–90	Rony Seikaly, Miami	1994–95	Dana Barros, Philadelphia

IBM AWARD
Determined by Computer Formula

1983–84 Magic Johnson, Los Angeles	1989–90 David Robinson, San Antonio
1984–85 Michael Jordan, Chicago	1990–91 David Robinson, San Antonio
1985–86 Charles Barkley, Philadelphia	1991–92 Dennis Rodman, Detroit
1986–87 Charles Barkley, Philadelphia	1992–93 Hakeem Olajuwon, Houston
1987–88 Charles Barkley, Philadelphia	1993–94 David Robinson, San Antonio
1988–89 Michael Jordan, Chicago	1994–95 David Robinson, San Antonio

COACH OF THE YEAR

1962–63 Harry Gallatin, St. Louis	1979–80 Bill Fitch, Boston
1963–64 Alex Hannum, San Francisco	1980–81 Jack McKinney, Indiana
1964–65 Red Auerbach, Boston	1981–82 Gene Shue, Washington
1965–66 Dolph Schayes, Philadelphia	1982–83 Don Nelson, Milwaukee
1966–67 Johnny Kerr, Chicago	1983–84 Frank Layden, Utah
1967–68 Richie Guerin, St. Louis	1984–85 Don Nelson, Milwaukee
1968–69 Gene Shue, Baltimore	1985–86 Mike Fratello, Atlanta
1969–70 Red Holzman, New York	1986–87 Mike Schuler, Portland
1970–71 Dick Motta, Chicago	1987–88 Doug Moe, Denver
1971–72 Bill Sharman, Los Angeles	1988–89 Cotton Fitzsimmons, Phoenix
1972–73 Tom Heinsohn, Boston	1989–90 Pat Riley, L.A. Lakers
1973–74 Ray Scott, Detroit	1990–91 Don Chaney, Houston
1974–75 Phil Johnson, Kansas City-Omaha	1991–92 Don Nelson, Golden State
1975–76 Bill Fitch, Cleveland	1992–93 Pat Riley, New York
1976–77 Tom Nissalke, Houston	1993–94 Lenny Wilkens, Atlanta
1977–78 Hubie Brown, Atlanta	1994–95 Del Harris, L.A. Lakers
1978–79 Cotton Fitzsimmons, Kansas City	

J. WALTER KENNEDY CITIZENSHIP AWARD

1974–75 Wes Unseld, Washington	1985–86 Michael Cooper, L.A. Lakers
1975–76 Slick Watts, Seattle	Rory Sparrow, New York
1976–77 Dave Bing, Washington	1986–87 Isiah Thomas, Detroit
1977–78 Bob Lanier, Detroit	1987–88 Alex English, Denver
1978–79 Calvin Murphy, Houston	1988–89 Thurl Bailey, Utah
1979–80 Austin Carr, Cleveland	1989–90 Glenn Rivers, Atlanta
1980–81 Mike Glenn, New York	1990–91 Kevin Johnson, Phoenix
1981–82 Kent Benson, Detroit	1991–92 Magic Johnson, L.A. Lakers
1982–83 Julius Erving, Philadelphia	1992–93 Terry Porter, Portland
1983–84 Frank Layden, Utah	1993–94 Joe Dumars, Detroit
1984–85 Dan Issel, Denver	1994–95 Joe O'Toole, Atlanta

NBA CHAMPIONS

Season	Championship	Eastern Division W. L.			Western Division W. L.		
1946–47	Philadelphia	35	25	Philadelphia	39	22	Chicago
1947–48	Baltimore	27	21	Philadelphia	28	20	Baltimore
1948–49	Minneapolis	38	22	Washington	44	16	Minneapolis
1949–50	Minneapolis	51	13	Syracuse	51	17	Minneapolis
1950–51	Rochester	36	30	New York	41	27	Rochester
1951–52	Minneapolis	37	29	New York	40	26	Minneapolis
1952–53	Minneapolis	47	23	New York	48	22	Minneapolis
1953–54	Minneapolis	42	30	Syracuse	46	26	Minneapolis
1954–55	Syracuse	43	29	Syracuse	43	29	Ft. Wayne
1955–56	Philadelphia	45	27	Philadelphia	37	35	Ft. Wayne
1956–57	Boston	44	28	Boston	34	38	St. Louis
1957–58	St. Louis	49	23	Boston	41	31	St. Louis
1958–59	Boston	52	20	Boston	33	39	Minneapolis
1959–60	Boston	59	16	Boston	46	29	St. Louis
1960–61	Boston	57	22	Boston	51	28	St. Louis
1961–62	Boston	60	20	Boston	54	26	Los Angeles
1962–63	Boston	58	22	Boston	53	27	Los Angeles
1963–64	Boston	59	21	Boston	48	32	San Francisco
1964–65	Boston	62	18	Boston	49	31	Los Angeles
1965–66	Boston	54	26	Boston	45	35	Los Angeles
1966–67	Philadelphia	68	13	Philadelphia	44	37	San Fran.
1967–68	Boston	54	28	Boston	52	30	Los Angeles
1968–69	Boston	48	34	Boston	55	27	Los Angeles
1969–70	New York	60	22	New York	46	36	Los Angeles
1970–71	Milwaukee	42	40	Baltimore	66	16	Milwaukee
1971–72	Los Angeles	48	34	New York	69	13	Los Angeles
1972–73	New York	57	25	New York	60	22	Los Angeles
1973–74	Boston	56	26	Boston	59	23	Milwaukee
1974–75	Golden State	60	22	Washington	48	34	Golden State
1975–76	Boston	54	28	Boston	42	40	Phoenix
1976–77	Portland	50	32	Philadelphia	49	33	Portland
1977–78	Washington	44	38	Washington	47	35	Seattle
1978–79	Seattle	54	28	Washington	52	30	Seattle
1979–80	Los angeles	59	23	Philadelphia	60	22	Los Angeles
1980–81	Boston	62	20	Boston	40	42	Houston
1981–82	Los Angeles	58	24	Philadelphia	57	25	Los Angeles
1982–83	Philadelphia	65	17	Philadelphia	58	24	Los Angeles
1983–84	Boston	62	20	Boston	54	28	Los Angeles

Season	Championship	Eastern Division W. L.			Western Division W. L.		
1984–85	L.A. Lakers	63	19	Boston	62	20	L.A. Lakers
1985–86	Boston	67	15	Boston	51	31	Houston
1986–87	L.A. Lakers	59	23	Boston	65	17	L.A. Lakers
1987–88	L.A. Lakers	54	28	Detroit	62	20	L.A. Lakers
1988–89	Detroit	63	19	Detroit	57	25	L.A. Lakers
1989–90	Detroit	59	23	Detroit	59	23	Portland
1990–91	Chicago	61	21	Chicago	58	24	L.A. Lakers
1991–92	Chicago	67	15	Chicago	57	25	Portland
1992–93	Chicago	57	25	Chicago	62	20	Phoenix
1993–94	Houston	57	25	New York	58	24	Houston
1994–95	Houston	57	25	Orlando	47	35	Houston

NBA SCORING CHAMPIONS

Season	Pts./Avg.	Top Scorer	Team
1946–47	1389	Joe Fulks	Philadelphia
1947–48	1007	Max Zaslofsky	Chicago
1948–48	1698	George Mikan	Minneapolis
1949–50	1865	George Mikan	Minneapolis
1950–51	1932	George Mikan	Minneapolis
1951–52	1674	Paul Arizin	Philadelphia
1952–53	1564	Neil Johnston	Philadelphia
1953–54	1759	Neil Johnston	Philadelphia
1954–55	1631	Neil Johnston	Philadelphia
1955–56	1849	Bob Pettit	St. Louis
1956–57	1817	Paul Arizin	Philadelphia
1957–58	2001	George Yardley	Detroit
1958–59	2105	Bob Pettit	St. Louis
1959–60	2707	Wilt Chamberlain	Philadelphia
1960–61	3033	Wilt Chamberlain	Philadelphia
1961–62	4029	Wilt Chamberlain	Philadelphia
1962–63	3586	Wilt Chamberlain	San Francisco
1963–64	2948	Wilt Chamberlain	San Francisco
1964–65	2534	Wilt Chamberlain	San Fran.-Phila.
1965–66	2649	Wilt Chamberlain	Philadelphia
1966–67	2775	Rick Barry	San Francisco
1967–68	2142	Dave Bing	Detroit
1968–69	2327	Elvin Hayes	San Diego

Season	Pts./Avg.	Top Scorer	Team
1969–70	*31.2	Jerry West	Los Angeles
1970–71	*31.7	Lew Alcindor	Milwaukee
1971–72	*34.8	K. Abdul-Jabbar	Milwaukee
1972–73	*34.0	Nate Archibald	K.C.-Omaha
1973–74	*30.6	Bob McAdoo	Buffalo
1974–75	*34.5	Bob McAdoo	Buffalo
1975–76	*31.1	Bob McAdoo	Buffalo
1976–77	*31.1	Pete Maravich	New Orleans
1977–77	*27.2	George Gervin	San Antonio
1978–79	*29.6	George Gervin	San Antonio
1979–80	*33.1	George Gervin	San Antonio
1980–81	*30.7	Adrian Dantley	Utah
1981–82	*32.3	George Gervin	San Antonio
1982–83	*28.4	Alex English	Denver
1983–84	*30.6	Adrian Dantley	Utah
1984–85	*32.9	Bernard King	New York
1985–86	*30.3	Dominique Wilkins	Atlanta
1986–87	*37.1	Michael Jordan	Chicago
1987–88	*35.0	Michael Jordan	Chicago
1988–89	*32.5	Michael Jordan	Chicago
1989–90	*33.6	Michael Jordan	Chicago
1990–91	*31.2	Michael Jordan	Chicago
1991–92	*30.1	Michael Jordan	Chicago
1992–93	*32.6	Michael Jordan	Chicago
1993–94	*29.8	David Robinson	San Antonio
1994–95	*29.3	Shaquille O'Neal	Orlando

*Scoring title based on best average with at least 70 games played or 1,400 points

ALL-TIME NBA REGULAR-SEASON RECORDS

INDIVIDUAL
Single Game
Most Points: 100, Wilt Chamberlain, Philadelphia vs. New York, at Hershey, Pa., March 2, 1962
Most FG Attempted: 63, Wilt Chamberlain, Philadelphia vs. New York, at Hershey, Pa., March 2, 1962
Most FG Made: 36, Wilt Chamberlain, Philadelphia vs. New York, at Hershey, Pa., March 2, 1962
Most Consecutive FG Made: 18, Wilt Chamberlain, San Francisco

vs New York, at Boston, Nov. 27, 1963; Wilt Chamberlain, Philadelphia vs. Baltimore, at Pittsburgh, Feb. 24, 1967

Most 3-Pt FG Attempted: 20, Michael Adams, Denver vs L.A. Clippers, April 12, 1991

Most 3-Pt FG Made: 10, Brian Shaw, Miami at Milwaukee, April 8, 1993; Joe Dumars, Detroit vs Minnesota, at Detroit, Nov. 8, 1994

Most FT Attempted: 34, Wilt Chamberlain, Philadelphia vs St. Louis, at Philadelphia, Feb. 22, 1962

Most FT Made: 28, Wilt Chamberlain, Philadelphia vs New York, at Hershey, Pa., March 2, 1962; Adrian Dantley, Utah vs Houston at Las Vegas, Nev., Jan. 4, 1984

Most Consecutive FT Made: 19, Bob Pettit, St. Louis vs Boston, at Boston, Nov. 22, 1961; Bill Cartright, New York vs Kansas City, at N.Y., Nov. 17, 1981; Adrian Dantley, Detroit vs Chicago, at Chicago, Dec. 15, 1987 (OT)

Most FT Missed: 22, Wilt Chamberlain, Philadelphia vs Seattle, at Boston, Dec. 1, 1967

Most Rebounds: 55, Wilt Chamberlain, Philadelphia vs Boston, Nov. 24, 1960

Most Assists: 30, Scott Skiles, Orlando vs Denver, at Orlando, Dec. 30, 1990

Most Blocked Shots: 17, Elmore Smith, Los Angeles vs Portland, Oct. 28, 1973

Most Steals: 11, Larry Kenon, San Antonio at Kansas City, Dec. 26, 1976

Most Personal Fouls: 8, Don Otten, Tri-Cities at Sheboygan, Nov. 24, 1949

Season

Most Points: 4,029, Wilt Chamberlain, Philadelphia, 1961–62

Highest Average: 50.4, Wilt Chamberlain, Philadelphia, 1961–62

Most FG Attempted: 3,159, Wilt Chamberlain, Philadelphia, 1961–62

Most FG Made: 1,597, Wilt Chamberlain, Philadelphia, 1961–62

Highest FG Percentage: .727, Wilt Chamberlain, Los Angeles, 1972–73

Most 3-Pt. FG Attempted: 611, John Starks, New York, 1994–95

Most 3-Pt FG Made: 217, John Starks, New York, 1994–95

Most FT Attempted: 1,363, Wilt Chamberlain, Philadelphia, 1961–62

Most FT Made: 840, Jerry West, Los Angeles, 1965–66

Highest FT Percentage: .958, Calvin Murphy, Houston, 1980–81

Most Rebounds: 2,149, Wilt Chamberlain, Philadelphia, 1960–61

Most Assists: 1,164, John Stockton, Utah, 1990–91
Most Blocked Shots: 456, Mark Eaton, Utah, 1984–85
Most Steals: 301, Alvin Robertson, San Antonio, 1985–86
Most Personal Fouls: 386, Darryl Dawkins, New Jersey, 1983–84
Most Disqualifications: 26, Don Meineke, Fort Wayne, 1952–53

Career
Most Games: 1,560, Kareem Abdul-Jabbar, Milwaukee and Los Angeles Lakers, 1969–89
Most Minutes: 57,446, Kareem Abdul-Jabbar, Milwaukee and Los Angeles Lakers, 1969–89
Most Points Scored: 38,387, Kareem Abdul-Jabbar, Milwaukee and Los Angeles Lakers, 1969–89
Highest Scoring Average: 32.2, Michael Jordan, Chicago, 1984–95
Most FG Attempted: 28,307, Kareem Abdul-Jabbar, Milwaukee and Los Angeles Lakers, 1969–89
Most FG Made: 15,837, Kareem Abdul-Jabbar, 1969–89
Highest FG Percentage: .599, Artis Gilmore, Chicago, San Antonio, Boston, 1976–88
Most 3-Pt FG Attempted: 2,816, Michael Adams, Sacramento, Denver, Washington, 1985–95
Most 3-Pt FG Made: 1,119, Dale Ellis, Dallas, Seattle, Milwaukee, San Antonio, 1983–95
Most FT Attempted: 11,862, Wilt Chamberlain, 1960–73
Most FT Made: 8,531, Moses Malone, Buffalo, Houston, Philadelphia, Washington, Atlanta, Milwaukee, San Antonio, 1976–95
Highest FT Percentage: .906, Mark Price, Cleveland, 1986–95
Most Rebounds: 23,924, Wilt Chamberlain, 1960–73
Most Assists: 10,394, John Stockton, Utah, 1984–95
Most Blocked Shots: 3,189, Kareem Abdul-Jabbar, Milwaukee and Los Angeles Lakers, 1969–89
Most Steals: 2,310, Maurice Cheeks, Philadelphia, San Antonio, New York, Atlanta and New Jersey, 1978–93
Most Personal Fouls: 4,657, Kareem Abdul-Jabbar, Milwaukee and Los Angeles Lakers, 1970–89
Most Times Disqualified: 127, Vern Mikkelsen, Minneapolis, 1950–59

TEAM RECORDS
Single Game
Most Points, One Team: 173, Boston, vs Minneapolis at Boston, Feb. 27, 1959; Phoenix, vs Denver at Phoenix, Nov. 10, 1990; 186, Detroit, vs Denver at Denver, Dec. 13, 1983 (3 overtimes)

Mark Price has mark for highest FT percentage.

442 • THE COMPLETE HANDBOOK OF PRO BASKETBALL

Most Points, Two Teams: 320, Golden State 162 vs Denver 158 at Denver, Nov. 2, 1990; 370, Detroit 186 vs Denver 184 at Denver, Dec. 13, 1983 (3 overtimes)

Most FG Attempted, One Team: 153, Philadelphia, vs Los Angeles at Philadelphia (3 overtimes), Dec. 8, 1961; 150, Boston, vs Philadelphia at Philadelphia, March 2, 1960

Most FG Attempted, Two Teams: 291, Philadelphia 153 vs Los Angeles 138 at Philadelphia (3 overtimes), Dec. 8, 1961; 274, Boston 149 vs Detroit 125 at Boston, Jan. 27, 1961; Philadelphia 141 vs Boston 133 at Boston, March 5, 1961

Most FG Made, One Team: 74, Denver, vs Detroit at Denver, Dec. 13, 1983 (3 overtimes); 72, Boston, vs Minneapolis at Boston, Feb. 27, 1959

Most FG Made, Two Teams: 142, Detroit 74 vs Denver 68 at Denver, Dec. 13, 1983 (3 overtimes); 134, San Diego 67 vs Cincinnati 67 at Cincinnati, March 12, 1970

Most FT Attempted, One Team: 86, Syracuse, vs Anderson at Syracuse (5 overtimes), Nov. 24, 1949; 71, Chicago, vs Phoenix at Chicago, Jan. 8, 1970

Most FT Attempted, Two Teams: 160, Syracuse 86 vs Anderson 74 at Syracuse (5 overtimes), Nov. 24, 1949; 127, Fort Wayne 67 vs Minneapolis 60 at Fort Wayne. Dec. 31, 1954

Most FT Made, One Team: 61, Phoenix, vs Utah, April 4, 1990 (1 overtime); 60, Washington, vs New York at New York, Nov. 13, 1987

Most FT Made, Two Teams: 116, Syracuse 59 vs Anderson 57 at Syracuse (5 overtimes), Nov. 24, 1949; 103, Boston 56 vs Minneapolis 47 at Minneapolis, Nov. 28, 1954

Most Rebounds, One Team: 109, Boston, vs Denver at Boston, Dec. 24, 1960

Most Rebounds, Two Teams: 188, Philadelphia 98 vs Los Angeles 90 at Philadelphia, Dec. 8, 1961 (3 overtimes); 177, Philadelphia 104 vs Syracuse 73 at Philadelphia, Nov. 4, 1959; Boston 89 vs Philadelphia 88 at Philadelphia, Dec. 27, 1960

Most Assists, One Team: 53, Milwaukee, vs Detroit at Milwaukee, Dec. 26, 1978

Most Assists, Two Teams: 93, Detroit 47 vs Denver 46 at Denver, Dec. 13, 1983 (3 overtimes); 88, Phoenix 47 vs San Diego 41 at Tucson, Ariz., March 15, 1969; San Antonio 50 vs Denver 38 at San Antonio, April 15, 1984

Most Blocked Shots, One Team: 22, New Jersey, vs Denver at New Jersey, Dec. 12, 1991

Most Blocked Shots, Two Teams: 34, Detroit 19 vs Washington 15 at Washington, Nov. 19, 1981

Jerry West: Most free throws in a season.

Most Steals, One Team: 25, Golden State, vs San Antonio at Golden State, Feb. 15, 1989

Most Steals, Two Teams: 40, Golden State 24 vs Los Angeles 16 at Golden State, Jan. 21, 1975; Philadelphia 24 vs Detroit 16 at Philadelphia, Nov. 11, 1978; Golden State 25 vs San Antonio 15 at Golden State, Feb. 15, 1989

Most Personal Fouls, One Team: 66, Anderson, at Syracuse (5 overtimes), Nov. 24, 1949; 55, Milwaukee vs Baltimore at Baltimore, Nov. 12, 1952

Most Personal Fouls, Two Teams: 122, Anderson 66 vs Syracuse 56 at Syracuse (5 overtimes), Nov. 24, 1949; 97, Syracuse 50 vs New York 47 at Syracuse, Feb. 15, 1953

Most Disqualifications, One Team: 8, Syracuse, vs Baltimore at Syracuse (1 overtime), Nov. 15, 1952; 6, Syracuse vs Boston at Boston, Dec. 26, 1950

Most Disqualifications, Two Teams: 13, Syracuse 8 vs Baltimore 5 at Syracuse (1 overtime), Nov. 15, 1952; 11, Syracuse 6 vs Boston 5, Dec. 26, 1950

Most Points in a Losing Game: 184, Denver, vs Detroit at Denver Dec. 13, 1983 (3 overtimes); 158, Denver vs Golden State at Golden State, Nov. 2, 1990

Widest Point Spread: 68, Cleveland 148 vs Miami 80 at Miami, Dec. 17, 1991

Season

Most Games Won: 69, Los Angeles, 1971–72
Most Games Lost: 73, Philadelphia, 1972–73
Longest Winning Streak: 33, Los Angeles, Nov. 5, 1971 to Jan. 7, 1972
Longest Losing Streak: 20, Philadelphia, Jan. 9, 1973 to Feb. 11, 1973; Dallas, Nov. 13 to Dec. 22, 1993
Most Points Scored: 10,731, Denver, 1981–82
Most Points Allowed: 10,723, Denver, 1990–91
Highest Scoring Average: 126.5, Denver, 1981–82
Highest Average, Points Allowed: 130.8, Denver, 1990–91
Most FG Attempted: 9,295, Boston, 1960–61
Most FG Made: 3,980, Denver, 1981–82

ALL-TIME NBA PLAYOFF RECORDS

INDIVIDUAL
Single Game

Most Points: 63, Michael Jordan, Chicago, at Boston, April 20, 1986 (2 overtimes); 61, Elgin Baylor, Los Angeles, at Boston, April 14, 1962

Most FG Attempted; 48, Wilt Chamberlain, Philadelphia, vs. Syracuse at Philadelphia, March 22, 1962; Rick Barry, San Francisco, vs. Philadelphia at San Francisco, April 18, 1967

Most FG Made: 24, Wilt Chamberlain, Philadelphia, vs. Syracuse at Philadelphia, March 14, 1960; John Havlicek, Boston, vs. Atlanta, at Boston, April 1, 1973; Michael Jordan, Chicago, vs. Cleveland, at Chicago, May 1, 1988

Most 3-Point FG Attempted: 15, Dennis Scott, Orlando, vs. Indiana, May 25, 1995; Nick Van Exel, Los Angeles Lakers, vs. Seattle, May 4, 1995

Most 3-Point FG Made: 8, Dan Majerle, Phoenix, vs. Seattle at Phoenix, June 1, 1993

Most FT Attempted: 32, Bob Cousy, Boston, vs. Syracuse at Boston, March 21, 1953 (4 overtimes); 28, Michael Jordan, Chicago, vs. New York at Chicago, March 14, 1989

Most FT Made: 30, Bob Cousy, Boston, vs. Syracuse at Boston, March 21, 1953 (4 overtimes); 23, Michael Jordan, Chicago, vs. New York at Chicago, March 14, 1989

Most Rebounds: 41, Wilt Chamberlain, Philadelphia, vs. Boston at Philadelphia, April 5, 1967

Most Blocked Shots: 10, Mark Eaton, Utah, vs. Houston at Utah, April 26, 1985; Hakeem Olajuwon, Houston, at Los Angeles Lakers, April 29, 1990

Most Assists: 24, Magic Johnson, L.A. Lakers vs. Phoenix at Los Angeles, May 15, 1984; John Stockton, Utah, at L.A. Lakers, May 17, 1988

Most Steals: 8, done 6 times, most recently by Tim Hardaway, Golden State, at Seattle, April 30, 1992

Most Personal Fouls: 8, Jack Toomay, at New York, March 26, 1949 (overtime)

TEAM
Single Game

Most Points, One Team: 157, Boston, vs. New York at Boston, April 28, 1990

Most Points, Two Teams: 304, Portland 153 at Phoenix 151, May 11, 1992 (2 overtimes); 285, San Antonio 152 vs. Denver 133 at San Antonio, April 26, 1983; Boston 157 vs. New York 128, at Boston, April 28, 1990

Fewest Points, One Team: 70, Golden State, vs. Los Angeles at Golden State, April 21, 1973; Seattle, at Houston, April 23, 1982

Fewest Points, Two Teams: 145, Fort Wayne 74 vs. Syracuse 71, at Indianapolis, April 7, 1955

Most FG Attempted, One Team: 140, Boston, vs. Syracuse at Boston, March 18, 1959; San Francisco, at Philadelphia, April 14, 1967 (overtime)

Most FG Attempted, Two Teams: 257, Boston 135 vs. Philadelphia 122, at Boston, March 22, 1960

Most FG Made, One Team: 67, Milwaukee, at Philadelphia, March 30, 1970; San Antonio, vs. Denver at San Antonio, May 4, 1983; Los Angeles Lakers, vs. Denver at Los Angeles, May 22, 1985

Most FG Made, Two Teams: 119, Milwaukee 67 at Philadelphia 52, March 30, 1970

Most 3-Point FG Attempted, One Team: 32, Houston, at Orlando June 7, 1995

Most 3-Point FG Attempted, Two Teams: 62, Houston 32 at Orlando 30, June 7, 1995

Most 3-Point FG Made, One Team: 19, Houston, vs. Utah, April 29, 1995

Most 3-Point FG Made, Two Teams: 28, Houston 19 vs. Utah 9, April 29, 1995

Most FT Attempted, One Team: 70, St. Louis, vs. Minneapolis at St. Louis, March 17, 1956

Most FT Attempted, Two Teams: 128, Syracuse 64 at Boston 64, March 21, 1953 (4 overtimes); 122, St. Louis 70 vs. Minneapolis 52, at St. Louis, March 17, 1956; Minneapolis 68 vs. St. Louis 54, at Minneapolis, March 21, 1956

Most FT Made, One Team: 57, Boston, vs. Syracuse at Boston, March 21, 1953 (4 overtimes); Phoenix, vs. Seattle at Phoenix, June 5, 1993

Most FT Made, Two Teams: 108, Boston 57 vs. Syracuse 51 at Boston, March 21, 1953 (4 overtimes); 91, St. Louis 54 vs. Minneapolis 37 at St. Louis, March 17, 1956

Most Rebounds, One Team: 97, Boston, vs. Philadelphia at Boston, March 19, 1960

Most Rebounds, Two Teams; 169, Boston 89 vs. Philadelphia 80 at Boston, March 22, 1960; San Francisco 93 at Philadelphia 76, April 16, 1967

Most Assists, One Team: 51, San Antonio, vs. Denver at San Antonio, May 4, 1983

Most Assists, Two Teams: 79, Los Angeles Lakers 44 vs. Boston 35, at Los Angeles, June 4, 1987

Most Blocked Shots, One Team: 20, Philadelphia, vs. Milwaukee at Philadelphia, April 5, 1981

Most Blocked Shots, Two Teams: 29, Philadelphia 20 vs. Milwaukee 9, at Philadelphia, April 5, 1981

Most Steals, One Team: 22, Golden State, vs. Seattle at Golden State, April 14, 1975

Most Steals, Two Teams: 35, Golden State 22 vs. Seattle 13, at Golden State, April 14, 1975

Most Personal Fouls, One Team: 55, Syracuse, at Boston, March 21, 1953 (4 overtimes); 45, Syracuse, at New York, April 8, 1952

Most Personal Fouls, Two Teams: 106, Syracuse 55 at Boston 51, March 21, 1953 (4 overtimes); 82, Syracuse 45 at New York 37, April 8, 1952

Most Disqualifications, One Team: 7, Syracuse, at Boston, March 21, 1953 (4 overtimes)

Most Disqualifications, Two Teams: 12, Syracuse 7 at Boston 5, March 21, 1953 (4 overtimes); 7, Los Angeles 4 at Detroit 3, April 3, 1962

Widest Point Spread: 58, Minneapolis 133 vs. St. Louis 75, at Minneapolis, March 19, 1956

Official 1995-96 NBA Schedule

*Afternoon (Local Time)

Fri Nov 3
Mil at Bos
Wash at Phil
Cle at Orl
Ind at Atl
NJ at Tor
NY at Det
Char at Chi
GS at Hou
Dal at SA
Sea at Utah
Phoe at LAC
Den at LAL
Minn at Sac
Van at Port

Sat Nov 4
Det at Wash
Cle at Mia
Phil at Char
Orl at Atl
Tor at Ind
Bos at Chi
NY at Mil
GS at Dal
SA at Den
LAL at Sea

Sun Nov 5
Hou at Phoe
LAC at Sac
Utah at Port
Minn at Van

Mon Nov 6
Wash at Orl
Atl at Utah

Tue Nov 7
Phoe at NY
Port at NJ
Sac at Phil
Det at Char
Ind at Cle
Tor at Chi
LAL at Minn
Van at Dal
Mil at Hou

Den at GS
LAC at Sea

Wed Nov 8
Phoe at Bos
Char at Wash
NJ at Orl
Hou at Mia
Sac at Tor
Port at Det
Van at SA
Sea at Den
LAL at Utah
Atl at LAC

Thu Nov 9
Ind at NY
Chi at Cle
Mil at Dal
Atl at GS

Fri Nov 10
Orl at Bos
Char at Phil
NY at Wash
NJ at Mia
Phoe at Tor
Cle at Det
Sac at Ind
Port at Minn
Mil at SA
Den at Utah
Sea at LAL
LAC at Van

Sat Nov 11
Sac at NJ
Mia at Orl
Tor at Char
Port at Chi
Atl at Dal
Minn at Hou
LAL at GS
Van at Sea

Sun Nov 12
Utah at NY
SA at Cle

GS at Phoe
Den at LAC

Mon Nov 13
Utah at Tor
Dal at Van

Tue Nov 14
Sea at Phil
Chi at Orl
Char at Atl
SA at Mil
LAC at GS
LAL at Sac
NY at Port

Wed Nov 15
Utah at Bos
Char at NJ
Phil at Wash
Ind at Mia
Hou at Tor
Sea at Det
Cle at Chi
SA at Minn
Den at Phoe
Dal at LAL

Thu Nov 16
Ind at Orl
Hou at Mil
Van vs LAC
 at Anaheim
NY at GS
Sac at Port

Fri Nov 17
Wash at Bos
Cle at Phil
Sea at Char
Mia at Atl
Minn at Tor
Utah at Det
NJ at Chi
NY at Den
Dal at LAC
Phoe at Sac
LAL at Van

Sat Nov 18
Phil at NJ
Tor at Wash
Orl at Mia
Det at Cle
Sea at Ind
Bos at Mil
Utah at Minn
Den at Hou
Char at SA
Port at Phoe
Dal at GS

Sun Nov 19
Van at NY
LAC at LAL
Atl at Sac

Mon Nov 20
Hou at Bos
GS at Orl
NJ at Utah
LAC at Port

Tue Nov 21
Sea at Tor
Chi at Dal
Atl at Den
Port at LAL

Wed Nov 22
Hou at Phil
Van at Orl
GS at Mia
Bos at Char
NY at Cle
Wash at Det
Tor at Mil
Sea at Minn
Chi at SA
Sac at Utah
Atl at Phoe
NJ at LAC

Thu Nov 23
Hou at Ind

Latrell Sprewell again led Warriors in scoring.

Fri Nov 24
GS at Bos
Mia vs Wash
  at Balt
Van at Char
Phil at Det
Cle at Ind
Orl at Minn
Den at Dal
Chi at Utah
Sac at LAL
NJ at Port
SA at Sea

Sat Nov 25
*Hou at NY
GS at Phil
Orl at Wash
Van at Mia
Tor at Atl
Mil at Cle
Utah at Den
LAL at Phoe
SA at LAC

Sun Nov 26
Char at Bos
Hou at Det
Minn at Mil
NJ at Sac
Chi at Sea

Mon Nov 27
Det at Orl
GS at Tor
Utah at Phoe
Chi at Port

Tue Nov 28
Atl at NY
Wash at NJ
Dal at Mia
Tor at Cle
Char at Mil
Van at Minn
LAC at Hou
Den at Sac
Ind at Sea

Wed Nov 29
Det at Bos
NY at Char
Phil at Atl
LAC at SA

Phoe at LAL
Port at GS

Thu Nov 30
Cle at Wash
Dal at Orl
Mia at Det
Utah at Hou
Ind at Sac
Mil at Port
Chi at Van

Fri Dec 1
NJ at Bos
Char at Mia
Dal at Atl
Phil at Tor
Minn at Phoe
Van at LAL
Mil at Sea

Sat Dec 2
Cle at NJ
NY at Phil
Bos vs Wash
  at Balt
Atl at Det
Char at Hou
Phoe at SA
Minn at Den
Chi vs LAC
  at Anaheim
Ind at GS
Orl at Sac

Sun Dec 3
Wash at NY
Mia at Tor
Dal at Cle
Ind at LAL
Orl at Port
*Mil at Van

Mon Dec 4
Mia at Bos
Det at Den

Tue Dec 5
Dal at NY
Phil at Ind
LAL at SA
Hou at Utah
Van at Phoe
Orl at LAC
Tor at Sea

Wed Dec 6
Dal at Phil
Atl at Wash
Bos at Mia
Cle at Char
NY at Chi
NJ at Minn
LAL at Hou
Orl at GS

Thu Dec 7
SA at Atl
LAC at Mil
Den at Utah
Tor at Port
Det at Van

Fri Dec 8
Ind at NJ
Char at Orl
Phil at Cle
SA at Chi
LAC at Minn
Wash at Hou
Phoe at Den
Tor at LAL
Det at GS
Sea at Sac

Sat Dec 9
Bos at Phil
Minn at Char
NY at Atl
NJ at Cle
Chi at Mil
Wash at Dal
GS at Utah
Mia at Phoe
Port at Sea

Sun Dec 10
SA at NY
*LAC at Ind
Det at LAL
Mia at Sac
Hou at Port
Tor at Van

Mon Dec 11
Den at Phil
Char at Utah

Tue Dec 12
LAL at NY
Orl at NJ

Mil at Wash
Minn at Atl
Bos at Tor
LAC at Cle
Den at Ind
Sea at Dal
Char at Phoe
Mia at GS
Hou at Sac

Wed Dec 13
Phil at Bos
LAL at Det
Orl at Chi
Sea at SA
Hou at Van

Thu Dec 14
Den at NY
Chi at Atl
Ind at Tor
SA at Dal
Mia at LAC
Char at Port

Fri Dec 15
Tor at Bos
LAL at Wash
Utah at Orl
NJ at Det
Mil at Ind
Cle at Minn
Sac at Hou
GS at Sea
Port at Van

Sat Dec 16
Det at NY
Utah at Mia
Den at Atl
LAL at Chi
Phoe at Dal
Sac at SA
Char at LAC
GS at Van

Sun Dec 17
Orl at Tor
Den at Cle
Ind at Mil
Phil at Minn
*Wash at Port

Mon Dec 18
Chi at Bos

Rik Smits' playoff performance highlighted best season.

Brian Grant made the All-NBA Rookie team.

Jamal Mashburn was fifth in the league in scoring.

NBA SCHEDULE • 453

Utah at NJ
Van at Sac

Tue Dec 19
Mia at NY
Det at Tor
Minn at Cle
Dal at Chi
LAL at Mil
Phoe at Hou
Port at SA
Wash at LAC
Char at GS
Sea at Van

Wed Dec 20
Mia at NJ
Utah at Phil
Minn at Orl
Mil at Det
LAL at Ind
GS at Den
Wash at Phoe

Thu Dec 21
Bos at Char
Utah at Cle
Port at Hou
Den at SA
Sac at LAC
Van at Sea

Fri Dec 22
Minn at Bos
Mil at Phil
NY at Orl
Det at Mia
NJ at Atl
Dal at Ind
Tor at Chi
Sac at LAL
Wash at GS
Phoe at Van

Sat Dec 23
Tor at NY
NJ at Phil
Mia at Char
Ind at Cle
Orl at Det
Utah at Chi
Atl at Mil
Dal at Minn
Hou at SA
LAC at Den

LAL at Port
Wash at Sea

Mon Dec 25
Hou at Orl
*SA at Phoe

Tue Dec 26
NJ at Mia
LAC at Atl
*Mil vs Tor
 at Hamilton,
 Ontario
GS at Det
Chi at Ind
Van at Hou
Dal at Den
Port at Utah
Bos at LAL
SA at Sac

Wed Dec 27
GS at Wash
LAC at Char
Mil at Minn
Phil at Phoe
Bos at Port
Den at Sea

Thu Dec 28
Cle at NY
Tor at Det
Mia at Ind
Van at Dal
NJ at Hou
Minn at Utah
SA at LAL

Fri Dec 29
NY at Wash
LAC at Orl
Port at Char
GS at Atl
Ind at Chi
Den at Phoe
Phil at Sac
Bos at Sea

Sat Dec 30
GS at NJ
LAC at Mia
Port at Cle
Char at Det
Atl at Chi
Wash at Mil

Hou at Dal
Minn at SA
Phil at Den
*LAL at Utah
Sea at Phoe
Bos at Van

Tue Jan 2
Port at NY
Mil at NJ
Cle at Wash
Sea at Atl
Hou at Minn
Utah at Dal
Ind at Den
Phil at LAL

Wed Jan 3
Port at Bos
Tor at Orl
Hou at Chi
Det at Mil
Utah at SA
Ind at LAC
Phil at GS

Thu Jan 4
NJ at NY
Dal at Wash
Sea at Mia
Chi at Char
Tor at Atl
Minn at Phoe
Den at Sac

Fri Jan 5
Cle at Bos
Dal at NJ
Sea at Orl
Port at Mil
Ind at SA
Phoe at LAC
Utah at LAL
Minn at GS
Phil at Van

Sat Jan 6
Atl at Char
Orl at Cle
Wash at Det
Mil at Chi
Ind at Hou
Mia at Den
GS at Sac

Sun Jan 7
Dal at Bos
Sea at NY
Atl at NJ
Den at LAL
Minn at Port
*LAC at Van

Mon Jan 8
Orl at Phil
Wash at Cle
Mia at Utah

Tue Jan 9
Bos at NY
NJ at Orl
Sac at Atl
Char at Tor
Sea at Mil
Ind at Dal
SA at Hou
LAC at Phoe
Minn at LAL
Van at GS

Wed Jan 10
Sac at Bos
NY at NJ
Wash at Phil
Sea at Chi
Cle at SA
Mia at Port
Den at Van

Thu Jan 11
Det at Char
Atl at Tor
Mil at Ind
Minn at LAC
Phoe at GS

Fri Jan 12
NY at Bos
Phil at NJ
Sac at Wash
Mil at Orl
Cle at Den
SA at Utah
Dal at Phoe
Hou at LAL
Mia at Sea
GS at Van

Sat Jan 13
Sac at NY

Det at NJ
Chi at Phil
Bos at Atl
Wash at Tor
*Minn at Ind
Char at Dal
Orl at SA
Port at Den
Hou at LAC
Mia at Van

Sun Jan 14
Cle at Phoe

Mon Jan 15
*Mil at NY
Tor at NJ
*Chi at Wash
*Det at Atl
*Sac at Minn
Orl at Dal
Utah at Hou
*Mia at LAL
*Sea at GS

Tue Jan 16
Ind at Tor
Phil at Chi
Bos at SA
Den at Port
Cle at Sea

Wed Jan 17
Mil at Phil
Wash at Mia
NJ at Char
Ind at Atl
GS at Minn
Hou at Den
Orl at Phoe
NY at LAC

Thu Jan 18
Chi at Tor
SA at Det
GS at Mil
Bos at Hou
Port at Sac
Cle at Van

Fri Jan 19
Atl at Phil
NJ vs Wash
 at Balt
Char at Mia

Det at Ind
SA at Minn
Bos at Dal
Orl at Utah
LAL at LAC
Phoe at Port
NY at Sea

Sat Jan 20
Minn at NJ
GS at Char
Mia at Atl
Sac at Den
Utah vs LAC
 at Anaheim
Cle at LAL
NY at Van

Sun Jan 21
SA at Phil
*Bos at Tor
*Chi at Det
*Wash at Ind
*Orl at Hou
Sac at Phoe
Cle at Port
Dal at Sea

Mon Jan 22
SA at Mia
Hou at Atl
Van at Mil

Tue Jan 23
Chi at NY
Phil at Orl
NJ at Tor
Atl at Cle
Phoe at Ind
Port at Utah
Dal at Sac

Wed Jan 24
LAL at Bos
Hou at NJ
Cle at Phil
NY at Mia
Wash at Char
Van at Chi
Ind at Mil
Phoe at Minn
Det at SA
Utah at GS
Den at Sea

Thu Jan 25
Hou at Wash
Van at Tor
Det at Dal
Den at LAC

Fri Jan 26
Ind at Bos
Char at NJ
LAL at Phil
Orl at Atl
Mia at Chi
Phoe at Mil
Port at SA
Sac at GS
Utah at Sea

Sat Jan 27
Atl at Bos
Minn at NY
LAL at NJ
Van at Wash
Phil at Char
Mia at Cle
Orl at Ind
Port at Dal
Det at Hou
Tor at Den
GS at Utah
Sea vs LAC
 at Anaheim

Sun Jan 28
*Phoe at Chi

Mon Jan 29
Mia at NY
Van at Phil
Cle at Char
Det at Utah
Sea at Port

Tue Jan 30
Bos at Orl
Phoe at Mia
Atl at Ind
Den at Minn
LAC at Dal
Chi at Hou
GS at LAL
Tor at Sac
NJ at Sea

Wed Jan 31
Van at Bos

Phoe at Atl
Mil at Cle
LAC at SA
Utah at Port

Thu Feb 1
Orl at NY
Phil at Mia
Hou at Char
Ind at Det
Den at Mil
Sea at Dal
Chi at Sac

Fri Feb 2
Port at Wash
Atl at Orl
Phoe at Cle
Bos at Ind
Minn at SA
LAC at Utah
Chi at LAL
Tor at GS
NJ at Van

Sat Feb 3
Port at Phil
Bos at Mia
Sac at Det
Cle at Mil
Minn at Dal
Sea at Hou
Tor at LAC

Sun Feb 4
*Phoe at Wash
*SA at Orl
Char at Atl
*NY at Ind
Chi at Den
Utah at LAL
NJ at GS

Mon Feb 5
Det at NY
Sac at Mia
Port at Tor
Dal at Minn
GS at LAC
Utah at Van

Tue Feb 6
Sac at Orl
SA at Char
Bos at Cle

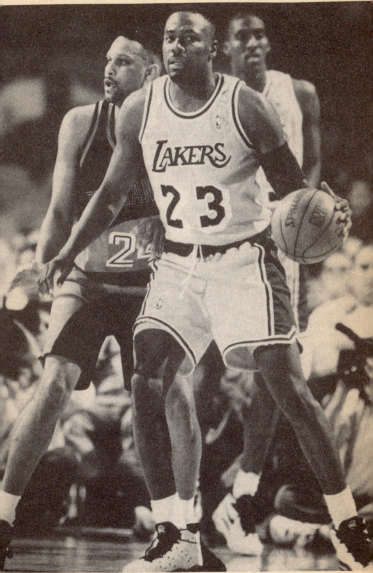
Cedric Ceballos produced a 50-point game.

Dal at Mil
LAL at Den
Chi at Phoe
Hou at Sea

Wed Feb 7
SA at Bos
Wash at NY
Ind at Phil
Atl at Mia
Mil at Tor
Orl at Det
Port at Minn
Van at Utah
Hou at LAC
NJ at LAL
Chi at GS

Thu Feb 8
Sac at Char
Wash at Atl
Utah at Dal
LAC at Den
NJ at Phoe

Sun Feb 11
ALL-STAR GAME
at SA

Tue Feb 13
Den at Orl
Tor at Mia
Char at Cle
NJ at Ind
Wash at Chi
Phil at Mil
Dal at Hou
Utah at SA
Sea at Phoe
Bos at LAC
Minn at Sac
GS at Port

Wed Feb 14
Ind at NJ
Det at Phil
NY at Char
Atl at LAL
Bos at GS
Minn at Sea
Sac at Van

Thu Feb 15
Den at Mia

Cle vs Tor
 at Hamilton,
 Ontario
Chi at Det
Wash at Mil
SA at Hou
Dal at Utah
Phoe at Port

Fri Feb 16
Phil at NY
Ind vs Wash
 at Balt
Mil at Orl
Den at Char
Chi at Minn
GS at SA
Dal at LAL
Bos at Sac
Phoe at Sea
Atl at Van

Sat Feb 17
NY at NJ
Orl at Mia
Phil at Cle
Tor at Det
Port vs LAC
 at Anaheim

Sun Feb 18
*Mil at Char
*Chi at Ind
*Wash at Minn
*Hou at SA
Bos at Den
Atl at Port
*Sea at Van

Mon Feb 19
*NJ at Wash
*Mia at Cle
Minn at Det
GS at Dal
Sac at Hou
Van at Phoe
Atl at Sea

Tue Feb 20
Mil at NY
Phil at Orl
Cle at Chi
Bos at Utah
LAC at LAL
SA at Port

Wed Feb 21
Mia at Phil
Wash at Char
NY at Det
Orl at Ind
NJ at Mil
Hou at Minn
Sac at Dal
Bos at Phoe
LAL at LAC
SA at GS

Thu Feb 22
Chi at Atl
Hou at Cle
Tor at Utah
Den at Port
GS at Sea

Fri Feb 23
Atl at NY
Char at Wash
Chi at Mia
Phil at Ind
Orl at Mil
Det at Minn
LAL at Dal
Tor at Phoe
SA at Sac

Sat Feb 24
Ind at Char
NJ at Cle
LAL at Hou
Utah at Den
LAC at GS
Sac at Sea

Sun Feb 25
Bos at NJ
*Mil at Wash
Phil at Mia
*Orl at Chi
*Atl at Minn
Tor at Dal
*NY at Phoe
Sea at LAC
*Det at Port
*SA at Van

Mon Feb 26
Ind at Bos
Phoe at Utah
NY at LAL
Det at Sac

Tue Feb 27
Mia at NJ
GS at Cle
Port at Ind
Minn at Chi
Char at Mil
Phil at Dal
Tor at Hou
Wash at Den
SA vs LAC
 at Anaheim

Wed Feb 28
Char at Bos
Mia at Orl
Port at Atl
Phoe at Minn
Wash at Utah
NY at Sac
Det at Sea
LAL at Van

Thu Feb 29
Orl at NJ
GS at Ind
Cle at Mil
Phil at Hou
Tor at SA
Dal at Den
Sac at LAC

Fri Mar 1
Sea at Bos
Port at Mia
Cle at Atl
GS at Chi
Char at Minn
NY at Utah
Det at Phoe
Wash at LAL
Dal at Van

Sat Mar 2
Sea at NJ
Port at Orl
Bos at Chi
Atl at Mil
Phil at SA
Van at Den
Det at LAC

Sun Mar 3
GS at NY
*Tor at Cle
*Char at Ind

*Mia at Minn
*Phoe at Dal
*Hou at LAL
Wash at Sac

Mon Mar 4
Mil at Bos
Atl at Det
SA at Den
Wash at Van

Tue Mar 5
LAC at NY
Minn at Mia
Orl at Char
Det at Tor
Sea at Cle
Mil at Chi
NJ at Dal
Ind at Phoe
Van at GS
Utah at Sac
Hou at Port

Wed Mar 6
LAC at Bos
Minn at Phil
Sea at Wash
NY at Tor
Den at SA
Ind at Utah

Thu Mar 7
Dal at Char
Atl at Cle
Det at Chi
Phoe at Den
Hou at GS
LAL at Sac

Fri Mar 8
Cle at Bos
NY at Phil
LAC at Wash
Char at Orl
Tor at Mia
Mil at Atl
Sea at Minn
NJ at SA
Hou at Utah
LAL at Phoe
Sac at Port
Ind at Van

Sat Mar 9
Dal at Det
GS at Den

Sun Mar 10
Chi at NY
*LAC at Phil
*Atl at Wash
*Phoe at Orl
*Cle at Mia
Dal at Tor
*Bos at Mil
*Utah at Minn
NJ at Den
Sac at GS
Ind at Port
SA at Sea
*Hou at Van

Mon Mar 11
LAC at Det
Van at Sac

Tue Mar 12
Phoe at NJ
Tor at Phil
Utah at Atl
Mia at Dal
Orl at Den
Port at LAL
SA at GS

Wed Mar 13
Phil at Bos
Utah at Char
Phoe at Det
Wash at Chi
NY at Minn
Mil at Sac
Orl at Sea

Thu Mar 14
Wash at NJ
Bos at Cle
Atl at Hou
Mia at SA
Dal vs LAC
  at Anaheim
LAL at GS

Fri Mar 15
Phoe at Phil
Tor at Char
Cle at Det
Utah at Ind

Den at Chi
Sac at Minn
Mil at LAL
LAC at Port
Dal at Sea
Orl at Van

Sat Mar 16
Phil at NY
Chi at NJ
Utah at Wash
Mia at Hou
Atl at SA
Mil at GS

Sun Mar 17
NJ at Bos
Phoe at Char
*Sac at Cle
*Den at Det
*Tor at Ind
*Van at Minn
Orl at LAL
*Dal at Port

Mon Mar 18
Chi at Phil
Den at Tor
Utah at Mil
GS at SA
LAC at Sea

Tue Mar 19
Van at NJ
Det at Orl
Ind at Char
Sac at Chi
Cle at Dal
GS at Hou
Sea at LAL
Minn at Port

Wed Mar 20
Orl at Bos
Ind at NY
SA at Wash
Det at Mia
Van at Atl
Char at Tor
Sac at Mil
Phil at Utah
Minn at LAC

Thu Mar 21
Den at NJ

NY at Chi
Cle at Hou
GS at Phoe
LAL at Sea

Fri Mar 22
Den at Bos
Orl at Wash
Atl at Char
SA at Tor
NJ at Det
Van at Ind
Mia at Mil
Minn at Dal
Cle at Utah
Phil at LAC
Port at Sac

Sat Mar 23
Det at Atl
Minn at Hou
Phoe at GS
Phil at Sea

Sun Mar 24
Mia at Bos
*Den at Wash
*Chi at Tor
*Van at Cle
*SA at Ind
*NJ at Mil
*NY at Dal
LAC at Phoe
Char at LAL
Sea at Sac

Mon Mar 25
SA at NJ
Dal at Utah
Phil at Port

Tue Mar 26
LAL at Orl
Atl at Tor
Wash at Cle
Van at Det
Bos at Ind
NY at Hou
Char at Den
Sac at Phoe
Mil at LAC
Sea at GS

Wed Mar 27
Tor at Phil

Ind at Wash
LAL at Mia
Bos at Minn
Hou at Dal
NY at SA
Mil at Utah
Char at Sea

Thu Mar 28
Atl at Chi
Cle at LAC
GS at Port
Den at Van

Fri Mar 29
NJ at NY
Bos at Phil
Wash at Mia
LAL at Atl
Orl at Tor
Ind at Minn
SA at Dal
Van at Utah
Mil at Phoe
Char at Sac

Sat Mar 30
Phil at Wash
Mia at Det
LAC at Chi
Port at Hou
Mil at Den
Cle at GS
Utah at Sea

Sun Mar 31
*Atl at Bos
*NY at Orl
*LAL at Tor
*NJ at Ind
*LAC at Minn
Port at Dal
*Phoe at SA
Cle at Sac
*Char at Van

Tue Apr 2
Chi at Mia
LAL at Char
Bos at Atl
LAC at Tor
NY at Ind
Det at Mil
Sac at Dal
Minn at Den

Sea at Utah
SA at Phoe
Hou at GS
Van at Port

Wed Apr 3
Orl at NY
LAC at NJ
Ind at Phil
LAL at Chi
Char at Det
Sac at SA
Hou at Sea
Minn at Van

Thu Apr 4
Bos at Orl
Wash at Atl
Cle at Tor
Mia at Chi
Utah at Phoe
Den at GS

Fri April 5
Det at Phil
Chi at Char
NY at Mil
Wash at SA
Port at Den
Minn at Utah
Van at LAL
Hou at Sac
Phoe at Sea

Sat Apr 6
Mil at NJ
Phil at Atl
NY at Tor
Char at Cle
Mia at Ind
LAC at Dal
Minn at GS
Sea at Port

Sun Apr 7
*Det at Bos
Chi at Orl
*Hou at Den
*SA at LAL
Utah at Sac
*Phoe at Van

Mon Apr 8
NJ at Phil
Mia at Wash

Atl at Ind
Char at Chi
Tor at Minn
SA at Utah
Port at LAC
Dal at GS

Tue Apr 9
Bos at NY
Det at NJ
Tor at Mil
Van at Hou
LAL at Den
Port at Phoe
Dal at Sac

Wed Apr 10
Wash at Bos
Cle at Orl
Mia at Char
Phil at Det
LAL at Minn
Van at SA
Phoe at Utah
Sac at Sea

Thu Apr 11
Cle at NY
Chi at NJ
Mil at Mia
Den at Hou
GS vs LAC
  at Anaheim
Dal at Port

Fri Apr 12
Tor at Bos
Minn at Wash
Ind at Orl
Mil at Atl
Phil at Chi
GS at LAL
Sac at Van

Sat Apr 13
*NY at Mia
Det at Ind
*Dal at Hou
*Sea at SA
Utah at LAC

Sun Apr 14
*Atl at NJ
*Char at Phil
*Tor at Wash

*Chi at Cle
Bos at Det
Orl at Mil
*Den at Minn
Phoe at LAL
Utah at GS
LAC at Sac
*Port at Van

Mon Apr 15
Tor at NY
NJ at Mia
Char at Ind
Sea at Hou
Sac at Den
SA at Port

Tue Apr 16
Wash at Orl
Cle at Atl
Chi at Mil
LAL at Dal
LAC at Utah
Hou at Phoe
SA at Van

Wed Apr 17
Tor at NJ
Mia at Phil
Bos at Wash
Ind at Det
GS at Minn
Phoe at Sac
Port at Sea

Thu Apr 18
Atl at Orl
Mil at Char
NY at Cle
Det at Chi
Den at Dal
LAC at Hou
LAL at SA
Utah at Van

Fri Apr 19
Char at NY
Bos at NJ
Orl at Phil
Wash at Tor
Mia at Mil
Van at Den
Dal at Phoe
Port at GS
Minn at Sea

NBA SCHEDULE • 459

Sat Apr 20
NJ at Atl
*Det at Cle
*Ind at Chi
Sac at Utah
Minn at LAL

Sun Apr 21
*NY at Bos
*Chi at Wash
Atl at Mia
*Orl at Char
*Phil at Tor

*Mil at Det
*Cle at Ind
*Phoe at Hou
*Dal at SA

*Sea at Den
*Van at LAC
GS at Sac
LAL at Port

Dennis Rodman: Led NBA again in rebounds and antics.

1995-96 NBA ON NBC
(Starting Time Eastern)

Day	Date	Game	Time
Mon	Dec 25	San Antonio at Phoenix	3:30
Mon	Dec 25	Houston at Orlando	6:00
Sun	Jan 21	Chicago at Detroit	12:00
Sun	Jan 21	Orlando at Houston	2:30
Sun	Jan 28	Phoenix at Chicago	1:00
Sun	Feb 4	New York at Indiana	1:00
Sun	Feb 4	San Antonio at Orlando	3:30
Sun	Feb 11	NBA ALL-STAR GAME at San Antonio	6:00
Sun	Feb 18	Chicago at Indiana	1:00
Sun	Feb 18	Houston at San Antonio*	3:30
Sun	Feb 18	Milwaukee at Charlotte*	3:30
Sun	Feb 25	Orlando at Chicago	1:00
Sun	Feb 25	New York at Phoenix	3:30
Sun	Mar 3	Phoenix at Dallas	1:00
Sun	Mar 3	Charlotte at Indiana*	3:30
Sun	Mar 3	Houston at L.A. Lakers*	3:30
Sun	Mar 10	Phoenix at Orlando	12:30
Sun	Mar 10	Chicago at New York	5:30
Sun	Mar 17	Phoenix at Charlotte*	12:00
Sun	Mar 17	Denver at Detroit*	12:00
Sun	Mar 24	San Antonio at Indiana*	1:00
Sun	Mar 24	New York at Dallas*	1:00
Sun	Mar 31	New York at Orlando	12:00
Sun	Apr 7	San Antonio at L.A. Lakers*	3:00
Sun	Apr 7	Houston at Denver*	3:00
Sun	Apr 7	Chicago at Orlando	5:30
Sat	Apr 13	New York at Miami**	3:30
Sat	Apr 13	Dallas at Houston**	3:30
Sat	Apr 13	Seattle at San Antonio**	3:30
Sun	Apr 14	Chicago at Cleveland	1:00
Sun	Apr 14	Phoenix at L.A. Lakers	3:30
Sat	Apr 20	Indiana at Chicago	3:30
Sun	Apr 21	Orlando at Charlotte**	3:30
Sun	Apr 21	Phoenix at Houston**	3:30
Sun	Apr 21	Milwaukee at Detroit**	3:30
Sun	Apr 21	Dallas at San Antonio**	3:30
Sun	Apr 21	Seattle at Denver**	3:30

*Regional Coverage
**Alternate

Glenn Robinson's 21.9 ppg led to All-Rookie team.

1995-96 TURNER/NBA SCHEDULE
(Starting Times Eastern)

Day	Date	Game	Network	Time
Fri	Nov 3	Charlotte at Chicago	TNT	8:00
Tue	Nov 7	Phoenix at New York	TNT	8:00
Fri	Nov 10	Orlando at Boston	TNT	8:00
Fri	Nov 10	L.A. Clippers at Vancouver	TNT	10:30
Tue	Nov 14	Chicago at Orlando	TNT	8:00
Wed	Nov 15	Denver at Phoenix	TBS	8:00
Wed	Nov 15	Dallas at L.A. Lakers	TBS	10:30
Fri	Nov 17	Utah at Detroit	TNT	8:00
Tue	Nov 21	Seattle at Toronto	TNT	8:00
Wed	Nov 22	Chicago at San Antonio	TBS	8:00
Fri	Nov 24	Chicago at Utah	TNT	8:00
Tue	Nov 28	Charlotte at Milwaukee	TNT	8:00
Wed	Nov 29	New York at Charlotte	TBS	8:00
Fri	Dec 1	Dallas at Atlanta	TNT	8:00
Tue	Dec 5	Houston at Utah	TNT	8:00
Wed	Dec 6	New York Chicago	TBS	8:00
Fri	Dec 8	Charlotte at Orlando	TNT	8:00
Tue	Dec 12	L.A. Lakers at New York	TNT	8:00
Wed	Dec 13	Orlando at Chicago	TBS	8:00
Fri	Dec 15	Utah at Orlando	TNT	8:00
Tue	Dec 19	Phoenix at Houston	TNT	8:00
Wed	Dec 20	Milwaukee at Detroit	TBS	8:00
Fri	Dec 22	New York at Orlando	TNT	8:00
Fri	Dec 22	Sacramento at L.A. Lakers	TNT	10:30
Tue	Dec 26	Chicago at Indiana	TNT	8:00
Wed	Dec 27	Golden State at Washington	TBS	8:00
Wed	Jan 3	Houston at Chicago	TBS	8:00
Fri	Jan 5	Indiana at San Antonio	TNT	8:00
Tue	Jan 9	San Antonio at Houston	TNT	8:00
Wed	Jan 10	Seattle at Chicago	TBS	8:00
Fri	Jan 12	Dallas at Phoenix	TNT	8:00
Tue	Jan 16	Cleveland at Seattle	TNT	8:00
Wed	Jan 17	Orlando at Phoenix	TBS	8:00
Fri	Jan 19	Charlotte at Miami	TNT	8:00
Tue	Jan 23	Chicago at New York	TNT	8:00
Wed	Jan 24	Phoenix at Minnesota	TBS	8:00
Fri	Jan 26	L.A. Lakers at Philadelphia	TNT	8:00
Tue	Jan 30	Chicago at Houston	TNT	8:00
Wed	Jan 31	Utah at Portland	TBS	8:00
Fri	Feb 2	Phoenix at Cleveland	TNT	8:00
Tue	Feb 6	Chicago at Phoenix	TNT	8:00
Wed	Feb 7	Orlando at Detroit	TBS	8:00
Wed	Feb 7	New Jersey at L.A. Lakers	TBS	10:30
Fri	Feb 9	NBA All-Star Friday at San Antonio	TNT	10:00
Sat	Feb 10	NBA Stay-in-School at San Antonio	TNT	12:00
		NBA All-Star Saturday at San Antonio	TNT	7:00
Tue	Feb 13	Dallas at Houston	TNT	8:00
Wed	Feb 14	New York at Charlotte	TBS	8:00
Fri	Feb 16	Denver at Charlotte	TNT	8:00
Tue	Feb 20	Cleveland at Chicago	TNT	8:00
Wed	Feb 21	Orlando at Indiana	TBS	8:00
Fri	Feb 23	L.A. Lakers at Dallas	TNT	8:00

NBA TV SCHEDULE • 463

Day	Date	Game	Network	Time
Tue	Feb 27	Charlotte at Milwaukee	TNT	8:00
Wed	Feb 28	Detroit at Seattle	TBS	8:00
Fri	Mar 1	New York at Utah	TNT	8:00
Tue	Mar 5	Orlando at Charlotte	TNT	8:00
Wed	Mar 6	Denver at San Antonio	TBS	8:00
Tue	Mar 12	Orlando at Denver	TNT	8:00
Wed	Mar 13	Phoenix at Detroit	TBS	8:00
Tue	Mar 19	Golden State at Houston	TNT	8:00
Wed	Mar 20	Indiana at New York	TBS	8:00
Tue	Mar 26	L.A. Lakers at Orlando	TNT	8:00
Wed	Mar 27	New York at San Antonio	TBS	8:00
Fri	Mar 29	San Antonio at Dallas	TNT	8:00
Tue	Apr 2	L.A. Lakers at Charlotte	TNT	8:00
Wed	Apr 3	Orlando at New York	TBS	8:00
Fri	Apr 5	Chicago at Charlotte	TNT	8:00
Tue	Apr 9	L.A. Lakers at Denver	TNT	8:00
Wed	Apr 10	Phoenix at Utah	TBS	8:00
Fri	Apr 12	Indiana at Orlando	TNT	8:00
Tue	Apr 16	Houston at Phoenix	TNT	9:00
Wed	Apr 17	Indiana at Detroit	TBS	8:00
Fri	Apr 19	Charlotte at New York	TNT	8:00

1995-96 NBA ON CTV
(Starting Times Eastern)

Day	Date	Game	Network	Time
Fri	Nov 3	New Jersey at Toronto	CTV	9:00
Sun	Nov 5	Minnesota at Vancouver	CTV	9:00
Sun	Dec 10	Toronto at Vancouver	CTV	8:30
Sun	Jan 21	Boston at Toronto	CTV	12:00
Sun	Jan 21	Orlando at Houston	CTV/NBC	2:30
Thu	Jan 25	Vancouver at Toronto	CTV	8:30
Sun	Jan 28	Phoenix at Chicago	CTV/NBC	1:00
Sun	Feb 4	San Antonio at Orlando	CTV/NBC	3:30
Sun	Feb 11	NBA ALL-STAR GAME at San Antonio	CTV	6:00
Sun	Feb 18	Seattle at Vancouver	CTV	3:30
Sun	Feb 25	Orlando at Chicago	CTV/NBC	1:00
Sun	Feb 25	San Antonio at Vancouver	CTV	3:30
Sun	Mar 3	Toronto at Cleveland	CTV	3:00
Sun	Mar 10	Houston at Vancouver	CTV	3:00
Sun	Mar 17	Toronto at Indiana	CTV	3:00
Sun	Mar 24	Chicago at Toronto	CTV	3:30
Sun	Mar 31	L.A. Lakers at Toronto	CTV	3:00
Sun	Apr 7	Phoenix at Vancouver	CTV	3:00
Sun	Apr 14	Portland at Vancouver	CTV	3:00
Sun	Apr 21	Orlando at Charlotte**	CTV/NBC	3:30
Sun	Apr 21	Phoenix at Houston**	CTV/NBC	3:30
Sun	Apr 21	Milwaukee at Detroit**	CTV/NBC	3:30
Sun	Apr 21	Dallas at San Antonio**	CTV/NBC	3:30
Sun	Apr 21	Seattle at Denver**	CTV/NBC	3:30

**Alternate

Revised and updated third edition!

THE ILLUSTRATED SPORTS RECORD BOOK
Zander Hollander and David Schulz

Here, in a single book, are more than 400 all-time—and current—sports records with 50 new stories and 125 action photos so vivid, it's like "being there." Featured is an all-star cast that includes Martina Navratilova, Joe DiMaggio, Joe Montana, Michael Jordan, Jack Nicklaus, Mark Spitz, Wayne Gretzky, Nolan Ryan, Muhammad Ali, Greg LeMond, Hank Aaron, Carl Lewis and Magic Johnson. This is *the* authoritative book that sets the record straight and recreates the feats at the time of achievement!

Buy them at your local bookstore or use this convenient coupon for ordering.

PENGUIN USA
P.O. Box 999 — Dept. #17109
Bergenfield, New Jersey 07621

Please send me _____ paperback copies of THE ILLUSTRATED SPORTS RECORD BOOK 0-451-17117-9 at $5.99 ($6.99 in Canada) each. Please enclose $2.00 per order to cover postage and handling. I enclose ☐ check ☐ money order.

Name_____

Address_____

City _____ State _____ Zip Code _____

Allow a minimum of 4-6 weeks for delivery.
This offer prices and numbers are subject to change without notice.